The Common Man, Oklahoma City and Life in Post-Freedom America

History has clearly shown that when the common man is cornered, unjustly treated, wounded and dispirited, he eventually reaches a breaking point. That is when he fights back. But in recent history, the American common man has taken this concept much further. When he fights back, he does so with an unparalleled, uncompromising ferocity — especially when his very survival, and that of his family and friends, hangs in the balance.

James D. Nichols is such a common man. His story echoes of Elijah, Socrates, Thomas Paine and Peter Zenger. James D. Nichols, like the common men of old, uses words, not weapons, to inflict the mortal blow upon the enemies of truth.

With a little help from his friends, and with much good humor and self-effacing charm, James D. Nichols has helped prepare Americans for *Freedom's End*. May we all benefit from this modern vision from the common man.

— **Gerald A. Carroll,**
contributing editor,
Media Bypass

For permissions, or serializations, condensations, adaptations, or for information about other products and services, write the Publisher at the address below.

Library of Congress Cataloguing-in-Publication Data

Nichols, James D., 1954-
Papovich, Robert S., 1945-
Papovich, Sandra G., 1946-
Carroll, Gerald A., 1954-
  Freedom's End: Conspiracy in Oklahoma
  by James D. Nichols as told to Robert S. Papovich
  Includes index.
  ISBN 0-9660439-0-01
  1. Biography/Autobiography/Letters. 2. Current Affairs. 3. History, 20th Century. 4. Political Science and Government. 5. True Crime.

Published by
FREEDOM'S END
P.O. Box 145, Decker, MI 48426

Printed in the [u]nited States of America
10 9 8 7 6 5 4 3 2 1

Freedom's End:
Conspiracy in Oklahoma

Photo by Debby Racine

Co-authors James Nichols, foreground, and Bob Papovich, to the
right of Nichols, share some time with friends in Michigan.

"Many books require no thought from those who read them, for a very simple reason: They made no such demand upon those who wrote them. Those works, therefore, are the most valuable that set our thinking faculties in the fullest operation."

— Colton

Introduction and Acknowledgments

People write books for many different reasons. Some authors write out of a sense of need or, perhaps, of artistic expression. Others write because they believe they have such an entertaining idea that the idea must be passed along to entertain others. Many write just because that's what they do. That's how they make their living. Authors for profit, you might say, and we certainly don't have a problem with that or any other honest reason for writing a book.

We also have our reasons for writing this book. Reasons with which many people, particularly government agents and investigators, will probably disagree. Some of this information will alarm many of you. Some readers who think their government is incapable of intentional wrongdoing will refuse to believe the words that grace these pages. The truth will be disagreeable to those people because it will not support what they want to believe. But isn't it better to know the truth than to live under a delusion? Isn't it better to know the facts than to be manipulated by lies?

As noted author and syndicated columnist Dr. Thomas Sowell has so eloquently stated: "One of the most common reasons for believing that things are not true — and for continuing to believe them as facts pile up against them — is that the belief flatters the ego of the believer. So, if you find yourself getting a special glow from something you believe, then it's time to start checking the facts."

We've checked the facts.

Considering all the stories that have been surfacing recently about government cover-ups, evidence planting, and evidence falsification, it's hard to imagine anyone still naive enough to think that government can do no wrong. Unbelievable as it may seem, these people do exist. In the past several months we have been confronted by numerous doubters, many in the news media, who have challenged us on our contention that the April 19, 1995, bombing of the Alfred P. Murrah Federal Building in Oklahoma City had to be some kind of an inside job.

All we ask is that you maintain a "thinking" mind. We want you to use a thinking mind as opposed to an "open" mind, because a thinking mind will evaluate all of the information available surrounding this investigation and will use that information to form an intelligent, objective opinion. Conversely, government agents would much prefer you keep an "open" mind which is generally subject to someone else's thoughts, however convoluted those thoughts may be. An open mind will accept as "truth" the propaganda and disinformation leaked by those "unnamed sources" in the FBI who are never held accountable for their lies. A thinking mind will not. Detroit-based Mark Scott, one of America's best radio talk-show hosts, has been presenting to his listeners this important distinction between a thinking mind and an open mind for the past 15 years.

The truth cannot be changed by our knowledge, or by our ignorance, although our knowledge and ignorance can be changed by the truth. What we *want* to believe has no bearing on the facts. But, as we all know, public opinion can have a great deal of influence on the decision of a jury. Consequently, what we want to believe can have a great deal of influence on the outcome of a trial, whether we want to believe it or not. We can assure you that government propagandists are acutely aware of the correlation between public opinion and the decision of a potential juror. After all, a jury is, and should be, nothing more than a cross-section of the public. As a result, a jury's decision will generally be a reflection of public opinion, particularly in high-profile cases. Most assuredly, that was the case when alleged Oklahoma City bomber Timothy McVeigh was "convicted" of single-handedly carrying out that act and a death sentence rendered against him.

The question we all have to ask ourselves concerning this tragic incident is: *What is the truth?* We have been told by many that we will never get to the bottom of this thing. Since the cover-up apparently runs so deep, and the people involved in the cover-up have so much power and control, we are just wasting our time trying to get to the truth, they say. That thought is unacceptable to a thinking mind. When you apply reason, logic, and common sense and evaluate all of the information you're about to read, we are confident that you will not only agree with many of our conclusions but will also realize why this book had to be written.

This book is for you, the American people. The people have a right to know the truth about this tragedy, not the gossip, half-truths, leaks by "anonymous" sources and just downright lies from "unnamed" agents in the FBI to which we're being exposed on a daily basis via the phony sensationalism in newspapers, magazines, television and other media constructed by government disinformation specialists. When this false information is reported it is seldom, if ever, retracted. Under these conditions the most grossly misrepresented false information will live on to be repeated over and over again, despite readily available facts that prove these rumors untrue. One hard lesson we have learned during this investigation is that "trying to squash a rumor is like trying to unring a bell." So says writer and television personality Shana Alexander, and we could not agree more with her very astute observation.

The victims of this unconscionable crime not only need to know what really happened in Oklahoma City, they especially have a *right* to know. The only chance we have of preventing this from ever happening again is for all of us to find out what, in fact, did happen — and that is precisely why we're writing this book. The only way to honor the victims of this tragedy is to prosecute and punish all of those who are actually responsible. Anything less would amount to the ultimate slap in the face to the victims and their families and would also dishonor our nation. We have certainly experienced national dishonor from past investigations carried out by the government. This act of terrorism has already claimed far too many victims. We must exercise caution to be certain that it claims no more innocent lives.

We can only hope that readers will appreciate the difficulty we have encountered while gathering and organizing the information in this book during an ongoing investigation. Particularly challenging was the task of trying to determine whether each piece of information was in reality misinformation, disinformation — or a genuine fact that might help us solve this crime. Please keep in mind that it has taken nearly two years to compile this information and to write this book. The allegations from federal prosecutors have changed many times during the past two years, as has much of their so-called "evidence." It has been a constant battle trying to counter all of the leaks, disinformation and rumors.

As you can probably imagine, we have also faced the monumental task of trying to make certain that our information was correct before passing it along to you. New information surfaces daily generally confirming our original opinions and conclusions. We have attempted to organize and present this information in a way that would make it easy to understand for those readers who are totally unfamiliar with this case. This is a new encounter for all of us. We can only pray that we have succeeded.

We do need to thank honest and concerned politicians like Oklahoma State Rep. Charles Key and those employees working in various government agencies whose conscience will not allow them to falsify evidence or to take part in an immoral cover-up. Rep. Key has been doggedly pursuing a state-sponsored investigation in Oklahoma — including new grand jury proceedings — and has been rewarded for his efforts with ridicule and criticism from former FBI, BATF and Secret Service supervisor Frank Keating, Oklahoma's current governor.

Gov. Keating, many feel, is being groomed for the presidency. We need to point out that, in our opinion, Gov. Keating has done his best to block any independent investigation which attempted to uncover the truth and has publicly criticized and personally insulted anyone who had the courage to doubt the government's "story." At least one of his ethnic insults suggesting that a courageous grand juror should go "back to the reservation" would have resulted in public humiliation and permanent unemployment had the distasteful statement been made by someone like Cincinnati Reds owner Marge Schott, the late sportscaster Howard Cosell, the late Las Vegas oddsmaker Jimmy "The Greek" Snyder or any other non-insider. The national media has successfully kept a lid on it, so to speak.

We especially need to thank WXYT (Detroit) talk show host Mark Scott for helping us get this information out to the public and for consistently campaigning on the side of "objectivism." We also need to thank former television talk-show host Phil Donahue for letting us "speak our peace," even though Phil was tougher than the FBI and BATF interrogators. We still owe him and many others a debt of gratitude for their generosity and for their hospitality. We are deeply indebted to the many producers and hosts on talk radio who were willing to listen to the "rest of the story."

We also need to thank Chris Hansen, Wendy Segal (Ms. Persistent), Suzy Stein, Jill Milliken (It's a girl! Congratulations!), Emily Barsh, Linda from *Nightline* (we tried), Dan Rather, David Fitzpatrick and Bill Cunningham (Fitzpatrick and Cunningham are two of the most objective producers in the business), *Hannity & Colmes* and the FOX News Channel and all of the other fine people working behind the scenes, going virtually unnoticed, who at least tried to give us an opportunity to speak out and who actually bring these shows to the American people. Viewers might be unaware of your dedication and your efforts. We can assure you we are aware, and we noticed.

We would like to thank Maryann Struman from *The Detroit News* and

Ann Stewart from *The Daily News* in Ann Arbor, Mich., for their honest reporting, their company at the Libertarian Party dinner and for many hours of very interesting conversation. Maryann offered her assistance on any literary advice that we needed and, without that assistance, we would still be groping in the dark trying to figure out what to do next. She has, on many occasions, located details about certain aspects of our investigation that we could not have found by ourselves. Meeting Maryann was a real godsend. We The People could certainly benefit from the talents of these excellent journalists in many of our national papers and magazines.

We also had the pleasure of meeting two other fine TV reporters who did their best to report the truth. One was John Noel from TV 2 News in Detroit and the other was Jay Brandow from TV 5 in Saginaw, Mich. Your honesty is also greatly appreciated.

I need to thank my friends Jim and Phil for retaining my brilliant attorney, Robert Elsey. I owe an immeasurable debt of gratitude to Elsey, who hails from Grosse Point Park, Mich. Without his services, I may well have been kept in prison for a crime I did not commit. His integrity as an attorney is impeccable. His courage and his ability to challenge the jurisdiction of the federal government and their army of prosecutors, we are certain, surprised many of his colleagues, including many on the federal payroll, who were unaware of his vast capabilities. His oral arguments and his cross-examinations of FBI special agents in open court make Matlock and Perry Mason look like rank amateurs. It was, at the very least, exhilarating. We cannot in words express our appreciation for your expertise, your courage, your patience and, most of all, for your friendship. Thank you, Mr. Elsey.

We need to express our appreciation to Richard and Donna B. for being there first to help with unsolicited financial assistance, to the organization Justice Pro Se for its support and for their unbelievable generosity, to Eugene and Joann for always being there for any help we may need, to Edie from Morning Star for never being late, to Doug Bennett and Stefani Godsey for their legal research, to Kathé Tidwell for her efforts in correcting our numerous mistakes during many, many days of editing and for her assistance in organizing the information in this book.

We are deeply indebted to my dad for being able to tolerate us during our many weeks of travel, staying in motel rooms, talking to investigators and interviewing witnesses. He had to spend what little money he had for travel expenses, neglecting his farm chores and literally going into debt to help the investigation. We were very fortunate that he was able to remain totally level headed and that he offered his 70-plus years of wisdom and experience in assisting our investigation, noticing some of the little details that we may have missed, and for keeping us "in line" those times when we began to lose focus.

We need to thank my mother, sister and brother for maintaining a collective "thinking mind" while considering the shocking allegations against us. Before this all started they never really understood or agreed with our political philosophy and probably never really gave it much thought. Like most people, they had complete confidence and faith in the government. I believe it's human nature to want to trust your government because the alternative is just too difficult to deal with. Knowledge is a great thing but too much knowledge about corruption and deceit among our political leaders and federal law enforcement agencies can be very stressful and can make your life extremely miserable. I believe my mother, sister and brother had a very crude awakening once they had the opportunity to experience, first hand, the deceptive, lying nature of the feds in and out of court.

We have to make special mention of and express our sincere appreciation to Glen, Kathy and Edye for your courage in this tragedy. Our hearts go out to you for your incomprehensible losses. This nation owes all of you a debt of gratitude for having the guts to speak out publicly and to challenge the federal government's ridiculous contentions as to what happened in this tragedy. If not for your courage in a time of crisis, quite probably, no one would have paid any attention to those of us who were skeptical of the government's account from the very beginning. Edye is still asking questions that federal investigators do not want to answer. We can only pray that our efforts will help you find those answers. We haven't always arrived at the same conclusions as Glen on some of the particulars in this case, but we can assure you that we are all working toward the same goal: The Truth.

Special consideration should go to Chuck Allen for his production of the videos, *Oklahoma City: What Really Happened?* This superb video is guaranteed to raise some eyebrows and send a chill up your spine. Chuck has uncovered much information through his own objective investigation and we believe much of that information will be instrumental in eventually solving this crime. During this past year Chuck and his lovely wife Feeny have become very close friends. We appreciate your friendship, your dedication to the truth and especially Feeny's fantastic home cookin'.

We also need to extend special thanks to Hoppy Heidelberg, the only one of 23 grand jurors alert enough to realize that government prosecutors were trying to keep pertinent information from the grand jury during the indictment hearings. He was inquisitive enough to ask: *Why?* He had the audacity to challenge the prosecution's phony instructions to the jurors. For that challenge and for his tenacity in demanding that the grand jury be allowed to exercise its right to investigate and to subpoena witnesses, a great and courageous American patriot will be forever persecuted by his own government.

We need to express our appreciation to the good people of Oklahoma for their hospitality and well-wishers. During all of our travels in and around Oklahoma City we were approached by informed citizens who voiced their suspicions about a cover-up and setup of monumental proportions surrounding this tragedy. These concerned citizens were privy to much information that has been virtually ignored by network news. Their exposure to the real news is evident in their opinions about what really happened in Oklahoma City on April 19, 1995. Thank you all for your support in our investigation.

Let us also acknowledge the work of Gerald A. Carroll, an adjunct assistant professor of journalism at the University of Iowa, who has acted as a valuable consultant and editor for this manuscript along with Ms. Tidwell. Mr. Carroll also conceived the idea of *Freedom's End* as the book's title and name of our new company. In rushing to make a nearly impossible deadline to get this book out before the start of Terry's trial, Mr. Carroll is also responsible for the primary design of this book and its cover. Mr. Carroll serves as a contributing editor for *Media Bypass* magazine (1-800-4BYPASS) based in Evansville, Ind., and author of *Project Seek: Onassis, Kennedy and the Gemstone Thesis* (1-800-729-4131). A second book from Mr. Carroll, *Militia Nation*, is due out in early 1998 from Commonwealth Publishers, Edmonton, Alberta, Canada.

We're certain, using the information and evidence we have been able to gather from friends and investigators like Michele Moore, Lawrence Myers, J. D. Cash, Karl Granse, Chuck and Feeny Allen, Glen Wilburn, You Know Who, and independent investigators and experts like Gen. Benton Partin and numerous others, in spite of a concerted effort by the government to hinder these investigations and to keep evidence from defense attorneys and from scientists in private laboratories, we believe we know what did happen.

Now, you will know. •

— **James D. Nichols** and **Bob Papovich,**
With a little help from our friends.

Photo courtesy Bob and Sandy Papovich

James Nichols strikes a stoic pose in front of his Decker, Mich., farmhouse .

Part I:

The
Decker
Connection?

Photo by Debby Racine

Invasion by sky: A Michigan state police helicopter buzzes the property of James Nichols during the April 21, 1995 raid.

Photo by Debby Racine

Law-enforcement vehicles of all stripes surround the James Nichols home on April 21, 1995, two days after the Oklahoma City bombing.

"He has erected a multitude of New Offices, and sent hither swarms of Officers to harass our people and eat out their substance."
— **The Declaration of Independence**

CHAPTER 1: DAY ONE (FOR ME)

Friday, April 21, 1995 started out as just an average spring day in the life of a farmer in rural America. Always too many things to do and never enough time to do all of them. There are hundreds of acres of fields to prepare for planting and seeds to buy, among other things. Many other things. It seems that no matter how much work you do on your farm equipment in the winter, something is always inoperable just when you need it in the spring.

This spring would not be an exception to that rule.

It was about 1:45 in the afternoon and I had been talking to my neighbor, Don Bullock, on the phone for awhile. We were talking about spring planting and just generally "shootin' the breeze."

Don jokingly said, "I've heard there was supposed to be some kind of a raid on a farmhouse in Decker. Maybe it's your house."

Needless to say, I was overwhelmed with laughter. At the time that statement seemed pretty funny, not to mention farfetched. Then Don told me he had heard that there was some kind of Decker connection to the bombing in Oklahoma. That didn't seem possible but, then again, I can't say that I know everyone in or around the Decker area so I guess it could be possible. But Decker, Michigan? The Oklahoma City bombing? I don't quite think so. I mean, everyone knows that's the kind of thing a terrorist or an intelligence agent would do in a foreign country, not something a hick from Podunk, U.S.A. would do to his fellow citizens; his own countrymen. Not a chance! Of course, I can't say for certain that a foreign terrorist or rogue Government agent hasn't moved to the Decker area lately so it could be possible. Maybe ... No, I don't think so.

Anyway, Don said he had lots of things to do so he had to get going, and I agreed. So did I. After all, it was spring. Never enough hours in the day. A few minutes after we hung up, I got in my car and headed for Marlette, a small town about a dozen miles due south of my house on a country road known only as M53, to run some errands. About nine or 10 miles down the road I saw several helicopters traveling north. There must be some kind of a practice run from one of the Air Force or National Guard bases in the area. Then I met some large trucks carrying satellite dishes also traveling north and wondered what their destination might be. I thought perhaps some major broadcasting company might be in the process of installing a large satellite dish network here in the geographic region known on maps as the "Thumb of Michigan." As they got closer I could see their news station logos on the sides of the trucks.

"Hmmm. I wonder what they're doing here?" I asked myself.

Before I could dwell on that thought, the lights from an ambulance came into view, again, traveling north on M53. Then I remembered what Don had said on the phone about a raid in Decker. When the ambulance sped by, rapidly closing the distance between it and the satellite trucks, my first thought was that the person they were after had already been shot. But if that was the case, why weren't they taking him or her to the hospital in Marlette which is just a few miles south of here? Maybe the ambulance was on its way to the location of the raid. The ambulance could just be going to a car accident. Oh well, I guess I'll hear it all from neighbors or on the news pretty soon. Nothing much ever happens around here and if something exciting does happen, you generally know who it's happening to while it's happening. Unfortunately, this time would prove to be an exception.

Out here you know just about everyone except for a few new people here and there. The new people aren't new for very long. Most everybody is friendly out here in the country. Neighbors help neighbors, often without even being asked. A good neighbor can live across the street or 10 miles away. I think that people have to depend on each other more directly out here in farm country than they do in the city. It makes for a nice place to raise a family. Not that we don't have our share of problems, but a major incident around here is a couple of kids involved in minor vandalism or taking a car for a joy ride, not a drive-by shooting that someone does just for kicks.

Driving into Marlette, my first stop was the bank. As soon as I got through the door I told the ladies inside to turn on the radio, there was something going on nearby. We were talking about the possibility of a Decker connection to the Oklahoma bombing. I told Connie, one of the bank employees, that I had just passed some emergency vehicles a couple of miles north of here so the raid may actually be closer to her house in Snover, four miles east of Decker, than to my farm which is six miles from Decker. We were joking about who the ill-fated farm may belong to. I realized that this was no laughing matter, but at the time it seemed funny that federal agents would be raiding any place in Decker for any reason.

I mean, this is Decker, Michigan — not New York, Detroit, Chicago or L.A. This is just Decker, Michigan, which consists of a small country type church, a backroad bar and a tiny post office.. What would federal agents be doing in Decker? Not *Decker*. There has to be some mistake. Right?

I'd have to guess that anyone in a rural small town could relate to the joke, but I can also understand how that humor might elude some people from a large city. After the normal small-town humor was expressed, they again mentioned on the radio that there was a Decker connection to the Oklahoma City bombing. At that point the humor disappeared and the disbelief set in. Apparently they were serious. The feds really thought there were terrorists living out here in God's country. That thought was just too far-fetched to even comprehend. There was no way anyone in the Decker area could even be remotely connected to the bombing in Oklahoma. I knew these guys had to be making a mistake. A big mistake.

I ran a few more errands in Marlette before making my last stop at the auto parts store. I had to give them a $2,000 deposit on a tractor engine they were rebuilding for me. Farming can be very expensive. On my way home I visually checked all the fields as I drove north on M-53. That's just something all farmers do, I guess. It just becomes a habit. We watch other farmers' fields to see how wet or dry they are, at what stage they are in preparation for planting, what they're planting this year, and a variety of other things. As I proceeded down the road, there seemed to be an abnormal amount of traffic. Then, a couple of miles from my farm, the number of vehicles increased drastically. It was obvious that whoever the Feds were raiding lived somewhere near here. As I drove, I tried to imagine who in this area could be involved in anything nasty enough to interest federal law enforcement agencies. I couldn't think of anyone. This must be a mistake.

Who could it possibly be? •

Photo by Debby Racine

Satellite television trucks like this one were prevalent for days around the James Nichols farm in April of 1995.

Photo by Debby Racine

Media descended like Old Testament locusts along M53, also known as VanDyke Road, and Deckerville Road.

"He has affected to render the Military independent of and superior to the Civil power."

— **The Declaration of Independence**

CHAPTER 2: THE RAID

Getting closer to my house, I could see satellite trucks belonging to news stations, vehicles representing every police agency imaginable and helicopters circling. I kept wondering: Who in the world could be the target of such an enormous raid? Through the process of elimination, thinking of everybody who lived right here close by my farm, I deleted all potential subjects. The closer I came to my house the more intense the traffic became. More police cars. More news media cars and trucks. There were some stations there that I had never even heard of. It looked as if they were raiding one of my close neighbors. I know all of my neighbors. It couldn't be anyone that I know.

"Well, wait a minute," I thought. "Where are they? What were these guys doing? My God, they're at my house!" Now I knew they had made a big mistake. They had the wrong house!

I drove up to the corner of Deckerville Road and Van Dyke, trying to get through the massive people/traffic jam and around the officer directing traffic. I motioned for an officer to come to my car. My electric windows didn't work so I had to open the door to talk.

"What's going on here!" I asked a Michigan state trooper.

"What's your business here and who are you?" He replied.

"I want to know what's going on here?" I asked again.

"Who are you?" He asked.

"I want to know what's going on here, that's my house!" I said.

"Who are you?" asked the officer again.

I then told the officer who I was and he seemed to be momentarily confused. I think at the time most of the law officers and federal agents involved in this raid didn't realize that I wasn't at home. He looked one way, then another, then at me and then to each side again. It almost seemed as if he didn't quite know what to with the most wanted criminal on the planet now that he'd "caught" him. He eventually waved to the FBI for back-up who then proceeded to search me and ask some questions.

"What's in your trunk?" an FBI agent asked.

"I don't know. The regular stuff, I guess. A spare tire, a jack, some jumper cables," I answered while they slowly and cautiously opened my trunk. I could not imagine what in the world they'd be looking for in my trunk or why they would be so paranoid about opening it. After the brief search and interrogation I was told to get back in my car and drive to the farmhouse; they'd be following right behind me.

"We'll call ahead on the radio to let the other agents know what the situation is. We'll be right behind you."

I wondered: "How can they tell the other agents what the situation is? I don't know what the situation is. I don't even know what the hell is going on here." I asked them to clarify their instructions again so I would be certain to understand their intentions. After all, I am just a dumb farmer livin' out here in the boondocks, so I'm not used to getting involved in any of these high-falutin complexities with which these highly-skilled, brilliant government agents deal on a daily basis.

"Get in your car and drive to the farmhouse. We'll phone ahead and we'll be right behind you," the agent said again.

Considering that it was immediately apparent that the government agents surrounding my farm possessed enough fire-power to easily defeat a small planet, and taking into consideration that the reason for this whole situation was still, somehow, eluding my senses, I felt compelled to again ask the agent to repeat the instructions so there would be no mistake on my part. Making a mistake did not appear as if it would add consideraby to my health or longevity under these circumstances.

For the third time, the FBI agent repeated the same instructions. Now I knew for sure what I was supposed to do. No doubt about it. I know how to follow orders. I had to get in my car and drive to the farmhouse. They'd radio ahead to let the other agents know what the situation was and they'd be following right behind me. Now I was sure. I could do that. No problem.

And I did. But unfortunately, as I approached my driveway, a BATF agent who mistakenly thought he was in a Ninja movie (I could tell by the way he was dressed and by the way he acted) jumped into my car and ordered me not to move while pointing an assault rifle at my face in a very menacing manner. This guy seemed to be a recruit from the KGB or Gestapo or something and was obviously a loose cannon who was also a few bricks short of a full load which just happens to be a prerequisite for any adult who wants to dress and act like a Ninja Turtle. Not wanting to be the object of this particular Ninja Turtle's apparent belief that he was "born to kill" I immediately informed him that I was with those guys, pointing behind me.

Glancing back over my shoulder, I suddenly realized that there was no one behind me. It appeared as if I was left "hung out to dry." Staring down the barrel of a fully automatic assault rifle and into the cold eyes of a fanatic who had been trained to kill unarmed citizens who could not fight back, sent a shudder up my spine. Many thoughts raced through my mind. "Does this guy want to take it out on me because he wasn't fortunate enough to be involved in the 'turkey shoots' at Waco and Ruby Ridge? Was I just manipulated into a situation which had a high probability of ending in my demise?"

I started doing some fast talking and convinced my newly found, very dangerous looking BATF buddy to check with the other guys before he used me for point blank target practice. Needless to say my fast talking paid off because Mr. BATF didn't shoot me. This problem was eventually resolved allowing the Feds to continue with their interrogation and investigation of the living suspected guru behind the Oklahoma City bombing, the total destruction of my farm and the harassment of the entire "Thumb of Michigan," not to mention the media's attempt to discredit the militia, the patriot movement, talk radio, and all Constitutionists, nationally.

Realistically, I'll never know how the militia fit into this situation other than affording the government's agents of deceit, via the news media, a.k.a. Ted Koppel, etc., an opportunity to destroy the American citizens' Constitutionally guaranteed last bastion of defense against a potentially oppressive and tyrannical government. An opportunity which, I might add, was and is being "milked to the max" by those agents of deceit in the "theater of operations" of politics as well as in the media.

Government agents asked all kinds of questions of me and I answered any and all questions that were asked. I had nothing to hide and I told them so. They asked me why I had $60,000 cash in my house. They wanted to know what I was doing with that kind of money. Not realizing the significance of that number at the time, I told them I didn't have $60,000 and if I did I wouldn't be driving an old, rusty junk truck that barely runs. I asked them to show me a search warrant but they could not produce one. An agent told me that a warrant was on the way.

I guess that's what they call "putting the cart before the horse." It was always my understanding, according to the Constitution, that the search warrant was supposed to come before the search. If the authorities could search first and then get a warrant after the fact, they could conceivably search anyone or anyplace at any time without a warrant and then if they found anything illegal they could secure a warrant. Under those circumstances, we would probably have a near criminal-free society, except for the criminals in government and their agents armed with assault weapons committing crimes against the citizens, of course. You could say that we then would have "licensed public criminals." Come to think of it, there are many countries currently living under that kind of oppression and they still have a high crime rate so I guess tyranny and oppression don't really eliminate "private" crime but actually add considerably to "public" crime. As Benjamin Franklin accurately observed: "They that will give up a little liberty to obtain temporary safety, deserve neither liberty nor safety."

Without a warrant they took me to the police station in Cass City, a quaint little town about ten miles northwest of my farm, and had me fingerprinted. They dissected everything on my farm and searched everything with a fine-tooth comb. Patrick Wease, the FBI's special-agent-in-charge of the raid, told me that he and the other three agents in command didn't see any evidence on my farm that would in any way suggest I was involved in the Oklahoma City bombing. He also said they didn't think I had done anything illegal.

I then asked agent Wease, "Why are you carrying out such an enormous raid if you already know that I had no involvement in the bombing, have done nothing illegal and have nothing illegal here at the farm?"

"Orders from above," he said.

"You mean orders from Detroit?" I asked naively.

"No, from Washington," he answered.

I was surprised and shocked. Why would anyone in Washington's "District of Criminals" be interested in raiding a farmer named James Nichols, especially when they knew that I wasn't guilty of anything? Looking back now and putting it all into perspective, I shouldn't have been surprised. But under the circumstances, I think any average, hard-working American citizen would've been pretty shook up in a similar situation. Most of us feel an enormous amount of anxiety just getting pulled over for a traffic violation and at the time I was unaware of any of the details surrounding this investigation or anything at all about the case other than what I'd heard briefly on the news. As a matter of fact, I believe the first time I heard anything at all about the Oklahoma City bombing was on April 19, later in the day when I was at the Self-Serve Lumber store. The second time was on the 20th when Paul and I stopped by the Decker Bar for a beer after a long,, hard work day.

You have to realize that I seldom watched television or listened to the radio before this all took place. I still very rarely have the time to watch television. Consequently, I either get my news word-of-mouth or by reading political magazines like *Relevance* or *Media Bypass*. Often, days go by before I'm aware of what's happening in other parts of the world. Until the raid on my farm this was basically an unfamiliar news story other than that I knew a bombing had taken place in Oklahoma City and that many people were killed.

One thing in particular that the FBI agents wanted me to do was to call my brother, Terry, and ask him if he knew anything about the bombing. I didn't have a problem with that. Like I've said before, I had nothing to hide and I had absolute confidence in Terry's innocence as well. There was no way in this world that my brother could even be remotely involved in any act of terrorism especially an action that would result in people dying.

Unfortunately, before the feds got everything in order to make and monitor that call Terry walked into the Herington, Kan., police station to inquire why he had heard his name on the radio. I really regret not being able to make that call because it would have shed a whole new light on the FBI's perception of Terry's involvement in this horrendous crime. Terry wouldn't have known that the FBI was at my house monitoring the call so he would have spoken to me freely and openly about anything and everything. To some people, calling Terry may not have seemed like the right thing to do at the time. It could be misconstrued as deceiving my own brother. An attorney may even consider such an act as having the potential of incriminating Terry.

But we have to put this all into perspective. This was an extremely grave situation, not your run-of-the-mill wrongdoing. I had such absolute, unwavering confidence in Terry's innocence that I guess you could say I was somewhat willing to deceive him into proving the validity of that confidence to FBI investigators. As you must now realize, I was so certain of my brother's innocence that I was also willing to temporarily relinquish our Fifth Amendment rights to prove to the FBI that which I already knew. TERRY WASN'T THERE. I certainly wish I could have made that call.

Needless to say, the day of the raid was a rather hectic ordeal for a farmer who had planned on getting greasy and twisting a few nuts and bolts for excitement. This whole situation seemed like walking into a swinging baseball bat that you could see coming in slow motion but just couldn't get out of the way. It was the kind of problem one may encounter in a dream, only I could touch and feel it. Unfortunately, my eyes were open and it was really happening to me!

At one point during the raid the FBI had me handcuffed and sitting in the back seat of a car. Realizing that this was not exactly a fair situation since I was outnumbered by at least 100 well-armed thugs to 1 unarmed and handcuffed farmer, I attempted to recruit some assistance. It occurred to me that these federal agents had no jurisdiction on my farm and that the local county sheriff had a responsibility to protect me from these thugs. I demanded to see the sheriff. When he finally came to talk to me I let him know in no uncertain terms that they had no probable cause to do this to me. They had no warrant to search my farm or to take me into custody. They were literally stealing my property. When the sheriff asked what property they were stealing, I answered, "Me." After a few moments of thought, Sheriff Strickler apparently realized the logic in what I was saying because the Feds removed the handcuffs which resulted in a tremendous reduction of anxiety, on my part anyway.

After some hours had passed and after experiencing considerable turmoil and commotion on my farm, I was informed that I would be taken into protective custody. Yep, they were going to cart me off to jail for my own good. I guess I should've really been grateful to them for being so concerned about my well-being, but at the time I just didn't quite understand of whom or of what I was supposed to be afraid. Soon, very soon, I would come to understand.

Realizing that I was going to depart from the comforts of my humble environment in the very near future, and remembering that I had all of my available liquid assets stashed under my mattress, I asked a BATF agent inside my house if I might be allowed to retrieve my money before they took me into custody for my own good. He told me that I could. I then asked if one of the BATF agents could go into my bedroom and get the money for me. Keep in mind that at the time there were no FBI agents or local law enforcement personnel anywhere in my house. Only BATF agents fully dressed in their "black battle gear," and there were many of them.

"My money is stashed under my mattress, and under my pillow is a loaded pistol. You have to move the pistol to get my money," I explained to the BATF agent.

"That's all right, go on and get it," the agent responded

"No, there's a loaded gun under my pillow that has to be moved. I think you should send one or two of your agents in there to get my money," I said.

"Go on and get your money. No problem," the agent said again.

"I don't think I want to do that. I think you should send one of your agents in there to get it for me," I answered for the second time.

My mind seemed like it was spinning a million miles a minute. A thousand thoughts raced through my brain in what seemed to be several minutes but couldn't have been more than a few seconds; i.e., "Am I watching a movie or is this some kind of a dream, maybe a nightmare? Isn't there something wrong with this picture? Wasn't I the most wanted and hunted man on the planet just a few hours ago? Why would a BATF agent tell someone who he perceived to be one of the most vicious criminals in the world to go pick up a loaded gun? Was he just an opportunist trying to take advantage of an opportunity that just happened to pop up? Was this all part of a plan to look for some reason, any reason, to eliminate me? Why would they want to eliminate me? Don't they want to find out the truth? I guess if they wanted to kill me right now they could, but I'm certainly not going to make it easy for them. If they did kill me in cold blood, someone outside with a telephoto camcorder just might see it through one of the windows and get it on tape. These guys can't take that kind of chance, but once I go into the bedroom I'm out of view from any window or the possibility of being seen by a media camera."

Common sense told me that I should not go in that bedroom and put my hand on that gun for any reason — under any circumstances.

"Go on in and get your money," the agent replied as he nonchalantly turned his back on me.

"I don't think so," I responded again as I pounded my fist on the countertop. "You send an agent in there right now. I told you that my gun has to be moved to get my money and I'm not going to touch that gun!"

"Go on and get your money," he said again.

"I'm not going in there," I shouted for the final time.

At this point, the agent apparently realized that I was not going to fall into his obvious trap. He sent another agent in to get my money and soon I was on the road to the county jail to be held in protective custody, for my own good. Now I knew of whom — and of what — I had to be afraid.

In the Sanilac County Jail, where I was incarcerated for my own good, I was treated pretty decently by the local police. They allowed me the liberty to make some phone calls and I took advantage of that liberty. I called Bob Papovich and his wife Sandy to let them know that I had survived this mess and gave them a list of names of friends to call and pass along the knowledge that I was all right. They told me they had complete confidence in my innocence and in Terry's innocence and that they would do everything they could to bring the truth to the attention of the media who had already convicted us. They said they'd be there for anything I needed. I made several other calls to close friends and family and basically got the same response which was extremely reassuring.

When the raid was taking place, the media, and consequently my friends, didn't know that I was not in FBI custody or that I wasn't even at home. I learned that Sandy had called me from work warning me on my answering machine to turn on the news and to look outside. After making several calls she still got no response. When she heard a news report that I had fled on foot she left work and started driving the back roads around my farm. Considering the possibility that I may be hiding somewhere in the woods she hoped that if I was in the woods I might recognize her car and come out in an attempt to go someplace that may have provided some temporary safety until we found out what in the world was going on here. No one here really knew what was happening but my close friends knew that I was innocent and apparently that was enough for them. You never really know which friends will actually stand by your side when the wrath of the entire federal government will inevitably be their reward for doing so.

At that particular point in time I had no idea what the future had in store for me but I will never be able to express in words what a relief it was to know that I had the support of many of my close friends. •

"He has combined with others to subject us to a jurisdiction foreign to our constitution, and unacknowledged by our laws; giving his Assent to their Acts of pretended Legislation."
                                   — The Declaration of Independence

CHAPTER 3: DAY TWO AND BEYOND

The next day, the FBI questioned almost everyone in the area who knew me. Bob and Sandy were questioned by two government agents, "Bill" from the FBI and "Mark" from the BATF. When Bob asked them where they got his name, they said that they didn't know. His name was just on a list of people they had to interview.

Bob said that these two agents didn't "interrogate" them, they just carried on a cordial conversation and, over a period of about three hours, asked questions about things that Bob didn't even remember had happened until the question was asked. Fortunately, Sandy remembered the details about the sequence of events and the dates of particular occurrences. They were two very courteous, professional federal agents who took their jobs seriously and harbored no apparent prejudices about anyone's guilt or innocence. They did a follow-up interview several days later, probably to retrieve any other bits of information that Bob and Sandy had forgotten the first time and, undoubtedly, to make certain that the information didn't change. That's all part of their job and probably the easiest most efficient way of getting to the truth.

Because of their certainty concerning our innocence, and because they had nothing to hide themselves, my friends cooperated fully with the federal investigators. Bob told me that his experience with Bill and Mark changed his opinion about all federal agents being the bad guys. He said that these two fellows seemed more like clean-cut, well-educated, next-door neighbors and not at all what he expected them to be. Like I said earlier, there are many honest, hard working intelligence agency employees who will not compromise their principles or "sell their souls," so to speak, for the Company. Unfortunately, many of their fearless leaders who are in positions of enormous power will, and have.

On April 22, 1995, after spending a nearly sleepless night in the Sanilac County Jail, I was interrogated by two Secret Service (SS) agents for about two hours. They had heard from a local resident that I had threatened the life of the President. This vindictive "neighbor", who was obviously seizing any opportunity to carry out his promise to "get me," has a nasty habit of taking things to the extreme. It has been rumored that he averages at least one law suit annually, and at least one physical assault on some unlucky neighbor biannually. His credibility around this area is below zero, and I'm certain that the feds were already aware of that fact. Of course, the facts don't really matter to people with an obsession so they still opted to collect some handwriting samples from me. Apparently they wanted to see if my handwriting matched any of the 217,345,894 threatening letters that Bill Clinton received during the week prior to my unlawful arrest and that he probably receives during most any other week (you're probably wondering how I knew the exact number, aren't you?).

Seriously, I can't read my own handwriting, so why should I think that the President would be able to read it? And if I ever did decided to type the President a letter, I'd sign the bugger. I don't try to hide my political opinions from anyone. I just don't understand the logic of sending someone an anonymous letter. I've received some of those since this ordeal started. That I have not been executed by the SS and that I have not been charged with the offense of threatening the President is the *ipso facto* evidence that these allegations were untrue.

After spending the night in the Sanilac County Jail I was escorted to the federal courthouse in Detroit for arraignment on the charge of "conspiracy to make and possess illegal firearms." I was appointed a federal defender, Miriam Siefer — a very competent, not to mention very attractive young lady. I have been told that she is the "cream of the crop" of federal defenders in this district. After many hours of conversation with Miriam I am convinced that these rumors are true.

Looking back on that first week, I have to admit that most of it was just a blur. The whole thing didn't seem real to me. I had to be in shock and, to be honest with you, I just wanted to go to sleep and wake up to find that this was all just a bad dream, a very bad dream. Terry told us that he experienced exactly the same thing that first week. Everything was very confusing and he had a hard time grasping what was really happening. I have been told by war veterans that the first week in a war zone kind of numbs your mind the same way. It just seems like you're dazed and walking around in a nightmare that just won't go away. The reality eventually sets in but, unfortunately, the numbness never seems to stop. I have to believe that many of the surviving victims of this horrendous crime and many of their family members have experienced these feelings also.

After the arraignment in Detroit I was transferred to Milan Federal Penitentiary in Milan, Mich., a small town about a 45-minute drive southwest of Detroit. That was where I would be incarcerated for my own good for the next 32 days. During that time and for sometime thereafter I had a rare opportunity to experience many new and unique things that I could've never even imagined just a few short weeks before.

One of those experiences was to enjoy the spaciousness of an entire cell block all to myself. Terry and Tim have the distinction of enjoying similar isolation in their respective 6-by-10-foot cells. It wasn't quite a pristine white-collar federal resort complete with tennis courts, spas, cable TVs, VCRs, and conjugal visits from your favorite young lady or gentleman, etc., where they typically send politicians and their banker buddies. Milan is a blue-collar prison, and I can assure you there was absolutely nothing pleasurable or pristine about it.

Another unique experience to which I was subjected was 24-hour surveillance of my cell with absolutely zero privacy. When I say zero privacy I mean ZERO privacy anywhere in my cell at any time. This "openness" with the world where, apparently, all of my normal body functions were supposed to be at peace with nature, or anyone else who just happened to be present, included relieving myself, standing and sitting. Keep in mind that the around-the-clock surveillance of my cell was not just camera surveillance. There were also at least two live guards just outside my cell on duty always. It was, to say the least, very embarrassing.

And this whole situation, uncomfortable as it may seem, becomes more than just embarrassing when you take into consideration a fact of which I was previously unaware. The guards outside of my cell who were viewing all of my bodily functions, including relieving myself while standing and sitting, were not always male corrections officers. Often, women corrections officers were on duty directly outside of my cell guarding me. Some, but not all, of the women guards would walk away slightly out of view when it became obvious that I was on the verge of relieving myself.

I have to admit that I cannot remember a more humiliating or degrading experience in my entire life. I certainly don't have anything against women or anyone else having equal employment opportunities, but there are some things for which any person needs complete privacy — particularly from the opposite gender. I believe that only female guards should be in direct, private contact with women in women's prisons, and only male guards should be present in private situations in men's prisons. Women should be working in every other position in men's prisons, and *vise versa* for men in women's prisons.

One might theorize that these are just criminals who have, for the most part, been convicted of committing violent crimes and therefore should not be extended any particular privileges. To an extent, I have to agree with that opinion. I don't believe that criminals should be allowed to enjoy all of the modern conveniences of home like the politicians and their white-collar criminal associates who, as punishment for their crimes, are granted occasional vacations in a variety of "Clubs Fed" around the country. But I do believe that even criminals should be extended some human decency. We are supposed to be a civil society and a "civil"ization is expected to treat all beings in a civil manner even if those beings are themselves uncivil.

The major difference between my situation and the situation in prisons concerning convicted criminals is that I had never been convicted of anything and I was still subjected to the degradation and humiliation of, what I would consider to be, extremely uncivil conditions. Try imagining yourself in that prison experiencing the same things that I had to experience. Put yourself in the same small cell having to relieve yourself several times a day in a variety of ways in front of a stranger of the opposite sex. Exposure to anyone under those conditions, even of the same sex, goes far, far beyond cruel and unusual punishment for any INNOCENT CITIZEN and should be intolerable for the citizens of this great nation.

I must admit, for the most part, the guards were friendly toward me. The situation of which we were all a part in Milan Penitentiary was really no more their fault than mine. Of course, they were all there voluntarily and I was not. For some unknown reason I've just never quite understood why being in prison was "for my own good." If someone could have successfully explained why this humiliating and degrading experience which resulted in the temporary loss of all of my rights and freedoms and a permanent loss of my reputation was for my own good I might have volunteered. But I doubt it.

I must also admit that my stay in Milan was not without its humor. After several days had passed none of the guards wanted the night shift. In a conversation with some of the guards I was told why. They had to turn up the volume on their television because my snoring was so loud they couldn't hear the programs. According to the guards, when they turned up the volume on their television, I turned up the volume on my snoring. The louder the volume got on the television the louder my snoring got, so I was told. They said that I snored so loud they were arguing about who wouldn't get the night shift. Now I'm not going to admit to snoring louder than the maximum volume on their television. I think they were exaggerating to be honest, but I was asleep during every one of those nightly ordeals in question, so I guess I wouldn't really be considered a credible witness. I thought the event was just humorous enough to lighten the atmosphere of an otherwise uncomfortable situation.

Another event, if you could call it that, seemed to happen every Tuesday. Whenever I received bad news, it seemed to come on Tuesdays. Without fail, every time another Tuesday came along I could count on some kind of bad news coming with it. Eventually we just called them the "Terrible Tuesdays." I had the feeling very early on that the corrections officers who were on duty watching me in my cell realized they were guarding an innocent farmer who was doing unnecessary time in a federal penitentiary. In my opinion this also made for some uneasy feelings on their part so any conversation with them or any humorous situation helped reduce the tension to some extent.

I think my first and second hearings before a federal magistrate set some sort of precedent. Apparently someone assumed I was such a dangerous criminal that I should not be allowed to leave the penitentiary to attend my own hearings in a courthouse. Maybe the feds thought that if they escorted me from prison to a courtroom the Michigan Militia would come to my rescue engaging the feds in a major gun battle. Or maybe the feds were starting to believe their own propaganda. Possibly they were just trying to convince everyone else. For whatever reason, they brought a federal magistrate into the prison to conduct the hearings. Now I'm not saying for certain that it has never happened but I must admit that I am unfamiliar with any previous case in which the hearings were held in the prison. The guards told me that I made history because it had never happened in Milan before. They said that they didn't even do that for former Panamanian military dictator Manuel Noriega, the reputed international drug dealer who allegedly made those notorious deals with our over-zealous entrepreneurial CIA to help raise a multibillion-dollar "slush-fund" — then pocket a few billion for himself on the side.

The media apparently asked the authorities for a copy of the tape of that first hearing and were turned down. The *Detroit Free Press* eventually sued under the Freedom of Information Act and the tape was released but, low and behold, the tape recording of that hearing was blank. What a coincidence. It had been 30 years since anything like that had happened here. I didn't know things like that could happen in non-political cases. But, then again, that just might be a clue.

Another memorable experience was my first visit from members of my family. I first hugged my mother and she hugged me. I cried and she cried. I don't think there was a dry eye among us and we are not a family of criers. Generally when we suffer a tragedy as a family we spend our day of mourning and then get back out into the field the next day to get our work done kind of like they did in the old days. When the cow needs milking and the field needs plowing the chores just won't wait until you feel good about doing them. But that first meeting with my family was a very emotional experience for all of us that I will never forget.

During that first week or so I spent many hours discussing my situation with my court appointed attorney, Miriam Siefer. Technically, they were trying to charge me with conspiring to make and possess firearms, that is, destructive devices, that were not registered in the National Firearms Registration and Transfer Record in violation of the provisions of Chapter 53 of Title 26, Internal Revenue Code. And although Miriam is a very competent, knowledgeable counsel, I don't think she really understood the concept of defending oneself by challenging the jurisdiction of the government (her employer), or the concept of the individual sovereignty defense. I am in no way criticizing Miriam's capabilities as an attorney. However, few attorneys ever get involved in cases that differ considerably from the norm. We originally discussed challenging jurisdiction, and it seemed as if Miriam was willing to explore that possibility. At each meeting thereafter she expressed the desire to defend me in the more conventional manner, a defense strategy with which I totally disagreed. If I understood her intentions correctly, she planned on making some kind of deal with the prosecution which was guaranteed to net me only a couple of years, max (WHAT?).

Not that I didn't appreciate her effort, but considering the charges against me—and considering that I knew the charges were nothing more than a figment of the prosecution's vivid imagination — "a couple of years max" seemed to be just a little harsh for an innocent man. I had other, more intellectually and physically challenging plans for the next two years and those plans did not include holding down a cot in Milan. Besides, I had very strong suspicions about the lack of jurisdiction of government agents when they were raiding my farm and the more time I had to think about it the more those suspicions escalated. •

"For quartering large bodies of armed troops among us:
For protecting them, by a mock trial, from punishment for any Murders
which they should commit on the Inhabitants of these States:"
— The Declaration of Independence

CHAPTER 4: A DENIAL OF RIGHTS; ENTER, MR. ELSEY

When my friends, Jim LeValley and Phil Morowski, became aware of my dilemma they decided to retain a private attorney for me. Enter Robert Elsey, a very bright and aggressive counsel who refused to be intimidated by the wrath of the federal government and who, under enormous pressure, still refuses to compromise his Constitutional principles. After meeting with Mr. Elsey my first impression was that he seemed to be the right man for the job. The more we talked, the more convinced I became. And, after watching his performance in court, there was no doubt that my first impression was absolutely correct. His oral arguments and cross examination of witnesses for the prosecution were imposing, to say the least.

I must mention that I had two hearings during that period of incarceration in which my bail was denied. This denial of bail was a direct violation of my Constitutional rights. We filed a writ of habeas corpus which should have released me from unlawful imprisonment. A writ of habeas corpus simply presents the issue of whether a prisoner is restrained of his liberty by due process. If there has been no due process then it is considered unlawful imprisonment. Keep in mind that the so-called "anti-terrorism bill" that the President and his cronies in Congress have passed recently on the coattails of the Oklahoma City bombing suspends the writ of habeas corpus in direct violation of the U.S. Constitution, so now they can justify their actions and unlawfully do that to anyone they desire — including you. This is not "progressive" law, it is extremely "regressive." The writ of habeas corpus is one important part of our justice system that distinguishes free, civil societies from those societies whose oppression keeps them enveloped in the politics of the Dark Ages.

An article in the *Detroit News* on May 25, 1995, quoted several attorneys and former judges on the subject of a writ of habeas corpus concerning my case. These are some of their opinions.

• "Certainly he was treated differently because of the Oklahoma investigation. But no investigation is reason enough to suspend our rights." — Patrick Keenan, law professor at the University of Detroit.

• Michael Batchelor, a Detroit defense attorney said that my case set "a dangerous precedent. Why wasn't he let out on a writ of habeas corpus? That's our right under common (Constitutional) law." Objecting to my being required to wear an electronic tracking tether, he went on to say: "We have bonds to secure a court appearance. A tether is for ... after you've been convicted of a crime. This is the kind of thing that impacts on you and me. How many of us will now be tethered by the government, in place of a bond?"

• Former Recorder's Court Judge David Kertwin said: "My experience (with the federal government's lawyers) is that they will go to court and say someone is a bad person because he is associated with bad people. When you have the President and Attorney General talking about the death penalty, it sets up a climate of vigilante justice that puts all our rights in jeopardy."

• "I think Nichols' lengthy detention is a classic case of the legal system caving in to public pressure," said Howard Simon, executive director of the American Civil Liberties Union of Michigan.

• "It's somewhat scary to think of a government that can arrest and hold you for one month or longer, then subsequently, a judge ... finds that you're not a threat to the community or a flight risk," said attorney Brian Legghio, who served six years as an assistant U.S. attorney in Detroit.

Considering the statements from these prominent officers of the court it is undeniable that my opinion concerning my unlawful detainment and the denial of my right to a writ of habeas corpus under the Constitution is shared by many, if not all, legal scholars.

During my successful bail-bond hearing before Judge Paul Borman, Mr. Elsey's cross examination of FBI Special Agent Patrick Wease was very enlightening, particularly for those members of the media who were somewhat uninformed about the so-called evidence on which the charges against me were based. After questioning Agent Wease for about ten or fifteen minutes, Mr. Elsey hesitated and walked away indicating that he was finished with the witness. Just as Agent Wease relaxed believing he had faired quite well answering all of the defense's questions with a professional evasiveness unequaled by any non-government persons, Mr. Elsey turned and suggested that he had one more minor question and that he wouldn't take much more time asking that question.

One thing led to another, as things have a tendency to do during cross-examination, at which point Mr. Elsey proceeded to hammer Agent Wease for another 45 minutes, extracting much information that Agent Wease undoubtedly would've rather not revealed in open court. After Agent Wease contradicted his original testimony on about four different occasions, it became apparent that his original statements were not exactly forthright. It also became apparent that Mr. Elsey was a force to be reckoned with and that these FBI agents, most of whom had law degrees themselves, were not in the same league as Robert Elsey. Neither were the prosecutors.

I'm not necessarily trying to criticize the courtroom capabilities of the prosecutors or agents for the FBI who have law degrees. I doubt that there are many attorneys anywhere who could match the abilities of Robert Elsey, so it's not exactly an insult to have been "outdone" by Mr. Elsey in court. Having the truth on our side definitely made Mr. Elsey's job easier but being right doesn't always mean that you will succeed in court. I do think it is necessary to criticize the FBI's evasive answers under cross-examination. Particularly disheartening was their aversion for telling the truth. I would have thought that the truth would be the FBI's ultimate goal. I sure was wrong about that thought. Live and learn!

The truth came out in court about several issues that had been misrepresented by the media who had been disinformed by "unnamed sources" in the FBI who had leaked this false information. One bit of information that finally saw the light of day was the aluminum powder; four whole ounces of aluminum powder, that I kept on hand for plugging leaky radiators. The FBI, through the media, made a real big deal about the aluminum powder suggesting that it could have been used to enhance the explosions in the Murrah Building. Of course, since I just happened to have a half-pint of aluminum powder in my shed it must have meant that I was involved in the conspiracy. It didn't really matter that the amount I had on hand would've only been enough aluminum powder to plug one radiator in a large tractor. It didn't matter that any other farmer or backyard mechanic anywhere would've had the same substance on hand and, generally speaking, much more than four ounces of the stuff. Many painters keep aluminum powder on hand for mixing paint. All of this information and much more information about aluminum powder was revealed in court proving how ridiculous the prosecution's allegations actually were.

More disinformation leaked by unverifiable, a.k.a. unaccountable, sources in the FBI concerned the alleged ammonium nitrate fertilizer found in my tool shed. The feds were persistent in feeding erroneous information to the press about the "suspect fertilizer" and the press eagerly reported every little piece of false information they were duped into believing. I tried to tell everyone from the very beginning that I had no ammonium nitrate fertilizer on hand. Not that it would've even been a big deal because many farmers keep many tons of ammonium nitrate in storage. The bags of fertilizer that I had were *calcium* nitrate which cannot be used as an explosive. I tried over and over again to show the FBI the difference, unfortunately, to no avail. They totally ignored the facts and the real evidence in this investigation and leaked incriminating accusations (lies) to the media even though they knew that there was no real evidence against me. Some people still think that I had ammonium nitrate fertilizer in my shed!

Another piece of "evidence" that the FBI tried to use to discredit me in court was an alias Social Security number. Agent Wease testified that I had used this phony Social Security number suggesting that I had been up to something sinister and didn't want my real identity to be known. Keep in mind that this is the same special agent who was in charge of the raid on my farm and the same special agent who admitted to me that he and the other three agents in charge knew that I had no involvement in the bombing or anything else illegal.   During cross-examination Mr. Elsey asked Agent Wease if the FBI had checked out this alias number (that I had allegedly used) in an attempt to discover to whom it really belonged?   Agent Wease replied, under oath, "That wasn't part of our investigation."

The FBI had that Social Security number for more than a month. The FBI said they suspected that the person who they claimed to be the "guru" behind the worst act of terrorism in U. S. history was fraudulently using this number to avoid being identified while carrying on secret and possibly sinister activities. The FBI actually expects us to believe that among the hundreds and perhaps thousands of federal agents involved in this investigation the thought never occurred to even one of those agents to take ten seconds of their time and punch that number into their computer to see if they could match a name to that number. That wasn't part of their investigation? That expectation by the FBI was, at the least, very insulting. I didn't believe them for a minute and I don't think anyone else did either. Doesn't it make you wonder: If FBI agents didn't ever punch that number into their computer, how did they know for certain that it wasn't my number?

Anyway, it appeared as if the FBI took a chance hoping, maybe even assuming, that it wouldn't be brought to task on its accusations concerning the false Social Security number. If their allegations weren't challenged, the rumor would continue, thereby discrediting me in court in front of many members of the local and national media. Fortunately, Mr. Elsey did challenge the FBI allegations and, fortunately, my mother was in the courtroom to identify the number for Mr. Elsey. The farm and properties are in my mother's name and the Social Security number in question was also her number. Since the farm was in her name, whose Social Security number would any reasonable person expect to appear on a contract involving her farm's business? Of course, no one has ever claimed that federal investigators or prosecutors are reasonable people.

After reading the real facts about this particular testimony in court, is there anyone naive enough to believe that identifying the real owner of that Social Security number wasn't really a part of the FBI's investigation? Assuming that none of the people who are reading this book are that naive, what might any "thinking" person conclude concerning the FBI agent's testimony under oath and in open court before a federal Judge? Might a thinking person conclude that the agent committed perjury? I personally do not want to believe that any law enforcement agent, especially a special agent for the FBI, would lie on the witness stand in federal court. But even more alarming than doing it is that they could actually get away with it and that their actions would go unpunished and, worse yet, unreported. And, if they can get away with perjury in such a high-profile case, what can and are they getting away with in all of the less visible cases? If federal agents have no fear of being prosecuted for perjury what's going to keep them from lying about Terry or Tim when their trials start? Honesty and morality certainly haven't been a determining factor in dictating that they "tell the whole truth and nothing but the truth" in the past, so we shouldn't expect compliance on their part any time in the near future.

Many legal issues were clarified at my bail-bond hearing. One point on which Judge Borman took issue with the prosecution was their assertion that I needed a license and then a permit to blow off any type of explosive devise on my farm. Everyone knows that farmers often use dynamite, ANFO (ammonium nitrate/fuel oil), and a variety of other explosives for ditching, removing boulders, tree stumps, etc. During one of the prosecution's tirades challenging the potential release of that evil farmer, James D. Nichols, Judge Borman interjected (not exactly verbatim), "Do you mean to tell me, Mr. Prosecutor, that any time Mr. Nichols wants to put gun powder into a little pill bottle to get his soybeans from his grain bin, he first has to contact the Secretary of the Treasury to secure a license so he can get a permit to loosen and remove his beans?"

Mr. Prosecutor responded with considerably more of the same rhetoric at which point it became apparent that Judge Borman was getting a little annoyed at the prosecution's ridiculous allegations. Judge Borman, obviously a very knowledgeable and wise federal judge, again asked, "Do you mean to tell me, Mr. Prosecutor, that any time Mr. Nichols or any other farmer wants to use some kind of explosive to blow a stump or move a rock in his field, he first has to contact the Secretary of the Treasury to secure a license so he can get a permit to remove those rocks or stumps?" (not exactly verbatim)

According to Bob Papovich, at that point some members of the press put their face down in their hands to hide their laughter and to keep from laughing aloud in federal court. Even prior to that particular fiasco I think everyone realized that the government's case against me was a joke. Unfortunately, after spending 32 days in a federal penitentiary and after being accused, although not formally charged, by government agents and prosecutors of being involved in a vicious act of terrorism for which the penalty would be death, none of this seemed like much of a joke to me. Nor did I find particularly humorous all of the accusations coming from every imaginable source in the media even after these hearings clarified all of those false accusations. I can assure you that all facets of the media were very well represented at my hearings so from that time forward they had no excuse for not reporting the truth. Many still do not report the truth and they still have no excuse.

There was another crucial point that Judge Borman clarified during my bail-bond hearing. The prosecutor, while launching into another tirade attempting to destroy my character with numerous false accusations, argued that I should be denied bail because I would be a flight risk. Since, according to the prosecutor, it was a matter of record that I had denounced my citizenship thereby having no ties to this country, I would feel no obligation to obey the court's travel restrictions and could not be trusted to stay within the boundaries of the United States.

Judge Borman corrected the prosecution's allegations with some legal wisdom that absolutely astounded me. He said, but not exactly verbatim, "It appears to me, Mr. Prosecutor, that Mr. Nichols renounced his citizenship to the *de facto*, illegitimate government of the United States. He did not renounce his citizenship to the *de jure*, lawful government of the united States."

Now this statement may shock many of you who had no idea that their precious government was illegitimate. This information is not new to many millions of patriotic American citizens who have had the opportunity to read and understand our Constitution. Technically, our current government doesn't even exist unless you agree to acknowledge its existence. You have to volunteer into a contract with that illegitimate entity and I certainly don't want to volunteer. Do you? If you don't want to believe these facts in law I will be happy to print for you, in part, some definitions from Black's Law Dictionary:

a. *Government de facto.* A government actually exercising power and control, as opposed to the true and lawful government; a government not established according to the Constitution of the nation, or not lawfully entitled to recognition or supremacy, but which has nevertheless supplanted or displaced the government de jure. A government deemed unlawful, or deemed wrongful or unjust, which, nevertheless, receives presently habitual obedience from the bulk of the community.

The distinguishing characteristic of such a government is that adherents to it in WAR against the government de jure DO NOT INCUR THE PENALTIES OF TREASON. (emphasis mine) Such a government might be more aptly denominated a "government of paramount force," being maintained by active military power against the rightful authority of an established and lawful government; and obeyed in civil matters by private citizens.

b. *Government de jure.* A government of right; the true and lawful government; a government established according to the constitution of the nation, and lawfully entitled to recognition and supremacy and the administration of the nation, but which is actually cut off from power or control (by the *de facto* government).

The current condition of the United States government and these definitions kind of remind me of a quote that I once read. "Treason doth never prosper, what's the reason? For if it prosper, none dare call it treason." Sir John Harrington, 1561 - 1612

Considering the current state of affairs concerning this de facto corporate United States government and taking into consideration these legal definitions in Black's Law Dictionary, a thinking person may have a tendency to conclude that the persons who have been responsible for "displacing by force or by fraud" the de jure lawful [u]nited States government may well be guilty of treason. I certainly can't think of any argument to dispel that conclusion.

Karl Granse (612-431-1845), the founder of citizens for a Constitutional republic, has been giving legal seminars teaching concerned citizens about the legal concept of limited jurisdiction for the bureaucrats in Washington's "District of Criminals" for quite some time. In reality, according to the law, they only have jurisdiction over the citizens of the United States, its possessions (military bases or other land ceded to it by the States), and its territories (Guam, Puerto Rico, etc.). So when Congress passes a law the only ones bound by that law are the citizens of

Washington D.C., its possessions and territories and, believe it or not, Congress. The sovereign citizens of the [u]nited States are not bound by the laws, treaties, foreign or domestic welfare entitlements, or even the national debt that Congress has incurred over the past few decades.

Do you remember that the charges against me were under Title 26 USC ? Doesn't it make you wonder why "firearms and destructive devices" would fall under Title 26 of the Federal Income Tax Code? I'll tell you why. The Bureau of Alcohol Tobacco and Firearms works directly for the IRS. The IRS exists directly under the Department of the Treasury, Puerto Rico, specifically to remove from circulation as much unlawful money as possible which is being put into circulation by the Federal Reserve which is not really federal but is, in fact, a private bank corporation. The BATF exists under Title 26 and is really nothing more than a strong arm (Gestapo) for the IRS, the Department of the Treasury, Puerto Rico, and the private Federal Reserve Bank. And remember that Judge Borman asked Mr. Prosecutor if he thought it was necessary for me to get a license from the "Secretary of the Treasury" to blow off a vile of black powder to loosen my beans. Shouldn't at least some of those curious journalists present have wondered just what the Treasury Department had to do with explosive devices and the BATF?

Judge Borman's judicial admission proved this information to be true. This all has to do with corporate law and a de facto government which has no jurisdiction over [u]nited States Citizens. The Dept. of the Treasury, Puerto Rico, the IRS and the BATF have no authority to act in the united States or against the citizens of the several States. It really makes you feel safe to know that these "jack booted thugs" (i.e., Corporate Federal Reserve/IRS Nazis) are out here protecting you, doesn't it? "But," says the Feds, "they only want to help us!" All I can say is, "Please, don't be so good to us."

You must keep in mind that the brilliant scoundrels who have imposed this definition scam upon us have used any and all means necessary to deceive the American public into believing and then admitting by contractual agreement that they were citizens of the United States, a little legal technicality that brings into Congressional (*de facto*) jurisdiction all of those individuals who previously, by birth, were sovereign citizens. All means necessary includes a constant media blitz and controlling certain information contained within the textbooks in our government schools. Were you taught the truth about your citizenship in your government school?

Keep in mind that you cannot be lawfully deceived into relinquishing your Rights. If all of the facts about losing your rights are made known to you and you still willfully and knowingly enter into a contract or agreement that will result in the loss of those rights, you have a problem. If all the details were not made known to you then the perpetrator of the fraud has a problem because, according to law, any contract entered into under fraud is null and void. It never existed. Were you told that you were relinquishing your sovereignty under constitutional law and entering into an admiralty jurisdiction controlled by a *de facto*, illegitimate corporate United States government when you applied for a Social Security card? I didn't think so.

Coincidentally, there is an article by Jim Thomas in the October, 1996, issue of *Media Bypass* concerning some aspects of this very issue. It's short, to the point, easy to read and understand if you're interested. Many more details on this subject have appeared in more recent issues of *Media Bypass*. Attending a Karl Granse seminar is necessary if you really want to understand the laws pertaining to these issues of law but reading Jim Thomas's article should whet your appetite. As you will soon see, my case would eventually prove these facts of law to be true.

What really shocked me and many of my friends who just happened to be present at the hearing was that a federal judge actually had the courage to make that statement in open court in front of members of the media. It appeared that the three dozen or so members of the media who were present in the courtroom either didn't understand what Judge Borman was talking about or just chose to ignore it. What really disappointed us was that the most important words spoken during the entire hearing never got quoted anywhere on television or in print.

Now it could be that those who are in control of the media don't want the American citizens to know that their government is not a lawful, Constitutional government but simply has the same status as a corporation. They may not want the people to know that that corporation's jurisdiction extends only to the 100 square miles (10 mi. x 10 mi.) of Washington's "District of Criminals" and its possessions and territories. They may not want the American citizens to know that the United States government has no jurisdiction over the sovereign citizens of the [u]nited States unless those Citizens give up their sovereignty and voluntarily "join the corporation" of the United States, so to speak.

Or it could just be that the information to which I'm referring never made it to the nightly news or anywhere in print because the only non-airheads in that courtroom were the Judge, Robert Elsey, yours truly, and my friends. We could hope that this extremely valuable information was never reported because no one else in the courtroom had the foggiest idea of what the hell Judge Borman was even talking about, but I really doubt that was the case.

The prosecutor also charged that my background at previous court proceedings proved that I had a total disregard for the law and there was no reason to believe that I would obey the law or the orders of the court at this particular time. Mr. Elsey dispelled that allegation by pointing out that I had always respected the law, appearing before the court any and every time that an appearance had been required of me. Mr. Elsey further solidified Judge Borman's opinion that I was not a flight risk by making mention of the fact that I had been living in the same house and working the same farm for about twenty years. He also accurately stated that almost all of my family and friends lived in or near Sanilac County where my farm is located.

At the end of the hearing Judge Borman indicated that he would release me with some restrictions. I could work at my farm, but could not stay overnight at my farmhouse. Fortunately, several of my close friends stated in court that I could stay at their homes until this problem was resolved. The judge selected Les and Rhonda Roggenbuck of Snover, Mich., as my temporary guardians. I had to be at their house no later than 10 p.m. every night and could leave no earlier than 6 a.m. every morning. There could be no firearms of any type at my farmhouse or at the dwelling where I was to reside. Considering that, at the time, Les and Rhonda were a young married couple with a two-year-old daughter and another baby on the way, the swarming press and constant surveillance and phone taps by the FBI had to be a very trying experience. Being a young family man and realizing the potential for danger, that he would've still agreed to those unpredictable circumstances, Les displayed a degree of intestinal fortitude that few people can even imagine.

And Rhonda. I can't possibly say enough about her. She's beautiful, feisty, tough, high-strung, yet she has an unbelievable sense of humor. This gutsy young lady had a small child and was five months pregnant when she agreed to accept a boarder who was accused of the worst act of terrorism in the history of this country. I can't really think of a word to describe the courage of Rhonda Roggenbuck. Rhonda, Saint Rhonda. How can I ever thank her for sacrificing her privacy, her subjection to potential danger and for her absolute confidence in my innocence? She has the "stuff" that our Founding Fathers were made of. The same "stuff" that is nonexistent in the current political structure of this great country. Our politicians and government agents could certainly learn a lesson in principles from this courageous young American mother.

Since it had been thoroughly established that I had no previous record of any kind and that I was not a flight risk Judge Borman concluded that

I could be released on my own recognizance. In his comments he also stated that "There is not one iota of evidence of dangerous acts toward others." The statement was obviously made about me.

The prosecutor then argued, with much persistence, that there should be some restrictions placed upon me by the court. Thanks to Mr. Prosecutor, my ability to travel was limited to a nine county area and, believe it or not, an electronic tether was fastened to my ankle. He and everyone else on the government's team knew that these restrictions were not necessary to secure any and all future appearances that may be required of me, but I'm sure he had his reasons, and his orders.

As we now know, exaggeration and deception is not beneath the moral character of nearly all U.S. prosecutors, and many other prosecutors for that matter and that character flaw is precisely why they have become U.S. prosecutors. It's kind of like a person who has a desire to steal and becomes a thief, or a person with a desire to rape who becomes a rapist. You may be thinking, "My God, how can you categorize prosecutors with thieves and rapists?" When you consider that periodically information surfaces in the news that an innocent person has been in prison for many years and, after reviewing the evidence in the case, it becomes apparent that the "public saviors" who prosecuted him knew they were sending an innocent man to prison, how else might one categorize these criminals?

It is estimated that, in this country, approximately 8,000 innocent people are sent to prison annually for serious crimes. Just by applying what we have learned in our own experiences in court, we would have to guess that the prosecutors were aware of the innocence of the accused in many, if not most of those 8,000 cases. The objective of many prosecutors is not to determine the guilt or innocence of the accused, but to get a conviction at any cost.

On Feb. 3, 1996, an article appeared in the *Daily Oklahoman* concerning a death penalty case in Oklahoma wherein it would appear as if this sort of cover-up occurred. Following is information from that article which helps to prove our point in addition to raising other issues.

Bill Devinney, past president of the Oklahoma Criminal Defense Lawyers Association, said he represented an Oklahoma death row inmate who would have been executed if HR 2768 (so-called anti-terrorism bill) had been in effect. That man, Adolph "Abe" Munson, was later found innocent at a 1995 re-trial — about 10 years after he was "convicted."

"By luck and by accident ... our investigator located two boxes of documents that had been withheld from the defense for a decade,"

Devinney said. "Those documents ultimately proved that Mr. Munson was innocent of the crime and he had spent nearly 10 years on death row here for a crime he did not commit."

If a new state post-conviction law and the proposed federal law had been in place, "Mr. Munson would have been executed in 1988 before anybody found out about any of this, " Devinney said.

"It's not worth the price to execute innocent people. Abe Munson wasn't the first (innocent) person found on death row in Oklahoma. I doubt he will be the last. It happens in other states, too." he said.

Now the first question that comes to my mind is: These documents that ultimately proved Mr. Munson was innocent had been withheld from the defense by *whom*? This is obviously a rhetorical question. These documents were certainly not withheld from Mr. Munson's defense team by Mr. Munson's defense team. Who else does that leave in a position to withhold documents from the defense? Only the prosecution. The prosecutor and quite possibly the prosecution's entire team and perhaps even some law-enforcement personnel were willing to send an innocent man to prison and, ultimately, to his death just so they could win a case. Unbelievable as it may seem, this is not necessarily an uncommon incident concerning the prosecution of accused defendants and it is not an uncommon mindset of prosecutors.

We must reason that if there are innocent people in prison and on death row, who were knowingly railroaded by a prosecutor, then it is not unreasonable to assume that there have been many innocent people who have been placed on death row and consequently executed. How would you describe persons who would knowingly and willingly send an innocent man to his death just to receive the rewards of promotion and glory for winning a case? To realize that this is a matter of fact one only needs to pay attention to the occasional exposé by a variety of investigative journalists on several popular news programs which we regularly enjoy on television during prime-time viewing.

One program recently covered another case many years old in which it was shown that the prosecutor had interviewed witnesses who would have proved his "victim" was innocent had it been known to the defense that these witnesses existed. The prosecutor never disclosed that information to the court or to the defense thereby securing a conviction of an innocent man. That disclosure was required by law under the rules of discovery. You could say that this particular prosecutor may have been a little overzealous in his attempt to get the bad guy and just got "caught up in the chase," so to speak.

Personally, I think the whole scenario is just a little simpler than that.

I would have to say that the prosecutor, and perhaps his whole team, are no different than cold, calculating, premeditated murderers. Basically, sub-human. It's kind of scary when you come to the realization that the reason these public servants have pursued their positions of employment is to protect the citizens from people with whom these public servants have much in common. "Who will protect us from our protectors?" asks Mark Scott on WXYT (Detroit) talk radio.

In a recent issue of *Media Bypass* we had the opportunity to read an excellent and informative article by Michael Brown titled, "Grand Jury Secrecy." In that article, Mr. Brown comments on a similar issue:

"What actually happens, as Hoppy Heidelberg discovered, is that grand jury secrecy is used to prevent the systematic misbehavior of government attorneys from coming to light. Since most federal judges are appointed from the ranks of these miscreants, you readily see why the rest of the behavior of the federal judiciary is so erratic, unpredictable, unconstitutional, and in many cases, criminal."

He goes on to say: "It is my own opinion that you cannot make a defender and upholder of the Constitution (what a federal judge is supposed to be) out of an individual who spent a great deal of his career trampling the very cornerstone of that Constitution ... as a federal prosecutor."

Let's see now. Didn't Mr. Brown mention that his observation of the federal judiciary was one of "systematic misbehavior, erratic, unpredictable, unconstitutional, and criminal?" Apparently we are not alone in our observations or opinions of federal prosecutors. I believe it could be said with some degree of certainty that many thousands of patriotic citizens who are reading these words right now could tell us thousands of horror stories involving federal prosecutors and federal judges.

At the time we didn't really understand why our Mr. Prosecutor was so insistent on limiting my travel, other than the fact that he based his arguments on the lies that he told about me while trying to deceive the court, which is not really untypical for a person in his position of employment. Eventually the reasons for Mr. Prosecutor's insistence would become very clear to us. It also became very clear that these guys seldom play with a full deck and generally deal from the bottom when they do play.

"Erratic" and "criminal" sound like pretty accurate descriptions once you've actually had some first-hand experience with these public saviors on a federal level. •

Photo by Debby Racine

Newly released and displaying a smile that reflects exhilaration and exhaustion, James Nichols enters the home of Les and Rhonda Roggenbuck.

Photoby Debby Racine

This home owned by Les and Rhonda Roggenbuck provided sanctuary for James Nichols from late May to Aug. 10, 1995.

"The Privilege of the Writ of Habeas Corpus shall not be suspended, unless when in Cases of Rebellion or Invasion the public Safety may require it."
— **Article 1, Section 9, U.S. Constitution**

Chapter 5: Limited Freedom — and Some Wild Times!

I was released to the custody of Les and Rhonda the day after my bail-bond hearing. When we left the courthouse in downtown Detroit we got a little lost, which turned out for the best because we were being followed by several vehicles some of which, we assumed, were driven by FBI agents and some by members of the media. We made so many wrong turns and got going around in circles so many times that we unintentionally lost those who were following us. Had we been driving anyplace other than a busy downtown area we would have never lost the FBI agents who were tailing us. And I'm speaking from experience when I make that statement. Of course they knew where we were going so it wasn't exactly a life-or-death situation that they stayed within eyesight of our vehicle. Besides, I was already wearing their "collar" so they were probably tracking me, anyway.

On the way home, we stopped and had some lunch at a restaurant without the intrusion of the media which was a welcomed break for all of us. On the way to Les and Rhonda's, we stopped in Marlette to switch cars and at that point, Rhonda headed for home. We had already determined that it may be less chaotic if I did not arrive during daylight hours so we stopped by Don Bullock's for awhile to visit and to gather our thoughts. From there we went to Paul's house to get my car and we were spotted by the FBI who then began following me.

We knew there would be members of the media and some law enforcement personnel stationed around Les and Rhonda's farm but in our wildest dreams we never could have imagined how many would actually be there waiting for us. I was about a mile away when the media's satellite trucks first became visible. The lights from police cars and from the media's camera equipment were reflecting off the large satellite dishes sitting atop the trucks making them very visible and unusual looking from a distance. Several county sheriff's patrol cars that were parked close to the house were directing traffic. It also appeared as if they were visually checking people who drove by to make certain the area remained safe and secure for everyone. Other police cars, State and local, were stationed several hundred yards from the farmhouse on each of the four roads so that anyone approaching could be seen before they actually got close. It was a very unusual scene on a dark rainy night out here in the middle of farm country where there are generally no lights other than your headlights or a security light on a barn.

Needless to say, the FBI had their agents parked around in inconspicuous places keeping a watchful eye. Actually, some of them were obvious but to the average passing motorist their presence probably would not have been noticed because they generally drove an unmarked Ford Taurus sedan which is one of the most popular, commonly driven cars in this country.

I took a side road to the farm which had a back entrance, which is really nothing more than a cow path, that the media didn't know about. It was really the only way to get into the yard and to the house without causing an accident, running somebody over, creating a major stampede or all of the above. The reporters all came running with the bright camera lights glaring in my eyes making it difficult to see where I was going. After a brief conversation with some microphones I entered the back door of Les and Rhonda's to be greeted by several close friends who were waiting inside.

The reason I said that I had a brief conversation with microphones is because of the effect that the bright lights had on my eyes in the darkness. Although there must have been several media people in the crowd who knew me, I didn't acknowledge them because I couldn't see any faces, only bright, blinding lights. We had a great deal of sympathy for all the reporters who had been waiting patiently in the cold, dark rain for several hours. I realize that they had a job to do and that they really didn't get much for their efforts. I can only hope that we did not offend any of them and that they understood my dilemma. We even talked about inviting them in out of the cold rain but that was obviously impossible because the number of reporters who were there could not possibly have fit in Rhonda's house. We could not invite inside those few reporters who we knew while leaving everyone else out in the cold. Had I been at my own farmhouse I probably would've invited all of these dedicated, hardworking citizens inside and just worried about cleaning up the muddy mess later.

When I entered Les and Rhonda's house I was greeted by many hugs and handshakes from all of my friends. Rhonda had chairs arranged in a large circle in the living room where we could all sit and rehash the experiences of the past month and discuss what we would do from this point forward. Later in the evening during a casual conversation in the kitchen, Rhonda and Sandy Papovich were talking about the restrictions that the court had imposed upon Les and Rhonda, on their home and on my farmhouse. Rhonda was saying that among the Court's demands was a restriction on firearms in their house and at my farmhouse. There could be no guns of any kind kept at either location. Right in the middle of the sentence Les walked into the kitchen and immediately "tuned in" to the conversation at hand.

"Yea, I'm gonna have to take our hunting rifles down to my dad's farm tomorrow for safekeeping when I get a chance to go over there," Les said, joining in on the discussion.

"You mean your guns are still here?" screamed Rhonda. "My God, Les, I told you that we couldn't have any guns anywhere while James is staying here. We have to get those guns out of here, now!"

The obvious question was: How? The entire area was surrounded by news media, crawling with state and local police officers, and even worse, an undetermined number of federal agents. We had no idea what kind of "surveillance technology" they had positioned around Les and Rhonda's house, or if they had any at all. We had no idea whether or not they were listening to our conversations inside the house. We're all just workin' people living in rural America and don't have the foggiest about any of this spying stuff.

Apparently Les didn't realize just how serious the restrictions of the court were and how important it was to comply with those restrictions from moment one, not until this conversation anyway. Now he knew and we all knew that we had a very serious problem. How in the world would we get the guns out of the house without being seen? They may already know that we have them if they were listening to our conversations. Needless to say, at that very moment we were all suffering from an acute case of panic attack! We couldn't waste any time, we had to get those guns out of the house and off the premises without being seen. If we tried that now we would most certainly be seen by someone and would then have a major problem on our hands. If we waited, we risked the possibility that the feds could get into position outside and bust us as we came out the door with Les' hunting rifles.

Realizing that we had to move quickly but could not afford to be seen, we decided to wait just a little while until things settled down outside. After some time passed, we checked around outside to see if there was anyone hiding nearby the house. It was so dark outside that there could've been twenty agents hiding out there within 100 feet of the house without ever being detected. Anyway, after checking around a little and trying not to be obvious about what we were doing, it appeared as if the coast was clear. Les bundled up all of his rifles and hustled out the door as quickly as possible, jumped in his truck and drove from his property a fast as he could. Once on the road we didn't know if the FBI could still cause trouble for us, but there was no doubt that the guns being on his property would cause some major trouble. From the window in the house we could see the taillights of Les' truck disappear into the dark, rainy night and we knew we were safe, for awhile anyway.

Over the next two months, my movements were monitored 24 hours a day by FBI agents. They followed me everywhere. Sometimes there were two cars and sometimes as many as eight cars. At times it seemed like I was part of a convoy. When I went home there were always two FBI vehicles parked in clear view of my house. My friends could always locate which field I was working on any particular day because there were always at least two FBI cars parked in a spot where the agents could watch me.

Every night they followed me back to Les and Rhonda's and parked down the road for awhile. My ankle tether had to be within 100 feet of a receiver and monitor inside the house by 10 p.m. or a signal would be sent through the phone lines to a law enforcement officer's location. An attempt would be made to contact me and if contact was not made immediately agents would come to the Roggenbucks' home. It wasn't really necessary for the feds to stand guard all night because if my tether was removed or if I strayed beyond 100 feet from the electronic device an alarm would be sent to the FBI. That didn't seem to matter because for the first thirty days at least one agent occupied an all night position to keep a watchful eye. Even after thirty days one agent may have been on guard all night watching from a neighbor's yard across the street but I'm not absolutely certain.

Friends and acquaintances expressed many different opinions about the constant presence of the FBI. Some thought I should be offended by the constant surveillance and what they perceived to be an invasion of privacy. Some thought that the presence of the FBI insured my security against some wacko who might decide to take a few pot shots at me. In the beginning, that certainly was a concern and there was no way I could have afforded the kind of security that the FBI provided for me. On the other hand you could rationalize that, since I was completely innocent, if not for the Feds, I wouldn't have needed any security and I definitely couldn't argue with that rationalization.

Personally, I have to believe that all of those concerns had some validity, although I must admit hindsight dictates that the whole thing was a big waste of taxpayers' money. I must also admit that there are some very attractive female agents working for the FBI, some of whom were assigned to my case from time to time. And, now that you're no longer assigned to my case, I'm still single.

During that 80 days of wearing Mr. Prosecutor's shock collar, we had some memorable experiences. On our way back to the federal courthouse in Detroit we had the opportunity to see just how determined these FBI agents can be when they're on your tail. Driving on a two-way highway where the posted speed limit was 55 mph, we had no choice but to go through a yellow traffic light which was about to turn red at one of the intersections. At that intersection, coming from the other direction, was a large semi-truck and trailer already in motion and about to make a left turn immediately after we had passed.

The first FBI car was about three or four seconds behind us and the second FBI car was about two or three seconds behind the first. Believe it or not, both of these guys went through that light! Keep in mind that these were unmarked cars. They had no special lights, no sirens and no markings of any kind. They didn't even lay on their horns! The second agent was about six seconds into a red light and had to swerve sharply to avoid a collision with that semi. That guy had more guts than sense, that's for sure. If the fellow who was driving that semi is reading this book there is no doubt in my mind that he will remember that incident on the M53 highway that bypasses Romeo and will now know why that crazy guy in a Ford Taurus had the audacity to play "chicken" with a kazillion-ton semi.

Another hair-raising (I still have a few) experience occurred when we were driving back from a July 4 picnic given by my friends Dave and Laurie. They live near Armada, a small town about 60 miles southeast of here located in the northern most tip of Macomb County. If you drove to their house from my farm you would normally drive through a part of St. Clair County. Unfortunately, the Blue Water Bridge to Canada is in St. Clair County. The FBI, pretending to assume that I would flee, excluded St. Clair County from my travel limitation list. It doesn't take a brainiac to realize that "escaping" to Canada would be the equivalent of escaping to ... Ohio! As a result we had to drive considerably further south than necessary and then drive east and north again to get there.

Dave had arranged for the farmer next door to take all volunteers on an early evening hayride. Needless to say, there were FBI agents parked at different locations on the road keeping a watchful eye on their house so when we went on the hayride we occasionally passed an agent parked just off the road where he could view us as we passed. Since I only knew a few people out of the sixty or so who were at the party, the FBI's presence made for some very interesting conversations. Someone even invited one of the agents to the party and we gestured for them to come along with us on the hayride, but to no avail. A simple smile and headshake was their response. They probably could have had more fun than they'd had in years, and I know that nobody there would have squealed on them. We were already having a blast on the hayride engaging in hay fights with people occasionally falling off the wagon. It would have added considerably to the excitement and to the pleasure if we could have had hay fights with a couple of government agents in suits.

Since the 10 o'clock hour was rapidly approaching ,and since we had some extra distance to travel to get back to the Roggenbucks' because of the St. Clair County deletion, the hayride was cut a little short. When we got back to Dave's house I realized that I had given my car keys to Sandy so she could get in the trunk for some Defense Fund T-shirts. To keep her hands free to pick up the box of T-shirts she inadvertently put the keys in her pocket and forgot to give them back to me. It wouldn't have been a big deal but, unfortunately, Sandy and Janell had already gone home in their car leaving Chase, Bob and me stranded with no keys.

Panic started setting in. If I violated my curfew the Court would automatically impose a $5,000 fine each on Rhonda and me and I may even be sent back to prison. Excuses wouldn't have carried much weight. There was no chance of not getting caught because there were FBI agents all over, not to mention the electronic alarm that would be sent if I didn't make it back to the Roggenbucks' by 10 p. m. We desperately needed a ride home and were in the process of determining of whom could we ask such an imposition. This wouldn't be a leisurely drive in the country. It would be at least 150 - 160 miles, round-trip, and really kickin' butt for the first 75 or 80 miles. Precious minutes were passing and we needed to fly, literally.

Then it occurred to me that I had a spare key stashed in one of those magnetic boxes under my car. I put it under there years ago. Would it still be there? I crawled under my car and after much searching finally found the metal container and pulled it loose. I couldn't believe it was still there. Even though the container was muddy and rusty the key was clean and in good shape. Without hesitation, we were on the road.

Our optimism was strong that we would beat the deadline but, realistically, we knew that having to stop for a red light in the town of Almont, Imlay City or Marlette might be the determining factor that would cost Rhonda and me $10,000 and could possibly send me back to prison. That's real justice isn't it? An innocent man going to prison because he had to stop for a red light. Ten thousand bucks and prison would have been an irresistible temptation for running a red light. Fortunately, that temptation never became an issue. Like it or not, that was the reality of our situation. We drove as fast as possible while still maintaining some degree of safety. Fortunately, the entire trip was country driving allowing us to safely drive above the speed limit. Had the police pulled us over for speeding our chance of beating the clock would have ended. If the police stopped us for a traffic violation one would think they would have to give the same violation to the FBI agents who were following me so a traffic ticket was not really my concern. Ten thousand dollars and going back to prison was most definitely a concern.

When we turned onto Snover Road from M53 we still had five miles to go. The seconds were ticking away on the clock. If my clock in the car was in time with the FBI's clock, we had about four and a half minutes to get to Les and Rhonda's. We were praying that our clock was just a little faster than theirs. It wasn't. Pulling into the driveway we thought for certain that we were late. I turned the car off and was out of the car and running for the house before the motor stopped spinning. We beat the clock by 30 seconds! After driving for more than 75 miles at breakneck speeds, in addition to driving through three small towns, we still had 30 big seconds to spare. You must be asking: "With all that time left, what was the big hurry?" •

Photo by Debby Racine

James Nichols talks with Michigan State Rep. Jim Barcia, right, in the aftermath of the April, 1995 raid and Nichols' imprisonment.

Photo courtesy Bob and Sandy Papovich

A "NO TRESPASSING" sign and another sign for "oats and spelt" is evidence that the scene at Nichols farm has calmed down.

"The Constitution is not an instrument for the government to restrain the people, it is an instrument for the people to restrain the government — lest it come to dominate our lives and interests."

— **Patrick Henry**

CHAPTER 6: JURISDICTION? WE'LL SEE ABOUT THAT!

Sometime in May or June 1995, my attorney, Robert Elsey, filed a motion to dismiss on jurisdictional grounds. Our motion stated, in part, that the BATF had no jurisdiction on my farm or over me. It was based on the simple rule of law that in this country, the government exists not as a matter of right but as a matter of privilege — by permission. Government exists because the people allow it to exist. The government, or agents working for the government, have no rights as agents, they only have powers granted to them by We The People. Any time such agents engage in activities or actions against the people that go beyond their designated powers, they are acting under the rules of criminal force, not under the rules of law. This is a very important legal issue of which many people are unaware. It is the same principle of jurisdiction which we discussed earlier concerning the commerce laws, treaties, a variety of tax laws and many other "deals and arrangements" that the players at "Disneyland on the Potomac" have made with We The People and a variety of other foreign entities. Do you reside within the jurisdiction of the agency in question, and if you do not, did you knowingly and willingly relinquish your sovereignty to them through a jurisdictional contract?

According to the law, the BATF only has jurisdiction over those people who are importers, manufacturers or distributors of alcohol, tobacco or firearms. In other words, involved in "commerce" with these items. I am none of the above, so when the BATF came into my house with a show of force and searched it, ransacked my farm and threatened me at the point of a gun, they were acting under the same authority as a common criminal or thug who forces his way into your home to rob you or worse. The phrase "jack-booted thug" thus becomes an extremely accurate technical description of the Ninja-suited BATF agents commonly used by the government (similar to communists and/or Nazis) to strike fear into the hearts of We The People. If you are not commercially involved in the import, manufacture or sales of alcohol, tobacco or firearms, they have no more "lawful" authority over you than your next door neighbor has over you.

The same legal principle applies to the Department of Natural Resources (DNR), Fish and Game or whatever it's called in your state. Do you have a fishing license or hunting license? If you have either, then you have voluntarily given them jurisdiction over you. If you do not, they have no jurisdiction over you whatsoever. They can't pull you over. They can't search your car. And, no, they cannot enter your house and search your refrigerator even if you are a licensed hunter or fisherman. Not without a warrant. They cannot lawfully do any of those things unless you let them, of course. They thrive upon our ignorance of the laws that govern We The People and restrict the powers of government. Like Detroit-based radio talk-show host Mark Scott says: "If you don't know what your rights are, you don't have any."

But if you open your door and invite a thief into your house and he tells you he's going to take your TV and VCR and you do not object, it's going to be extremely difficult to prove that he committed a crime. If you open the door for the guy and show him where you keep the items that he wants it would be impossible to prove a crime was committed unless you could somehow establish that he threatened you with physical harm. If you voiced no objection and the threat of physical harm was not apparent, as far as the law is concerned you let him.

It's the same rule of law that applies to government agents. You have to object in a timely manner. I'm not suggesting that you physically resist unless physical harm is imminent. We all have the right to defend ourselves and our families if we are physically threatened. But if a government agent wants to impose his jurisdictional will upon you, the only safe and legal thing to do is to voice your objections. Your recourse of action against these agents who are ignorant of the legal principles which govern this country and place limitations on their powers is in the courts — not in the battlefield.

Let's get back to the court's opinions concerning our motion to dismiss. On the surface, it seemed that when the prosecution realized exactly what we were challenging, they dropped the charges against me to avoid that challenge or confrontation in open court. They could not win and they knew it. Actually it was U.S. Attorney General Janet Reno who dropped the charges against me. The judge acted upon that motion, and not ours, even though our motion was filed first which made it incumbent upon the judge to act upon our motion.

It would seem to me that, by their actions, the government's prosecutors admitted that their charges against me were false. They never submitted a counter to our jurisdictional challenge. The judge never made a determination on our motion because he would have had to have made his decision in compliance with the law, admitting that the government agents never had any jurisdiction on my farm and never had probable cause to search. That would open up a whole new can of worms for the Attorney General — federal judge determining in a federal court that Janet Reno's henchmen were on my property illegally and made an unlawful arrest and an unlawful detention. That would be an impossible obstacle to overcome for the "Just-Us Department" if they had to defend their actions. No evidence existed to lead them to believe that I had broken any laws or taken part in any conspiracy. The only things that even remotely tied me in to this situation were my address on Tim' McVeigh's driver's license and a couple of habitual liars in the area who have a vendetta against me and have publicly expressed their desire to "get me." These simple facts were obvious to most people in the area who know me and most certainly were not a secret to the FBI investigators.

Do you realize the implications for the BATF and FBI if Judge Paul Borman had ruled on our motion? I can only believe that Judge Borman's integrity would've dictated that he follow the law and dismiss my case on the legal principles of our motion thereby admitting in federal court that these government agents violated my rights and never had any jurisdiction over me, not to mention that they literally kidnapped me, kept me incarcerated for 32 days and restricted my travels for almost three more months.

Which brings us back to another point of interest.

By keeping me in prison, the government made it impossible for me to travel to Oklahoma City and make contact with Tim or Terry. Their actions also made it impossible to go out there shortly after the bombing when there was still a chance of obtaining some "virgin evidence." Was it a coincidence that I was kept in prison until the exact same day that the implosion of the Murrah Building tainted and destroyed most, if not all, of the evidence? There was a good possibility that the judge would not restrict my travels which would have allowed me an opportunity to at least try to retrieve some evidence. Keeping me incarcerated until after the evidence was destroyed was their insurance policy. Had I known at the time that the feds were not even allowing the defense teams access to any evidence my dad and Bob could have gone out there and tried to obtain something, anything that would help us prove the truth about these explosions.

Was it a coincidence that the charges against me were dropped at exactly the same time the indictments were handed down against Tim and Terry? Once they were formally charged all the rules of the game changed. I no longer had any chance of getting in to see Tim without first getting permission from Stephen Jones, his lead attorney. It just seemed like all of these coincidences kept me away from Oklahoma until all of the evidence was buried and until Tim was kept solidly isolated from anyone he could trust. What a coincidence.

When I heard it reported on the news that the charges against me were dropped it brought to mind a conversation that took place during the raid. My house was swarming with FBI and BATF agents, and I hadn't been shown a search warrant even though I'd asked to see one on several occasions. During one of our very heated disagreements I was pounding my fist on the counter, demanding that they produce a search warrant, demanding to talk to Janet Reno, demanding my rights and demanding that they leave my home unless they could produce a warrant. Right in the middle of one of my tirades a very imposing-looking BATF Refrigerator pushed his way through the front door at which time I started voicing my complaints towards him.

"You people have no right to be in here," I shouted. "I demand to see a Fourth Amendment warrant. I demand to talk with Janet Reno."

"Oh shut up. We have more rights in here than you do," he responded in a deep, commanding voice.

"We'll see about that," I answered in a submissive, unchallenging tone. Were you paying attention Mr. BATF Refrigerator? It was made very clear in a confession by your ultimate boss, Janet Reno, that they had no evidence against me. It was the decision of a Federal Judge that you had no right to be in my house. On Aug. 10, 1995, WE SAW ABOUT THAT! •

"When you begin with so much pomp and show, why is the end so little and so low?"

— **Roscommon**

Part II:

Conspiracy?
You Be
the Judge

Photo by Debby Racine

When James Nichols, left, finally received his personal property seized by the FBI, the media was right there to record the event.

Photo by Debby Racine

All manner of belongings were returned by truck to James Nichols, who had to sign for the property as it was unloaded.

"I am only one, but I am one. I cannot do everything, but I can do something. What I can do, I should do and, with the help of God, I will do!"
— **Everett Hale**

CHAPTER 7: THE FACTS, PLEASE, JUST THE FACTS

After sitting in prison for a month unable to effectively research the problems with the prosecution's investigation and then being restricted on an electronic tether for nearly three more months — and unable to talk freely about the information and discrepancies we've uncovered — going to Oklahoma City in August 1995 for Terry's and Tim's arraignments was a welcome opportunity to be removed from the limitations of my restricted area. The freedom to travel is a right that we all enjoy in this beautiful land of ours and I believe, for the most part, a freedom that we all take for granted. I certainly did and I also know that I never will again. The old saying "you don't know what you've got until you lose it" is especially true when it concerns your rights and your freedoms.

Most of us, as free American citizens, have never had travel restrictions of any kind imposed upon us. Not since childhood, anyway. But even more annoying than travel restrictions were the limitations on my First Amendment right to speak freely — which became a necessary imposition because of the charges against me. I had to be careful about everything I said which, by now, everyone knows is a nearly impossible restriction to obey for a person who loves to debate any issue, who was put on this earth to discuss politics, who has an opinion on almost everything, and who can't keep a secret to save his life.

Needless to say, when U.S. Attorney General Janet Reno confessed to the nation that the FBI didn't have any evidence against me which forced the prosecution to drop all charges against me, the freedom to exercise all of my rights to their Constitutional limits was like a "born again" experience. Not that I took any of my rights to their Constitutional limits, but it felt great just to know that I could without fear of repercussion. One of the first examples of those new-found freedoms was a very emotional public speech that I gave at the Fitzgerald High School auditorium in Warren, Mich., on Sept. 14, 1995. The program was sponsored by Justice Pro Se, a group dedicated to Constitutional preservation, and I spoke before an audience of approximately 800 people. This was my first public appearance since my release and the first public speech that I had ever given in my whole life.

This group of patriotic Americans, in addition to being the first audience on which I would nervously practice my first-ever speech, gave generous donations to my defense fund to help pay some of my legal fees for which I will be forever grateful. Thank you for your generosity and your patience. All of you.

After the speech, my friend Kathy, who was handling the T-shirt detail, was asked by many of those in attendance for a copy of my speech so that they could then make copies and pass them around because of the new and alarming information that had just been brought to their attention. I did not give the speech exactly as it was written. I left some out here and added some there so I can't repeat exactly what was said on that night. I will include the first few pages of the speech because it has an appropriate message at this particular point.

You will soon realize the relationship and it will become apparent why we thought it necessary to include the beginning of the speech as an introduction to the questions and discrepancies surrounding the FBI's investigation. More than a year has passed since that night at the Fitzgerald auditorium and many new issues have surfaced which were not known to us at that time. The remainder of that speech will not be included because it asked only a fraction of the same questions we will ask and attempt to answer throughout this book.

> **September 14, 1995**
> **Fitzgerald High School**
> **Warren, Mich.**
>
> I'd like to take this opportunity to thank all of you for coming tonight, for your moral support, and for your interest in discovering the truth about this tragedy in Oklahoma City. I'd also like to thank Robert Elsey for his brilliant effort in defending me, Karl Granse and Stefani Godsey for their assistance in that defense, all of the other people who have supported me, and all of my friends who helped take care of the farm and other things while the government had me in Milan Federal Penitentiary.
>
> As you probably know by now, on Aug. 10, Attorney General Janet Reno confessed to the entire nation and to the world that government prosecutors had no evidence against me. I think that we all have to ask: If they had no evidence against me on Aug. 10, what evidence did they have in April and May when they assaulted my farm and accused me of being the "guru" behind the most vicious act of terrorism in the history of this great nation? They marched me bound and

shackled in front of everyone on world-wide television, show-ing the same embarrassing scenes over and over again: The same film clip that the news media still considers necessary to show the public. Even after I have been totally exonerated, they find it necessary to shame and discredit me in front of the whole country. My country. My republic ... and your republic.

I have experienced humiliation and embarrassment that few innocent people on this planet will ever experience. I have been incarcerated in a federal penitentiary for 32 days, kept on an electronic tether and restricted for nearly three more months. My home has been ransacked, my life threatened, and my reputation nearly destroyed. My property was confiscated for five months. My privacy and the privacy of my close friends have been invaded by telephone taps. We have and will in the future experience major financial burdens. They have intimi-dated and imposed emotional and economic hardships on my entire family and it is very possible that, before this is all over, my mother will have experienced medical problems that did not previously exist. Even with no evidence, they have tried to destroy me. I didn't hurt anyone or do anything wrong. I didn't tell any lies trying to destroy innocent people's lives. The government did. I think that I deserve to have my life put back where it was before the Government started making all these mistakes.

President Clinton expressed his apologies to the Jorda-nian/American man who was detained in London and sent back to the United States. He certainly suffered some discom-fort for a couple of days. A precedent has been set by Bill Clinton. I believe that Bill Clinton and Janet Reno owe me a personal public apology for the needless turmoil that I've been through. They owe me an apology and much, much more. They and the news media owe this entire nation an apology for their total disregard for the "presumption of innocence" guar-anteed by our Constitution and for their "rush to judgment," not only on me, but on my brother Terry and, I believe, Tim McVeigh as well. I believe when the evidence surfaces about this tragedy, people will not only be surprised, they will be angry. Angry about what really happened and angry because there has been a concerted effort by the major media to not report the truth to the American people.

There seems to be an effort to conceal the truth or to report only half of the truth, either of which will cause people to come to inappropriate conclusions. One example of this is the notorious letter that Terry left for Tim when he was leaving for the Philippines. In the letter Terry told Tim that if he didn't come back for Tim to "clear everything out of the storage shed." That's where the media ended the sentence and it sounded like they may have been up to something sinister, but that's not how the sentence ended. It actually continued, "or

> pay to keep it longer." It has a completely different meaning
> when you put it into context. Why didn't the news media
> finish the sentence? Is it their job to report the truth or to
> spread government propaganda? There are a lot of unan-
> swered questions about this tragic incident.

As you can see, my speech had just begun to ask many of the
unanswered questions about this tragedy. I can assure you that we will
attempt to answer all of those questions and many others that have
surfaced as thoroughly and as accurately as we possibly can throughout
the remainder of this book. We will also ask questions that have never
been asked before and will bring to your attention much information that
has been "overlooked" by the mainstream media. To anyone with a
thinking mind, the discrepancies surrounding this "rush to judgment"
defy all logic and common sense. Some of the more enlightened journalists across this country started raising questions about the government's
handling of this incident right from the very beginning.

One magazine in particular, *Relevance* of Birmingham, Mich. (1-800-
626-8944), reasonably challenged the major media's reports via FBI
"leaks" about the so-called facts or evidence in this case. They published
a special issue called "The Oklahoma City Bombing: America's Reichstag
Fire?" *For The People News Reporter* printed an article, by our friend and
fellow patriot Pat Shannan, titled" "Did Feds Repeat Reichstag Fire?"

Obviously, more than one person realized the similarities between
the so-called Reichstag Fire in Nazi Germany — which galvanized public
outrage against opponents of the Nazi party — and the Oklahoma City
bombing,. Many people see the similarities in deception between the
people in power in Germany at that time, the late 1930s, and the current
administration in the U. S. Shannan has also submitted four other
superbly written articles on this subject which the *For The People News
Reporter* has published.

The New American (1-800-727-TRUE) also issued a special report by
William Jasper titled "Explosive Evidence, Cover-up In Oklahoma City,"
which brought forth some very important detailed technical information
concerning the discrepancies in information surrounding this disaster.
The technical explosives information was offered by General Benton
Partin.

Media Bypass (1-800-4BYPASS), an absolutely necessary news journal
for anyone who wants to stay informed, has also published some very
interesting articles concerning this tragedy including an objective interview with Tim McVeigh written by Lawrence Myers, one of the brightest
and most aggressive investigative journalists we've met.

We feel that reading all of these special magazines is an absolute must for anyone wanting to know about the real FACTS, PLEASE, JUST THE FACTS in this case. We realize that most magazines and newspapers across this country published special issues concerning this bombing, but it has been our observation that the only thing the other printed media special editions have in common with these very informative and enlightening journals is that they also were published as "special editions."

There have been many books written about the Oklahoma City bombing long before any of the real facts were known. The only information available to these "authors-before-the-fact" had been spoon fed by the government propagandists through leaks to the media and the inaccuracies in their works are evidence of their sources of information. There will be many books written in the future about this senseless tragedy and we're certain some authors will dedicate their works to accuracy. However, history dictates that most will concentrate on sensationalism not really caring about the facts in the case.

A perfect example of this sensationalism and not really caring about the facts is a recently published unauthorized biography of Timothy McVeigh. We will not in any way justify the legitimacy this work by mentioning it by name. It appears as if the author simply read all of the disinformation available in the news, put it into his own disinformed words and then used as much filler as he could get his hands on to make up for his total lack of substance. Instead of being an accurate biography of Tim written by an author who's intentions are to present the truth, the book reads like all the other volumes of government propaganda which have been circulating since April of '95.

The author begins his book by declaring the presumption of innocence of Tim McVeigh and Terry Nichols yet, throughout the book, his own presumption of guilt is unavoidably obvious. He completely ignores the eyewitnesses and the facts that are available for any objective journalist to discover. He goes out of his way to criticize any legitimate information surfacing from private investigations without actually challenging the information. He drives his point home by making subtle personal insults against the investigator with critical catch words like "Amerinoid" with the intention of prejudicing the reader against the investigator, thereby discrediting the investigator's information. Certainly not an original technique.

This author makes it a point to talk about the possible existence of some Ku Klux Klan members near the area in New York where Tim grew up. Of course the KKK was there more than 100 years before Tim was born, but just mentioning them in the same breath with McVeigh is an obvious attempt to make the subconscious "link" in the readers mind. It is a tactic typically used by agents of deceit when they want to avoid the real issues. He totally avoids any and all of the facts in these investigations which would expose his book for the work of fiction that it is. The author has included some correct information and some "name dropping" in an attempt to lend credibility to all of the propaganda.

The use of the words "unauthorized biography" on the cover makes it sound as if the author has written an exposé about the deep dark secrets surrounding Timothy McVeigh's background. Realistically, nothing could be further from the truth. All of the thoughts in his book that are supposed to be coming from Tim are nothing more than a figment of the author's pathetic little imagination. The result is basically a fiction novel based upon inaccuracies with a title that is meant to deceive. Why did he bother? If we didn't know any better we may be inclined to believe that this guy was just another damage control agent working for the Government. But then again, maybe we don't know any better.

One of this fiction author's subtle personal insults was aimed at a dedicated investigator who just happens to be a good personal friend of ours. While referring to Chuck Allen's video, *Oklahoma City: What Really Happened?*, this fiction author suggested that there was a lot of money to be made selling this Oklahoma City bombing information. We know Chuck to be an honest, hard-working American patriot who has invested an enormous amount of time and effort trying to gather as many facts as possible about this crime. Chuck has found witnesses in downtown Oklahoma City whom the feds did not want found. He has invested his time and effort because he feels it is his responsibility as an American to find out the truth about this act of terror. We can assure you that Chuck is not making a bundle on his video.

And since the fiction author brought up the issue of money, we must ask why he decided to write a fictional book about McVeigh if not for the money? He certainly did not take on this task because of his "thirst for the truth." If you decide to read this fictional unauthorized biography of McVeigh because of your thirst for the truth, you can reasonably expect to die from dehydration long before you've finished reading. And if you're looking for some new, honest information, don't waste your money or your time. We do not mention the name of the fiction author or the title of his fictional book because he and his fictional book do not deserve that distinction.

In addition to using the names of Richard Burr, Tim's assistant counsel, and Lawrence Myers from *Media Bypass*, the author of this fiction novel also included a short interview with Jennifer McVeigh, Tim's sister. The author's intentions were to give his "unauthorized biography" even more credibility. By printing a cordial, accurate interview with Jennifer, the author expects the reader to assume that McVeigh's sister agrees with the contents of his book. Again, nothing could be further from the truth.

This is what Jen had to say about the book's content: "I could point out a mistake, false info, or downright lie on every page. He just took the newspaper stories and put them together in a book. Then he talked to people we barely know and called them our 'best friends.' His sources were far from credible." Apparently we are not the only ones who recognized the re-worded news stories in this poorly researched, fictional, unauthorized biography of Timothy McVeigh.

You can rest assured that the government propagandists will always be out there writing their books, attempting to continue their disinformation campaign, taking advantage of the extremely limited thought processes of the non-thinkers. They, unfortunately, will always have the advantage of unlimited budgets, unlimited connections and never-ending publicity. We all have a responsibility to at least make an attempt to sift through the hype, the speculation, the sensationalism, and the downright lies being told to We the People. We all owe it to the victims, their families, and to the accused to be eternally vigilant on this issue. THE FACTS, PLEASE, JUST THE FACTS!

But there will be one book in particular that we believe will eventually stand out as the "best among the best." It thoroughly covers the accurate information reported on the news in Oklahoma City before the "agents of deceit" had an opportunity to make their alterations. It is a documentary based upon the facts that have emerged in this case and upon what really happened right there at the site immediately after the explosions that destroyed the Murrah Building along with at least 168 lives and changed forever the lives of tens of thousands more.

We have had the privilege and have been honored to receive an original rough draft of this book, *Oklahoma City: Day One*, written by investigative author, Michele Moore of Norman, Okla. The information contained within the pages of this expertly written documentary will shock anyone who has not been intimately involved in the investigation of this case, and may even shock many who have. Reading it is a "must" for anyone who wants to know what really happened that first day in Oklahoma City and insists upon documentation. The author has elaborated on many points which we make in this book and will bring to your attention other very important and interesting facts which we did not cover in this book.

As a matter of fact, Michele's book has much information that you may never see in print anywhere else. After reading this accurate documentary we have concluded that *Oklahoma City: Day One* and the book you are currently reading will undoubtedly be used as "the" encyclopedias of information on the investigation and on the bombing of the Murrah Building. Over the past 12 months we have received more accurate information from Michele than from any other single source. She has become a much needed, appreciated and trusted friend. You can order her book by sending a money order for $35 to Harvest, P.O. Box 1970, Eagar, AZ 85925.

As we mentioned earlier, there are some very informative videos available that bring to light some frightening information about the explosions inside the Murrah Building. Chuck Allen has interviewed investigators, victims and witnesses who saw some alarming things that have been conveniently left out of the media coverage of this disaster. He makes these interviews available for your viewing in *Oklahoma City: What Really Happened?* by calling 1-800-954-1122. These videos include interviews with Oklahoma State Rep. Charles Key who has the distinction of being the only politician we know of who has been willing to risk his political career by raising issues that are considered "taboo" by everyone else in the political arena and, consequently, by the national media. Another excellent video suggesting official complicity is *Murder in the Heartland* produced by our friend Pat Shannan, and can be ordered by sending $25 to: Center For Historical Analysis, Suite 163, 6069 Old Canton Rd., Jackson, MS 39211.

In spite of some honest journalists, media in general, with very few exceptions, has been nothing more than an instant, all-encompassing outlet for government propaganda and disinformation. The citizens of this country have been inundated with this disinformation and propaganda right from the very start. Within minutes after the explosions at the Alfred P. Murrah Federal Building in Oklahoma City, the disinformation campaign began. Actually, some evidence seems to indicate that the campaign was planned to disinform even before the explosions at the Murrah Federal Building took place. •

"One strategy of those who seek increased control over our lives is to manufacture a crisis."

— **Dr. Walter Williams**

Chapter 8: Reasonable Doubt

It has been reported that since early in 1994, the BATF and the Army Corps of Engineers have been experimenting with ANFO/car/truck bombs at the White Sands Proving Grounds in New Mexico. This project has been code-named DIPOLE MIGHT and, according to Lawrence Myers of *Media Bypass*, was sanctioned by the Clinton administration and funded by the National Security Council. These tests were said to have been designed to help these agencies learn better ways to avoid or disrupt potential terrorist attacks using car or truck bombs made with ammonium nitrate and fuel oil as was allegedly used in the World Trade Center bombing in New York City, or so they would have us believe.

Myers says the FBI records clearly indicate that Urea Nitrate was used in the World Trade Center bombing and not ANFO as has been reported. He also said that the FBI's man on the inside literally showed the potential terrorists how to construct the bomb. Because of his concern that something might go wrong the informant wanted to substitute the real explosives with non explosive material that could pass for the real stuff. His supervisors wouldn't let him make the switch and we are all aware of the result of that executive decision. How many of us have heard the truth about this evidence on network news? Had Lawrence Myers not filed a Freedom of Information Act request for this information we can assure you that it never would have been reported. *Media Bypass* doesn't exactly have tens of millions of readers, although it should, so even though this information appeared in Myers' article we cannot reasonably expect the people of this nation to instantly know that they have been disinformed. You're not going to get this kind of accurate reporting from *Time* and *Newsweek*. Definitely subscribe to *Media Bypass*.

It didn't seem to matter that ANFO has not exactly been the choice of terrorists in the U.S. when Clinton's National Security Council decided to fund these "experiments." Myers states in his article that according to FBI records there have been no ANFO bombings on U.S. soil in nearly 25 years and prior to that one, there were none. Those records might encourage one to ask: "If there was no apparent threat from an ANFO attack why did the Clinton administration deem it necessary to conduct these tests using ANFO car/truck bombs?" And: "Was it just a coincidence that even though there had been no ANFO attacks in more than two and one half decades, the worst act of terrorism in the history of this country was allegedly carried out with an ANFO truck bomb immediately after government agents practiced and became experts at ANFO explosions?" We believe these are both reasonable questions for which we would like to hear some responsible and honest answers.

We have to keep in mind that, contrary to the disinformation that has been circulating since April 21, 1995, no evidence exists which would indicate that either of the accused have, in any way, experimented with ANFO bombs or ANFO explosions. Mixing swimming pool granules in a plastic pop bottle with a variety of automotive petroleum derivatives and watching it expand until it goes BANG! is not exactly experimenting with ANFO and honing to perfection your efficiency with ANFO or with any other explosives.

We think that it is very important at this particular time to read what some experts have to say about the mixing and handling of ANFO. Occasionally accurate information surfaces within some of the articles written for our national magazines which inadvertently weakens the government's case against Tim and Terry. An example of this is an article appearing in *Time* magazine, May 1, 1995 which stated in part:

"But just because anyone can buy ammonium nitrate for 11 cents a pound doesn't mean that anyone can make it explode at a particular time and place. The act of terror that demolished the Murrah Building and destroyed scores of human lives required a basic understanding of chemistry (?), skill at bomb-making (?), and some technical know-how to jury-rig a few key components that are not easy to get."

The article goes on to say: "The fertilizer is not as pure a preparation as what is used for demolition work and has to be treated before it can be converted into an explosive substance. Moreover, it is almost impossible for amateurs to mix thoroughly the ammonium nitrate with the fuel oil. (Commercial manufacturers use industrial-size blenders for the job.)"

In the same article Jeffrey Dean, executive director of the International Society of Explosives Engineers, said; "ANFO is easy to make if you know how to do it, but it takes years of experience to work with it safely."

After reading the opinions of these explosives experts don't we have to wonder just who the "experts" in the manufacture of ANFO bombs might be? It has been stated that to build a successful ANFO bomb a person would need some chemistry background, have considerable skills at bomb making, access to uncommon components and an industrial-size blender in addition to having years of experience at making such bombs.

It has been established that Tim and Terry are not chemists or bomb makers, do not have an industrial-size blender and do not have years, months or even days of experience mixing ANFO. On the other hand, several BATF agents do have access to any components they would need, are bomb makers, probably have a commercial blender to mix some of their very large "practice" bombs, and obviously have much experience with ANFO in scientifically monitored experiments. And being that their ANFO tests were so closely monitored they could most certainly learn much more from their experiments and become experts in a much shorter time than a person who was using ANFO on occasion for some type of excavation work. This information certainly should, at the very least, be considered when one tries to determine who may have been capable of building such a device. Even Frank Keating, governor of Oklahoma, prior to being briefed stated: "Obviously, no amateur did this." We could not agree more with Mr. Keating's very astute observation.

Now another minor detail to which we must give some consideration occurred in downtown Oklahoma City almost immediately after the explosions. Coincidentally, and we use this term very loosely, a BATF agent named Harry Everhart who had been assigned to DIPOLE MIGHT just happened to be in Oklahoma City working in the Federal Courthouse across the street from the Murrah Building on the side opposite of the blasts when the explosions occurred. He immediately called Ralph Ostrowski at the Dallas BATF office reporting that the Murrah Building had been hit by an ANFO bomb. CNN, ABC, CBS, NBC and every other news network in this country and every other country on this planet immediately picked up on this story and never even questioned it.

Now, we don't want to sound like skeptics or anything and we're sure that the BATF agent who called in the report on the ANFO is a very competent, knowledgeable professional who has totally dedicated his whole life to government service and was born to offer that service to the citizens of the United States of America. But doesn't it seem a little curious that this guy would have known exactly what type of bomb it was before any samples were taken for laboratory diagnosis? We would have to say that his phoned-in report rated considerably higher than a little curious. We're not suggesting that this particular BATF agent knew that this bombing was going to take place before it happened because we all know that no government agents would knowingly be involved in something as evil as murder and conspiracy. Although it does seem quite peculiar that Tim and Terry have no experience in ANFO bomb manufacture while several agents in the BATF have much experience with these materials, particularly since the Feds claim that this was a very efficient ANFO explosion. Coincidental also is the fact that the BATF started practicing and experimenting with ANFO just months before the Murrah Building was destroyed and prior to the BATF practice sessions there hadn't really been any problem with ANFO explosions due to terrorism.

And shouldn't it also, at the very least, raise suspicions that one of the few BATF agents specially trained in ANFO bombs just happened to be across the street from the only federal building in the United States that has ever allegedly been blown up by an ANFO bomb? We have to wonder, what are the odds? Boy, did this guy luck out, huh? He just happened to be in the right place at the right time to immediately use his very recently acquired expertise in telling the world what kind of explosives were responsible for the worst act of terrorism in this country's history. He seemed to know just about how large it was (it did grow several times when skeptics expressed doubt), exactly what it was made of, and precisely how it was implemented before lab tests of any kind were done.

The government really trained Harry Everhart very well. This BATF agent is so exceptionally well-trained, it would seem as if we no longer need scientists or laboratories or even investigators to solve crimes. Again, we are not suggesting or even implying that Agent Everhart had anything to do with this bombing or that he had any prior knowledge that it might happen. Although it does not seem inconceivable that someone, somewhere could have made certain that an expert in ANFO was in the right place at precisely the right time. Of course that is only a speculative possibility but it cannot be denied that Agent Everhart's being there at that location was e-x-t-r-e-m-e-l-y coincidental.

Did it ever occur to anyone in the news media, those great bastions of our individual liberties, those watchdogs for the people who exercise eternal vigilance making certain that every aspect of government corruption and deception is brought out into the light of day, those guardians of the truth who expose the officials involved in corruption and deception, to ask for proof? Did it ever occur to any of them to ask for proof that there was, in fact, an ammonium nitrate/fuel oil explosion? Apparently, it did not.

Had the question of proof been raised by anyone in the media, the lack of answers and the lack of evidence may have "raised" some eyebrows as well. According to all of the experts who have not yet been intimidated into silence by the FBI for "national security" or some other equally nauseous reason, an ANFO explosion always leaves certain "signatures." One of these signatures is a nitric acid cloud that would be present in the area for a considerable time after an ANFO explosion. None of the rescue workers could have possibly entered the area without appropriate breathing apparatus, not just dust masks. They would've had to have been wearing gas masks or some other type of quality breathing apparatus to avoid serious respiratory injuries due to nitric acid which is a very strong corrosive.

Now, a skeptic might say, "Well, maybe it was a windy day. Could the wind have blown the nitric acid cloud away quickly allowing rescue workers to enter the bombed out structure immediately?"

Gee, we're glad you asked that question. Nitric acid is actually a transparent, highly reactive, corrosive liquid which would rapidly settle downward. Keeping that in mind, we will pass along to you some more very important facts regarding this issue. Nitric oxide is a colorless, poisonous gas, produced as an "intermediate" during the manufacture or transformation of nitric acid from ammonia or atmospheric nitrogen. Now remember, people, in the beginning of this book all we asked is that you maintain a "thinking" mind.

Please put on your thinking caps. We have an ammonium nitrate explosion. Nitric acid, a corrosive liquid, is a by-product of this explosion. Nitric oxide, a poisonous gas, is an intermediate, a substance formed in the middle of these two extremes, which are ammonium nitrate and nitric acid. There would have been no escape. Wind would not have been a factor. Nitric acid would have moved downward, covering everything, including people, at all of the lower levels in the area. Nitric oxide would have floated through the air, getting into every crevice. In the air or on the ground, if this had been an ammonium nitrate bomb responsible for all the massive damage to the Murrah Building, everyone who was inside and everyone who entered the building within an hour or so after the explosion would have been exposed and would have suffered from skin and/or respiratory burns due to the presence of nitric acid and nitric oxide.

Another skeptic might say, "But I saw rescuers wearing some sort of breathing masks when they entered the bombing site."

Okay, we can also address this issue by applying simple logic to our observations As a matter of fact, there were some rescuers wearing masks while working in the damaged structure shortly after the explosions. We personally didn't see more than a few people wearing equipment adequate enough to protect them from nitric oxide and none were wearing equipment which would have protected them from nitric acid, but let's give this issue the benefit of the doubt. Let us assume that every one of those people who was wearing a mask had the appropriate equipment for adequate protection from nitric acid and nitric oxide. What about all of the other workers who did not? And a more important question is; what about the survivors of the blasts? People who were inside the Murrah building at the time? People who were rescued from the rubble and lived to tell about it?

None of those people experienced respiratory problems due to nitric acid or nitric oxide inhalation. None of the area hospitals has any record of admissions due to respiratory injuries or skin injuries caused by exposure to nitric acid or nitric oxide gas. There were some people whose hospital stay included treatment for smoke and dust inhalation but not for burns from nitric acid. There is a big difference.

Jim Ferguson is a maintenance foreman for some of the federal buildings in Oklahoma City. His office is in the basement of the federal courthouse across the street from the back of the Murrah Building. Being so close to the explosions he, along with many others, heroically entered the bombed out structure within a minute or two after the blasts in an attempt to assist in rescuing the survivors. In an interview with Pat Shannan, Ferguson said that he had trouble breathing because of the dust, but there was no gas and there was no fire inside of the Murrah Building. The presence of poisonous gas and fire, according to all explosives experts familiar with ammonium nitrate/fuel oil bombs, is absolutely unavoidable after an ANFO explosion.

Taking this information into consideration, and realizing that there was no "signature" of any kind indicating the occurrence of an ANFO explosion, and realizing that Special Agent Harry Everhart from the BATF is an expert in ANFO explosions, doesn't it seem even more curious that he would hastily report that the explosion was absolutely and positively the result of an ANFO car/truck bomb? If there was no apparent evidence, why ANFO? Why not some other explosive like C-4 or maybe even a gas leak?

Interesting also is that Jim said he heard two distinct explosions several seconds apart. There was no mistaking that there were two separate blasts, an observation confirmed by many other witnesses including Jim's wife and his mother who were in downtown Oklahoma City just about a mile away from the Murrah Building. They said when they heard the first blast, they looked in that direction to see the smoke rising from the explosion and seconds later heard the second blast and observed another mushroom cloud rise from the Murrah Building. Jim has been interviewed by members of the national media but his interviews have never aired. Have you seen Jim giving his account of what he saw on any network news program? Are we to assume that what Jim and his wife and mother witnessed wouldn't be considered pertinent information concerning this incident?

Immediately after the bombing, many people who were interviewed also said they heard two separate blasts several seconds apart and have since been totally ignored by the media and by federal investigators. Apparently someone would prefer to just sweep this information under the carpet. Who might that someone be? Just where have our eternally vigilant great bastions of liberty been hiding? Inquiring minds would like to know.

Another point of interest brought to our attention by some observant Oklahomans was that immediately after the bombing, their local media were telling a different story from that of the national media. The local media in Oklahoma City interviewed witnesses and generally reported the information as it came from eye witnesses and local police agencies at the scene. With few exceptions, the national media was getting most of their information spoon-fed by federal agents. What began as two different stories in the morning became the same story by the end of the day and that "same story" did not reflect what Oklahomans viewed on their local news that Wednesday morning. Many competent eyewitnesses were totally ignored by network news because what they saw didn't correspond with the government's story. They are still being ignored, not only by the national media, but by government prosecutors as well.

You should also be made aware that the seismograph readings taken at the University of Oklahoma Department of Geology verify the multiple explosions heard by Jim Ferguson, his wife, his mother, and many others. Dr. Ken Louzza from the Geology Department was absolutely positive that there were two distinct explosions approximately ten seconds apart. After being contacted by the FBI and after having his seismograph readings confiscated, it has been leaked by the FBI that Dr. Louzza changed his story. We don't know for sure if he has officially changed his interpretations of the seismograph readings because we have been told by "reliable" sources that Dr. Louzza has not changed his findings.

Actually, when you look closely at the seismogram, it appears as if there was a small disruption of tranquillity just before the two large explosions took place, a very important point which we will discuss later in the book. Why would the FBI confiscate all of the seismographic information recorded during the bombing? Fortunately for those of us who have this hang-up about wanting to know the real truth, copies of this information were obtained by investigators before it occurred to the FBI that they should confiscate this evidence from the University.

On May 23, 1995, test instruments at several locations, including the Omniplex Science Museum and the University of Oklahoma in Norman, were set up to record the implosion of the Murrah Building. This experiment, according to the experts, would produce seismic recordings similar to the original blasts recorded on April 19, 1995. The Associated Press reported an interview with Thomas Holzer, a United States Geological Survey (USGS) geologist from Menlo Park, Calif., and in the interview, reported extensively across the country, Dr. Holzer explained that even though there appeared to be to separate waves on the seismograms from two separate explosions on April 19, there had really only been one explosion. He said that the reason there appeared to be two separate explosions is that the shock waves from the explosion traveled through "different layers of the earth's crust" at different speeds.

As we know, sound travels faster through the ground than through the air and apparently the same principle is true for shock waves traveling through a variety of solid substances. Dr. Holzer explained that this discrepancy in velocity through a variety of substances would account for the 10-second delay recorded on the seismic readings at Norman. It was implied in the AP story that Dr. Charles Mankin, director of the Oklahoma Geological Survey, was in total agreement with the "findings" of Dr. Holzer (Source, *The New American*, August 7, 1995).

During an interview with *The New American*, Dr. Mankin said, "I had urged him (Dr. Holzer) to delay that press release. What they have proposed is a plausible interpretation, but there is a difference between a plausible interpretation and being able to support that interpretation with data, and you'll notice that at the end of that press release I note that development of a velocity model for this region is critical to the resolution of their hypothesis." Dr. Mankin is conducting a study of the different layers of rock in the area because different types of rock will conduct energy at different rates of speed. He went on to say, "While the work is not finished, I will say candidly that we are having trouble finding that velocity difference. We have not identified a pair of layers that could account for the 10-second difference."

Dr. Raymond Brown, assigned by Dr. Mankin to lead the OGS investigation, set up test instruments next to the original seismograph at the Omniplex and the Oklahoma Geological Survey Station near the

University of Oklahoma. His findings: "A portion of the ground movement [recorded] at the Omniplex was not directly related to the truck bomb. The extra time of ground motion at the Murrah Building is clearly indicated by the discrepancy between these two signals." The signal through the ground was considerably longer than the signal through the air which corresponds with eyewitness accounts.

Dr. Brown goes on to tell *The New American:* "*Now* I think that there is no longer a question that there was energy activity at the Murrah Building in addition to the original explosion, and we simply need to determine the source of that activity."

It has been widely reported that the "source of that activity" was actually the destroyed part of the Murrah Building that came crashing down after the alleged truck bomb explosion. The tests taken on May 23 proved beyond any doubt that those reports were in error. Keep in mind that the remaining three-fourths of the Murrah Building was brought down by no more than 150 pounds of dynamite strategically placed in drilled holes at about 400 different locations within the damaged structure. Even though dynamite, pound for pound, is much more potent than ANFO, nobody would disagree that 150 pounds of dynamite couldn't pack anywhere near the wallop of 4,800 pounds of ANFO. Commenting on those dynamite explosions, Dr. Brown stated, "Even the smallest of those detonations had a larger effect on the recording then the collapse of the building, which demonstrated that the explosives are much more efficient at exciting the ground motion than is the collapse of three-fourths of the building. So it is very unlikely that one-fourth of the building falling on April 19 could have created an energy wave similar to that caused by the large [truck bomb] explosion."

In his interview with William Jasper of *The New American*, Dr. Brown concludes that the most logical explanation for the second event is "a bomb on the inside of the building." Many other distinguished scientists concur with Dr. Brown's conclusions but, unfortunately, their opinions have never found their way to "government's network news."

Anyway, getting back to the topic of the alleged fertilizer bomb, we should bring to your attention another very interesting point that many in the media have conveniently overlooked in their coverage of this tragedy. An ammonium nitrate bomb is a rather slow-burning, low-velocity explosion, comparatively speaking. Whenever there is an ANFO explosion, there is always some remnant of the materials left over that did not explode. In other words, you can never get a complete "burn" like you would with high velocity explosives. Because of this commonly known fact concerning ANFO explosions, all non-government experts have stated that it would have been impossible for what was basically an open-air blast from an ANFO bomb to have caused that kind of destruction to a cement structure. Since this skepticism has been made public, the feds have come up with a counter allegation. They say that the ANFO bomb which allegedly destroyed the Murrah Building was enhanced with racing fuel and/or some other high velocity explosive, perhaps dynamite, which would have allowed for a very efficient burn of the ANFO adding considerably to the power of the blast. Since there was a complete burn due to this enhancement, the result was much greater destruction to the targeted building, say the Feds.

While exploring all of the theories about the alleged ammonium nitrate explosion it has become alarmingly apparent that the intentions of federal investigators are to keep all other investigators eternally confused and their goals have been accomplished with some degree of success. After giving all of their allegations and their theories some very serious thought, and after talking to many private investigators and viewing numerous still pictures and videos of the area immediately after the bombing we have concluded that none of their allegations make any sense.

One problem with the "enhanced complete burn" theory is that it has been rumored by some investigators that the entire area around the Murrah Building for many square blocks was covered with ammonium nitrate prills that did not disintegrate during the explosion. We have to assume that these "overdunit" rumors have been circulated to confirm the allegations of an ANFO explosion. Had this alleged bomb been enhanced like federal investigators claim, there still would have been some ammonium nitrate evidence. There should have been some remnants of ANFO prills (tiny ore-like bits) because you can never really get a "complete burn" and there should have been other signatures like nitric oxide and nitric acid. But ANFO certainly wouldn't have been splattered all over the downtown area. If this information is true it obviously would suggest that the alleged ANFO bomb was not enhanced to increase its potency and might even suggest the presence of ANFO without an actual ANFO explosion.

One thing we should also consider that apparently hasn't occurred to anyone who is rumoring this information is the size of the area that was allegedly splattered with these ammonium nitrate prills. When you apply some simple mathematics, 20 barrels measuring approximately three-and-a-half feet by one-and-a-half feet would be capable of, at the very most, covering one square block with 1/30th of an inch of dust. Over 10 square blocks, which would've been the minimum coverage of these prills, the layer would have been a humongus 1/300th of an inch thick!

Realistically, not even visible to the human eye. Both of these mathematical equations are based upon the total volume of the 20 barrels. If there had been an inefficient 50 percent burn, the layer of dust would've been 1/600th of an inch thick. A 90 percent, reasonably efficient burn would have left 1/3000th of an inch of residue. A good microscope would've been necessary for even the slightest detection. Now, we realize that these measurements are not necessarily representative of the remnants that would be left from an ammonium nitrate explosion because there should have been little beads of fertilizer scattered around. But considering these figures, if there had been an efficient ANFO explosion, there would have been some, but very few, remnants of solid beads of fertilizer left in the area.

But again, some reports suggest that there were ammonium nitrate prills scattered all over the entire area. These reports would bring us around to another very interesting bit of information concerning the government's allegations. The FBI alleges that Tim and Terry mixed this ANFO one or two days before the explosions occurred. Ammonium nitrate prills turn to mush within a couple of hours after mixing with fuel oil. Had the ammonium nitrate and fuel oil been mixed at the time and place that the FBI claims, there would've been no ammonium nitrate prills left in the mixture. The ammonium nitrate would've been mush. Considering the rumors that there were ammonium nitrate prills covering the entire area, this information would seem to indicate that the mixing would've had to have taken place immediately before the explosions if there was ever any mixing of these substances. The question then arises, when, where and by whom were these substances mixed because TERRY WASN'T THERE!

As we have previously brought to your attention, ANFO experts have said that the amount claimed to have been used in this tragedy could not be mixed by hand and still maintain even a minimum degree of efficiency during detonation. If a commercial mixer was not used to mix more than two tons of ammonium nitrate and fuel oil properly, the majority of the substance would have been splattered all over the entire area which was the case according to some investigators. Again, we must realize that the amount of ammonium nitrate prills claimed to be present in the multi square block area surrounding the Murrah Building would indicate, not only the probable inefficiency of the alleged ANFO explosion but, the fact that, if there actually had been an ANFO explosion it would have been a complete dud. Whatever kind of explosion tore the Murrah Building to pieces, killing and injuring hundreds of people, was most certainly not a dud.

We must state, for the record, that we have not yet seen any evidence that an ANFO explosion contributed in any way to the destruction of the Murrah Building. As a matter of fact, the first time we heard anyone say that they had seen remnants of ANFO in the area of the explosion was in February, 1996, a full 10 months after the fact. We found it rather curious, to say the least, that for ten months nobody mentioned anything about seeing any real "evidence" of an ANFO explosion. All the news and government reports of ANFO were based on Harry Everhart's opinion and not necessarily on hard evidence. We still have our doubts that there was any unexploded ANFO remnants splattered anywhere in the area. After viewing many photos and videos of the area taken immediately after the explosions it does not appear that there were any ANFO prills visible anywhere which just doesn't seem possible if the FBI's allegations are true. Since the rumor about the presence of ANFO prills has been circulating recently, we felt compelled to address this issue.

If there was an ANFO bomb involved, could it have been placed there to destroy the vehicle that was carrying it and to create a distraction from the expertly placed demolitions that really dropped the Murrah Building? There were burning cars in the area, which could indicate the presence of an ANFO explosion, but that alone is certainly not convincing evidence since all of those cars had gas tanks that may have exploded and/or caught fire. If there was an ANFO explosion with enough force to annihilate this massive structure, an "if" that experts say is impossible, one would think that remnants of ammonium nitrate would have been blown in toward the Murrah Building and fires would have been burning inside and at least some ANFO prills would have been visible inside the building.

According to Jim Ferguson in his interview with Pat Shannan, there were no fires or ANFO prills inside the building and, again, no skin or respiratory problems from nitric acid or nitric oxide. Had there been an ANFO explosion from the outside, the only thing that could've kept ammonium nitrate prills out of the building would have been massive explosions from inside the building that would have blown ANFO remnants out and away form the Murrah Building. Recently the Pentagon has released reports from two independent engineering firms that have studied the available information surrounding this tragedy. The reports indicated that these firms have concluded that the Murrah Building was blown from the inside by multiple and simultaneous detonation. This often ridiculed, far-fetched theory that, from the very beginning, has been so obvious to simple minded folks like us no longer seems quite so "far-fetched."

The dilemma we are facing concerning this issue of the existence of an ANFO bomb seems to be the conflicting reports by investigators. Until February of 1996, all of the information we received suggested that there were absolutely no remnants of an ANFO explosion in or around the Murrah Building. There were no reports of the presence of ANFO prills in the downtown area which would indicate two things. First, that there was no ANFO explosion in front of the Murrah Building. And second, that there was no ANFO bomb inside the alleged Ryder truck parked in front of the Murrah Building. We do know beyond any doubt that there was no signature of an ANFO explosion inside the Murrah Building and no reports of any injuries due to nitric acid or nitric oxide.

What we see here, looking at all of the evidence available, is a situation that is impossible to explain if you're trying to convince people that the government's version of this act of terrorism is accurate. If the area was covered with ANFO prills, which is one story, then the Government's allegations about an ANFO explosion being solely responsible for the damage to the Murrah Building couldn't possibly be true because of the inefficiency of the explosion. If there were no ANFO prills, which has been our observation, then the Government's allegations couldn't possibly be true because there would then be no evidence whatsoever of an ANFO explosion.

One might conclude that, since government investigators have had all of the physical evidence in their possession for more than ten months before their partial compliance with Judge Richard Matsch's order to disclose that information, it would probably be a pretty solid bet that some of their lab technicians have found material indicating that this was precisely what the BATF and FBI experts planted (sorry), said it would be.

THE FACTS, PLEASE, JUST THE FACTS! •

Photo courtesy Bob and Sandy Papovich

Co-authors James Nichols, left, and Bob Papovich sift through some of the thousands of pages of documents they have collected.

Photo courtesy Bob and Sandy Papovich

Of course, James Nichols does try and get some farming in whenever he gets a rare break from defending himself.

"I am a firm believer in the people. If given the truth, they can be depended upon to meet any national crisis. This great point is to bring them the real facts."
— **Abraham Lincoln**

CHAPTER 9: FLEXIBLE FACTS

If you think that evidence falsification is beneath the moral character of the BATF and the FBI, then you probably haven't been paying attention to the information surfacing lately. Some of the FBI's own scientists are coming forward and telling their horror stories about being ordered to falsify evidence and to create evidence where none existed. One technician has told reporters that much of the evidence which surfaced in the World Trade Center bombing was fabricated by FBI investigators. ABC's *Prime Time Live* recently aired a show in which chief investigative correspondent, Brian Ross, interviewed top FBI scientist, Frederick Whitehurst. Dr. Whitehurst's integrity dictated that he come forward and expose the fact that the FBI has been falsifying evidence for years. He said that it's common practice in the FBI crime lab and, believe it or not, other honest scientists have finally come forward and have confirmed what he's been saying. Thank you, Dr. Whitehurst.

Anyone who has an appreciation for the truth will find Dr. Whitehurst's testimony encouraging, but the circumstances surrounding his public statements are very discouraging when you take into consideration how long it took for this alarming and incriminating information to surface. Actually, Dr. Whitehurst began blowing the whistle on the corruption that was taking place within the FBI's scientific crime lab nearly two years ago! Why didn't anyone in the media jump on this story back then? Could it be that the feds have become experts at "silencing" anyone who might expose their criminal activities?

Dr. Whitehurst alleged that some individuals in the FBI's laboratory have deliberately falsified evidence to insure convictions of accused citizens. You might think that sometimes they have to stretch the law a little to get the bad guys, assuming they know who the bad guys are. But, put into perspective, how would you like to be falsely accused of a crime and have the FBI fabricate evidence against you to make it appear as if you were guilty as charged? We used to think that the situation about a secret group of corrupt small town cops framing some poor slob whom the Sheriff did not like only happened in the movies. We never realized that it's "standard operating procedure" for this nation's top bureau of investigation. How many innocent people are in prison right now because their case was not high profile enough or because they didn't possess the resources which would give them access to a Tigar, Jones, Cochran, Abramson, Elsey or Bailey?

The reason Dr. Whitehurst's allegations have been made public is not necessarily because of our watchdog media, but because of the O.J. Simpson trial. If O.J.'s defense attorneys hadn't decided to call on Dr. Whitehurst as a possible witness, the public may never have known about his statements concerning FBI misconduct. He claimed that the evidence and procedures for testing in the World Trade Center bombing and the mail bomb killing of a federal judge and a civil rights activist in Alabama had been tampered with. Dr. Whitehurst also said that some of the explosive components were intentionally left out of the laboratory reports concerning the World Trade Center bombing in New York City. FLEXIBLE FACTS!

The FBI coincidentally claimed that the World Trade Center was destroyed by an ANFO bomb also. As we now know, Lawrence Myers has reported that this claim was untrue. And, as coincidence would have it, the bomb was delivered in a Ryder truck! Shouldn't this raise some suspicions as to why Ryder seems to be the consistent choice of terrorists? Why not U-Haul or Hertz? What are the odds that two different groups of terrorists committing two separate terrorist attacks in the U.S. taking place a couple of years apart would not only use the exact same mode of transportation, but would rent that transportation from the same company and that the agents of deceit would falsely claim that the exact same method of destruction was used by those two different groups of terrorists?

Hasn't it piqued anyone's curiosity as to how Dr. Whitehurst's claims of wrongdoings by the FBI were kept from the public's attention for two whole years? There certainly appears to be at least a possibility that many very important players would have to be in some key positions within the media pulling some major strings to keep a story of this magnitude out of the news in a country where reporters and investigators like Lawrence Myers, Patrick Shannan, Maryann Struman (*Detroit News*) and William Jasper are always trying to get to the bottom of things and where all of its citizens assume that the press really does have the freedom to report the truth. The single equation that is obviously missing in this assumption is the belief that the press always knows the truth. But even if they do know the truth and even if they do try to enlighten the public, their information still has to meet the final approval of those very important and powerful players in the media who are really in control of what we see and hear on the news.

Since Dr. Whitehurst's challenge of their "evidence," the feds say they have not made a final determination concerning the type of bomb used in the World Trade Center bombing even though, according to Lawrence Myers, the FBI's records clearly indicate that that is not the case. Since the method of destruction is now being questioned in that act of terrorism, and since court documents also indicate that the FBI was intimately involved in the planning of the bombing at the World Trade Center which was allegedly a sting operation that went bad (yeah, right), we would say there's a strong possibility that the same type of explosives was actually used by the terrorists in Oklahoma City.

One might even speculate, considering the evidence and all of the similarities including the confiscation, falsification and intentional destruction of evidence, that the same group of people may have been responsible for planning both of these vicious acts of terrorism. And a well informed person might also speculate that both of these expertly planned, vicious acts of terrorism were carried out to accomplish a particular political goal. We can assure you, without speculation, that preservation of our Constitutional rights was not that "political goal."

At any rate, as a reward for being honest and doing what's right, Fred Whitehurst, who has a Ph.D. in Chemistry from Duke University and is the FBI crime lab's top bomb residue analyst, has received physical threats and intimidation from within the FBI. Being one of the FBI's top forensic scientists, and perhaps one of the top bomb residue analysts in the world, Dr. Whitehurst was also rewarded by receiving a demotion to the paint chips analysis division by the FBI's brilliant and fearless leader, Louis Freeh.

I guess one thing Louie just can't tolerate is honesty. Right, Louie? There's just no place for honesty, civility, morality, or patriotic decency on Louie's team. Just FLEXIBLE FACTS and OBSTRUCTION OF JUSTICE. Right, Louie? When you take a little time to look beneath the surface, you can see exactly what many of our "fearless leaders" are really made of. Generally what they're made of is discarded down our toilets with a simple push on a handle. Unfortunately, dangerous beings like Louie Freeh won't fit down our toilets, so their actions have to be exposed to eventually relieve them of their positions of power.

In the interview with Brian Ross on *Prime Time Live*, Dr. Whitehurst also claimed that he had submitted evidence to his superiors that FBI agent James T. Thurman, chief of the explosives unit at the FBI crime lab in Washington, had been altering test results in many different cases for several years by slanting the evidence to favor the prosecution. Whitehurst alleges that Thurman distorted the results of lab tests in the Alabama mail bomb case, for which Louis Freeh was the prosecutor. That single case was responsible for Freeh's eventual promotions within the Justice Department to FBI director, virtually catapulting him from obscurity into the national limelight overnight.

Interestingly, and unfortunately for Tim and Terry but very fortunate for John Does No. 1, 2, 3, 4, and 5, Thurman is also intimately involved in the prosecution's investigation into the Oklahoma City bombing case and heads the FBI's scientific investigation in that case. Considering his reputation for doing what he's told by his superiors without regard for the truth, this is a convenient position for a man who, along with his boss, may have already traded his soul for a paycheck and a position of authority. They apparently have their roots deeply tied with the political philosophies of the former Soviet Union and Nazi Germany. These are very sick and very dangerous men who are obviously living in the wrong country. The simple solution to our problem and to their philosophical problems with our Constitution may be that we could use some much, much larger toilets.

Mr. Moody, the accused and convicted man in the Alabama mail bomb case against whom James T. Thurman allegedly falsified evidence and who Louis Freeh prosecuted, is scheduled to be executed in the very near future. Considering all of the allegations surfacing about evidence falsification and lying under oath at Moody's trial, James and Louis are probably praying that Mr. Moody gets a stay of execution. According to the law, if it can be proven that evidence was falsified by Thurman and that Freeh knew the evidence had been falsified, after the execution Tom and Louis could also be brought up on charges which could result in the death penalty for both of them.

A perfect example of the prosecution's total disregard for the truth presented itself at Tim's and Terry's first hearing in Denver. Challenges were being made before the court by Stephen Jones concerning the prosecutions "so-called" evidence that had been withheld from the defense defying the rules of discovery which dictate that the prosecution supply the evidence to the defense. The allegations of evidence tampering by Dr. Frederick Whitehurst were brought to the court's attention by Mr. Jones. U.S. Attorney Beth Wilkinson argued the issue for the prosecution. She suggested that Dr. Whitehurst's claims of evidence tampering were nothing more than "sour grapes" because he had been demoted.

At that point, Stephen Jones came a little unglued. He pointed out that Dr. Whitehurst had been trying to blow the whistle about the improprieties in the FBI's crime lab for quite some time and his demotion was the direct result of his whistle blowing, not the other way around as Ms. Wilkinson had suggested. It was the first time that we saw Stephen Jones express his arguments with tremendous passion which, at the least, was very uplifting. Mr. Jones knew that Ms. Wilkinson was aware of the facts concerning this issue and he was also aware that she had intentionally misrepresented the truth in an attempt to discredit Dr. Whitehurst. That federal prosecutors can get away with lying in federal court is extremely discouraging to any objective person who has ever witnessed one of these professional deceivers in action. It certainly brought Stephen Jones off his seat in a hurry to expose the prosecution's deception.

Media Bypass recently printed an article in which an unnamed lab technician at the state medical examiner's office said that official reports on the Oklahoma City bombing concerning forensic records from the coroner's office are being "altered by the government in a number of substantive ways prior to release to the defense team or the public." That's interesting. How are these reports being altered and why would they need to be altered before the information was released to the defense teams if the evidence really does prove the prosecution's allegations that McVeigh committed this crime with Terry's assistance? If the evidence helps prove that the accused are guilty after the alterations were performed, what might that evidence have proven prior to the alterations? We would really appreciate it if a government representative would take the time to address these issues. Wouldn't you?

Another lab technician has told independent investigators in the Oklahoma City bombing that he was coerced by superiors into falsifying evidence, suggesting that he would find urea in samples taken from the bombing site when all of his tests showed that none existed. More FLEXIBLE FACTS! Had there been an ammonium nitrate explosion, all samples from the immediate area should have tested positively for urea. After several attempts using chemical analysis and still unable to find urea in any of the samples, under "pressure from above," he added his own urea. You can use your imaginations as to how he may have accomplished that feat. Most of us easily handle that task at least several times a day in our own little lavatory, and we're not even FBI laboratory technicians. These whistle blowers are all honest, patriotic Americans who are not only risking their jobs but are literally risking their lives coming forward with information that is potentially damaging to some of the powerful people in charge of directing these federally controlled agencies. There is a very interesting fact of which most people are unaware, or, should we say, some very interesting information has been intentionally kept out of the news. DEFENSE INVESTIGATORS HAVE NOT BEEN ALLOWED TO TAKE ONE LITTLE TEENSY SCRAP OF EVIDENCE FROM THAT ENTIRE BOMBING SITE FOR PRIVATE, INDEPENDENT   LABORATORY INSPECTION! Now everyone out there who still believes the government's story about how this building was blown up by patriotic American farmers and fertilizer, raise your hands. Raise them high and keep them up, because we don't want you to miss out on a once-in-a-lifetime opportunity to buy some bridges for which we have no deeds.   And they're not cheap either!   Are those Bryant's, Geraldo's and Greg's hands we see out there?

Read the big print once more so that we don't have to type it again. No, you're not mistaken. Unbelievable as it may seem, neither defense team has been able to secure even one single speck of virgin rubble. Lord knows that the government has plenty to go around. As a matter of fact, they have so much that they've hauled it away and buried it at the BFI Waste Systems landfill just outside of Oklahoma City and the discarded rubble is under guard at all times. We have recently heard that the feds have used three or more different areas to bury and hide the evidence, of course, under armed guard and lock and key at all times. Now wouldn't you think that if the rubble was no more valuable than so much garbage that you would bury in the ground at a landfill, perhaps hundreds of thousands of tons of the stuff, they could spare an ounce or two for the defense attorneys to do some private testing?

But nope. None. Not one little pebble of virgin evidence. In January and February of 1996, the prosecution finally released some evidence to the defense, only because they were ordered by the court under the rules of discovery to produce that evidence. They didn't give it up without a fight and every bit of evidence that was turned over to the defense had been in the hands of the feds for "safekeeping" for eight to 10 months. What might it have been that they did not want defense investigators to discover from this virgin evidence? If the original evidence really proved the prosecution's allegations a reasonable person would be inclined to believe that the federal prosecutors would have stumbled over each other trying to present this evidence to the defense teams and to the media. Instead they have leaked to the media disinformation about many issues while they were hoarding and jealously guarding the real evidence in this crime. As Bryant Gumble would so eloquently say: "*Whye?*"

Do you think it's fair to Terry and Tim or even remotely possible for their attorneys to defend them under these circumstances? Do you think they can get an adequate defense or a fair trial? Do you think that this policy of a FLEXIBLE FACTS cover-up is fair to the victims and their families who want to know the truth about this tragedy? How would you like to be in Tim's or Terry's shoes having to prove your innocence when the government prosecutors are stacking the deck against you like they are in this case, especially when you take into consideration that these two young men are facing the death penalty? And it does appear that these men have to prove their innocence, particularly since they have already been tried and convicted by the media. This kind of an investigation by the feds actually does violence to the Justice System in this country. Can you appreciate the frustration we've been experiencing for the past two years? •

"I have neither wit, nor words, nor worth, nor actions, nor utterance, nor the power of speech. To stir men's blood: I only speak right on."

— **Shakespeare**

Note that, in this photo taken almost immediately after the Murrah bomb, signs of a crater are evident at lower right.

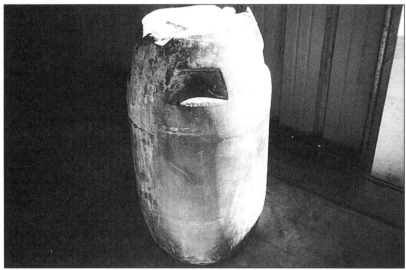

This blue plastic drum, containing only smelly, fishy fertilizer liquid, still provided enough "evidence" to permit federal authorities to charge James Nichols (see Appendices).

"Today the primary threat to the liberties of the American people comes not from communism, foreign tyrants or dictators. It comes from the tendency on our own shores to centralize power, to trust bureaucracies rather than people."
— **Gov. George Allen**

Chapter 10: Obstruction of Justice

Of course, the evidence hauled to the landfill couldn't possibly have shown that there wasn't ever an ammonium nitrate explosion, because if the evidence was really that important in finding out what actually happened in this bombing and who really murdered all of those beautiful, innocent people, the government wouldn't be burying it in a landfill, would it? And wouldn't you agree that if the rubble did not contain relevant evidence that might tend to incriminate someone whom government investigators did not want incriminated, and if it did not contain certain evidence that would totally clear the current suspects, they would not need to keep the evidence hidden and they would not need armed guards posted making sure that nobody, including the defense teams, could get samples of that rubble?

But they do have armed guards protecting that evidence. The defense investigators were allowed to inspect the site for a day before the remainder of the building was leveled with explosives. It was a full month after the fact and it was also the first time they were allowed to enter the scene of the crime for inspection and investigation. The armed guards were there watching to make sure that the defense team didn't remove anything. Why would the government do that? Wouldn't armed guards prove the inconsistency in the government's contention that the evidence in the rubble was irrelevant to the defense investigators? Wouldn't refusal of independent testing of samples prove the same thing? Wouldn't that be considered OBSTRUCTION OF JUSTICE? One might be inclined to believe that when falsifying evidence becomes "standard operating procedure," obstruction of justice is no big deal. It's just part of the routine setup, uh, investigation. Of course, not being a big deal depends totally upon who you are; the guys doing the investigating, or the guys getting setup, uh, investigated. We must keep in mind that one crime is usually concealed by the commission of another crime.

When we returned to Oklahoma City in December for the disclosure hearing the prosecution was still being quite stingy with the evidence (how much time does the FBI need to taint evidence?) so we decided to do a little disclosing of our own. By then the feds had moved the protective barrier inward surrounding only the Murrah Building and the front of the Athenian Restaurant directly across the street. We picked up small samples representative of most of the debris in the parking lot directly north of the Murrah Building, including some bark from the now-famous tree in that parking lot which had been scorched from the explosions.

We also collected some leaves from the bush on the southeast corner of the *Journal Record* building, and some paint chips from the south side of that building which would have been directly exposed to the explosions from the Murrah Building. This was something we had been wanting to do for a long time but had been denied the opportunity, in part, because we live in Michigan and seldom have access to the area, but mostly because a very large area had previously been fenced off and guarded making it inaccessible to private citizens. We certainly would have preferred evidence taken directly from the rubble in the Murrah Building, but had we attempted to secure any of that rubble we're certain we would have either been shot and killed or prosecuted for some kind of federal violation and Tim and Terry may have had a couple of cellmates.

The rubble we did gather was almost an acceptable substitute, so we proceeded to have a laboratory check out some pieces of the rubble we collected and guess what! No residue from an ANFO explosion! No nitrates! No urea! No byproducts of ammonium nitrate! Nothing! Absolutely clean. Even the bark from the tree, the leaves from the bush and the paint chips showed no evidence of ANFO and we have been told by lab technicians that it would have been impossible for the bark to be completely free from that kind of evidence. These tests are consistent with the absence of nitric acid and nitric oxide in the area immediately after the explosions. Are you surprised? Should you be? We can say without hesitation that we were not in the least bit surprised.

Both defense teams tried, unsuccessfully, for many months to obtain the alleged evidence against their clients promised to them by the prosecutors under the discovery rules of criminal prosecution. Most of the court records have been sealed and kept from public scrutiny. The reason for this, says the FBI, is that they don't want to influence the opinion of potential jurors who may read or hear this information in the news. If their excuse was really true then why has the FBI from the very beginning "leaked" so many lies and so much disinformation to the press? OBSTRUCTION OF JUSTICE?

Prosecutors claim to withhold evidence from the public record so as not to try the case in the media, yet constantly tell lies to the media to accomplish exactly that which they claim they are trying to avoid. Isn't slanting public opinion precisely the reason for lying and spreading disinformation? And when you really think about their excuse, it makes even less sense. If the prosecution disclosed "confidential" information to the defense teams only, why would that influence "public" opinion? Did the prosecution withhold evidence from the grand jury so as not to influence their opinion also? Why else would they withhold witnesses and information from the grand jury? "But the feds would never do that!" you say. Oh, really? Just listen to what Hoppy Heidelberg, one of 23 members of the grand jury who indicted Tim and Terry, has to say on this subject:

"They [prosecutors for indictments] kept promising and promising to answer all my questions, but ultimately they stalled me. I was had.

"Let's get the architects and engineers who built the building in there and question them. I demanded bomb experts and geologists and engineers. They [prosecutors] said they didn't have the money. I said I'd go down to the University of Oklahoma myself and bring some geologists back myself for free and they wouldn't let me." (You can see why they wanted Hoppy Heidelberg off the grand jury.)

"The various surveillance video tapes of the bombing from Southwest Bell and the *Journal Record* building, we don't know that they showed all the details of the bombing, including the perpetrators, but it's possible. None of this material was shown to us in the grand jury."

Are you still harboring some healthy skepticism? Hoppy's not shy about voicing his observations of prosecutorial and FBI misconduct. His overabundance of intestinal fortitude, evident in these next statements, is as fortunate for the American people who seek only the truth as it is unfortunate for the feds.

"The FBI has been able to get witnesses to shut up about important things they know. In certain instances the witnesses believe that concealing evidence is the right thing to do. They really believe it. The FBI has sold them a bill of goods about national security or something like that. In other cases the FBI has used straight-out intimidation on witnesses. They size people up. On one witness they'll use something like national security. On another they'll use intimidation."

"Eventually they brought in one [bomb expert]. They didn't count on the fact that anyone on the grand jury could spot this guy as a CIA type operator. I found out later he was CIA although he had lots of impressive credentials. His testimony was very effective, but the whole thing was bogus. A dog and pony show."

Doesn't it make you wonder just which way the prosecutors did not want the grand jury's opinion influenced?

For the prosecutors to take part in this kind of immoral activity is sad, but unfortunately it's true. They seem to justify their actions by claiming they have to catch the criminals at any cost. To exercise their philosophy the feds have to operate under the assumption that they, as an agent, investigator, or prosecutor, know exactly who the guilty people are. Their egotistical assumptions dictate that they routinely eavesdrop on conversations between attorneys and their clients, thereby negating the attorney client privilege. That's why they conceal or perhaps even destroy evidence that shines light on the truth. That's why they throw a bloody glove in a suspect's backyard to solidify their perceived case against him.

When you really think about it, that kind of activity does violence to our justice system by attempting to eliminate the jury system. And that's why these officers of the law who falsify evidence or OBSTRUCT JUSTICE are just as criminal as the perpetrators of this vicious act of terrorism in Oklahoma City. The victims of their actions are, inevitably, the innocent. •

"It is most unfortunate that the federal government has chosen to dispose of physical evidence, and has not mounted a more aggressive investigation and made all of the facts concerning this case public."
— **John W. Culbertson, President, Walker Aerospace Group, Inc. (Preliminary Event Analysis, Alfred P. Murrah Federal Building)**

Chapter 11: Destruction of Evidence — Who Benefits?

Now that we're on the subject of the falsification or DESTRUCTION OF EVIDENCE and how it relates to the implosion of the Murrah Building, one question we all have to ask is: Why? Why would anyone want to participate in the DESTRUCTION OF EVIDENCE in an ongoing criminal investigation? Honest government investigators still do not know exactly what happened inside this building. We believe it can be said with absolute certainty, considering the current ability of scientific investigators, that in time they could have easily discovered who the real perpetrators of this heinous crime were and precisely how they initiated their cowardly act of destruction. There is one question that we all need to ask: Who wanted this damaged building destroyed, and WHO BENEFITS by burying the evidence forever?

Certainly not the defense teams for Tim and Terry. We believe they initiated a vigorous effort to keep the Murrah Building standing until all of the facts were known — but their attempts at blocking the order to demolish the Murrah Building were in vain.

All of the arguments that we've heard in favor of dropping the damaged Murrah Building were very emotional yet very specious. Their "experts" came forward, all claiming precisely what the government investigators wanted to instill in everyone's mind. This building was too dangerous for any of the workers to continue their mission. It had to be demolished so the families of the victims could lay this horrible image forever to rest thereby getting on with their lives and not being reminded on a daily basis of the terrible tragedy they had endured and, hopefully, begin to ease the pain. As if destroying this building was going to change anything or make losing their loved ones any easier or less painful. In our opinion, many of the families of the victims and the surviving victims were extremely insulted by this phony cover-up and the premature implosion of the Murrah Building long before all of the facts were known and all of the evidence gathered. The government's contention that the damaged building had to be demolished because it was unsalvageable, unsafe, and dangerous to the public makes no sense when you really think about it. DESTRUCTION OF EVIDENCE: WHO BENEFITS?

First, the entire area was fenced in so the "public" couldn't even get close to the Murrah Building. And, second, what about the condition of the Athenian Restaurant directly across the street? The whole front of that building was blown off. Chunks of debris were hanging out all over the place. The inside of the building had been blown to smithereens and the building was easily accessible from the back for anyone, including children, who might want to go inside among the rubble to be injured or worse. That building was still standing in February 1996 when we were there, and it sure looked dangerous to us. If public safety truly was a factor for those who pressed the issue of implosion, the Athenian Restaurant also would have been demolished.

We believe this was another slap in the face to the whole nation. Basically what they were saying when they gave the order to implode the damaged Murrah Building was: The American people are too stupid to realize what's going on, so we'll just destroy the evidence on national television in front of tens of millions of people and give them a line of b.s. and play on their emotions. We'll even sucker some of the victims and survivors into demanding that we destroy the evidence. That way, no one can blame the agents in the government who orchestrated this scam. You have to give credit when credit's deserved.

These agents of deceit certainly deserve credit for their deception. So far, it has worked perfectly. Abe Lincoln said, "you can't fool all of the people all the time." Unfortunately, this time they only needed to fool enough of the people to justify burying the evidence very quickly while emotions still clouded our thought processes. Can you imagine the outcries from some of the more foolish members of the public if one of the defense teams wanted to help prove their clients' innocence by exhuming some of the rubble that is left buried under the sod where the Murrah Building once stood? The area will either be made a national monument, making it untouchable, or Congress will pass a specific law concerning that particular spot making it illegal to disturb anything above or beneath the ground.

And we certainly sympathize with the surviving victims and the families of victims. We understand that the families consider this area hallowed ground similar to a cemetery where we would bury our loved ones. We understand why the victims would not want this ground disturbed. But we must also understand the only way the victims and their families will ever realize any degree of closure on this horrendous act of terrorism is to find out exactly how it happened, exactly why it happened and even more important, who was actually responsible.

Think about the power that these "public servants" possess: The ability to destroy evidence in an ongoing criminal investigation on national TV, and with the blessings of the vast majority of the media giants. We must suggest that this is not only an indication of their power and connections but an indication of whose script these talking heads we see daily on national TV are reading, not to mention the influence they have on public opinion. As a nation relying on "network news" for most of our daily diet of information, wouldn't you agree that we may have some very serious problems with many of the very high paid phonies who are supposed to be giving us that news?

There was a universal sigh of relief in the national media when the Murrah Building was destroyed, forever burying and tainting the remaining evidence approximately one month after the fact. Common sense dictates that the only people relieved by the implosion were those scoundrels who were actually responsible for the explosions. The talking heads suggested that now the families of the victims could finally get on with their lives, as if this damaged structure was somehow keeping them from "getting on with their lives." We all know from experience, when you lose a loved one, it doesn't matter if the whole world is upside-down or rightside-up, nothing eases the pain. Time is the only elixir and sometimes that doesn't seem to help much either.

Looking at recent history, you can't really blame them for thinking we're that foolish. After all, the feds lied and destroyed and falsified evidence in both of the Kennedy assassinations, Martin Luther King's assassination, the Waco massacre, the Ruby Ridge murders, and the World Trade Center bombing. The government even lied and covered up evidence concerning American patriots who thought they were fighting for God, country, and baby in the Vietnam "conflict" and were captured by the enemy and abandoned by the cowards and traitors controlling the government. As a matter of fact, they lied about the entire war and we bought their lies, turning against each other, not realizing who the enemy really was. They concealed information and lied about the use of agent orange and the suffering and death it has inflicted upon thousands of Vietnam veterans and, in some cases, their offspring-to-be.

The feds have lied and are still lying about the Gulf War Syndrome even though thousands of Gulf War veterans have died or will soon die from this illness. All that is necessary to save the lives of these patriotic American citizens who literally put their lives on the line for their country is for our government to admit that they manufactured and shipped to Iraq the very chemicals or biological agents that are causing this illness. Once the feds own up to this "mistake" they could offer proper treatment to those soldiers who are still alive.

But it is unlikely that the Pentagon will ever admit to this damning information even though the truth is slowly being brought to the attention of those of us who are willing to pay attention. The feds would much prefer to sacrifice thousands or, if necessary, tens of thousands of good American citizens rather than admit to selling or giving weapons and chemicals to Iraq a few years ago when they were "our buddies" fighting with Iran, "the enemy." Ironically, the same chemicals manufactured in the United States that Iraq used against Iran were also used against U.S. troops in the Gulf War and that's one of the dirty little secrets that they're trying to hide.

We would like to believe that the government would gladly admit to wrong doing to save innocent lives. The evidence, unfortunately, does not confirm that desire and strongly suggests that just the opposite is true. As we have shown, the federal government would much rather sacrifice tens of thousands of lives or maybe even 168 lives than to be held accountable for the Gulf War Syndrome.

"What's that got to do with this?" you're thinking to yourself. "What do the deaths in the Murrah Building bombing have to do with Gulf War?" you ask. Well, recently it has been reported that the records of Gulf War Syndrome veterans who have died and information, quite possibly incriminating information, concerning the Gulf War Syndrome illness have come up missing. It has not yet been established by the national media just how those records got "misplaced" but for many months there has been information circulating about this story that has been successfully kept out of the news. The information we have heard indicates that those records were stored in a federal building in downtown Oklahoma City. Just coincidentally, the building where those records were stored was the Alfred P. Murrah Federal Building. And also, just coincidentally, all of those records were destroyed in the bombing. Convenient. Very convenient. After all, how can you prove that missing records have been destroyed if they are missing? There's really no evidence to prove or disprove.

Two brave Americans named Peter Kawaja and Joyce Riley have brought this information out into the light of day. Despite the loss of his wife, death threats against him and at least one nearly successful attempt on his life, Kawaja just won't go away. He has also been given the opportunity to experience that which all patriotic Americans will eventually experience. His reward for loving his country and speaking out about crimes against its citizens was constant harassment and then financial annihilation by the IRS. This patriotic citizen has been terrorized for attempting to bring forth the truth to the American people. He was to be the star witness before a grand jury and when he tried to present evidence to the grand jury of the CIA's involvement in weapons deals with Iraq he was immediately dismissed and his miserable ordeal began. You'll be hearing more about these patriots because they will not be intimidated into silence.

And we thought the government would have a big liability problem with the Oklahoma City bombing if the truth ever came out. Can you imagine the liability problem they're going to have when the truth comes out about the Gulf War Syndrome? You're probably suffering from an acute attack of skepticism as you're reading these words and that skepticism is absolutely what we want you to feel. We don't want you to accept as fact anything we're telling you. All we ask is that you use common sense and think about the information we are passing along to you in this book. When you take the time to put it all into perspective it will make sense. Just think of the de facto United States as a gigantic corporation, which is precisely what it really is. We covered that information in Part I of this book. Now ask yourself, Wouldn't any large, corrupt corporation be inclined to protect their corporate interests and their corporate checkbook at any cost? Anyone care to answer that one?

It isn't all that difficult to see why these corporate social planners think we really are stupid enough to buy their scam. They've gotten away with it so many times before. Since lying has been so easy for the feds and has worked so well in the past for their crimes and political campaigns (we're not sure there's a difference), why not try it again? Lord knows they've had enough practice. We must remember that none of this would have been possible without a great deal of influence within the national media, particularly the television media.

Anyway, getting back to the subject of the implosion, one man's opinion, James Loftis, the architect who designed the Murrah Federal Building, was kept out of the national news quite successfully. He thought that the building could be saved and would be much less costly to repair than to replace. He also said that the damaged building could easily be secured using conventional shoring techniques, making it safe for workers and investigators. He was not alone in his opinions. Other independent construction experts expressed similar opinions, none of which appeared on network news.

Whoever originated the order to implode this building should, most definitely, be the target of some sort of investigation. If that action does not raise suspicions among the leaders of our Justice Department, then we must suggest that it should raise suspicions among all vigilant citizens concerning those leaders. We may just need some new, competent, and honest leaders in our law-enforcement agencies who consider themselves accountable to the citizens. Apparently, it has not raised suspicions within our "Just-Us" Department so we as free citizens will eventually have to assume this responsibility and, in our opinion, the sooner the better.

You may find this hard to believe, but one of our investigators has been told "off the record" by an agent of the CIA that this so-called fertilizer bomb is an inside joke among all of the government intelligence agencies. He stated that all of the informed agents in the FBI, CIA, DEA, BATF, etc. know that it was not a fertilizer bomb that destroyed the Murrah Building. They know that a fertilizer bomb couldn't possibly cause that kind of destruction and that this was some kind of covert operation although they do not know exactly who was responsible for initiating the operation. That they admit the operation was covert suggests to us that this was a government operation. Which country's government? That is obviously the unanswered question.

They've been told by their superiors what to say to the news or in public about this disaster and about the ANFO villains, and they follow those instructions because that's what they're paid to do; it's their job. But in private this person said they have joked about how stupid people are to believe that this horrendous destruction could have been caused by a couple of amateurs with some plant food. He said they especially joke about the ignorance of the news reporters. They believe anything the Government agents tell them. Believe me, we have some first hand experience with that statement. DESTRUCTION OF EVIDENCE: WHO BENEFITS?

There have been some incidents recently that somewhat relate to what this CIA agent was saying which basically verify the awareness that government agents have of the cover-up in this particular case and of their attempts at concealing the cover-up (crime hidden by another crime). An example of this is the planned experiments by the Army Corps of Engineers to duplicate the explosion in Oklahoma City to prove to the world that it could have happened the way the government investigators say it happened. When Tim McVeigh's attorney, Stephen Jones, caught wind of what was going on — and said that he wanted to be present with his investigators to monitor these experiments — they were abruptly canceled.

As long as there weren't any objective investigators or demolitions experts monitoring these experiments, the barrels could've been packed with C-4 or some other potent explosive, even a limited nuclear device, and who would have known? An enhanced experimental explosion may have convinced all of the skeptics in the media or in a potential viewing audience that an ANFO bomb could have inflicted the extensive damage that was done to the Murrah Building and downtown Oklahoma City. Do you really think the "on the scene" reporters would have known the difference? These experiments, which were planned by the Army Corps of Engineers, were supposed to have made up for the unconvincing failures of previously aired television ANFO explosions.

Several months after the Murrah explosions, another demonstration of a fertilizer explosion aired on television. It was designed to convince skeptics of the vast capabilities of a fertilizer bomb, but couldn't have convinced anyone with any common sense that this was even remotely representative of the blasts that actually destroyed the Murrah Building in Oklahoma City. The explosion was impressive, but you have to realize that you could put a firecracker under a tin can and take a close up movie from the proper angle and it would be a very impressive explosion. Our world-renowned anchor man bought it. Surprise, surprise! (Maybe the reporter should have secretly recorded the VIN on the axle of the vehicle carrying the demonstration bomb to see if it showed up in the future at the scene of another act of terrorism.)

Recently, the CBS News "documentary" program *48 Hours* aired a program which was supposed to have demonstrated the awesome power of an ANFO explosion. They exploded a 1,000-1,500-lb. ammonium nitrate bomb inside a van sitting next to a small wall fabricated for the occasion. This demonstration took place at some remote desert location, and when the smoke cleared, the bomb had totally destroyed the van and demolished the small wall which was about 1/100th the size of the Murrah Building. It was a very impressive explosion. Very impressive. It also fell very short of proving that an ANFO bomb could've been responsible for the massive damage to the Murrah Building.

As a matter of fact, if you saw the program, nobody could ever convince you that the crater in front of the Murrah Building was caused by an ANFO bomb contained inside a truck above the pavement as government investigators claim. The explosion in this demonstration barely broke the surface of the ground. It created a slight impression in the sand and left a small mound of sand around the circumference of the impression. Now if a 1,500-lb. ANFO bomb sitting in a van above the surface can barely blow a shallow impression in the sand, how in the world could the same type explosion blow a mammoth crater through the asphalt and hardpan in front of the Murrah Building? Anyone want to take a guess at the answer to that one? Perhaps the reporter should have recorded that VIN also.

If certain agents and politicians can't get their anti-terrorism bill passed in Congress by playing on the emotions of the nation after the Oklahoma City bombing,, we'd say it would be a safe bet that there will be more acts of terrorism until they get what they want. The VINs of these destroyed vehicles could prove to be very important evidence in the future. (They have since passed the so-called "anti-terrorism" legislation and for obvious reasons we decided to leave this prediction in the book.)

It reminds us of a story we watched on PBS several years ago when Cuban troops were escorting a news man from the U.S. around a war zone somewhere in Africa, probably in Angola. The apparent purpose of the segment was to shine a bad light on the South African military who were apparently fighting with the Cuban communists over control of the area. As if the South African military weren't already doing quite well in the shining-the-bad-light-on-themselves department. As they drove into a small town with cameras rolling suddenly there was an assault by, what they claimed to be, South African artillery.

Our unbelievably naive news reporter started yelling in apparent horror, "Oh no, we're being hit, we're being hit by artillery rounds!" All the time, as his Cuban escorts accelerated their jeep to escape certain doom, the cameras were rolling to capture every second of this ridiculous sensationalism. They made it appear as if this innocent, peaceful little town in Angola was about to be destroyed by South African artillery.

Apparently, the observant news reporter never noticed that the town was completely void of people. Nor did he notice that the artillery shells were missing the town by at least a couple hundred yards, thumping the sandy terrain just on the outskirts of the small city. Like Bob said, you don't miss a city by a couple hundred yards with modern artillery. Maybe by a few feet from five miles away. Not a couple hundred yards. Impossible.

Bob also said that the explosions in the sand were absolutely not artillery rounds. He said that they appeared to be very small charges equivalent to, at the most, a one-half stick of dynamite and probably much less than that. A blasting cap placed a couple of inches under the sand would kick up a large enough cloud of dust to impress someone who's never played with firecrackers or witnessed a real explosion from a grenade, mortar or artillery round. More than likely, these devices were detonated electronically to make sure that the timing was right so this naive reporter would have the opportunity to get it all on film and to wet his pants. They got their point across and the news correspondent bought it completely and responded accordingly. This whole incident was obviously staged to sway public opinion against the South African government but, as we all know, the South African government is perfectly capable of accomplishing that feat without assistance. With the help of a well-meaning but ignorant reporter, sway they did.

The problem, unfortunately, is that we have to rely on many reporters who couldn't find their butt with both hands if their lives depended on it to tell us what's going on in the world, and what's going on in the Oklahoma City bombing investigation. That all too common problem is one reason we're writing this book and, quite probably, why you're reading it. •

Photos courtesy Bob and Sandy Papovich

These two country gentlemen, co-authors James Nichols, left, and Bob Papovich, deliver a visual message to federal authorities. The cards read: "TERRY WASN'T THERE" and "NEITHER WAS TIM."

"We're taking over now and it would be advisable and recommendable that you keep your mouth shut."
— **FBI agent to Toni Garrett, registered nurse and rescuer at bombing site (from video documentary,** *Oklahoma City: What Really Happened?***)**

Chapter 12: The Grand Cover-Up

In light of the actions by the government to conceal and destroy pertinent evidence in this investigation, we have no choice at this point but to look at and to evaluate the evidence and eyewitness testimony that is available. We have an enormous number of pictures and numerous people who have seen many things that do not match the government's explanation of what happened. We can and will use the pictures and eyewitness reports to accurately piece together what really happened that fateful day inside the Murrah Building. The government has very carefully guarded the physical evidence from the bombed out building, but the pictures taken by investigators and the statements given by victims and eyewitnesses will eventually expose some of the evidence that has been concealed in this disaster. It almost seems as if the FBI, in their haste to prevent investigators from finding out what did happen in THE GRAND COVER-UP, didn't realize that the pictures being taken would eventually allow defense investigators to prove what did not happen.

Another inconsistent, or "flexible," story by the FBI has been troubling us for quite some time. Their investigators originally stated that the fuse for the ANFO bomb inside the Ryder truck was set off by hand. They also said that there were approximately twenty barrels filled with the substance inside the truck. They have also stated that these fertilizer-filled barrels were wrapped with a special detonator cord and that it would have been necessary to wrap the barrels three times each to realize some efficiency in detonation. It is also known that the particular detonator cord that FBI investigators claim was used is nearly impossible to obtain unless you're BATF, FBI or very well connected in the military. This is not an item that Tim McVeigh or Terry Nichols could have purchased in large quantities at the local military auction. It is a very closely guarded item and someone has to be accountable for it, although to obtain a very small quantity would not necessarily be an impossible task particularly at military type trade shows.

Now, let's put on our thinking caps again. We have 20 barrels with a circumference of approximately seven feet each. Wrapped 3 times it would take about 21 feet of cord for each barrel. That would be a total of 420 feet of detonator cord that is nearly impossible to obtain even in small quantities. In addition to that, you would need extra cord for the lead fuse for each barrel, say 5 feet. I don't think that 520 feet of detonator cord would be easily obtainable unless you were an agent of the BATF, FBI, DEA, or a member of one of the other alphabet soup gangs. And I don't think anyone would consider 520 feet a small quantity. Now apparently the FBI investigators have confidence in their contentions that this explosion was caused by an ANFO bomb set off by detonator cord and since this cord is only available to certain government agencies, wouldn't their claims raise even more doubts and suspicions about who may have really been the culprits in this tragedy? The FBI realized the problem with Tim or Terry having access to detonator cord and ... enter into the picture the robbery of the Marion, Kan., construction site to explain how they acquired this cord.

This technique has become typical for the prosecutors in this case. If their story doesn't make sense, they make up another story to cover the voids in the first story and then make certain that the evidence that they have "discovered" substantiates these voids, sometimes many days or weeks after the fact. Occasionally this evidence mysteriously surfaces from an area weeks after that area has been searched or after the evidence has been in the feds' possession for months. The more we learn about the facts in their investigation, the more difficult it becomes to accept or to even understand their theories when logic is used as a basis for trying to understand those theories. You might think that computer technology can help law enforcement to more easily track criminals and solve crimes, and we agree. But you must also realize that the same technology can and is being used to easily fabricate cases against accused citizens.

There's another point of interest concerning this issue that deserves equal consideration. The feds originally said that their evidence indicated that the fuse to the bomb was ignited by hand. Now let's give this idea some serious thought. We know that because of the properties of a fertilizer bomb, each of these barrels had to have had its own detonation device. We also know that if one of these barrels of destruction was ignited before any of the others, even by 1/10th of a second, none of the others would have exploded. They would have been blown to pieces, the explosion would've been a total dud, and the unexploded ammonium nitrate fertilizer would have been scattered all over the entire area. Whatever kind of explosion it was, it obviously was not a dud.

And try to imagine this: Tim McVeigh exited a very large, yellow Ryder truck in downtown Oklahoma City at 9:00 in the morning, undeniably a busy time of the day. He went around to the back of the truck, opened the big yellow back door and proceeded to light 20 matches all at the same time igniting 20 fuses all at precisely the same time and these fuses are all exactly the same length, exact to within 1/1,000th of an inch. Obviously this guy's really good, maybe even a magician. He then had time to walk over and jump into his car and as he's driving away his license plate gets blown off in the explosion. Of course, none of the rest of the car shows any indication that it was ever exposed to any type of an explosion. Now that must have been magic. There was enough force to rip the license plate off his car and it didn't even scorch the paint. Try ripping the license plate off your car, even if it is hanging by one loose bolt. You'll soon realize how ridiculous that idea was. (Apparently the FBI eventually realized it, too, in their attempt at THE GRAND COVER-UP!.)

"Oh," you say, "Tim is a 1990s-style terrorist. He used a disposable lighter instead of matches." That would make it much easier for one man or even 20 men to light 20 fuses all within 1/100th of a second of each other, right? Of course, nobody saw this happen in downtown Oklahoma City at 9:00 in the morning even though Daina Bradley was standing inside the Murrah Building looking at the Ryder truck (she did see John Doe No. 2). And none of the surveillance tapes that the government has confiscated caught this on camera either, at least we have to assume the cameras didn't catch this on film because two years after the fact we're still looking at composite drawings. Does the government think that the people in this country are really foolish enough to swallow the allegations in THE GRAND COVER-UP? Now if you can buy this scenario please raise your hands again because, believe it or not, we have just acquired some more bridges, again, with no deeds. The first ones have already been sold to the previous hand raisers.

Government investigators at some point realized that their story as to how Tim ignited this concoction had, shall we say, enough holes to make a sieve look like it would hold water. And as usual, their story has conveniently changed to fit their accusations against McVeigh. It would appear as if the FLEXIBLE FACTS in this disaster are changed any time the government investigators find it convenient to do so.

In the next story the feds fabricated, they claimed that this kid was so stupid he made numerous errors that a kindergarten criminal would not make, but he somehow put together common farm supplies which created an explosion equal to and resembling a small nuclear blast and detonated it electronically from a distance as he was escaping the scene of the most vicious and expertly executed one-man crime (TERRY WAS NOT THERE) in history, a-a-a-and drove for 60 miles before anyone noticed that he didn't have a license plate on his vehicle. I believe they have progressed from historical revisionists to current event revisionists with more FLEXIBLE FACTS!

Apparently it works for the government. And do you know what's really disheartening? We haven't seen one reporter in the major national media bring them to task on any of these inconsistencies in their stories. Oh yes, one minor detail that's always puzzled us about this particular story. What happened to the electronic device that Tim allegedly used for his expertly calculated remote detonation? Inquiring minds want to know. And, correct us if we're wrong, but wouldn't it be rather dangerous to take a chance on electronic detonation in an area with countless car phones, radio transmitters, microwaves, garage door openers and numerous other devices that might unexpectedly set off an electronically controlled detonator?

Needless to say, the feds have another theory as to how this plant food was ignited. The FBI's top explosives fabrication expert, James T. Thurman, testified that he did not know exactly how the bomb was detonated. However, Thurman did express the FBI's theory which suggests that the suspects drilled a hole through the floor beneath the seat and then drilled another hole in the cargo trailer through which a water-proof cannon fuse was fed to a non-electric blasting cap placed inside the "primadet" cord and explosives wrapped around the barrels of ANFO (source: *Media Bypass*). Since this "theory" is, in fact, right out of *The Turner Diaries*, we have a question. "Who was reading and acted upon this information in *The Turner Diaries*, McVeigh or the FBI?" Considering his track record for evidence falsification, perhaps Mr. Thurman should be given a polygraph test to determine if he's telling the truth about not knowing exactly how the bomb was detonated.

Either *The Turner Diaries* or Mr. Thurman — or both — have a great theory unless you are aware of all the eyewitness observations concerning the Ryder truck. Eyewitnesses say that John Doe No. 2 got out of the truck, walked around to the back of the truck and actually stayed there for a few minutes. Now we know that you can't speak for anyone else, but if you had just lit a fuse to a 4,800-pound bomb, would you mosey around close by for a few minutes or would you have rapidly left the scene without any hesitation? And even if their purely speculative theory about the fuse being lit from inside the cab was true, the fuse length would have to be so accurate that blowing 20 barrels at precisely the same time seems like it would have been physically impossible. This idea really does sound like something that would come out of Hollywood or from a "fiction" novel because it just doesn't represent reality. Being in separate containers would've insured that the explosion, at best, would have destroyed the vehicle carrying it and only caused superficial damage to the Murrah Building and other buildings close by.

According to FBI records, Michael Fortier has also stated that McVeigh drilled a hole in the cab and then into the box of the Ryder truck to accommodate the fuse to the bomb. The problem with Fortier's "statement" is that it was made after the FBI made public their "theory" about how the bomb was ignited. It really makes us wonder: Would they have fabricated this story if any of their previous stories had gone unchallenged? Could Fortier have concocted this story on his own without the "power of suggestion and coercion" from the feds who obviously got their idea from *The Turner Diaries*, or maybe from past experiments. When challenged, their case appears very weak indeed.

The biggest problem with Thurman's theory about how the bomb was ignited is that no evidence exists which would support his theory. The FBI claims to have found traces of bomb residue and PETN, an explosive found in detonator cord, or "detcord," on McVeigh's clothing, a claim which is vigorously disputed by the first FBI scientist who tested Tim's clothes. But even if the traces of PETN were on his clothes, so what? If there is no evidence of detcord being involved in the explosions, it wouldn't matter if Tim's whole body was wrapped in detcord when he was pulled over for a missing license plate, would it?

(Incidentally, traces of PETN were found near the front of the wings of the TWA Flight 800 that exploded and crashed mysteriously on July 17, 1996, in the ocean near Long Island, N.Y. These traces were reported by the *New York Times* — then the story was abruptly dropped.)

We must also keep in mind that only John Doe No. 2 was seen exiting the Ryder truck. Only John Doe No. 2 was seen walking around to the back of the truck. Only John Doe No. 2 was seen hanging around the back of the truck for a few minutes. Only John Doe No. 2 could have lit a fuse to a bomb in the Ryder truck if there was a bomb in the Ryder truck. Only John Doe No. 2 is not being sought by the FBI. Until very recently, nobody claimed to have seen Timothy James McVeigh inside the Ryder truck or saw him exit the Ryder truck that was parked in front of the Murrah Building just before 9 a.m. on April 19, 1995. And TERRY

WASN'T EVEN THERE! Why is Terry in prison? Where is John Doe No. 2? Daina Bradley, testifying in the Tim McVeigh trial earlier in 1997, did change her testimony and told jurors that she saw a second man exiting the Ryder truck — a man that "could have been" Timothy McVeigh. Bradley made this statement despite saying on innumerable talk shows and in other interviews that stated just the opposite — that only John Doe No. 2 exited the truck. The change in testimony appeared to be a pivotal moment in the McVeigh trial, in which Tim was found guilty and subsequently sentenced to death. His case is currently under appeal.

Many people had the opportunity to publicly express their horror about the tragedy in Oklahoma. One person to whom the media paid particular attention was Lt. Colonel James "Bo" Gritz when he expressed a "real" expert's opinion about the bombing. He stated, in part, that this bombing "was a Rembrandt, a masterpiece of science and art put together." Of course, that was the only part of his statement that the media reported, making it sound as if he was praising the slimeballs who were responsible for this tragedy.

Putting that sentence into context, the point which Col. Gritz was attempting to make was that this crime was so skillfully executed there was no way in the world that a couple of amateurs could have possibly accomplished that kind of destruction with a fertilizer bomb in the back of a truck sitting out in the street. It had to have been done by experts specifically trained in demolitions who had access to the building when it was empty. To an experienced combat veteran and Special Forces commander like Col. Gritz, this fact was obvious, and he tried to inform all of us who are not experienced. It's too bad that the news media intentionally took his statements out of context — thereby giving those statements a completely different meaning. Would that be considered a media lie?

Eventually the truth about the media taking Col. Gritz out of context started circulating on talk radio and on the pages of the more enlightened news journals across the country. But a nationally known military hero who had the courage to publicly dispute the allegations by the feds had to be silenced. Since Col. Gritz has more combat medals than can possibly fit on any one uniform, no matter how wide the chest, finding someone to silence him proved to be a task for which they could find no volunteers, so they moved on to plan "B" which was to discredit him through media propaganda.

Taking Col. Gritz out of context was not enough for some members of the media and the chance to discredit someone whose courage and patriotism they envied yet despised was an opportunity which some, not only willingly but enthusiastically embraced. For reasons that are known to us yet still remain incomprehensible, those members of our society who harbor resentment, animosity, and jealousy towards our patriotic military heroes take great delight in criticizing and attempting to discredit them. That resentment and jealousy was obvious during an interview with Bo Gritz by John McKenzie of the TV program *Day One*. McKenzie suggested that Bo Gritz had turned against his own government when, in fact, Col. Gritz has devoted his entire life to defending his government until he realized that the government for whom he had put his life on the line hundreds of times was diametrically opposed to the Constitutional republic which he thought he was defending. (Have you ever put your life on the line for your country, John?)

And anyone with a thinking mind knows that this government has turned against its own people through oppressive taxation, evidence manufacturing and falsification, the CIA's long-standing involvement in drug smuggling, the attempted undermining of our Constitution and the violation of our basic property rights via the "drug war" partially due to that smuggling and taxation and, more recently, through the induced threat of terrorism. It is also common knowledge to anyone with a thinking mind, John, that the U.S. government has a total disregard for the lives of the sovereign citizens of this great nation, apparent during the massacres at Waco and Ruby Ridge, the intentional prolongation of the Vietnam War which was responsible for the loss of no less than an additional 50,000 young Americans, the abandonment of the POWs and MIAs from that war and finally, the denial of the existence of the Gulf War Syndrome — allowing even more American patriots and their families to suffer needlessly and eventually, to die a miserable death. Do you need any more proof, John?

And then John, who in the realm of patriotism and service to one's country would not qualify to clean the Colonel's boots, made his second attempt to discredit one of this nation's bravest, most honored war veterans by suggesting that Bo Gritz was anti-Semitic. John concluded this some of the literature being sold by someone else at one of Bo's rallies allegedly contained some negative statements about Jews. This attack was very typical of mainstream media illogic. If someone within John's network made a racist statement would that make John a racist? Apparently, if we believe in the "Logic of John," it would.

To confirm their accusations that Col. Gritz was a dangerous militant, John interviewed a person from the area who was more than willing to express an uneducated opinion about the Colonel and his friends who were living in the other neighborhood on a hill in the woods. It was obvious that this person was suffering from paranoia as a result of being uninformed. She seized the opportunity to criticize the Colonel's religious beliefs saying that he was running a "cult" up there and that she was afraid of those people.

Once any group of people is labeled a "religious cult," the door is wide open for the public's acceptance of a government massacre just like in Waco. So now the stage had been set and it appeared as if their ultimate objective had been accomplished. Gritz and his friends were a violent religious cult, let's send in the BATF to slaughter them. Never mind that they haven't ever threatened or injured anyone. Just ignore the fact that they haven't broken any laws. It's easy to forget that freedom of religion is the very first declaration in the Bill of Rights, even before free speech, a free press, freedom to peaceably assemble, and to petition government, John. As a matter of fact, Col. Gritz and his friends are exercising all of their rights under the First Amendment as are the majority of the informed people in this country. And from what we've seen and heard, it would appear as if the Colonel and his friends are fundamentalist Christians. Just remember, John, the freedoms declared by our Constitution under which you practice your profession appear in the same Amendment as freedom of religion. So, now that you know John, how does it feel to have unwittingly (?) planted the seed of self-destruction?

You know John, we have some first hand experience with the same tactics that you used against Bo Gritz and his neighbors so you can't really take credit for coming up with an original idea. Ted Koppel aired his "town meeting" here in Decker and the original plan, devised by Linda B. from *Nightline* and a local friend, was to bring into my church many people from the area who know me and maybe some who know Terry. One problem was that my church wasn't in Decker, it was in Deford. I had never even attended the church in Decker. Ted and crew just kind of did their own thing and actually manufactured the subject at hand. They filled the church in Decker to maximum capacity mostly with people whom I did not know and left many people standing outside who have known me for a long time.

The *Nightline* team brought to the church, in a limousine, some of the more famous members of the Michigan Militia Corps who did not really represent the Corps. As requested by the *Nightline* crew, they were dressed in camos which did nothing to enhance their image. They were more than willing to voice their own personal opinions and display their negative attitudes on national television which, in our humble opinion, did not help the image of the hard working citizens in the militia in any way whatsoever. These non-representatives jumped at the chance to get on national television and were not alert enough to realize that the stage was being set for them to discredit the entire militia in front of a national audience and to link the militia movement with the Oklahoma City bombing.

The self-proclaimed militia "leaders" seemingly did everything they could to insure the success of the Koppel-and-crew ambush. These particular militia leaders were subsequently booted out of their respective leadership positions in the Michigan Militia Corps and began another militia group of their own. We've heard it said that this self-promoted militia general (?) was the general of none and the commander of one. It has also been reported that these particular militia leaders claim that Tim, Terry and me were kicked out of the militia because we were trying to insight violence. This rumor is absolutely untrue.

I only went to one or two militia meetings and was not kicked out as the legend-in-his-own-mind-general claims. We have many friends in the organized militia but we're not members. We understand and appreciate what they are doing and they appreciate what we are doing in the court system. That's really all there ever was to the militia "connection."

There was another problem with this "town meeting." Not only was this not my church, but I had never even met the vast majority of the people who attended by invite only. One of those people who didn't know me was a local woman who has a history of severe paranoia and "other problems" which she was more than eager to display with much emotionalism on national television. She claimed to be extremely afraid of us and afraid that she could be injured from all of the bombs going off on my farm (?) which she referred to as "in her own backyard." Unless her own backyard is several miles long and several miles wide she exaggerated just a little because her house is many miles from my farm. Realistically, she never heard any "bombs" explode anywhere and, to my knowledge, she's never even met me. Koppel took advantage of the ignorance and paranoia of this woman for the sake of sensationalism just like John McKenzie did in his story about Bo Gritz.

In fact, the paranoid woman in Idaho has nothing to fear from Bo Gritz and friends — but she does have much to fear from government terrorists should they decide to pay Bo and friends a visit. And the paranoid woman who expressed her emotions at the "staged" town meeting here in Decker never had anything to fear from any of us here at the farm. She had nothing to fear until the feds brought in helicopters, fully-suited Ninja Turtles, hundreds of machine guns and who knows what else. She has had absolutely nothing to fear since the feds left the farm.

John's climax, and almost a broken nose, came when he subtly accused Col. Gritz of being a Nazi. To back that accusation John showed some pictures and then a movie of Bo as he was giving what John considered to be a Nazi salute to some supporters of Randy Weaver. These people, depicted as Nazi skinheads (naturally), had written Bo letters asking him to help Randy Weaver before the feds murdered Randy and the rest of his family. The salute from Bo was basically an appreciative gesture requested by Weaver. Again, John tried to take it out of context implying that Bo was a Nazi. Now Colonel Gritz is not the kind of guy that a rational person would want to insult. Certainly not to his face anyway. John narrowly escaped with his skin and, in all honesty, he shouldn't have.

Shall we try to put this situation into perspective making it relatively simple for John to understand? Well John, since the "yes" votes won by an overwhelming margin, we shall. Now, if you and your family were about to be burned alive by terrorists, and some neighbors perceived by John McKenzie to be Nazi skinheads called 911 to save your lives, would you:

1. Refuse the assistance because the call was made by some people who John McKenzie perceived to be Nazi skinheads?

Or would you:

2. After escaping to safety, thank whoever was responsible for saving the lives of your family members who were lucky enough to survive?

This was really a rhetorical question for everyone but John. Actually, we shouldn't give a crap if they were Nazis, Communists, Darth Vader or even Janet Reno for that matter. If someone assisted in saving the lives of members of our families, they would receive our most sincere appreciation. Can you understand that logic, John?

It is becoming more and more obvious that some members of our society feel the need to insult and discredit our true patriotic American heroes so they can justify their own anti-American shortcomings generally resulting from their own cowardice or from the shame they are harboring because of that cowardice. Their lack of courage and character generally dictates that these cowards not only run away from the defense of their country but often times side with the enemy to save their own skins and to even stoop so low as to collude with the enemy taking part in demonstrations against their country in a treasonous manner (i.e. Bill Clinton and "Hanoi" Jane Fonda) which results in the deaths of many more of their own countrymen.

If you will recall, before Jane Fonda married a good portion of the media (Ted Turner) and before Bill Clinton stole the Presidency with far less than a majority of the popular vote, being called a "patriot" was something that would make any American proud. Today, we are afraid to be called "patriots" because that title has been intentionally mis-aligned with some bad groups of people, not limited to, but including terrorists. Anytime anybody does anything violent and anti-government they are labeled a "patriot" in an attempt to make patriot a four-letter-word.

The U.S. now has a president who dodged the draft, lied to a high-ranking officer whom he befriended specifically to avoid the draft, helped organize demonstrations against his own country on foreign soil, and then traveled to a country which presented the biggest threat in history to the security of the [u]nited States. He was welcomed to that country (why?), the most oppressive, violent and murderous tyranny in history, and enjoyed the most luxurious accommodations in the entire Soviet Union while many people in that nation were freezing and starving. Clinton aided and abetted communist organizers who, like Jane Fonda, were not only calling for peace in Southeast Asia, but for a Marxist communist victory and for the defeat of the United States armed forces, which, when you really think about it, translates into the killing of our very young men and women in the military service, i.e. OUR CHILDREN!

He learned much about Marxist philosophy during his visit, which apparently had a strong influence on his political "sense of direction." And to top it all off, at the time of Bill's visit, that country was building war equipment and supplying advisors for another country which was killing American troops who were doing that which our fearless leader did not have the courage to do. He's not exactly what any honest American would consider a patriot. We have our doubts that any honest American would even consider him an honest American. One might be inclined to believe that some people want draft dodging, lying and treason to be considered admirable qualities which should be held in high esteem. Those people also seem to want to redefine the word PATRIOT so that it is generally accepted as a description of someone who is bad instead of someone who is good. Now who might those people be? Could this be the "new speak" to which George Orwell referred in his book, *1984* ?

Patriot: A person who loves, supports and DEFENDS his country. (emphasis ours) This definition is from *The American Heritage Dictionary, Second College Edition.* We could rest our case about Bill on this definition alone.

We want to state right here and now, for the record, that we love our country and we consider ourselves PATRIOTS. We will never buy into this notion that being a PATRIOT is a bad thing just because the president and Hanoi Jane think that being a PATRIOT is an undesirable quality for an American. This country was founded on patriotism and designed by PATRIOTS. Throughout history our country has been defended by PATRIOTS and, if it ever needs defending in the future, will again be defended by PATRIOTS.

We must keep in mind that Col. Gritz is the quintessential PATRIOT. He is probably the most decorated Green Beret in history and is literally a living "Rambo." He is precisely the kind of guy who the Commander-in-Chief loathes. And when you really think about it, the very existence of MEN like Bo Gritz may cause cowards to feel a degree of shame and embarrassment that is and should be reserved for them exclusively. Wouldn't you agree, John?

If you take the time to review the original statements concerning this disaster, many government agents and high ranking officials, including Gov. Keating, agreed with Col. Gritz in stating that this was definitely a very complex, expertly planned and calculated act of terrorism. This massive destruction was definitely the result of some very sophisticated explosives. Their first statements on April 19, 1995, also included opinions that this was a very well financed crime with some major players involved in the planning. We could fill several pages with quotes to that effect from government and media personalities, but after that fateful Wednesday morning in April, these opinions would never again be expressed by those persons, not publicly anyway. Apparently, prior to briefing, these officials were unaware that the feds intended on pinning this one on patriotic former soldiers, farmers and a fertilizer company. Not only have these "servants of the people" been briefed (muzzled), the Feds have gone out of their way to deny these very astute observations unwittingly expressed in those first few important hours after the tragedy. FLEXIBLE FACTS?

One thing that we have to realize about this investigation is that the government's only circumstantial link between this bombing and Timothy McVeigh and Terry Nichols is the fertilizer. Everything else is really nothing more than rumors and accusations, at best, with many of those accusations coming from known liars. Actually the fertilizer is nothing more than an accusation also but, as you've probably noticed by now, we always give the government propagandists the benefit of the doubt.

"What about the Ryder truck?", you ask. Well, if the Ryder truck was empty, so what! "What about Tim being seen in the area?" There were hundreds of thousands of other people seen in that area. The only circumstance that they have successfully rumored is that the bomb was made of fertilizer and that is precisely why the FBI and BATF have been so adamant about their ANFO bomb disinformation. They still have not shown any evidence that this was a fertilizer explosion. If it was not a fertilizer explosion, then there isn't even a weak link to Tim. And if there is no link to Tim, then there is no link to Terry —not that a weak link to Tim is necessarily a link to Terry. If recent investigations are any indication of their actions, given enough time we can be sure that the FBI's dedicated scientists will use any means necessary to fabricate whatever evidence they need to prove the prosecution's case. That is most certainly why the feds have so jealously guarded the evidence and why they have refused any independent, objective tests.....using original, untainted evidence.

We believe that the original evidence taken from the Murrah Building would have proven to be evidence for the defense. If anyone disagrees with that statement then explain to us the unusual activities of the Feds concerning the evidence. THEY HAD NO CASE! ◆

Photo courtesy David Longstreath

Damage to the Alfred P. Murrah Federal Building in Oklahoma City was far more extensive than could have been done by a single open-air ANFO explosion, many experts contend.

"I think they blew the building up because they wanted to get rid of the crime scene. What else do you know [about] that the crime scene is destroyed before they even go to trial or before a thorough investigation is done on it?"
— **Earl Garrett (from the documentary video,** *Oklahoma City: What Really Happened?***)**

CHAPTER 13: THE DAMAGED STRUCTURE: WHAT HAPPENED TO THE EVIDENCE?

Another issue of evidence that deserves scrutiny is that portion of the Murrah Building still standing after the explosions.

We first have to examine the interior of the bombed-out structure to get some kind of understanding about what might have happened there. Under close observation, pictures of the inside of the building reveal some very alarming information. The more obvious evidence is that it appears that the most damaged part of the building does not line up with the crater in the street that was allegedly made by the truck bomb. It appears as if the explosion had to turn a corner to create the type of damage that was done to a particular part of the building commonly referred to as the "pit area." Another apparent discrepancy at the crime scene was that the damage to some parts of the building was much more severe farther from the crater in the street than areas in the building that were closer to the crater.

Now try to imagine a firecracker sitting on the ground, and you have one hand two inches from the firecracker and the other hand two feet away. The firecracker explodes and stings the hand two feet away, but the hand two inches away feels no pain! That's basically what the prosecutors in this case expect us to believe, and that is why there has been an enormous effort by the feds to use the media, who are more than willing, to appeal to the emotions of people when the information about this case is discussed. They would much prefer that people did not use their common sense when considering the erroneous information they have been given about this case by the media which has been leaked to them by the FBI or by the prosecutors.

They do not want the public to be exposed to the real facts in this case, because the feds know that if the people are given all of the information about any particular issue, in the long run, common sense will prevail.

Again, they do not want us to rely on our senses, only on our emotions. The feds consider it preferable that the general populace remain uninformed that way their opinions can be swayed in whatever direction the swayers desire. That's why they seldom talk about specific issues in political campaign speeches and that is why they've been concealing the facts and evading the issues in this investigation — THE GRAND COVER-UP!

Our intentions are to make available that heretofore unavailable information.

Viewing the pattern of damage to the building,, it appears to be asymmetrical which, under the circumstances, would have been physically impossible. You certainly wouldn't expect a perfect circle of destruction from any explosion, but we can reasonably expect to see a near-circular pattern of similar damage at equal distances from the center of an explosion. Aerial photographs indicate three distinct circular patterns of destruction, the least of which is the closest to the center of the alleged truck bomb crater.

Again, the most severe damage appears to be the farthest from the center of the crater in the street which couldn't possibly have been the location for the explosion that caused that particular damage. Many of the pictures being portrayed in books and magazines have been taken from angles which misrepresent the location of the crater. These photos lead you to believe that the crater lines up perfectly with the most severe damage to the Murrah Building. BUT DO NOT BE DECEIVED. There are many aerial photographs that accurately depict the location of the crater which does not line up with the most severe damage to the building. This unusual damage would indicate the probability of multiple explosions inside the building and would also seem to answer the question of why there was an attempt to deceive the public concerning the location of the crater. The most extensive damage doesn't seem to match the damage in any other part of the building which makes for some very interesting theories, many of which we will explore.

We are certainly not alone in our observation of the inconsistent damage to the Murrah Building. One of the more outspoken critics of the federal investigators' claim as to what actually destroyed the Murrah Building is retired Gen. Benton K. Partin. Much of Gen. Partin's 31 years of active military service in the U. S. Air Force was spent in research and development of weapons design and accuracy and in the testing of explosives. Gen. Partin was a command pilot and a command missile man and has received the Distinguished Service Medal and the Legion of Merit. He is considered to be one of this country's leading experts in high-tech weapons and explosives. In the video *Oklahoma City: What Really Happened?* produced by Chuck Allen, Gen. Partin stated:

"When I first saw the pictures of the truck bombs asymmetrical damage to the Federal Building, my immediate reaction was that the pattern of damage would have been technically impossible without supplementing demolition charges at some of the reinforced concrete column bases, a standard demolition technique."

Gen. Partin has confirmed many of our observations and, because of his expertise on these issues, has brought to light many other points of interest which a thinking mind might find curious and possibly even inexplicable. Many of the discrepancies noticed by Gen. Partin were also brought to the attention of a limited number of alert and informed citizens in an article titled "Explosive Evidence: Cover-up in Oklahoma City," appearing in *The New American* and written by William Jasper. If you want to be informed and do not receive *The New American,* you should subscribe.

In Jasper's article, Gen. Partin points out that in some of the photos taken inside the building after the explosions much of the visible evidence tends to arouse one's suspicion. In viewing many of these pictures you can clearly see the dry wall that surrounded each of the massive columns within the building was still in place facing the crater in the street, yet, on the side of the columns opposite the alleged truck bomb, the drywall was blown off. That obviously would indicate that there was some type of explosion or explosions near those columns on the side opposite the crater in the street. In a photo taken from the front of the building, dry wall is still in place on the columns that are standing, yet a column was sheared between two of those drywall covered standing columns.

Even more suspicious is that at least two of the columns still wrapped in dry wall is closer to the alleged truck bomb than the column that was destroyed. That bit of evidence may also lead a person to believe that explosions might have taken place inside the building. If anyone thinks that an explosion powerful enough to shear a steel reinforced concrete column two feet thick couldn't strip half-inch of drywall from a column closer to the explosion, please raise your hands. Are those FBI hands that we see?

Now let us consider the information available concerning the first row of columns destroyed by the explosions. It has been reported by demolitions experts that it would take a blast pressure of approximately 3,500 pounds per square inch to shear those steel reinforced concrete columns. We have to keep in mind that blast pressure dissipates rapidly in an open-air explosion as with the alleged truck bomb.

According to Gen. Partin's calculations, by the time the open-air blast reached the first column that was destroyed, the pressure was only one-quarter of what was needed to actually blow over or destroy that column. By the time it reached the second closest column, the blast pressure was only 1/10 of the necessary impact per square inch. If the blast from the alleged truck bomb reached "around the corner" and brought down the column in the second row inside the building,, it would have needed 130 times as much pressure as could have possibly been available to destroy that column. When you realize that the blast pressure from the alleged truck bomb at that destroyed column inside the Murrah Building was only 27 pounds per square inch, assuming that the bomb was at maximum efficiency, it suddenly becomes obvious why the two columns on either side of the missing column were still wearing their coats of drywall. Again, there wasn't even enough blast pressure to strip the dry wall, so what was it that destroyed that two foot thick column of steel-reinforced concrete?

We have to look again at the photos to answer that question. The doors on many of the offices were blown to the north, out toward the street where the alleged truck bomb exploded and were not blown inward like they should have been if the bomb outside created the most damaging blast. Surviving victims inside the building noticed that the same thing happened to the stairwell doors. We have heard the same reports concerning flying glass being blown out and away from the building although there could be another reason if the glass was blown out of the east, west or south ends of the building.

Much of the debris blown out of the Murrah Building, including large chunks of the building, was blown over the alleged truck bomb and appeared to have landed near the *Journal Record* building which is at least 150 feet to the north. Large chunks of concrete were blown over the alleged truck bomb northward and into the parking lot across the street from the Murrah Building. There can be no explanation for those chunks of concrete landing where they were found other than explosions from within the building itself. Much of the damage inside the building was done to the wrong side of the walls, according to investigators and rescue workers. In some areas the walls on the north side of a room were blown to the north out of the building while the inside walls on the south side of a room collapsed northward crushing the victims occupying the room.

All of this evidence tends to solidify the theory of inside explosions causing the collapse of the building and, when all of the facts are known, this theory has more credibility than most people realize. Much more evidence and eyewitness testimony will eventually surface about the explosions inside of the building which will more than convince the skeptics. THE FACTS, PLEASE, JUST THE FACTS!

According to Gen. Partin, under close examination some of the photos reveal even more information to the experienced, skillful eye. Some of the columns that were destroyed had fractures or rough type breaks, the type of damage that should have occurred on all of the columns if they were blasted over by an explosion or by other falling columns or falling debris. The problem is what was supposed to have happened in this type of explosion, didn't happen.

On some of the key columns, the areas of failure are relatively smooth — indicating that these concrete supports were severed by contact explosives. And those particular columns appear to have fallen or collapsed almost straight down instead of falling over sideways from an explosion that blasted them over. According to Gen. Partin, there's virtually no other way to drop those columns vertically and to achieve a smooth break without an expertly placed, military style, high velocity contact explosive typically used in the "shear and drop method. If the truck-bomb explosion had enough force to destroy all of those columns, it would certainly have enough force to knock them over.

Gen. Partin said: "When I saw the damage to the building, and with my knowledge of explosives, demolitions and what you can do and what you can't do, I had a problem, a big problem very quickly. You can't destroy hard targets with blasts. It just doesn't work. And reinforced columns in this building are hard targets. I spent much of my career working on precision-guided weapons because I know what you can do and what you can't do with explosives against hard targets. A 24-inch reinforced concrete column is a hard target. It's a very hard target (from the documentary video *Oklahoma City: What Really Happened?*)."

Even more interesting is the fact that the only column that was "sheared" in the second row back from the alleged truck bomb, the one that the explosion turned the corner to take out, also had a smooth break that was obviously caused by some sort of contact charge. One thing we want you to keep in mind is that a high velocity contact charge set up to take out a concrete pillar doesn't necessarily have to create a large explosion. Properly placed, a very small explosive charge can easily shear a large chunk of concrete. You should now begin to realize how important that slight "disruption of tranquillity" is to this investigation. It all ties in to some of the information we have already covered and is a significant factor in piecing together this puzzle that government investigators have scattered in the wind in their attempt to create   THE

GRAND COVER-UP!

In viewing photos of the scene and by gathering information from investigators, it becomes apparent that the charges which sheared these support columns were not placed into position on the ground floor which would have been the case if an "outsider" had entered the building to do his dirty work. According to Gen. Partin, it appears as if some of the explosive charges that sheared these columns were set in place on the third floor of the Murrah Building. A large concrete header across the front of the building, approximately three feet by five feet, supported every other column from the third floor up. The header was supported from the third floor to the ground by columns much larger than the standard two-feet-by-two-feet columns. Even the massive support columns and the 3' X 5' feet header, which were close to the alleged truck bomb, were not blown over by the blast, but collapsed straight down which is a typical result of the shear and drop method of destruction.

That these support structures were sheared at the third floor level clearly indicates a strong probability of an inside job, since the explosives obviously were placed into position long before the alleged big yellow truck made its grand entrance and exit, however that exit may have taken place. As Gen. Partin said in his interview with *The New American*, "You just don't walk in off the street through security with explosives like this."

Gen. Partin is certainly not alone in his assessment as to what transpired in the Murrah Building on the morning of April 19, 1995. In an interview with *The New American*, Sam Gronning, a professional blaster with 30 years experience, explained that Partin's report "states in very precise technical terms what everyone in this business knows: No truck bomb of ANFO out in the open is going to cause the kind of damage we had there. In 30 years of blasting, using everything from 100 percent nitrogel to ANFO, I've not seen anything to support that story."

Mr. Gronning also stated that he had recently set off an ANFO charge of 16,000 pounds and that even an ANFO blast that size would not have been capable of causing the damage that the Murrah Building received.

Another expert interviewed by *The New American*, physical chemist Dr. Roger Raubach, confirmed Mr. Gronning's statements when he said, "Gen. Partin's assessment is absolutely correct. I don't care if they pulled up a semi-trailer truck with 20 tons of ammonium nitrate; it wouldn't do the damage we saw there."

Other evidence, and other witnesses, indicate the possibility of alterations made at the basement or parking garage level under the building just days prior to the bombing. At that time at least two people witnessed a construction or maintenance crew apparently drilling holes in the underground supports for the Murrah Building, but nobody really paid much attention to the "work" being done because it was not uncommon for maintenance or construction crews to be working somewhere in or around the building. Keep in mind also that this parking garage was only partially accessible to the public. Travel northward, beyond the center of the building where the underground parking garage extended even beyond the northern most boundaries of the Murrah Building, was limited to certain people. Only government employees with the proper passes or appropriate clearances would have had access to the street directly under the alleged truck bomb. Yes, the area under the Ryder truck where the 30-feet-wide and eight-feet-deep crater appeared to have been blown from underground, was accessible from underground by certain government employees only. It is very possible that the construction crew that was seen was just there doing some legitimate work — but the timing is rather curious.

It seems that the damage to the Murrah Building is very inconsistent with the government's explanation of this tragedy. Now that's a real shocker, isn't it? We just can't believe that the government's story doesn't correspond with the evidence. They do have all the best investigators and all the state-of-the-art equipment so we can't think of any good reason why the actual evidence can't verify their alleged findings, can you? •

Photo courtesy *Newsweek* magazine

This May 1, 1995, cover of *Newsweek* magazine kicked off a parade of media that might have adequately covered the grief and anguish of the families caught up in the Murrah Federal Building bombing, but neglected critical issues related to the cause of the explosions and the perpetrators.

"If you want to show someone that ANFO is powerful, show a film of a truck and blow the hell out of it and then say you used only five pounds of ANFO to do it. But how could the Grand Jurors be sure that it was only five pounds? All the demonstrations the prosecution used were like that. Obviously to dupe an unsophisticated audience. But it's easy to see through this."

— **Hoppy Heidelberg, grand juror**

CHAPTER 14: THE CRATER

Now let's move on to another issue that has been misrepresented since the very beginning of this massive disinformation campaign: The crater. The mammoth crater in the front of the Murrah Building. This crater was reported to be eight feet deep and 30 feet across, blown through six to eight inches of asphalt and another eight feet of hardpan. It would appear as if they expected us to believe that a fertilizer bomb made by farmers sitting above the ground inside a truck blew this massive hole in the ground. After all, the media believed it and never even questioned it. Why wouldn't they just assume that all of the "sheeple"out here who believe everything they see on TV would swallow this story, hook, line and stinker? We believe they made a big mistake underestimating the intelligence of the average American citizen and we will do our best to make absolutely certain that this time their mistake comes back to haunt them.

To begin with, anyone who has ever been in a war zone and who has actually seen what kind of a crater rockets, mortars, artillery rounds, land mines, and bombs can create would realize that blowing this size hole through concrete cannot be accomplished by any open-air explosion, short of a nuclear blast, without accelerated penetration of the ground or without being planted under the ground — very deeply underground.

Bob Papovich, my co-author, says that when he was in Vietnam he saw craters from land mines powerful enough to blow a large military truck into pieces so small that the truck was unrecognizable and the crater wasn't 1/10th the size of the crater in front of the Murrah Building. And we all know that a land mine is planted under the surface of the ground which adds considerably to its excavation capabilities. If anyone without first hand experience doubts Bob's assertions, take a look at the Sept. 18, 1995 issue of *Time*. Turn to page 77 and observe the crater from the smart bomb gone astray. The damage to the building in this photo certainly resembles the type of damage that the Murrah Building suffered, doesn't it? Pay particular attention to the crater. Keep in mind that this crater was made by a device traveling, at the very least, hundreds of miles per hour penetrating what appears to be a few inches of asphalt.

Take note that the crater in Oklahoma was about eight times the size of the crater in this Serbian war zone and probably 15 times the volume when you also consider the depth. And we're supposed to believe that this gigantic crater in the Oklahoma City tragedy was made by an open air blast from a bomb manufactured from common farm supplies by amateurs with absolutely no training in demolitions or explosives?

We must also realize that an explosive device properly placed inside or under a building is capable of doing 100 times the destruction as the same amount of explosives detonated in the open outside of the building. One stick of dynamite buried under the surface of the ground would make a hole many times larger than ten sticks of dynamite sitting in the open air above the ground.

We can assure you that military explosives, particularly those explosives used in the manufacture of bombs and rockets or missiles, are considerably more potent than a fertilizer/fuel oil bomb. As a matter of fact, military explosives possess approximately three times the velocity (25,000 feet per second) on the average as an ANFO bomb (8,000 fps). When you apply common sense, which apparently is not very common among government agents and many members of the media, you come to the realization that it would have been impossible for a fertilizer bomb sitting above the asphalt and hard pan to blow a hole downward the size of the crater in front of the Murrah Building.

We also need to consider that the FBI investigators stated that the reason this fertilizer bomb had such a devastating effect on the Murrah Building is because it was sandbagged to direct the explosion up and toward the building. Let us for a moment assume that they're telling the truth for a change. This blast was sandbagged to direct it up and away from the street underneath the truck they say. Their explanation for the force of the explosion further proves that blowing that size crater through the asphalt and hard pan would have been impossible under the circumstances. The sandbags would have acted as a barrier between the pavement and the bomb and would have protected the street from the blast. Soldiers sandbagged the backs of Claymore mines in Vietnam to help direct the blast and to considerably reduce the "backblast" from the explosion. The FBI investigators, in their haste to convince skeptics that the impossible suddenly becomes possible, have contradicted themselves again. Liars they are, but we never said they were smart liars.

We would like to know if anyone out there recognized the similarities between the pictures of the building that was bombed in Saudi Arabia on June 25, 1996, killing 19 U.S. soldiers, and the pictures taken of the front of the Murrah Building after the explosions? When we saw those pictures on the news, we thought we were looking at pictures of the Oklahoma City bombing. A red flag went up immediately when we realized we were not. From the very beginning of this investigation we have publicly stated on national television and on national radio that there was no way an above the ground fertilizer explosion could have blown that large hole in the street in front of the Murrah Building. We only used common sense to form our opinions, but many demolitions experts, using years of experience, agreed with us. We do not believe the similarities between these two bombings are in any way a coincidence. The identical visual appearance was not a coincidence. The timing was not a coincidence. The relatively low number of casualties was not a coincidence. The gigantic crater in front of that building was absolutely not a coincidence. The fact that it happened in Saudi Arabia was not a coincidence.

There has been so much skepticism about the crater in front of the Murrah Building that the public needed to be convinced that an open air explosion could, in fact, have blown a crater in the ground and the bombing in Saudi Arabia certainly proved that. Or did it? Whatever was in that truck in Saudi Arabia it was definitely not ANFO. We do not know what caused that crater in front of that building and we probably never will know for certain.

There will never be a private, independent investigation to find out what really happened over there. It's a foreign country and their intelligence agencies, who are intimately involved with our intelligence agencies, have investigated and they have told us what their investigators have discovered. In other words, we have been told exactly what they wanted us to be told. We have seen exactly what they wanted us to see: A lasting image of a situation which is supposed to be identical to the situation in downtown Oklahoma City. We have seen the front of a structure which, after it was blown up, looked just like the Murrah Building and in front of that building in Saudi Arabia was a crater that made the crater in downtown Oklahoma City look very small by comparison. And all of this was accomplished by terrorists with a truck bomb. Now everyone has been convinced; what was once considered impossible by the experts suddenly becomes not only possible, but a reality. The whole world saw it on television. It must be true.

We know that we're going out on a limb here, but we've been going out on a limb since the beginning of this investigation and our opinions have consistently been considered extreme, off-the-wall, wacky, crazy, etc., etc., etc. — until the truth came out and other investigators, journalists and even defense attorneys eventually discovered the same things that we had been saying all along. In the past year and a half this has happened more times than we can count.

We have voiced our opinions about what seemed obvious to us, what we thought was really happening and have received remarks from many journalists and television personalities implying that we were conspiracy nuts and didn't know what we were talking about. Then, months later, when their own investigation proved what we had been saying was absolutely correct, this "new" information was reported as if it was some kind of a great revelation, some great discovery by that particular reporter or investigator.

Oklahoma City bombing researcher and author Michele Moore has had similar experiences, being shunned by other investigators because her conclusions about the information available, like ours, were termed "off-the-wall." You will see many of these wacky and crazy ideas of ours and Michele's eventually become accepted as facts in this case when the conscience of some of the government workers who were eyewitnesses forces them to come forward and tell the truth about what they saw. We are hopeful that by the time you are reading this book that "attack of the conscience" will have happened.

We believe that the building in Saudi Arabia was picked specifically because it so closely resembled the Murrah Building in size, shape and overall appearance. We believe that the act of terrorism in Saudi Arabia was perfectly timed to take place just when it appeared as if too many people were expressing doubt about the government's allegations concerning the Oklahoma City bombing and to keep the threat of terrorism fresh in everyone's mind and to maintain a high level of fear in everyone's heart. We believe that the crater was created by an extraordinary explosive device designed to create an extra-large crater. It could have been made by an underground charge but with all the technology that exists today, it's anyone's guess. We believe that this act of terrorism was executed on foreign soil so that only government investigators would ever be exposed to the crime scene. We believe that it happened in Saudi Arabia because Saudi intelligence has worked hand-in-hand with our intelligence agencies in setting up other acts of terrorism which were pawned off as blown sting operations. We believe that a particular time of day was picked when there would be the least number of American casualties, not because of any conscience that these sub-humans may have or of any guilt that they may be harboring, but because they didn't want too much attention.

Two or three hundred American deaths would have attracted too broad of an investigation. Nineteen could soon be forgotten but the mission of the terrorists and all of their expected results would have been realized. Unfortunately, the families of those 19 innocent, unsuspecting, sacrificial, patriotic, servicemen will never forget.

We believe that our thoughts about this bombing in Saudi Arabia could prove to be another of those instances where our opinions are on the "cutting edge." We can only pray the someday the truth will be told by someone who was involved in this tragedy but, realistically, the odds are very much against that happening in our lifetime. Governments in this century have become very good at hiding information that may tend to be self-incriminating by simply classifying such information as "national security" and not to be unsealed for 75 years just like they did with the real findings in the Kennedy assassination. That way all of the guilty miscreants involved will have died long before anyone can actually prove what really happened and who was actually responsible. Whatever oppressive goal that the government intended to be a result of the crime in question will have been accomplished without the publics knowledge.

We've been asking another question about the crater in front of the Murrah Building that has raised some suspicions among independent investigators. Why did they find it necessary to fill in the crater before any independent tests could be made on the contents inside that massive hole in the ground? Why did they fill in the crater the day before McVeigh's defense investigators were to have gone into the hole to conduct their own tests? OBSTRUCTION OF JUSTICE! Oh, you mean you didn't know that? Well, now you do and we can assure you that we have received this information first-hand. It must have been an oversight by our vigilant media. Doesn't it make one wonder why an unnamed source in the FBI never leaked that information to the press? We have given the media that information, many times.

Why hasn't anyone taken responsibility for giving the order to fill in that crater, coincidentally, just in the nick of time? Would they have allowed a similar action at any other crime scene or would government investigators have secured the crime scene, making certain that all the original evidence was preserved in its original state until the investigation was completed and all of the facts were known? Was there some sort of evidence in that crater that government investigators did not want discovered? DESTRUCTION OF EVIDENCE! WHO BENEFITS? Remember that the area beneath the Murrah Building was accessible via the underground parking garage. Some reports have ANFO scattered everywhere except inside of the Murrah Building. But there was no nitric acid or nitric oxide signature of an ANFO explosion which may indicate the presence of an underground explosion blowing ammonium nitrate and the vehicle carrying it to kingdom come without ever having an actual ANFO explosion. Could that be why someone was in such a rush to fill in the crater before defense investigators could make their discoveries? Could that be why the axle of that large truck was blown up instead of down? Could that be why two eyewitnesses saw what appeared to be a construction or maintenance crew working under the building just days before the explosions. One question that really deserves answering is: If there was nothing to hide, why did someone OBSTRUCT JUSTICE to hide it?

Since government agencies have had a monopoly on the evidence for eight to 10 months, can we trust any of the evidence in their possession considering the recent reports about evidence falsification in the FBI's crime lab being a rather routine procedure? We have yet to find out who was responsible for giving the order to fill in the crater with no warning to the defense teams. Nobody on the government's payroll wants to accept that responsibility. You can be sure that some expendable employee will end up taking the blame if this issue comes out during future trial and appeals, and federal investigators find it necessary to blame someone.

What exactly is it that someone is obviously trying to conceal? Is this pattern of occurrences beginning to sound familiar? In your wildest thoughts can you imagine that any of this evidence is being destroyed, concealed or altered to benefit Timothy McVeigh or Terry Nichols? Neither can we. And if all of this evidence could really prove Tim and Terry are guilty as charged, which is what the GOVERNMENT prosecutors are alleging, why are GOVERNMENT agents destroying, concealing and altering it? •

"Nothing in politics (government) happens by chance."
— **Franklin D. Roosevelt**

CHAPTER 15: THE AXLE

Another of the FLEXIBLE FACTS in this case which really deserves dissecting is the location of the axle from the alleged Ryder truck. According to the Feds this enormous truck bomb was supposedly sitting above the axle in the truck and there probably were sandbags packed somewhere between the bomb and the axle. This blast managed to blow a crater in the street eight to 12 feet deep and 30 feet across but the now famous axle which was sitting between the bomb and the crater somehow got blown backward through the explosion and landed several hundred feet away. Now that's really confusing.

Common sense tells us that this axle would have gone in whatever direction the blast dictated. You cannot defy the laws of physics. It would seem to us that the only way the axle could have gone up and away was if there was an explosion under the axle unless, of course, the axle hit the pavement with such force that it bounced several hundred feet. But we know that couldn't have happened because there was a 30-foot hole blown through the pavement. If this explosion came from above the axle, wouldn't the axle have been blown down into the hole like a very large bullet?

Would a government damage-control agent please make up a reasonably believable lie for a change and explain how this blast could have had enough power to blow the hole beneath the axle and not drive the axle in the direction of the blast? Perhaps this was a special-type explosion, a "smart explosion" designed by farmers using plant food, that went around the axle first and then came back later to throw the axle up and away — kind of like that part of the explosion which turned the corner to take out the large concrete support column in the second row inside of the Murrah Building and then blow more craters inside the building. If we try real hard we can believe that one, although the explosion from under the axle does make a little more sense. Not that the government agents need to make sense while bringing forth the results of their investigation. Lord knows they haven't made an effort to make any sense about anything yet.

Interesting, too, are all of the amazing stories about how this alleged axle was discovered. We're not going to elaborate on all of those stories, just the most curious. None other than Oklahoma Gov. Frank Keating takes the credit for finding the notorious axle which was the one single most important piece of evidence that would break this case wide open and lead the FBI to Elliott's Body Shop, then to the Dreamland Motel and, within minutes, to John Doe No. 1. Our hero, Frank Keating, who just happened to be in the right spot at the right time for this incriminating piece of evidence to have fallen at his feet. Frank Keating, whose background as an FBI agent and supervisor of the U.S. Customs Service, the Secret Service, and the BATF, certainly qualified him for knowing how to take advantage of being in the right spot at the right time. Yes, our candidate being groomed for the White House, whose brother, Martin, wrote about how, when, where, and almost exactly (Tom McVey) the name of the person who would be blamed for this heinous crime some years before the fact in his fictional book, *The Final Jihad*.

Some agents of the FBI read Martin's book years before it was published and years before the Oklahoma City bombing. It has been suggested that possibly some rouge agents took Martin's fictional novel and turned parts of it into a reality. Martin Keating even suggested that possibility when he admitted that some of his brother's FBI friends read his pre-published manuscript several years ago. He acknowledged the unbelievable coincidences between his book and the bombing.

Another coincidental "find" that we have read about was that of a bomb-squad employee running to the scene of the explosion to assist in the rescue. He noticed that a large truck axle had crashed into a building a few hundred feet away from the Murrah Building. Later, while he was helping in the rescue efforts, he remembered seeing the axle and thought it might be an important clue to the bombing. He then reported what he had seen. Another story has a law-enforcement employee finding the axle laying in the street after it had apparently crashed into a car some blocks away from the explosions. That may have just been a variation of the report about the same bomb-squad employee, but we don't know for certain. There have been many other reports about how this axle was discovered. The bomb-squad employee and the governor's find seemed to us to be the most coincidental.

Coincidental also is that almost the exact same piece of evidence, the axle from a Ryder truck, solved the World Trade Center bombing case. Of course, we now know that the evidence in that case was falsified. There is no longer a final statement on exactly what happened in that bombing. The how, why or with what doesn't really matter, but having the "who" they want seems to be good enough for the Feds. It's also very interesting that Ryder trucks have become the consistent choice among terrorists planning a bombing. And again, the vehicle identification number (VIN) — big, bold, and clearly stamped on the axle housing on these Ryder trucks — is just a shear stroke of luck. There have been a lot of rumors floating around about Ryder being a front organization for the CIA, but we find that very hard to believe. It has been reported that the CEO of the Ryder company just happens to be a Trilateralist, but even if that's true we can't imagine how his commitment to that organization or to the New World Order could in any way have any influence on his decisions concerning the activities of the truck rental company. Of course, key people in certain corporate positions could certainly assist the international intelligence agencies in their quest to march, or run, to the New World Order.

And maybe it was just our imagination but when we saw a picture of the alleged axle from this truck laying in the street ripped open from the explosion, it looked remarkably clean having gone through the ordeal that government investigators claim. One thing that caught our attention immediately was how perfectly clean and visible the VIN was on the outside of the axle housing. If we didn't know better, at first glance we would have to say it appeared as if someone had actually placed the axle there for evidence. Nobody saw this huge chunk of evidence bounce down the street or land after a long flight. It didn't hit anyone. We don't recall seeing any indication that it damaged the cement where it landed. Can someone please explain to us these unusual occurrences? Can someone give us a "final" story on how this alleged axle was really found?

Still another claim as to how this large piece of evidence got discovered was that an FBI agent found it while he was searching the area for clues and evidence. That makes the most sense of any of the stories thus far. It still does not explain just how that axle was blown up through the alleged truck bomb explosion. A possible explanation was brought to our attention very early in this investigation by Karl Granse, founder of Citizens for a Constitutional Republic. According to Karl there is some evidence suggesting that a small rocket or missile may have been fired from directly above. At first thought that suggestion seems far-fetched, until you take into consideration the facts about the location of the axle, some eyewitness reports and some other peculiar actions by the Feds concerning evidence confiscation.

First, we have the location of the axle, a location which seems impossible under the circumstances. Second, there are eyewitnesses who claim to have seen a military-type helicopter circling high above the Murrah Building moments before the explosions. Third, it has been reported that the FBI has confiscated all of the radar records concerning that area at the time of the bombing.

Doesn't it make you wonder why the FBI would need to confiscate and then conceal the radar records of that area? What might those radar records have shown? Whatever it was we can rest assured that "it" is no more. Fourth, we have been told by a confidential informant stationed in another country that the informant had access to satellite photos of the area when the bombing occurred and that the informant would, in time, make those photos available to us. Even though these were private conversations between our contact and the informant concerning the acquisition of evidence about the bombing, the informant was immediately transferred from that station to another location where satellite information was not available. Another coincidence? Enough time has passed that all of the satellite photos of that area for that particular time could have been altered or destroyed by now. Our confidential informant may have been our only opportunity to actually see what happened on April 19, 1995. That opportunity has been effectively "cut off at the pass."

Again, we are not necessarily saying that this truck was destroyed by a rocket fired from a helicopter from above, but when you consider some of the information surrounding this valuable piece of evidence allegedly blown from the Ryder truck, it makes you wonder. Was it just a coincidence that witnesses saw a helicopter directly above the building before the explosions? Was it a coincidence that the FBI was very interested in the radar records which would've provided no information about anything that happened below an altitude of at least 600 feet? Was it just a coincidence that witnesses saw a construction crew working under the building a few days before the bombing? Was it just a coincidence that a potential informant was transferred for no apparent reason making it impossible for that informant to expose satellite photos to the world? Was it just a coincidence that the axle was allegedly found by former FBI, SS, and BATF supervisor Frank Keating? Is it just a coincidence that common sense demands that we ask how that axle got blown backward through the explosion?

We need some answers. •

"I saw a lot that day I wish I hadn't. I can't talk about it. I have a family. I have a job."
— **Journalist J.D. Cash, quoting bomb-squad employee.**

Chapter 16: John Doe No. 1— Still At Large

Now that we have at least reasonably convinced you that the "facts" do not always correspond with what the FBI tells the news media to report, let's move on to a bit of interesting information that started a lot of people thinking and raised some serious doubts about the stories and information that the FBI was leaking to the press. This will include many more FLEXIBLE FACTS which have been increasing in number on a daily basis.

In the CNN special, *Road To Oklahoma,* it was stated that on the Friday morning just 48 hours after the bombing, a BATF agent punched Timothy McVeigh's name into a national crime computer and discovered that Jerry Cook, the Sheriff in Perry, Okla., had sent in a routine inquiry about a man who was in his jail. Sheriff Cook said that the agent picked up the phone and (in an obvious expression of surprise and jubilation), "... he was going yes, yes, yes, you know and I heard him talking to someone there, and they got him in Perry!"

ABC News anchor Peter Jennings originally reported that the local police did not know Timothy McVeigh was a suspect until just before he was going to be released. He said the FBI got in touch with the police in Perry, Okla., just one hour before Tim was due to be released on bail. There were many similar reports about how the feds located McVeigh and how it was a stroke of luck that he was not released on bail just the day before. All of the "readers" on the national news networks told us exactly the same story as to how Tim was located. It was a "boy-did-we-get-lucky-with-a-little-help-from-God" report designed to make us all feel good that there may have been divine assistance in helping our great protectors capture this vicious terrorist. In our humble opinion, Tim's being picked up and held in Perry, Okla., is hardly a coincidence or the result of any assistance from above — but the fact that we are all still alive could very well be an indication of the possibility of divine intervention.

At the beginning of the smear campaign against Timothy McVeigh, the authorities stated that they got turned on to McVeigh from Oklahoma

State Trooper Charlie Hanger, the observant police officer who originally arrested him and took him to the Perry, Okla., jail. Now if this particular officer realized that Tim resembled the composite drawing of John Doe No. 1 and relayed this information to the FBI, logic would dictate that he would also tell the other police officers at the jail in Perry that he noticed the resemblance. To assume anything else, you would then have to assume that Trooper Hanger, who was observant enough to make this connection, wasn't sharp enough to realize that it was his responsibility to tell his fellow officers in Perry that they may have in their custody the nastiest criminal in the history of this Country. Such inaction would have amounted to an act of gross negligence on the part of this astute, observant, highly praised police officer. This information leads us to another case of FLEXIBLE FACTS!

The story about Charlie Hanger was inadvertently destroyed when Ted Koppel of ABC's *Nightline* program interviewed Mark Gibson, Assistant District Attorney for Noble County, Okla... When asked about the resemblance between John Doe No. 1 and Tim McVeigh, Mr. Gibson said that, "Although he looked similar to the sketch neither one of us (Gibson or Hanger) would have picked him out of a line-up and said, ' Yeah, that's the man they're looking for '." He went on to say, "Even now, having seen again the pictures and Mr. McVeigh, I would not necessarily think, I'm gonna pick up the phone and call somebody. I think that's the guy they're looking for. There's a similarity but not an incredible likeness." So much for the FBI's story as to how they got turned on to McVeigh by an observant police officer. Is it just us or are you beginning to realize a pattern developing here, too? Maybe Ted's bosses should've checked with the feds before they let him do that interview.

Realizing this story was no longer palatable to the average I.Q. because of the obvious discrepancies and because they hadn't taken the time to coordinate their stories with or put a gag order on local police agencies, the feds soon changed their story to comply with their FLEX-IBLE FACTS! Their second story, and the story which they temporarily decided to stick with, was that they got a phone call that tipped them off that John Doe No. 1 resembled a guy named Timothy McVeigh. Now this is going to get a bit involved so put on your thinking caps again and try not to nod off because this will prove to be a very important issue in untangling the web of deceit woven by the FBI.

Try to imagine yourself as an FBI agent sitting at your desk relentlessly working night and day on the biggest case in the history of the Bureau, searching for any clue that might lead you to John Doe No. 1, the most wanted criminal in the history of the world. You get a call and the caller claims that John Doe No. 1 may be a guy named Timothy McVeigh. What's your next move? Maybe a mid-morning break? Maybe a quick trip home to see the wife and kids whom you haven't seen in a couple of days because you're obsessed with catching this vicious killer before he can strike again? Maybe you could just complain about being over-worked and decide to follow-up this lead tomorrow? Not very likely.

The next obvious move, for any rational person, would be to punch that name into the computer and see what comes up. So, being a dedicated FBI agent and, we hope, a rational person, you punch Timothy McVeigh into the computer and find out that at least one Timothy McVeigh is being held in the Perry, Okla., jail. What's your next logical move? Now do you go out for a break, go home to see the wife and kids, take a sick leave because you feel overworked, or maybe, just maybe, do you call the Perry, Oklahoma jail, IMMEDIATELY? Since we all have our thinking caps on, this was an easy multiple choice quiz.

Now pay close attention because this gets real interesting.

We called the Perry, Okla., sheriff and asked him about what time the FBI first called them inquiring about Tim McVeigh on April 21. The Sheriff said the call came in just before 10:30 a.m. This was apparently the same call that Sheriff Jerry Cook mentioned on CNN, wherein he described the surprise in the BATF agent's voice when he realized that McVeigh was in custody. We then asked what time the FBI actually came out and made physical contact with McVeigh, the sheriff told us that the FBI came to his jail just before 12 noon to question McVeigh, but they didn't actually leave with him until about 6:30 p.m.

When you put this all into perspective, the discrepancies become alarmingly apparent. The FBI supposedly got a tip that John Doe No. 1 could be Timothy McVeigh. The FBI punched his name into the computer. The computer says McVeigh is in the Perry jail. The FBI immediately called the Perry jail. That call was made at approximately 10:30 a.m. Oklahoma time, 11:30 a.m. Michigan time. They got to the Perry jail and made physical contact with Tim around noon, 1 p.m. Michigan time. The FBI checked Tim's driver's license and observed an address in Decker, Mich., belonging to James Nichols.

James has a brother named Terry Nichols now living in Herington, Kan. The FBI immediately organized a raid on the notorious farm in Decker, which is about two hours north of the Detroit metropolitan area. Now how long do you think it would take the FBI and BATF to organize a hundred agents, many with masks, full battle gear with fully automatic weapons, several helicopters, airplanes, sniff dogs, more electronics equipment than Radio Shack, and all the news stations in the world complete with satellite trucks to beam their staged assault on this dangerous farm in Decker, Mich. — the bomb-manufacturing Mecca of the whole world — and then transport all the equipment and all of the over-dressed-in-black bullies from the Detroit area to a farm two hours away in Decker so that they could initiate an assault on the most dangerous organic farmer in America? Five or six hours you say? Guess again. Ten or 12 hours? Not quite.

Actually they got to the farm about 2 p.m. that afternoon. Considering that, under these circumstances they would've gotten my name and address off Tim's driver's license at around 1 p.m. Michigan time, this raid reflects the most efficient action that the U.S. government has ever initiated. They organized all these agents and all of this equipment and all the news media and, after getting all of these things together which would've taken no less than several hours, still managed to get to Decker by 2 p.m.. And they organized all of those people and all of that equipment in about one hour! You know, even if it only took one hour to organize all of the equipment and participants, they would've had to have made a 90-plus mile trip in, say, 10 seconds or less..

You say the last story that you heard was that the FBI said they got turned on to Tim McVeigh from the axle on the alleged Ryder truck? The FBI said they got the VIN off the axle, which we still consider a hard to believe coincidence, and traced it to a particular truck rented from Elliott's Body Shop in Junction City, Kan. They followed that lead to the rental agency and, with the help of a rental agent, got a basic description of the person who allegedly rented the truck. They then questioned anyone and everyone in Junction City until a clerk at the Dreamland Motel just outside of town and about a mile down the road on the same freeway claimed that she recognized the general description as looking like a guest who had stayed at the Dreamland a few days ago and the records indicated that his name was Timothy McVeigh.

Fortunately for the feds, this McVeigh character had temporary episodes of absolute ignorance at precisely the right time and place which would make him easy to locate. He conveniently used his real name and I.D. to register at the motel even before he allegedly used a fake I.D. to rent the truck just a mile down the road which he also parked at the motel because nobody would ever notice a big yellow Ryder truck parked by his room which he rented for $20 a night having talked Lea McGowan down from $28 a night to $20 a night drawing even more attention to himself. Brilliant plan for keeping a low profile. Anyway, they fed Tim's name into their national computer network and located him in the Perry, Okla., jail.

What's their next move? That's right. Call the jail to make certain that they didn't release Tim, the most wanted criminal on the planet. What time was that call made? That's right. April 21 at 10:30 a.m. Oklahoma time, 11:30 a.m. Michigan time. So what has changed? Only the method by which the FBI got Tim's name. The timing discrepancy still exists.

"But," you ask, "what if the FBI somehow got the information from McVeigh's driver's license via the computer as soon as they located him at 10:30 a.m.?" That's still only 11:30 a.m. Michigan time. But keep that thought because we're always willing to give the feds the benefit of the doubt.

Let's assume that they had access to Tim's driver's license at 11:30 a.m. Michigan time. And let us assume, just for the sake of argument, that they got my address off Tim's license immediately. That would only leave the storm troopers half an hour to organize one of the largest raids in history because it still would take them two hours to drive here. Not to mention the fact that local police have admitted to having my house under surveillance since early in the morning on April 21.

Now if they became aware of my address on Tim's license at 10:30 a.m., 11:30 a.m. Michigan time at the very earliest, then why were they watching my house since 5 o'clock that same morning? And why did they go to Kevin's house, who is another friend of Tim's, at exactly the same time they were raiding my house? His address wasn't on Tim's license. How did they get Kevin's name so quickly? Why did they appear at my mother's home at precisely the same time they came to my farm and Kevin's house? Why did they put a trace on Bob's phone at 4:14 p.m. on the April 21?

We hadn't talked on the phone in over a week. Why did they single him out of dozens of other people to whom I've talked on the phone? They didn't even secure a warrant to search my farm until 6:54 p.m. on the April 21, so how and why would they get a warrant to put a trace on Bob's phone two and one half hours earlier? We wouldn't have even known about the trace if the *Detroit Free Press* hadn't filed a suit under the Freedom of Information Act and forced the court to release the sealed documents. Also, some of the local people in small towns near here have told us that federal agents were already grouping in surrounding areas the day before the raid. Something in their story just didn't add up.

We also have to keep in mind that FBI agents contacted Lana Padilla, Terry's ex-wife, in Las Vegas at 8:30 Friday morning to question her and Josh. That would be 10:30 a.m. Oklahoma time. Now if the FBI got my address at 10:30 Oklahoma time, 8:30 Las Vegas time, how did they get to Lana's so quickly? How did they link Tim to Lana to Kevin to me all instantaneously? Why did they locate Lana before they located Terry? Terry's time zone is the same as Oklahoma's time zone. Considering the apparent magical timing of the FBI, one might think that we were all in the Twilight Zone.

We have had people in the media explain that one to us by suggesting the FBI had leaked to them that they were already aware of Tim McVeigh the day before the raid. Then may we suggest that the FBI would have been guilty of nothing less than incompetence and extreme gross negligence because if they had McVeigh positively identified on Thursday, April 20, why did they wait until Friday, April 21, to call the Perry, Okla., jail to make certain that McVeigh was still there and would not be released?

As we have shown, according to the sheriff in Perry, Okla., the call was made at 10:30 a.m. Oklahoma time. There is no mistaking this timing discrepancy. There is no explanation that can justify the timing of the actions by federal agents without either admitting to extreme gross negligence or just downright lying. Now if we had to make a choice between those two options, applying all of our past experience with federal agents, we'd have to choose the "just downright lying," although extreme gross negligence cannot be ruled out completely.

And as a matter of fact, we're going to prove beyond any doubt that the feds have routinely lied about every aspect of the investigation concerning this timing discrepancy. Detective Dave Hall of the Sanilac County Sheriff Department said the FBI first contacted them about the Decker address as being part of their investigation of the Oklahoma bombing incident on Thursday night at around 11 p.m., April 20. This information was confirmed in the *Sanilac News* in a special edition released on Saturday, April 22. Federal officers began arriving in Sandusky, the county seat, around 5 a.m. Friday, April 21. The FBI set up a command post in the county conference room and then established telephone communications between the command post and Washington D.C. and Oklahoma City.

Detective Hall said that federal and local officers set up surveillance on my farm early Friday morning. No one would have known that any of this information would even be significant if we hadn't called Perry, Okla., and found out when the feds located McVeigh. We have established that McVeigh was located at 10:30 a.m. April 21.

Even if they had his license immediately, and got my address from McVeigh's license, how did they find me the day before they found McVeigh? That's a real puzzle isn't it? If you stop and think about it and are willing to accept reality for what it really is, it appears as if somebody had this thing planned long ahead of time. Someone knew who was selected to take the blame. This whole thing was staged for the media of the world. How efficient the government will be under a police state. We'll catch all of the bad guys. But that one little mistake got them caught. One little phone call. If someone just would've made that call to the Perry jail on Thursday instead of Friday, we probably would never have been suspicious and started raising these questions and the FBI wouldn't have had to make up so many lies about how, when, where and by whom.

Apparently, some people were so sure of themselves that they got careless. They were absolutely positive that certain things would happen that didn't happen. There is no other rational explanation. The planners knew whom they were going to assault before the bombing of the Murrah Building ever took place. Unfortunately for them and lucky for us, they got a little sloppy and very over anxious. Now that they know we've caught them in their little timing discrepancy and considerable time has passed, they have managed to come up with another GRAND COVER-UP! We're certain that by now the phone records could've been altered to show that the feds called Perry before 10:30 a.m. on April 21. Realistically there was no benefit for the feds to have altered those records because we already knew when the call was made and, unfortunately for the feds, so did the sheriff.

After changing their FLEXIBLE FACTS no less than four times, their most recent explanation of this timing discrepancy, which we discovered way back in May 1995, has finally surfaced. We have to assume that this is the story they'll stay with because we're certain that by now enough documentation has been created from another damage control agent's imagination to certify this lie, once and for all!

Here's the latest scoop, folks:

FBI agents, being the most competent investigators in the universe and obviously possessing ESP, traced the VIN which was conveniently clean and visible to Elliott's Body Shop where Tim allegedly rented the notorious Ryder truck brilliantly using a phony I.D. to avoid being positively identified. They got a basic description from the employees at Elliott's, made a rough sketch, and then went door-to-door until they found someone who also saw a tall, thin guy with a short haircut. Apparently, there had never been a tall, thin guy with a short haircut anywhere near Junction City, Kan., prior to the time in question. The someone who just happened to see a tall, thin guy with a short haircut was Lea McGowan at the Dreamland Motel just a mile down the road from Elliott's where Tim cautiously used a phony I.D. to rent the truck and, as luck would have it, a tall, thin guy with a short haircut stayed there just a few days before and he carelessly used his real name and I.D.!

And that's not the most remarkable part of this story.

Even more interesting is the fact that they didn't even do a detailed composite drawing of the man who rented the Ryder truck until the next day. The lady at the Dreamland made a positive I.D. on Tim from a verbal description and a rough sketch given to her by the FBI and immediately the FBI knew they had their "mad bomber." They were absolutely certain that they had their man. We do not know how they reached this degree of certainty, considering the description that the people at Elliott's gave them. Actually, the witnesses at Elliott's didn't say the guy who rented the truck was a tall, thin dude with a short haircut. We just threw that in to show you how ridiculous a positive I.D. would've been even if they did describe Tim's general appearance.

The description that the people from Elliott's gave was; 5'-10", 180-185 lbs., stocky build, brownish-green eyes, a rough complexion with acne, and a slightly crooked or deformed jaw.

Tim is about 6'-2" tall, 150-160 lbs. soaking wet, blue eyes, no acne and his jaw is not crooked. Basically, he's a tall, blue-eyed, clear-complected, straight-jawed beanpole.

The description of the renter of the Ryder truck identified as "Bob Kling" from South Dakota wasn't even close to resembling Tim McVeigh's appearance, so would someone please tell us how FBI agents were so certain that they had their man when the verbal description didn't even resemble McVeigh? This "description" of John Doe No. 1, which doesn't even vaguely resemble Tim, is not a figment of our imagination but a matter of court records if you'd care to check it out or if you'd care to debate the issue, Mr. or Ms. Fed.

Curiously, a question that we have not heard asked is: "Just what description of John Doe No. 1 did the feds actually give to Lea McGowan?" Did they give her the same description that the witnesses at Elliott's gave to them, or did they give her a description of a young man who stayed at her motel recently using his real name and I.D. with the address of the farm in Decker on it? Had they given Ms. McGowan the same description they received from the witnesses at Elliott's the likelihood of Ms. McGowan recognizing that description as being Tim McVeigh is slim to none. If they gave her a description which she would recognize as being Tim, from where did they get that description on April 19?

The FBI claims that, after getting a positive I.D. from Lea McGowan, then getting Tim's name and address from the motel register via computer, they located Tim in the Perry jail late afternoon or early evening of

April 19 but didn't notify the police in Perry of their discovery, hoping that when Tim left the jail, they could follow him to the other conspirators in the bombing. But, as luck would have it, the bungling, stupid, trip-over-their-own-feet BATF also found McVeigh the next day, April 18, and blew the whole operation. Blame it on the B-A-T-F! This story also conveniently covers their butts on finding everyone in the world, including me, before they physically contacted McVeigh.

And all of this flies in the face of the claims by some that the FBI has surveillance pictures of the men exiting the Ryder truck in front of the Murrah Building. Why didn't they show the witness at the Dreamland a picture if they had one? Wouldn't that be OBSTRUCTION OF JUS-TICE? If they had pictures, why did they have to wait until Thursday for a detailed composite drawing which the lady at the Dreamland helped create? And please tell us, how could the FBI be so certain that they had their man just by using an inaccurate verbal description? Keep in mind that they did not create the sketch that resembles McVeigh (and a million other guys) until after they got a verbal description of what could have been a different species than McVeigh considering that they had so little in common in the appearance department. They seemed to be very certain on Wednesday, April 19, that their description, which didn't even vaguely resemble Tim, was in fact Tim because they did not pursue the John Doe No. 1 who was 5'-10" tall, weighed 185 lbs., had a stocky build, brownish-green eyes, acne and a deformed jaw, or John Doe No. 2, his Middle Eastern looking accomplice with a tattoo on his left arm. Instead, they concentrated all of their efforts on blaming Tim, who doesn't look anything like the original description of John Doe No. 1 given by the employees at Elliott's, and then on my brother Terry, who doesn't look anything like John Doe No. 2. And TERRY WASN'T EVEN THERE!

Now let's apply a little logic to this situation.

If their most recent story is true, why didn't they just call the judge in Perry and tell him to hurry things along and release McVeigh so they could follow him? Why would the FBI bust their butts locating a man who they were absolutely certain was John Doe No. 1 — and then sit patiently for two days while the trail got cold for all of his alleged co-conspirators? In two days anyone else involved could have gone to the four corners of the earth with time to spare. Can you imagine hundreds of these brilliant, dedicated investigators, who want more than anything in the world to apprehend all of those involved in this unconscionable act of mass murder, taking a chance that some of the people responsible would escape punishment when a simple phone call to a judge in Perry may have helped solve this crime and may have allowed the FBI to capture everyone involved?

We can't imagine the FBI or any other investigators, professional or amateur, having that kind of patience or incompetence depending upon how you look at it. Not by accident anyway. We would consider that an extremely negligent act and OBSTRUCTION OF JUSTICE on the part of the FBI. If Tim really was John Doe No. 1, for the sake of a simple phone call, they may have allowed the most vicious criminals on this planet to escape. Shouldn't we be wondering; if the FBI already located John Doe No. 1 on April 19, and if the FBI really wanted him to lead them to his co-conspirators, why would they plaster his composite drawing all over the news taking a chance on his being identified by the police in Perry who would have then blown the FBI's whole plan? And it really makes a thinking person wonder; if their most recent explanation is true, why did they wait seven months to come up with the alibi? And equally important; who began spreading this excuse for the FBI? And do you know what? John Does No. 1, 2, 3, 4, 5 and 6 did run away and escape to the four corners of the earth because they are guilty as charged and because the feds concentrated all of their efforts on bogus leads. They've been led around by their noses because of some very carefully laid plans. Tim McVeigh was driving down the road, minding his own business, conveniently without a license plate, not resisting arrest, not getting excited, not getting nervous while being pulled over, and not having the foggiest idea about what was going on. Terry was at home, enjoying his wife and baby, not running anywhere because,   TERRY   WASN'T THERE!

Do you think that the FBI would have mistrusted a judge or prosecutor to the extent that they did not pass this information along to them for fear they may have "let the cat out of the bag?"   But then again, realistically, letting the cat out of the bag should've been their objective, shouldn't it?   When we were first given this most recent "excuse" explaining all of the timing discrepancies we didn't really know what to say. It seemed as if the FBI finally had an air-tight alibi although alibis are generally reserved for those who are trying to prove their innocence. It didn't take long to realize that their most recent "alibi" also defied logic and common sense when you applied some thought. It was by far the best explanation they had manufactured although nothing in their latest explanation seemed to breach national security or even slightly resembled confidential information so the question that first came to mind about the latest story was: Why wasn't this their first story instead of their fifth story?

Another interesting bit of information that we have to keep in mind is the fact that all of the witnesses who helped in the composite drawings and all of the witnesses who claimed McVeigh resembled the notorious drawing of John Doe No. 1 also identified other John Does accompanying John Doe No. 1, not only at the truck rental location but at the motel and at many different locations and at many different times, including in and around the Murrah Building. Do you remember the two million dollar reward for John Doe No. 2, the reward that was withdrawn for the guy whom everyone saw? The same guy whom the government now claims never existed. Please tell us: Should we consider the feds' denial of other John Does puzzling, insulting, or just another small part of THE GRAND COVER-UP?

Recently, driving back from Oklahoma City via the northern route through Herington and Junction City, Kan., we passed by the Dreamland Motel and Elliott's Body Shop. Both were conveniently located, very visible from the same freeway just a mile or so apart. It immediately occurred to us that, because of their high visibility, these would not be good places to frequent if a person were planning to commit a crime. It also occurred to us that these locations couldn't have been better for the sake of the media and TV cameras, kind of like searching for "bomb fragments" at my farm, not behind the barn but close to the road for the benefit of the media. After all, we shouldn't expect the media to truck all over the countryside looking for a little motel in some remote location where the alleged bomber stayed when you have a great motel with a big visible sign right next to the freeway.

Easy-on, easy-off. Very convenient. And it would be very inconvenient for media, unfamiliar with the area, to drive all over the side roads trying to find a truck rental business where the alleged bomber obtained his vehicle of destruction. Elliott's also has a large sign, very visible and very easy to find. Excellent choices for a group of terrorists trying to keep a low profile.

Timothy, Timothy, John Doe was lookin' at you. ◆

The John Doe Story

**STILL AT LARGE
JOHN DOE #1**

ALIAS ROBERT KLING

DESCRIPTION: 5'-10" - 185 POUNDS - CREW CUT, LIGHT BROWN HAIR - BROWNISH GREEN EYES - ROUGH COMPLEXION, ACNE - CROOKED, DEFORMED JAW...

LAST SEEN: APRIL 17, 1995, ELLIOT'S BODY SHOP, JUNCTION CITY, KANSAS RENTING RYDER TRUCK - ALSO ON APRIL 19, 1995, DOWN-TOWN OKLAHOMA CITY.

**STILL AT LARGE
JOHN DOE #2**

DESCRIPTION: 5'-9" - 185 + POUNDS - STOCKY BUILD - DARK HAIR - OLIVE COMPLEXION, - POSSIBLY MIDDLE EASTERN DESCENT - TATOO ON LEFT ARM.

LAST SEEN: APRIL 17, 1995, ELLIOT'S BODY SHOP, JUNCTION CITY, KANSAS RENTING RYDER TRUCK - ALSO ON APRIL 19, 1995, DOWN-TOWN OKLAHOMA CITY, EXITING RYDER TRUCK IN FRONT OF MURRAH BUILDING.

Drawings by Bob Papovich

**STILL AT LARGE
JOHN DOE #3**

DESCRIPTION: AVERAGE HEIGHT - MEDIUM BUILD - DARK, LONG HAIR - OLIVE COMPLEXION - POSSIBLY HAWAIIAN, HISPANIC OR MIDDLE EASTERN DESCENT.

LAST SEEN: BY DAVID SNIDER IN BRICKTOWN SECTION OF OKLA-HOMA CITY, APRIL 19, 1995, DRIVING RYDER TRUCK.

Co-author Bob Papovich has produced his own versions of the so-called "John Does" reportedly seen at or around the Murrah Federal Building on the day of the bombing. These John Does have also been reportedly seen else-where prior to the bombing. Why is it so hard for federal officials to track down the real perpetrators of this crime?

"Some day when you know what I know and what I have learned, and that day will come, you will never again think of the United States of America in the same way."
— **Stephen Jones , speech at University of Oklahoma, November, 1995**

Chapter 17: Dead Men Don't Testify

Someone made a major mistake assuming that Lee Harvey McVeigh would be eliminated in Perry, Oklahoma by some extremely irate Oklahoman. They certainly gave any number of would-be assassins enough time to organize their thoughts (six and one-half hours) before they exited out the front door at around 6:30 p.m. with McVeigh who was not wearing a bullet-proof vest, even though he'd asked for one several times. Tim also asked to be taken out the back of the building where he would not be such an easy target, but to no avail.

With McVeigh out of the picture, the timing discrepancy, and many other discrepancies, would have never come up. They would have had their man; case closed. The irate shooter would have become intimately acquainted with an assortment of psychobabblers. He or she would spend a year or two in prison and most of that time would have been spent having dinner with more "psychological profilers at Quantico" and then, finally, being the primary subject of the "ongoing investigation," he or she would've received considerable fame and fortune and, more than likely, some sort of certificate of appreciation from Frank Keating and the rest of the "good ol' boys" whose primary objective has been to block any honest investigation.

If the professional deceivers who planned this thing had any idea that no private citizen would attempt to kill McVeigh, we really believe they would have had Lon Horiuchi or some other cowardly, low-life assassin in position to begin the elimination process. The common sense restraint of the good people of Oklahoma was obviously underestimated by someone in charge. As we have already pointed out earlier in this book, the BATF tried to sucker me into a situation that would have allowed them to turn me into Swiss cheese. With Tim and me "guilty by elimination," Terry wouldn't have been a problem even if he did survive. Of course, Terry driving straight to the Herington Police Station was not exactly part of the plan. They obviously could not comprehend the actions of an innocent man, so they just assumed he would be so scared when he heard his name on the news that he'd take flight and turn himself into a target also.

DEAD MEN DON'T TESTIFY was most definitely the plan here. Considering the odds, the fact that I'm still here and able to tell this story to you, and that Terry and Tim are still alive, we can honestly attribute to nothing less than Divine Intervention.

There's another interesting issue that we'd like to point out here. You do realize that there really were helicopters involved in the raid on the farm in Decker, don't you? Now think about this. You're a government agent and you believe you have located the most wanted mad bomber in America. You have at your disposal any means of transportation that you could possibly want. You have orchestrated an enormous raid on him, the most wanted man in the history of this great country, obviously an extremely dangerous criminal. Not a minute to waste.

Do you:

a. Secretly fly in a S.W.A.T. team of special agents immediately surrounding the suspect's house in an attempt to apprehend said suspect taking all precautions to avoid any situation that may pose a danger to any innocent bystanders thereby taking this dangerous suspect into custody or eliminating him as quickly, safely and efficiently as possible.

Or do you:

b. Contact all the news media on the entire planet and then drive to the location more than 90 miles away making certain that you go slow enough so that all the big hoagie satellite trucks belonging to the news media can keep up so that they can arrive simultaneously with the FBI and the BATF at the farm on which the most vicious farmers in America are manufacturing bombs from cow poop or chemical fertilizer or something of that sort which have enough power to make the inventors of the atomic bomb green with envy?

And then, assault this bomb-manufacturing Mecca of the planet Earth with masked agents from the BATF making certain that all the innocent bystanders are viewing from a position close enough so they may also have the opportunity to get hit by an occasional stray bullet or maybe, just maybe, be lucky enough to be injured or killed by shrapnel from one or more of the many bombs that will probably be discovered at this poop bomb manufacturing center in Decker, Mich.? The fact that they were watching my farm since 5 o'clock that same morning proves beyond any doubt that this thing was staged so the media could beam a video of our masked wonders to the whole world.

We're not trying to make humor out of a pathetically sad situation, but to coin a phrase from one of America's most prominent talk-show hosts Rush Limbaugh: "We have pointed out the absurdities by being absurd." And speaking of Rush, some months ago he was talking about Richard Jewell's situation and how he had been falsely accused by an Atlanta newspaper called *The Atlanta Journal and Constitution* which resulted in the total destruction of Richard's reputation and the disruption of his life.

Rush predicted that Mr. Jewell will own the *"Atlanta Urinal and Constipation"* (Rush's characterization) for being in error in their "rush" to judgment (no pun intended Rush) about Richard being the Atlanta Olympic pipe-bomber. We agreed completely and that's why Bob Papovich called in and brought to Rush's attention a similar situation which was a hundred times worse than Mr. Jewell's ordeal.

Bob told Rush that, using the same logic, James Nichols should own almost every newspaper company and nearly every television and radio station on the planet. Applying Rush's logic, Bob's statement was absolutely true. Rush did not disagree. Personally, I think we should go straight to the source of the crimes against me and hold them and their employer criminally responsible and civilly accountable and then go after their partners in crime who are in the media.

You could defend the actions of these federal agencies who made certain that the media were there to catch their performance on camera by saying their plans were just a little sloppy. We could call that the "sloppy defense" if you wanted to use being sloppy as a defense. Knowing what we know about all that transpired during this raid, and pointing out all of the obvious "mistakes" by the directors of this assault, nothing they did happened by accident with one exception: I'm still alive. Everything else that occurred on that day was absolutely deliberate and very carefully planned.

The news media didn't just accidentally hear about this thing. They didn't just coincidentally arrive at the farm with all of their cameras and satellite trucks precisely when the FBI and BATF initiated their crimes against me. These government agencies wanted to be sure that the cameras caught every bit of sensationalism that the U.S Storm Troopers could possibly muster. They wanted to be certain that the entire world witnessed them turning into Swiss cheese the "guru" behind the Oklahoma City bombing. They wanted to be sure that everyone saw the biggest farm raid in history so that our heroes in black masks could receive the credit they deserved for doing battle with this vicious organic farmer from Decker, Mich., who had bad things like tractors, cultivators, combines, seeds, grain bins, grain dryers, diesel fuel, calcium nitrate fertilizer, four "big" ounces of aluminum powder (wow, that's scary), several stray cats, and at least one overly-friendly dog (I can't believe they didn't shoot my dog).

You could tell that this farmer was really prepared to do battle with and inflict much physical damage on the Army, Navy, Air Force, and Marines. Definitely a dangerous guy and those 50-plus BATF agents, armed with fully automatic assault weapons, helicopters and who knows what else, were in for the fight of their lives. But, as luck would have it, there was nobody home. Darn it! And they were really itchin' for a tough fight. Darn it anyway!

Assuming people would be so terrified by the almighty U.S. government that all of our friends and neighbors would run and hide or attempt to distance themselves from me was also a major error in judgment on the part of government agencies. Unlike the founders of this great country, some did. And to those who did I say, Shame on you! Fortunately, many did not. Those who did should thank God that many did not.

Like Detroit-area talk-show host Mark Scott always says: "I love my country, but I fear my government."

The *Citizens' Rule Book* says: "Where the people fear the government you have tyranny; where the government fears the people, you have liberty."

Ditto, and ditto. •

"To lie to Terry Nichols' mother and say he's not cooperating, and then to take her to the FBI office and record her as she talks to her son, I think is an outrage.

"To hold his wife for 34 days incommunicado and to tell her that the only way out for her husband is if she calls him up and reads to him a script written by FBI agents, I think is an outrage.

"Then to send his wife a Mother's Day card signed by FBI agents saying they're her only friends in the world and saying she should call the Kansas City Field office if she ever needs to cry ... What in the world are we coming to here?"
— **Michael Tigar, attorney for Terry Nichols, quoted in** *New York Times,* **Sept. 7, 1995**

CHAPTER 18: TERRY LYNN NICHOLS

I feel that it's necessary to take a little time to reflect on Terry's background and personality considering the misconceptions that many people have about him because of "false information for profit" that's been written about him. Terry is, without a doubt, the most private person I've ever known. His insistence on keeping personal affairs very personal is probably why there's been so much speculation about his character. Other than immediate family, only a few people have been fortunate enough to know Terry very well which creates an atmosphere of even more speculation and more curiosity. The desire to obtain information which is not readily available is probably why people are willing to believe anything that is said about Terry no matter how outrageous it may seem to those few of us who really know him well.

As I'm sure you already know, Terry Nichols is my younger brother. I am almost exactly one year older than Terry, which means that we grew up about as close to being twins as we could without being twins. Terry is more than just my brother. He is also a very close friend. I would have to say that I know him as well as anyone could possibly know him. As siblings we certainly had our differences, which is typical for two brothers so close in age. We also had and have a lot in common, particularly as adults and, as our friend Bob has said, we are probably a lot more alike than either of us will admit. Again, I believe this is a typical attitude for brothers.

I will state right here and now that I have absolute confidence that my brother Terry is incapable of initiating violence. I have no doubt about his innocence in this tragedy. He can not possibly be knowingly involved in any way whatsoever. After you get to know the real Terry Nichols, the Terry whom I grew up with and the Terry who has very close personal friends here in Michigan who are willing to stake their lives on his innocence, I'm certain that you will share our opinions and come to the same conclusions about Terry's peaceful nature.

Terry and I both spent the majority of our lives living and working on the family farm. Although Terry handled his jobs on the farm as well as anyone could and knows and understands the farm business, I don't think that his heart was ever really in it. He even sold insurance for a short while but when he realized that his job consisted of occasionally selling people something they didn't really need, his integrity dictated that he quit.

His first wife, Lana, excelled selling the same insurance. He was involved in real estate for a while, buying and selling and he made substantial profits on his investments. Some time ago, he and Lana owned about a half-dozen residential rental properties located in nearby communities. He's made a variety of investments involving land con-tracts, stocks, gold and silver and then — as you all must know by now — military surplus equipment and supplies.

These were all businesses to earn some sort of living which Terry has always been very capable of doing. Terry and Lana always had a considerable amount of gold and silver stashed as security against inflation, or the collapse of the dollar which is, in reality, exactly the same thing. Why Lana expressed any shock or surprise whatsoever about Terry having gold and silver coins and bullion leaves us completely baffled. I'd have to guess that they had tens of thousands of dollars in gold and silver at any given time and I don't remember them ever selling any of it.

Although he most certainly loves nature and the natural organic approach to farming and gardening, I don't believe he necessarily considered farming his vocation. Terry's diet for the past two decades distinctly represents his attitude and obvious love and appreciation for organically grown foods, free from chemicals and pesticides. He grinds his own organically grown wheat for flour to bake breads and for breakfast cereals. He had his own equipment for making distilled water for drinking. He does not voluntarily ingest preservatives or toxins of any nature and has been known to fast on occasion. We have always been fresh fruit and vegetable eaters, raw whenever possible. Needless to say, smoking or doing drugs is not even a temptation.

Terry and I married sisters. It was a rather unique situation, I guess. Two sisters marrying two brothers. Terry married Lana and a few years later I married Lana's younger sister, Kelly. Terry and Lana have one son, Josh, and Kelly and I have one son named Chase. Although Terry got married before I did, I had the distinction of having a much shorter marriage by getting divorced before he did. Lana was five years older than Terry and I was several years older than Kelly. The older sister married the younger brother and the younger sister married the older brother. Neither Terry or I initiated the divorces. As brothers, Terry and I have a firm family commitment in common. As sisters, Lana and Kelly had roving eyes in common. My marriage to Kelly was the first time for both of us. After some flings, then our divorce followed by a few more flings, she got remarried. I believe at the time there may have been too much of a difference in age and maturity between us in addition to a personal, emotional tragedy that weighed heavily on both of our minds. Especially hers.

When Terry and Lana married, it was Terry's first and Lana's third. She was an old pro at marriage by the time Terry met her, albeit unsuccessful, still very experienced. She did seem to benefit financially from her marriages though, so I guess you could say she realized some degree of marital success. I don't think we could say the same for her ex-husbands. Lana already had two children from her first marriage, Troy and Barry. Since Lana divorced Terry, she has remarried and divorced again for the fourth time.

When Lana and Terry were first married, they lived in their own house a couple of miles from the farm here in Decker. They sold the house in which they were living to Phil and Barb, some friends in the area, and moved into the farmhouse with me. Shortly thereafter, Kelly and I married. Needless to say, two families with kids living in the same house can become irritating after a while so Lana and Terry bought a very nice, brick, single story home just a mile west of here on Lamton Road and moved out of the farmhouse. They lived there for a couple of years, then sold it and moved into a farmhouse with eighty acres on Argyle Road. It was a beautiful setting a good long way from the road with fruit trees, I believe a couple of grapevines, some bush fruit, and a large, very clean barn with an extra cement block building for a workshop. I thought this was surely the place where Lana and Terry would finally settle. So did everyone else, including Terry.

We were wrong.

Not long after moving to the farm, their marriage seemed to be faltering. At the time I didn't really know why and I didn't ask. Some things are personal and aren't anyone else's business. I know they had some difficulties with Lana's oldest son, but I think it was a combination of many things including Lana's roving eyes. Somewhere along the way, Lana suggested to Terry that it may be a good idea to try a career in the military service. I still find it extremely odd that she would suggest such a thing unless she was having an affair or something and just figured this might be a neat, convenient way to get rid of her third husband.

Surprisingly, Terry took her up on it. It's still unbelievable but Terry joined the Army at age 33. That suggestion by Lana and decision by Terry didn't do anything to enhance an already faltering marriage. If anything, it allowed Lana the freedom to have the affair or whatever "something" she wanted which included moving to Bay City, a town about fifty miles west of here, without her children. She already had a business office in Bay City selling insurance so moving there almost immediately after Terry left for basic training made it much easier for her to operate her business, and other extra curricular activities, without her children and without her husband. Had Terry known of Lana's intentions of moving to Bay City without the kids, he would've never joined the Army.

She left Joshua, 7, with her brother and sister-in-law and she left Troy, 14, and Barry, 16, at the farmhouse. She would occasionally come by to drop off groceries and to see how things were going. This may seem strange to most of us that a mother would leave her two young teen-age sons alone and on their own. But you have to understand that Lana is a very independent woman so, I guess, expecting her sons to experience independence didn't seem unusual to her, although it wouldn't surprise me if leaving them alone may have been illegal. It was, inarguably, not in their best interests.

Terry came home shortly after basic training to take Josh back with him to his permanent station in Fort Riley, Kan. He had to hire someone to look after Josh while he was at work on the military base which led to some major problems. At least they were major problems for a father who deeply loved and wanted to be with his son. Terry was a driver for some high-ranking officers and his excursions often kept him away from home and away from Josh for days at a time. That was part of the reason Terry applied for a hardship discharge. The other part had to do with the fact that Lana's two boys back at the farm were living with virtually zero supervision and nobody was there to take care of the land, outbuildings, and farmhouse. From what I've been told, it was a 24-hour-a-day, 7-day-a-week party, and the once meticulously maintained farmhouse was being slowly but surely destroyed. What else might one expect from unsupervised teenagers?

When you put all of this into perspective, it's not difficult to realize just what kind of a person my brother is. He seemed to enjoy the military and it appeared as if he had found the career opportunity that he was looking for. He had the hardest part, basic training, behind him and he certainly had the brains to become a high-ranking officer. He gave up this career to look after his son and the sons of his soon-to-be ex-wife. Can you think of many young guys who would give up their careers to baby-sit someone else's teen-age sons? Terry always treated Lana's sons as his own to the extent that he could. Supervision over an older teenager by his mother's husband can create animosity and many problems within a household. This situation is certainly not unique in today's society, but being common doesn't make it any easier on the man of the house or on the teen-ager about to become an adult.

Terry did receive his hardship discharge and came back to the farm to live with Josh, Troy and Barry. He got a job as an assistant to a local carpenter named Danny and did quite well in that occupation. Terry generally was pretty good at anything he tried. I believe he worked with Danny for a little over a year while still exploring some investments in land contracts and a few other things. Barry didn't stick around for long, so for the majority of the time Terry lived at the farmhouse on Argyle road with just Troy and Joshua.

Sometime during this period, Terry's and Lana's divorce was finalized. The cause for the delay in their divorce was because of residency problems for Lana. She had moved out of Sanilac County and into Bay County, without her children, right after Terry left for basic training and then she moved to Las Vegas, without her children, just before he got his discharge from the Army so there was a problem with filing the paperwork. Again you have to put this all into perspective to realize the enormous responsibility that Terry had taken upon himself, part of which he had no legal obligation to do although he thought he had a moral obligation to accept this responsibility. Knowing these facts, and how Terry's mind works, is extremely important in understanding Terry's moral character and realizing that my brother is incapable of the evil that encouraged someone to destroy all of those precious, innocent lives in Oklahoma City.

It has been very frustrating reading all of the misinformation about Terry so I'd like to share with you a letter to the editor written by some friends of Terry's. They sent this letter to a variety of news sources, but I don't know when or if it ever got printed in any paper. Early on in this investigation they also experienced much frustration concerning the alarming, inaccurate, negative things that were being said about Terry.

I think that reading this letter is very important in realizing just what kind of person Terry really is.

May 17, 1995

Letter to the Editor,

Lately more and more people have been asking, "How well do you know Terry Nichols and what kind of a man is he?" It seems that not too many people really got to know Terry very well. My wife and I had the opportunity and good fortune to become best friends with Terry and his first wife Lana some time ago.

If you really want to know about Terry Nichols, I can assure you that he is not a vengeful, hate-filled terrorist as he is being portrayed.

Terry Nichols is our friend and neighbor who dearly loves his 12-year-old son Josh, his beautiful new wife Marife and his baby daughter Nicole. He is also dearly loved and desperately needed by all of them.

Terry Nichols is our good friend and neighbor who has never shown any prejudices of any kind in my presence. It has been my observation that he treated Lana's two sons as well as any good man would treat his own children.

Terry Nichols is a good friend and neighbor who I have never even heard utter the words "hell" or "damn," not to mention the broad assortment of vulgarities commonly spoken over the last thirty years.

Terry Nichols is our good friend and neighbor who, with his first wife Lana, gave us a lawn mower when we needed one and didn't have the money to buy one.

Terry Nichols is the thoughtful friend who, when moving to Las Vegas, called before his garage sale and offered us free first choice of clothes and jackets that he probably wouldn't need in a warmer climate.

Terry Nichols is the good friend who stopped by unannounced, on no special occasion, with a hand-operated stone wheat grinder and 50 pounds of organically grown wheat and wouldn't let us pay him for it.

Terry Nichols is a good member of the community who, with his first wife Lana, offered the use of their home on Van Dyke and the use of his time and effort to organize and host a combination garage/bake sale to help raise money for a local school project.

Terry Nichols is a sensitive, soft spoken man who was devastated when he lost his baby boy, Jason, in a tragic accident.

Terry Nichols is a friend and neighbor with whom we've had many dinners.

Our children have stayed at his home and his children at our home.

If you really want to know Terry Nichols, he is the friend and neighbor who stopped by uninvited, climbed to the top of a 40-foot TV tower that I was attempting to disassemble, and helped me take the antenna and tower apart, piece by piece, and carry the pieces to the ground one at a time. Had Terry not volunteered his help I'm certain I would have caused myself great bodily harm "going it alone."

We're not going to let Terry handle this one alone. We will support him and believe in him until he is proven innocent of any wrong doing no matter how unpopular that position may be. He has survived tragedies in his life and we're certain that he will survive this tragedy with our help.

If you want to hear about Terry Nichols being depicted as this hateful, disturbed, mad-bomber like the national media is portraying him and the government would like you to believe then I guess you have to keep talking to all of those people who don't even know Terry Nichols.

If you want to know the real Terry Nichols, he's the good friend and neighbor who falls asleep in our living room while watching TV. I know Terry Nichols to be a kind, gentle, generous man absolutely incapable of violence. Nobody really seems to be interested in the real Terry Nichols. The truth is sensationally good, but not very sensational.

Bob & Sandy Papovich

As you can see, I'm not the only one who thinks my brother is a pretty neat guy. I believe Bob and Sandy's letter accurately portrays Terry's real personality which obviously bears no resemblance to the disturbed-drifter-government-hater-with-a-chip-on-his-shoulder type that some-one has deemed necessary for you to believe so that you can accept their allegations of his involvement in this act of terrorism. I honestly believe that some people in our government don't really give a good crap who is responsible for this mass murder so long as they get someone to string up, just anybody convenient, so they can look good in the news and milk this thing for their own benefit of being re-elected or re-appointed to whatever office or position they're willing to sell their souls to hold.

I find it very interesting that they couldn't find the Unabomber for umpteen years but they seem to have known who the Oklahoma City bombers were and how they carried out their act of destruction before the tragedy even happened.

As I've said before, over the years Terry earned a good living in a variety of ways. One of his most recent endeavors was his partnership with Tim McVeigh going to government auctions and surplus sales with the intention of purchasing whatever items were available for pennies on the dollar and selling these same items for a substantial profit. Terry has always had a keen eye for a bargain, and I don't think I've ever seen anyone more capable of buying low, embarrassingly low, and selling high, embarrassingly high, which I'm certain was his goal at the trade shows he and Tim frequented. Terry has always had a considerable amount of money saved since he is the most frugal (cheapest, he's my brother so I can say that) person I know and he's always been able to realize a profit on investments. I'd have to guess that it was mostly Terry's money that kept their buying and selling business afloat.

It has been said that Terry was going to loan Tim a substantial amount of money earlier this year and, as usual, someone has put a sinister spin on that potential transaction. You have to realize that Terry and Tim were kind of informal business partners who were on the verge of going their separate ways. Tim is young and single and Terry has a wife and child and another on the way. Terry wanted to start settling down in one place and Tim wanted to remain foot-loose and fancy-free. Terry has substantial assets. Tim has few. These two men are friends. Why would anyone find it unusual that Terry had intentions of loaning money to Tim to help him get out on his own? These two were severing their partnership in business, not their friendship. Considering that these guys were close friends, it would seem much more unusual if Tim was planning to start his own trade show venture and Terry didn't loan him some money to get started, wouldn't it?

This unfounded suspicion about some covert plot between Tim and Terry to do something evil seems to have started with the package Terry left with Lana when he went to the Philippines to visit his second wife, Marife (pronounced MAR-i-fay), and her family. Remember, the package that Lana was only supposed to open if Terry didn't return in 60 days? Well, she wasn't too far off. She only missed the required instructions by 59 days! Anyway, I'd like to explain the apparent realization by Terry that there was a possibility, however slim, that he may not come back. I am hopeful that this information will finally put an end to all of the absolutely ignorant speculation.

Again, we have to begin by putting this entire situation into perspective. Terry was traveling to the Philippines to see Marife and his in-laws, Marife's family. These people were also little Jason's family. Jason was not Terry's flesh-and-blood boy; he was conceived to Marife via another man in the Philippines at the time that Terry, who had just returned from there, was trying to cut through the red tape to get his new wife back in the U.S. When Jason was born, Terry simply accepted him as his own, no questions asked. That is the kind of man Terry Nichols is. Jason died in a tragic accident, suffocating in a plastic bag in my house in November of 1993 when Terry and his family were staying there temporarily in between moves. Even the medical resuscitation efforts of military-trained Tim McVeigh, a house guest at the time, were not enough to save the boy. It was a tragic loss.

Jason's grandmother and grandfather, aunts, uncles, cousins and other relatives were going to be there in the Philippines to greet Terry. He had already indicated that some parts of the Philippine Islands were not exactly a safe place for an American or anyone else to visit. Like Terry's attorney Michael Tigar says, because of lawlessness in some parts of the Philippines, it's almost as dangerous there as in some of our major cities, like Washington, D.C. The people in that part of the world literally live in another world. Their superstitions might seem rather unusual to an average first-worlder.

Bob gave me an example of the superstitious mentality in that part of the world. He said he gave a little girl $40 for a new bike in Vietnam. The next day the bike was stolen from her. She explained that she had been told by her father that it was all right because if the bike hadn't been stolen, probably something bad would've happened. If you can understand that logic, please explain it to me and Bob. The obvious logic to us is that something bad had already happened. The bike was stolen!

Anyway, Terry had been to Marife's homeland enough to know that their thought processes don't necessarily have to be logical, at least not by our standards. Even though little Jason's death was an unfortunate accident back in Michigan, Terry knew there was a possibility that one of his relatives could somehow, by some convoluted thought process, blame him for Jason's death. Jason was not Terry's biological son, so you have to realize that Terry knew that there was a possibility of a confrontation with Jason's biological father which was, realistically, his primary concern and his reason for leaving the instructions with Lana.

These were all potential situations that Terry had to consider which would explain why, according to Lana, Terry took two stun guns with him to the Philippines — strictly for close-range self defense without having to permanently injure or kill someone. The stun guns would also protect him from being mugged or worse in bad neighborhoods in the Philippines. If Terry had been up to something sinister, he wouldn't have armed himself with stun guns. He would have had the real thing. Doesn't exactly sound like a vicious killer, does he? Fortunately, he didn't experience any problems with anyone, including Jason's biological father.

We want to emphasize here that we're not trying to criticize the beliefs of anyone from the Philippines. We would imagine that in most of the large metropolitan "first-world" areas of the Islands, people have similar beliefs to our general beliefs. In some of the more remote areas in the United States, some people still have strange superstitions, as do people in every corner of the globe. Our typical beliefs may seem just as unusual to them as their beliefs do to us. I'm just stating some facts so we can shine a proper light on this situation and put an end to the sensationalist disinformation campaign.

One issue that really needs clarification is that of the notorious letters Terry left in Lana's safekeeping — the same ones that were only to be opened upon his death, or if he didn't return in 60 days. Terry is a meticulously thorough person and these letters were basically Terry's last will and testament. If there was even a remote possibility of his not returning, he wanted to be certain that his affairs were in order.

In the letter he left for Tim, Terry told him if he received this letter to clean out a particular storage shed by Feb. 1, 1995, or pay to keep it longer. "Pay to keep it longer." Do you remember when I told you that Terry was frugal? This is typical Terry. He wanted to be sure that Tim knew when the paid-up time period ended so that he wouldn't have to pay any more for unnecessary storage space. That doesn't sound like some kind of plot when you put it into context and finish the sentence. This is the same sentence that the government propagandists in the news media conveniently failed to finish. In all of their reports they only included that part of the sentence in which Terry seemed to instruct Tim to "clean out the storage shed." It sure wouldn't have sounded very sensational if it had been honestly reported. Giving the public only half of the information made it sound like Terry was trying to hide something. But again, when we see the sentence in its entirety, there are no hidden messages concerning a conspiracy in his statements.

Even now, with the complete sentence displayed in a much-talked-about book written by Lana, how many of you who read her book actually realized what these instructions really meant before you read this last paragraph? Can you see what's been done to our minds through an intentional disinformation campaign? We have been given only half of that sentence so consistently, for so long, that we now believe what we have been told that it means. Even when we read this information in context, our minds have been programmed to believe what we have been told, over and over and over.

It reminds me of one of Hitler's old techniques for brainwashing. He said that if you tell people something often enough and long enough, you can convince them that "heaven is hell and hell is heaven." That's exactly what they're doing to us. We have to pay close attention to all of the information, evaluate it, and then apply reason and logic to form our conclusions. Don't believe anything you've been told about this case until you've given it some serious thought. We expect you to apply the same reason and logic to the information that we're passing along to you in this book. As a matter of fact, we insist upon it. Objectivity will get us to the truth and we all want the truth.

Another piece of information that has been used to implicate Terry is the alias name that he used. The storage shed was rented under a fictitious name and if you understand why Terry had to use an alias, it's not really much of a "spy thriller" story either. I know some people like to sensationalize these things to lend credibility to their accusations about whodunnit, or to promote their newspapers, magazines and books thereby appreciating a much larger profit by tantalizing a morbid curiosity. I really hate to pull the rug out from under all of the sensationalists for profit and all of those morbid morons who only want to hear the negative side of anything positive, but here it goes.

Terry was not exactly in good standing with the Chase Manhattan Bank. If Terry had stored anything of value in a storage room anywhere in his own name, it would have been susceptible to confiscation. Not very sensational, is it? Just very logical (typical Terry) and very simple. Now you may or may not agree with Terry's interpretation of Article 1, Section 8 and Section 10 of the U. S. Constitution which is really the foundation for his and many other people's problems with the banking system but, for the moment, put yourself in his shoes. If you had tens of thousand of dollars invested in real money, gold and silver, and you knew an omnipotent entity like the Chase Manhattan Bank would snatch it if they could find it, would you rent a storage room to hide it and then declare to the world that you rented the room to hide all of your valuables by using your own name?

I think you get the point. He also had a substantial amount of cash stashed at Lana's house. He obviously doesn't trust banks and apparently his strategy was working. The Chase Manhattan Bank wasn't putting any "heat" on Terry because they couldn't find his assets. Terry apparently answered a question from Tim asking if Terry was aware of any "heat." Terry answered: "As far as heat, none that I know of." Now you know what Terry really meant when he used the word "heat" in the letters he left in Lana's "safe keeping." By the way, you should try reading Article 1, Section 8 and Section 10 before you pass judgment on Terry's interpretation of the Constitution and his evaluation of the banking system.

Please, put on your thinking caps first.

In Terry's letter to Tim, he gave him instructions on repairing the brakes and doing an oil change on the truck and what to do with the storage shed. He said that this letter would be mailed to him by Lana because that's what he instructed her to do in writing. He went on to say: "That's all she knows." If you really stop and read these letters objectively, and try looking at it from Terry's point of view, why would she know any more than he told her in his instructions? He trusted her not to open Tim's letter, so why should she know anything more than the instructions he gave her? Should Lana have known what kind of brakes and oil and filter to use on his truck and how to get into the storage locker? It wasn't necessary to give that kind of information to Lana. Of course, Terry didn't realize it, but he had already given her that information and she read it the day after he left.

Terry continued his letter to Tim with the very controversial and now world-famous quote, *"You're on your own. Go for it!"* I think it's time to clarify and finally lay to rest the misinterpretation of this phrase for all of you who really want to know the truth. Keep in mind that, according to Lana, Terry had intended on loaning Tim a substantial amount of money to pursue his own business. As long as Terry returned safely from the Philippines in 60 days or less, Tim would never receive the letter Terry left for him. If necessary, Terry would make the loan to Tim and he would be on his own to the extent that he would be handling all of his own buying and selling. Even though Tim was "on his own" he would have still had some financial support and some general business advice from Terry.

If Tim were reading the letter, that would have meant that Terry had not come back and Tim would've been completely on his own. Terry left no provisions for Tim to receive any money in the event of Terry's untimely demise, so Terry basically told him, go for it kid, you're on your own. No loans. No advice. No help. Just a few odds and ends in one of the storage rooms. He meant it literally. You're on your own. How much more clearly could he say it and why wouldn't he say exactly that under the circumstances? All of the money was to go to Marife and Josh. He even told Lana not to tell anyone about the gold and silver in storage and the cash hidden at her home. The only ones who knew about the gold, silver and cash were Terry, Marife — and now Lana. Terry specifically states that in his letter to Lana.

The only items of any particular value in the storage shed were the gold and silver and the only thing of value he had hidden at Lana's house was the money stashed behind the kitchen drawer. The other items in the shed on which the sensationalists have put so much emphasis were insignificant. They had no value and were of no importance whatsoever. That's why they weren't mentioned. There was no plan to take part in any covert activity other than trying to keep his assets safe from the vultures at Chase Manhattan Bank if they applied any "heat." He instructed Lana not to tell anyone else about the gold, silver, and cash because he knew his assets were vulnerable because of his troubles with the bank.

Again, our intentions are not to disappoint all the sensationalists out there, but someone has to finally tell the truth about this thing. I have to assume that's why you're reading this book, to get to the truth. We're writing this book to finally clear the air on these misconceptions. We are not trying to capitalize on or market sensationalism or fact-based fiction like other people have done. We just want to bring forth the truth and THE FACTS, PLEASE, JUST THE FACTS about this case in addition to applying logic and common sense to the rumors being "leaked" by the FBI. Again, you may not agree with Terry's opinion about our "unlawful" money system (millions of informed patriots agree), but trying to live up to his oath* to uphold the Constitution by bucking the money system in court does not a terrorist make. (*When he joined the Army.)

The statements by Lana, that part of the money which Terry had hidden at Lana's house was to be used as a loan for Tim to start his own trade show venture also destroys the Government's allegations when you apply some logic. The prosecutors plan on using Lana's statements against Terry in his trial alleging that her statements prove that Terry was, at the very least, financially backing McVeigh in his scheme to blow up the Murrah Building. Keep in mind that the government claims that this act of terrorism was financed by the Arkansas gun robbery which the government also claims was committed by Tim and Terry.

When, in our search for the truth, we give the government's claims and allegations some serious thought, they become very contradictory. If the gun robbery had been committed by Tim and Terry doesn't it stand to reason that the money would've belonged to both of them? There is no evidence in the letters or any testimony whatsoever to indicate or even imply that Tim knew anything about the money, gold or silver that Terry had hidden. The statements by Lana indicate that Terry was going to loan Tim some money. Would Terry have to loan Tim his own money? Obviously not. Wouldn't Tim know about the money if he and Terry had actually committed a robbery? Obviously he would. This revelation, using the most simple of our thought processes, should prove to any thinking person that Terry was not involved in any robbery with Tim.

And, if Tim was involved in the gun robbery, why would he have needed a loan or any financial backing from Terry. Obviously, he would not.

Terry's instructions to Lana bring up another very interesting point. Lana was told not to say anything about these assets. When the FBI started accusing Terry and questioning Lana about him, she did not hesitate to tell them about the letters and what she had found in the storage shed. We're not trying to criticize Lana for doing that which most people would have done as a result of being frightened and intimidated during an FBI interrogation. How many of us Joe Lunchbuckets and Sally Housewives have ever been questioned by the FBI? I can assure you that it is intimidating, so I can relate to her anxiety. Lana had done nothing illegal that I'm aware of so she really had nothing to hide, although I still don't know why she would've made copies of the letters. Perhaps, not understanding the entire situation or the true meaning of Terry's letters, she may have thought that something was going on that shouldn't have been. If that had been true, having copies of the letters certainly would've given her something to hold over his head to, shall we say, twist his arm if it ever needed twisting. She could not, in her wildest dreams, have ever imagined how these letters would be misrepresented by the prosecutors and the press to suggest Terry's complicity in the worst act of terrorism in this country's history.

Under the pressure of an FBI interrogation, she may not have had the time to evaluate the situation and to give serious thought to the letters and the other information of which she was aware. All she wanted to do was get to the truth which she was sure would prove that she was not involved in anything. The FBI's suggestions of Terry's involvement all seem to make sense until you appeal to your "common" sense. At the time Lana wanted to make sure that the FBI knew she had no involvement in any type of conspiracy to commit a crime.

She did exactly what anyone with nothing to hide would have done. She came forward with anything and everything that she thought might be important. Lana told them everything she knew and cooperated with the investigators completely. Did her actions seem unusual to anyone? Did Lana's attempt to cooperate fully arouse suspicions that she may have been knowingly involved in some type of illegal activity? Absolutely not. Anyone not obsessed with their own pathetic little dream world of Agent 007s, and at least making an attempt to rationally analyze her situation, would realize that just the opposite was true. She, quite obviously, was totally innocent, which finally brings us to the very interesting point on which this small detail about Lana's predicament will inevitably allow us to focus.

I believe at this time all government agents should put on their thinking caps (probably not part of their normal inventory, but ...). They aren't necessary for anyone else. Now, we all know that Lana cooperated fully with the Feds and we have learned by applying common sense and logic that her actions would dictate that she had nothing to do with anything illegal.

When my brother, Terry, first heard his name mentioned on the radio, he immediately packed up his pregnant wife and baby and headed for the local police station to find out what was going on. He didn't even request an attorney and I think we can safely assume that he knew he was entitled to one. He cooperated fully with the FBI, just like Lana, and never even asked for an attorney when they interrogated him. His son, Josh, and his wife, Marife, have corroborated everything Terry has told the FBI, precisely, without exception.

Now the federal investigators apparently have enough sense to appreciate Lana's innocence in light of the circumstances. *Hello!* Hey there, federal investigators. In case you haven't figured it out yet, the same circumstances and the same logic applies to Terry's situation. He cooperated fully, just like Lana, because he had nothing to hide. With all that we've seen in the past two years, it wouldn't take much to convince us that if you took all of these federal agents and prosecutors, especially the prosecutors, with all of their law degrees, their combined common sense would fit on the sharp end of a pin! They get so hung up on what angles their superiors tell them to pursue that they can't see the obvious when it hits them in the nose.

We heard Terry's attorney, Michael Tigar, quote Proverbs 28:1 in defense of Terry on NBC's *Today* show: "The wicked flee when no man pursueth: but the righteous are bold as a lion." Did my brother flee, or did he come forward, bold as a lion? You know, people, there's a man's life in the balance and we cannot afford to make a mistake. God just may be trying to tell us something with this quote from His book and I've never found God to be wrong about anything yet. Have you?

When Terry drove to the police station in Herington, Kan., the police had already been watching his house for some time. When he left his house, the police thought at first that he was attempting to flee. They were rather surprised when he drove in the direction of the police station and even more surprised when he actually drove into the police parking lot. He walked into the station and said that he had heard his name on the radio and wondered what was going on. The chief of police didn't quite know what to do with Terry now that he had him, kind of like when I drove up to the raid on my farm. The chief tried calling the FBI and consistently got a busy signal. He finally decided to call the FBI's hot-line number to make his declaration to the feds that Terry Nichols was at his police station in Herington, Kan. After a short time the Herington chief of police got a phone call from the FBI.

"Chief, this is the FBI. Can you talk?"

"Sure, I can talk," said the chief.

" I mean, can you really talk?"

"Sure, I can really talk," replied the chief.

"I mean, can you REALLY talk?"

"Sure, I can REALLY talk. What's the problem?" asked the chief.

"Well, isn't Terry Nichols there?"

"Well, yeah, Terry Nichols is here."

"Aren't you being held hostage?"

"Hostage, nobody's being held hostage," the chief finally replied.

It seems that the FBI, in their blaze of glory, had the police station in Herington, Kan. completely surrounded, quite probably, by a S.W.A.T. team in full battle gear reminiscent of a raid on a farm in Decker earlier that day. Do these guys just sit around for days and weeks and months ready to pounce like a spider on any opportunity to flex their muscles on some tiny little prey? It's kind of funny when you think about it. Terry Nichols holding a police station hostage?

Yeah, right. If you knew Terry you would appreciate the humor. By the way, we met Dale Kuhn, the police chief in Herington, and we were pleasantly surprised to find that he is a compassionate, honest man endowed with a good amount of common sense. A good neighbor and guardian for the fortunate Citizens of Herington.

He also clarified the misconception that Terry "turned himself in." The "turned himself in" disinformation spread to the news media by the feds was meant to imply that Terry was guilty of something. The police chief said that Terry did not turn himself in, he simply came to the station asking questions about a name he had heard on the news and to find out if that name was actually him.

Anyway, when the feds took Terry into custody, they didn't tell Terry that he was in custody or that he was a suspect. They held Terry and questioned him as a material witness. As an innocent witness Terry assumed he would not need an attorney so he freely answered all of their questions. He had nothing to hide. Consequently, by not informing him that he was a suspect, the feds tricked about eight hours of testimony out of Terry with no attorney present. The FBI interrogators took written notes of their conversations with Terry and much of what they wrote concerning Terry's testimony did not accurately reflect what Terry told them. That's why they don't want a tape recording of interrogations. They would prefer to just write it down, that way if they don't like the way you say something, they can change it. Had an attorney been there to represent Terry, nothing he said could have been twisted or taken out of context or out of sequence. That was their reason for lying to Terry, to make certain there were no witnesses present to confirm or refute anything the feds wrote down. An attempt will be made in court to use much of what the FBI interrogators wrote down in their own words that night. There have been numerous instances when they have attempted to twist the words of the witnesses in this case.

The FBI tricked Marife into signing a consent form to search their house. The feds never advised her of her right to have an attorney, and when she asked if she would need a lawyer they told her that she'd be okay as long as she was telling the truth, she wouldn't need a lawyer. They also took Marife and daughter Nicole into "protective custody" — for a long time. They kept Marife and Nicole in hiding with FBI interrogators for five weeks. They moved them around from motel to motel so nobody could contact them. Marife called my sister, Sue, once and my dad once but couldn't tell them where she was because the FBI wouldn't let her. She said that they treated her pretty good for the first few weeks of the interrogation but after that, it got a little nasty. Can you imagine living with FBI investigators 24 hours a day for weeks on end?

Can you imagine the brainwash they imposed on this sweet, young lady who was unfamiliar with our justice system? When she asked for an attorney they told her that she could have one but it would cost her $10,000! She obviously didn't have that kind of money since the feds stole everything Terry and Marife had. She was never told that she had the right to have counsel present at all times so, consequently, she was alone during this entire five week interrogation! Take notice people. This happened right here in the U.S.A. If you think your Constitutional rights are safe, think again. If they can violate Marife's rights, they can also violate your rights. This appears to be a clear case of kidnapping, doesn't it? Holding two people against their will for five weeks, without charging them, and without the assistance of an attorney?

The odd thing about this intense questioning of Marife for five weeks in isolation was that, even though they did their best to convince her that Terry had something to do with this bombing, her story never changed from the very beginning. That got the FBI a little perturbed, to say the least. Here's this very young lady from another country, doesn't under-stand the legal system in this country, doesn't have the wherewithal to fabricate a story, hasn't had any opportunity to get her story "straight" with her husband, and specially trained FBI interrogators have held her illegally at their mercy in total isolation with no counsel for five weeks, subjecting her to intense interrogation and brainwash, and she never changed her story as to Terry's whereabouts for the time period in question.

The FBI got so upset with Marife that they sent her back to the Philippines. Did it ever occur to these over-zealous kidnappers that maybe, just maybe, this sweet, young, innocent, beautiful young lady was just plain telling the truth? Are these government agents so far removed from any form of truth that they can no longer recognize it when it hits them square in the face? Is it possible that they've been working with and taking orders from liars for so long that they cannot even comprehend an honest person? That thought is scary, but if you take a close look at Washington and politics in general, that thought is, unfortunately, a reality.

The really interesting thing about Marife's interrogation is not only that her story never changed, but that her story corroborated everything that Terry told them during his interrogation. And their stories matched everything that Joshua told them during his questioning. Hey there, FBI investigators! TERRY WAS NOT THERE! What inquiring minds would like to know is:

Why is Terry still in prison? •

"I can't believe all the people who want to get in the spotlight! They must feel some urgent need to get their 15 minutes of fame & fortune. You can see that some are outright liars. Some take normal innocent things and attempt to put a suspicious spin on it, and it sure looks like others were coached in what they may have heard or seen — leading questions."

— **Terry Nichols**

Chapter 19: Terry Wasn't There

In conversations with us, many people have brought up the issue about the blue plastic barrels. Government investigators admit that while Terry may not have physically been in the area when the actual bombing took place, they still believe he was involved in the conspiracy because of other evidence they have discovered — other evidence.

Now what evidence might that be? The storage locker "evidence" has been shown to be absolutely insignificant as far as this bombing is concerned, and we have explained the reason for the phony names on these storage rooms. We have, once and for all, put an end to the ridiculous "money grubbing" speculation about the letters Terry left in Lana's safe keeping. We have, in effect, line for line and word for word dissected and put into proper context the meaning behind all of Terry's instructions and the reasons he said what he said. We have rationally explained why Terry had concerns for his safety while traveling to the Philippines. You now know the real reason why Terry was going to loan Tim money and the real meaning behind the phrase, "You're on your own. Go for it." And now, for all of those who missed Michael Tigar's statements on the *Today* show and for those who have not had the opportunity to read the court documents, we will put an end to the ridiculous speculation about the blue plastic barrels and many other "items of evidence."

In searching Terry's residence in Herington, Kan., the FBI found many items, all of which were meticulously recorded on inventory sheets. During a court hearing in May of 1995, Michael Tigar raised the question about the 55-gallon blue plastic barrels while cross-examining an FBI agent. Mr. Tigar noted that, according to the inventory list, the infamous barrels were actually white and not blue. The agent replied that the barrels had blue plastic lids. Mr. Tigar then asked why the alleged blue lids were not listed on the inventory sheets. The agent replied that they did not list lids separately on an inventory sheet. Mr. Tigar then turned the page on the FBI's official inventory sheet and noted some five-gallon buckets that were on the list. Also listed separately, as Mr. Tigar pointed out, were lids for the five-gallon buckets. So much for that lie and so much for the totally fabricated and absolutely untrue rumor about the blue plastic barrels linking Terry to this disaster.

The blue barrels never existed and there never were any blue lids. And you didn't think that FBI agents would lie about evidence in open court? They lied about Terry, they lied about me, they will lie about Tim, and they will lie about you if their superiors ever consider it necessary.

As Michael Tigar also pointed out in his interview with NBC television correspondent and *Today* show co-host Katie Couric, the media was well-represented in the courtroom when he brought this FBI agent to task on the witness stand. This was not some sort of confidential information. It was a matter of public record. These facts were right there in the court transcripts. All members of the media had access to the transcripts and many have had those transcripts in their possession since May. Shouldn't we all wonder why the truth about the white plastic barrels with no blue lids didn't get out to the public until Michael Tigar appeared on the *Today* show in September 1995? WHO BENEFITS from keeping this information from the public?

When this disinformation about the blue plastic barrels was reported in the news and none of the members of the media discounted these lies, even though they knew they were lies, who was injured by these false reports? A typical example of this was a story in *The Daily Oklahoman* on Dec. 15, 1995, seven months after the court hearing which clarified this falsehood and three months after Michael Tigar made the correction on national television. *The Daily Oklahoman* reported that searches of Terry's home turned up; "four barrels with blue lids made from material resembling blue plastic fragments found at the bomb scene, an FBI affidavit said." If anyone out there thinks that public opinion doesn't matter, then tell us why the government investigators have made such an effort to sway public opinion by telling lie after lie after lie to the media.

We would like some members of the media to come forward and tell us who was responsible for the concerted effort to NOT report the facts about these white barrels with no blue plastic lids? Please explain to us why anyone would stoop to something so cowardly, unprofessional and immoral? Do a few corrupt people in high places really have that much power over you and what you report? Can your souls really be bought for a measly job? Two thousand years ago, a soul could be bought for 40 pieces of silver. Apparently the price of a person's soul has gone up in the 20th century. Now it's 40 pieces of silver an hour, or a day, or a week, or a month — depending upon the size of that particular soul's paycheck. It doesn't appear as if the principle has changed much, does it?

The news media has also reported that the FBI found an "anti-tank bazooka" at Terry's home in Herington. That certainly makes him sound like a dangerous criminal, doesn't it? For months there was much talk about this weapon and people asked why anyone would want to have anything like that in their possession. That's a good question. We would like to know why the VFW hall down in Brown City, Mich., has a three-story high Nike missile on their front lawn? We want to know why many businesses and City Halls have cannons in front of their buildings and why other VFWs have fighter jets on the lawn in front of their halls. Are they planning a small personal war of their own? Common sense dictates that they are not. The Nike missile obviously is just a shell, the cannons are plugged and the fighter jets are inoperable.

Terry's oft-described "anti-tank bazooka" enjoys those same qualifications. It was a spent piece of equipment. This item is a one-shot weapon so it really was nothing more than an empty casing used for displays at the trade shows where Terry was selling the goods that he purchased at military surplus auctions.

As recently as late February 1996, *American Journal*, a late night tabloid TV show, referred to this spent, harmless piece of equipment as an "anti-tank bazooka." There can be no doubt that *American Journal* knows the truth about this "piece of evidence," so one would have to conclude that they intentionally withheld half the truth to add more sensationalism to their story and to help the government propaganda machine spread their disinformation continuing on with their "media trial" or should we say, media lynching?

American Journal also went to the Philippines to bamboozle an interview from Terry's wife, Marife. After much persistence, with the assistance of a money-grubber who Marife knew and mistakenly trusted, they got that interview. Neither Marife's attorney nor any of the attorneys on Terry's defense team had any knowledge of the interview until after the fact which, at the very least, was a violation of legal ethics. I believe we already knew that ethics and honesty were not exactly strong points for *American Journal* or the money-grubber.

Back in April 1995, a crew from *American Journal* did an honest and, for a change, positive interview with Bob and Sandy about me and Terry. *AJ* wanted to take pictures of some pictures that Sandy had of Terry and me with our families. *AJ* was allowed to take pictures only if they were to be used with that positive interview. They had a verbal agreement (that means a promise, *AJ*) that the pictures were not to be used for any other interviews or given to anyone else. Sandy was very reluctant to let *AJ* take pictures of her pictures because she didn't trust them. She experienced much anxiety because of *AJ's* request. She had Bob call *AJ* on several occasions to re-confirm their promise, which they did. If the interview ever aired we never saw it, but the pictures have surfaced elsewhere in other negative programs which were based upon disinformation. A representative from *AJ* claimed that the pictures must have surfaced from other friends or family members. Sandy knows that's not true because the pictures were her own personal pictures and she has the negatives. Live and learn.

Also found at Terry's home was a fuel meter. This allowed the FBI via their disinformation campaign through the media to make it appear as if Terry was involved in the manufacturing of this alleged ANFO truck bomb. They said he used the meter to precisely measure the amount of fuel oil necessary for maximum detonation. It sounds like he was performing a highly sophisticated procedure, doesn't it? What they failed to tell us was that the fuel meter at Terry's home was inoperable. As a matter of fact, Terry purchased the broken fuel meter with the intention of repairing it and selling it at a trade show. The meter was disassembled when the FBI found it at Terry's home and apparently there was no evidence that it had been used recently. In his book *I Rode With Tupper*, our friend Pat Shannan refers to these agents as "professional deceivers." We couldn't agree more with his observation. Professional deceivers who contrive FLEXIBLE FACTS!

Let's see now. Terry purchased his fuel meter in an inoperable condition with the intention of repairing it. Two days after the bombing the FBI found it in his house, not only in an inoperable condition, but disassembled and with not even the slightest trace of "bomb-making residue." Gee, that's a real tough one to figure out, isn't it? You know, the old saying that "the FBI always gets their man" should actually be that the FBI always gets "a" man. They apparently don't give a darn who they get as long as they nail someone so they can impress their superiors who can impress the politicians who spend their whole lives thumping their own chests in front of their constituents even though very few have ever really accomplished anything or even held a real job. Do you see what we mean about their combined intellects fitting on the sharp end of a pin? The really alarming thing is that, again, the majority of the media didn't report the facts even though they had the facts which might lead one to believe that someone, somewhere in the upper echelons of the media is assisting in THE GRAND COVER-UP!

Another item that the FBI claims they found at Terry's home is a key to a safe-deposit box belonging to Roger Moore, the Arkansas gun dealer who was allegedly robbed. The first question we have to ask is: How do we know the key was actually found at Terry's? We do know from past investigations and from prior experience that the FBI has a tendency to plant evidence to insure a conviction, assuming the jury's "responsibility in their own minds."

Another question we have to ask is: What was in this alleged safe-deposit box? Did you know that the key was not listed on the inventory sheet of this alleged robbery of Roger Moore who is reported to have deep ties with government intelligence agencies? The contents of this safe-deposit box have never been disclosed to our knowledge. And what good would a safe-deposit key do if you didn't know where the box was located? How would one know that it was a safe deposit key? And why would anyone take a safe deposit key and not use it immediately? Anyone who had a safe deposit key stolen would most certainly change locks so what would be the purpose of stealing the key and then stashing it? And if you stole a safe deposit box key and didn't get around to using it immediately, why in the world would you keep it? And if you did keep it and were going to "turn yourself in" two days after the fact, why wouldn't you drop it down a sewer or something first? A key wouldn't be too hard to get rid of. And why didn't they find the key until two weeks after the fact and after Roger Moore claimed he'd been robbed by Tim? We'd like these questions answered by some of our brilliant government investigators. You have to admit that if it really was a key to Roger Moore's safe deposit box, it would have been a pretty good idea to plant it at Terry's house especially when you consider that they have no evidence against Terry. THEY HAVE NO CASE! TERRY WASN'T THERE!

One of the government's rock-solid "eyewitnesses," a clerk at a convenience gas stop, claims to have seen Terry at her gas station on April 18. She also says McVeigh was there in a yellow Ryder truck with two men in suits. The reason that she remembered for sure it was Terry was that he came in and bought eight burritos and some cigarettes. The eight burritos were an unusual purchase and that's why she remembered for positive that it was Terry Nichols. One minor problem is that Terry would never have bought any cigarettes and probably wouldn't eat a convenience store burrito unless maybe his life depended on it.

Another minor problem is that when this investigation first began, the same rock-solid eyewitness for the FBI said that the fellow who came into her store was James Nichols. She saw my picture on TV and remembered me well because I made such an unusual purchase of eight burritos and some cigarettes. She was absolutely positive that it was me. Well, we all know that it wasn't me because I was in Michigan. That's when this really credible, or incredible, eye witness changed her story to identify Terry. Terry and I don't look anything alike. He wears glasses; I don't. I have a beard; Terry doesn't. Terry has a pretty decent head of hair and I have a very shiny reflection on the top of my head.

Now, the really big problem with her identification of Terry is that the records show he checked in at Fort Riley, Kan., for a military auction on April 18, 1995, at exactly the same time this observant young lady claims to have seen him 200 miles away. We know she is mistaken about seeing me. We know she is mistaken about seeing Terry. Why in the world would anyone believe her story about seeing Tim? She got some attention and it looks like that's what she wanted. This lady's testimony has about as much credibility as Michael Fortier's testimony. None. Of course, she could be right about seeing the Ryder truck and the two men in suits.

Another "eyewitness" claims to have seen Terry early in the morning on April 18, the day before the bombing. She claims Terry came into her restaurant, the Santa Fe Trail Cafe, and had breakfast with Tim McVeigh and John Doe No. 2. She said that she knew Terry because he came in occasionally for dinner and coffee. My dad, Bob, and I stopped in Herington just to see this restaurant for ourselves. As soon as we laid eyes on the place there was no doubt whatsoever in our minds that Terry had never eaten at this particular restaurant.

Terry is very selective about what he eats and where he eats it. This restaurant is located just one block over from the end of Terry's street. I'd have to guess it's about one-third of a mile from Terry's house. Josh said that he's never even seen the place, and if you saw it you'd realize why he never noticed it. These false claims did get the restaurant's name in the *New York Times*, publicity on several radio shows and now in our book, so I guess their goal of some degree of notoriety has been realized. There are many similar situations like this one on which the media investigators rely for "first-hand" information. Each of these rumors leaked by the FBI which the media accepts as a "solid lead" has turned out to be bogus. Even though all of this information has turned out to be false, it has been extremely effective at creating negative public opinion which appears to have been the FBI's goal from the very beginning. They knew, and now we know, that countering a rumor or false accusation is nearly impossible.

More extremely incriminating pieces of evidence that the federal investigators seem to have compiled against Terry are receipts for the purchase of diesel fuel. This is also a real tough one to figure but, for the benefit of all the truly patriotic [u]nited States private citizens who are reading this book, including those dedicated patriotic FBI agents who just don't quite get it yet, we'll do our best to simplify the complexities of this very confusing issue. Now if our memories serve us correctly, the purchases were for amounts in the 20-gallon range. There may even have been occasions when he actually purchased that amount *two days in a row!* Let's see now, most pickup vehicles have a fuel tank capable of holding 20-plus gallons of fuel and Terry's pickup has a diesel motor, but gosh, that's no excuse for buying 15 to 20 gallons of diesel fuel two days in a row, is it? Wow, let's just forget it. We give up. They have all the hard evidence that they need for a conviction right there!

Since all of the skeptics out there who still believe in the presumption of innocence can now see the evil of their ways, let's address another "incriminating" rumor about Terry's activities that has been greatly exaggerated and falsely represented by the FBI via the media — the ammonium nitrate fertilizer. Keep in mind that Terry has been around farming most of his life so he knows the general price of bulk fertilizer. The average person living in or near the city with a few plants or a small garden buys a very small quantity of low potency plant food at the local nursery for a few dollars a pound and a pound of fertilizer doesn't really go very far. In a small city garden, the cost of the fertilizer doesn't matter because the city gardener only uses a few pounds. The average gardener in the country can go to the local feed or hardware store and buy a 50-pound bag of 19-19-19 high potency fertilizer for six or seven bucks.

When you figure the price and the difference in potency, the city dweller pays 20 to 40 times as much for his fertilizer. When a farmer buys fertilizer by the ton to farm hundreds of acres, his cost per pound goes down even further. A farmer buying by the ton pays about a dollar for nine pounds of ammonium nitrate. The person living in the city with a small backyard garden probably pays 50 to a 100 times as much per pound as the farmer buying by the ton. This simple fact was obvious to Terry who capitalized on the opportunity by buying bulk ammonium nitrate, a high-nitrogen fertilizer, placing it in small bags or containers — and was handsomely compensated for his efforts by small gardeners at various trade shows across the country.

Let's see now, is there any other "hard" evidence against Terry? Can you see why they wanted to make this a combination trial? THEY HAVE NO CASE because TERRY WASN'T THERE!

Right in the middle of writing about Terry, he called me from El Reno prison. We talked for at least an hour on the phone having, what we assumed would be, a non-public conversation. We know the prison authorities and certainly the FBI tape our conversations, read all of our letters and probably make copies of our letters. We find it rather peculiar that within a couple of days after Terry called me, friends heard a news report that Terry had confessed to me during a phone conversation? That's obviously a lie, but let's look at this situation. How did the media know that Terry even called me? Either the FBI or the prison authorities had to tell them. And where would they get information concerning the topics of our conversation? Either the FBI or the prison authorities had to tell them. Since the information the media received was false, guess who's lying again!

"New and incriminating evidence" has surfaced recently about Terry and Tim being seen in Missouri when they were down there inquiring about a piece of property. It was sensationally reported, mostly by the Cable News Network (CNN), that they were looking for a hideout in the wilderness. Again, we found that accusation very interesting. The "hideout" accusation really carries a lot of weight when you consider that Terry eventually found his hideout on a side street in Herington, Kan., with neighbors on all four sides. I can assure you that a hideout was not Terry's intentions when he was in Missouri looking for property. For some time Terry considered the possibility of starting a blueberry farm. After researching the idea, pricing real estate and the cost of special equipment, buying the blueberry plants, and then waiting several years for the plants to produce, I believe Terry discovered that it would have been impossible for him to finance the project.

By the time Terry and Marife went to Missouri in 1992, I believe his intention was to find property on which he could start a pick-your-own organically grown vegetable farm and I also believe that Tim traveled with them on one occasion. After the initial cost of the property, a small, old farm tractor, a source of free manure and some seeds, that kind of investment could start paying off in a matter of months if Terry timed it right. Hardly sensational, hardly incriminating, and not even a big deal once you know the truth.

For nearly two years the media has been clamoring for Terry to say something, anything. When, against his attorney's wishes, he finally released a statement to the press, it was swept under the carpet! The story was covered in Oklahoma City, Denver, and was mentioned by Dan Rather on the *CBS Evening News*. That was it. After two years of waiting for Terry to say something, that something was virtually ignored because the government's media didn't like what he said. Terry expressed to us his feelings about this matter quite some time ago and we agreed with him completely. We also voiced our feelings to some of the victims in person.

In case you missed it, and you probably did, here's Terry's first and only press statement:

"I feel that the victims do have a right to view/sit in on my trial. They are victims of a terrible crime that has affected them enormously for life. They have lost loved ones and some have even suffered physically not to mention emotionally from that tragedy. They were totally innocent victims, given no warning, and were unexpectedly subjected to an event that should never have happened. So if any of the victims can get some peace of mind and/or relief of pain by personally sitting in court (or viewing on TV in OKC) during my trial, it's the least I can do in not opposing their right to view my trial.

"In fact, I feel and believe that it would be best to waive my right (if I have any) that keeps the victims away from viewing my trial. I would rather have the victims in court watching my trial and hearing and seeing all the evidence in court personally rather than the victims getting their information second and third-hand by the media or even from government prosecutors."

Terry wants all the victims to view his trial and so do we. When the truth finally comes out, there won't be any doubt in anyone's mind about Terry's innocence. By the time this book is published Terry will have spent two years in prison for a crime he did not commit. By the time Terry goes to trial, he will have been in prison three years for a crime of which he had no prior knowledge. No evidence exists which would indicate that Terry was in any way involved or that he had any prior knowledge of this heinous crime. In light of all the evidence discovered by private investigators, and all of the unusual activities by government police agencies before and after the fact, can anyone honestly say the same about them? ●

Photo courtesy *Time* magazine

Timothy James McVeigh was tried and convicted in the mainstream media long before his Denver trial. In fact, this cover photo and headline in the May 1, 1995, edition of *Time* magazine pretty much cinched McVeigh's guilt in the eyes of the American people right from the day he was accused.

"The prosecution spent a lot of money bringing in witnesses who knew nothing about the bombing. How many witnesses do you need to say that McVeigh was at gun shows? Not ten witnesses! That's irrelevant! Many people go to gun shows and don't blow up buildings. These witnesses were used to get across the idea that McVeigh, because he went to gun shows, was a bad guy."
— **Hoppy Heidelberg, grand juror**

CHAPTER 20: TIMOTHY JAMES MCVEIGH

There has been much discussion over the past 20 months about the demeanor of Timothy McVeigh. They have paraded "old army buddies" across the tube who claim to have known him well from basic training (?) to tell the smut-thirsty journalists just exactly what they wanted to hear — i.e., McVeigh was obsessed with guns and things that went "boom" and couldn't wait to get into a firefight to waste someone, anyone!

Apparently, this was a once-in-a-lifetime chance for these former McVeigh "associates" to get their mugs on TV. It doesn't matter that they didn't know anything more about the guy than that his name was Tim, and they were in the same company or the same platoon. It doesn't matter that they got on national television by telling the media precisely what they wanted to hear, true or false, even though the falsehoods and exaggerations may tend to incriminate someone whom they don't even know. In a blatant attempt at character assassination, it has even been rumored by someone that he killed an Iraqi soldier who was surrendering.

If that "leak" was true, why did someone wait for Tim to become world-famous to report the murder? Wouldn't it make that "someone" an accomplice after the fact? They're just coming out of the woodwork, aren't they? What really happened — according to fellow soldiers who witnessed the incident and who were not overcome with jealousy because of Tim's accomplishments of excellence on the Bradley — is that Tim's pinpoint accuracy with one single shot from 1,500 meters, killing one Iraqi soldier, caused all of the other Iraqi soldiers to come out of their bunker and surrender. Had he been the gun-crazed maniac who he is accused of being, would he have fired just one — single — shot, forcing a surrender?

Did it ever occur to any of the interviewers to raise the issue: What exactly is it that soldiers do? I think we can apply common sense to answer that question with some degree of accuracy. Soldiers get paid to train with weapons and things that go boom. They train to defend themselves in hand-to-hand combat. They train to fight. Our soldiers train to do battle using a variety of weapons so that they can defend OUR country, thereby making it a safe and peaceful place to live, work and raise our families.

Do we want soldiers who don't like to handle and use weapons? Do we want soldiers who want no part of any fight? Did it ever occur to any of the interviewers to ask any of those soldiers who were critical of McVeigh exactly what it was that THEY were doing in the army since it was apparent that THEY didn't want to shoot guns and THEY wanted no part of combat? Could any of these soldiers have seized the opportunity to criticize a much more accomplished and more decorated soldier than themselves because of a little envy?

When former military buddies and friends who really knew Tim are interviewed, the stories are just a little different. His real Army buddies all said that he was a consummate soldier. His commanders said if they had a couple of hundred men like McVeigh, their jobs would be much easier. Some said they didn't agree with many of his political views. But many Republicans don't agree with the political views of many Democrats and vice versa. So what? Some said they would not necessarily be surprised if Tim had some kind of confrontation with the government. So what again. We are all, as citizens, supposed to be the final "check" on government by getting involved and confronting government if necessary. This country was founded by people who had the courage to "confront" government with grievances.

All of those who knew him well did agree upon one thing: Timothy James McVeigh was not singularly capable of this vicious act of terrorism. A terrorist is a sneak and a coward. Tim McVeigh would meet an enemy face-to-face, man-to-man, head-on. Bill Clinton even stated on *60 Minutes* that "this was an act of cowardice." We must then ask, who are the known cowards, Bill?

We have read and heard many accusations about McVeigh by many different people. In her recent book Lana Padilla, Terry's first wife, certainly didn't go out of her way to flatter Tim. Many statements she made could be construed as detrimental to Tim's defense if her statements were true. Most of what she wrote about Tim might lead a reader to believe that Lana thinks Tim is guilty of at least having some involvement in this bombing. We're not going to waste much precious time or space dispelling everything Lana has said about Tim because it can all be summed up very simply.

The subtitle of her book, *My Life with Terry Nichols and Timothy McVeigh*, is a deception. We realize the need for sensationalism when you lack substance, and here we have a clear case of absolute sensationalism which is also absolutely lacking in substance. The fact is, Lana Padilla never had a life with Tim McVeigh. She has recently clarified that misconception on a television interview. She talked to Tim on the phone a few times when Tim called her house looking for Terry. The conversations were short and simple. "Hi, how are you doing? Here's Terry."

She has remarked that Tim seemed like a happy-go-lucky guy with a good sense of humor. We don't know if she got that impression talking with Tim on the phone or if she heard someone else say it, but that is certainly descriptive of Tim's personality. Always joking around, putting a humorous slant on everything. Actually, Lana only met Tim once in her life, very briefly, when he stopped by her house in Las Vegas to pick up a TV to take to Terry's house for Joshua. Lana didn't really know Tim McVeigh, so any of her remarks, good or bad, have no validity in her book or on the witness stand. They are based upon speculative sensationalism, quite probably on the advice or instructions of her co-author or publishing agents, and have no foundation whatsoever.

It has also been reported that Joshua originally stated to his mother that he thought Tim did it. You have to realize that Joshua is only 14, and at the time he made that statement he was only 12. Being traumatized by intense FBI interrogation and filled with emotion, he made that statement simply to defend his father. It was just a statement blurted out during a very traumatic experience. This was not a statement of fact. It was a statement made out of fear and anxiety and out of defense. He felt a lot of pain and was striking out at the most convenient target, Tim McVeigh. After having some time to think about it, Josh realized that he didn't really mean what he had said and he corrected himself. Actually, the past two years have been a very traumatic experience for all of the adults affected by this situation. We really don't know how Josh has been able to handle it at his age. He's become a very mature and brave 14 year old and we're all very proud of him.

The negative rumors and accusations about Tim have been mounting for months, creating a mountain of psychobabble hell-bent on showing a dark side of this bright and friendly young man. A dark side that we've never seen. The portrait that these government investigators have painted of Timothy McVeigh, with the help of the news media, is exactly the opposite of his true character. Anyone who actually knows Tim and has something good to say about him has been virtually ignored by the media and government investigators.

A perfect example of the portrait being painted of McVeigh to heavily influence public opinion via a propaganda campaign stared at us from the magazine stands all over the country immediately after Tim was taken into federal custody. It was the cover of *Time* magazine May 1, 1995, which displayed his close-up portrait overlooking the now famous picture of a fireman holding a bloody baby in his arms. They used the familiar close-up of McVeigh's face while he was being escorted from the Noble County courthouse in Perry, Okla., bound and shackled, dressed in a bright orange target with no bullet-proof vest, in front of an angry Oklahoma mob that had more than six hours to gather. He wasn't scooted out the back door to avoid a potential Lee Harvey McVeigh. He was marched at least a hundred feet to a waiting vehicle in front of an angry mob of people not much more than an arm's length away who were shouting "baby killer" and other obscenities at him.

Time magazine labeled him "The Face of Terror." It was the face of terror, all right. Anyone who knows Tim could see that he was terrified out of his wits, waiting for the bullet that he knew would come. He just didn't know when. We realize that it may be difficult for some of us who have never been waiting for that bullet, but at least try to put yourself into that situation. Would you have been smiling? Would you have been crying? Would you have been screaming? If you ask combat veterans, most will tell you that this cold, blank stare accompanied by what seems to be a mental silence is typical of soldiers in combat waiting for the sniper's shot that they know will eventually come. Your mind separates from your body and it's as if you're watching someone else's experience, not your own. That was the blank look on the face of Timothy McVeigh. That was most definitely "The Face of Terror." He was absolutely TERRIFIED!

Time magazine had Tim tried, convicted and executed with just four little words: "The Face Of Terror." They didn't ask the question: "Is This The Face Of Terror?" They passed judgment. They made a definite statement designed to persuade, and persuade they did. At that particular time, under the circumstances, with emotionalism overriding all of our other senses, you could've probably counted on one hand all of the people on this entire planet who were still capable of looking objectively at the charges against this young man. And we can assure you that we know all four of those people.

The following week, *Newsweek* magazine came out with an issue entitled "The Plot" and subtitled "Cracking the Oklahoma Conspiracy." Again, the entire cover of the magazine was a close-up of Tim's face. This particular picture made him look vicious and it was just hazy enough to give you an eerie feeling when you looked at him. This publication, and most of the others, jumped the gun by assuming that they had a handle on what actually happened in Oklahoma City.

Over a period of time, they told their stories as if they were a matter of fact and not speculation. THE FACTS, PLEASE, JUST THE FACTS! They talked of the ammonium nitrate fertilizer bomb that had destroyed the Murrah Building without ever having seen any evidence to confirm that speculation. They believed, without question, everything federal investigators told them. They showed how Tim, Terry and I began practicing our career in bomb manufacturing back here at the farm in Decker without ever confirming that disinformation. The media's "investigators" originally reported that James Nichols was the "guru" behind this conspiracy because that's what they were told to say by the feds. Some repeated the "guru" story even after it was dispelled in federal court because that's what they wanted to say for the sake of sensationalism. They believed the "stories" of a few vindictive people in the area because that's what they wanted to believe. They believed those people who wanted their 15 minutes of fame because their fabricated stories were sensational. They ignored the truth from people who really knew the suspects because it didn't match the "potential terrorist" profile that they were attempting to create to discredit us and to convince an uninformed public that three average, patriotic citizens were capable of such horror.

Representatives for the feds seized every opportunity to voice their "rehearsed" speeches about the so-called evidence surrounding this disaster. From the television, the radio, the newspapers and magazines, the same disinformation was shown and repeated over and over again, echoing loudly in our ears, like the bell that could not be un-rung. But, as Shakespeare once said, "The empty vessel makes the greatest sound."

Recently, an interesting story has surfaced about something that happened in Tim's not-too-distant past. Lawrence Myers from *Media Bypass* did an interview in El Reno prison with McVeigh back in December of '95 and, all in all, we thought the story was objectively written. Myers laid to rest many of the rumors that have been circulating about Tim. Rumors designed to assassinate his character making it much easier for the nation, including potential jurors, to despise this young man. Rumors designed to open our minds to the suggestion that a young, clean-cut, patriotic American war veteran could lash out with unconscionable vengeance, murdering innocent fellow patriots and their children.

In his article Myers told a story about an incident in which Tim got involved, and I can say with absolute certainty that the federal prosecutors would prefer that you did not know about this particular incident, because it doesn't match the profile of McVeigh which they have attempted to convey through the media.

As Myers reported, one night Tim was traveling down I-70 somewhere near the Illinois-Indiana border. He was still in the service and was on his way home to Pendleton, N.Y., for a short leave. In the darkness he happened upon a bad accident that had just taken place. No police or medical personnel were there yet but two men in a semi-truck had stopped to offer their help. Because of the darkness, the two men in the semi were unable to locate the victim who had been thrown from his vehicle and onto the median.

Tim pulled over and stopped to see if he could be of any assistance and immediately located the seriously injured young man who was suffering from a compound fracture and numerous other injuries resulting in a major loss of blood. Complicating the situation was the fact that the man was panicking. Tim, using the training he had received in the service, proceeded to calm the man down while he bandaged his wounds and started an I-V in the man's arm which probably saved his life.

Tim was not supposed to have taken his medical pack off base, but Tim's stretching the rules this one time probably saved the young man's life. Some believe that there is a reason for everything and that fate plays a role in many things that happen. I don't know one way or the other, but if that's the case, then fate wanted this young man to survive a crash that may have been fatal if Tim hadn't broken the rules just a little and if he hadn't felt that it was his humanitarian responsibility to stop and offer his assistance.

When the situation was under control, Tim just got up and left, never taking credit for his act of compassion and for possibly saving the young strangers life. The rumors about Tim wanting all this attention and about his wanting to be a martyr don't carry much weight when you are aware of this particular incident. Keep in mind also that Tim didn't go around bragging about this story. He didn't volunteer this story to Lawrence Myers. As a matter of fact, I only know of one person who was aware of this story and that person enlightened Larry during a breakfast conversation on the morning of the same day Myers interviewed Tim.

I know for sure because that person is me.

Had I not told Myers about the incident it would have never been reported. Tim revealed the information only because he was asked, not because he was thumping his own chest. So much for this hate-filled loner who was looking for attention. So much for the rumors that Tim wanted to be a martyr. These "martyrdom" accusations have been made by a certain person in a certain position of employment who shouldn't have been making those kind of accusations. Some of these issues will be clarified in great detail in Michele Moore's book, *Oklahoma City: Day One*. Reading her book is an absolute must for anyone who wants to know the real truth surrounding this tragedy, particularly the information which has not been reported on network news by our extravagantly paid talking heads who make an ungodly amount of money for simply reading what someone else wants to indoctrinate into American minds.

Lawrence Myers has done a very detailed investigation into Tim McVeigh's background. There is one thing we have noticed about Myers. Other than being a very aggressive journalist, he is extremely thorough. He told us that Tim's entire "criminal record" consists of a traffic ticket for going over the yellow line or something of the sort, and an overdue library book.

To quote Larry about Tim, tongue-in-cheek: "He's a friggin' one-man crime wave." He also said: "The clean cut, bright, funny and friendly kid who I met in that box couldn't possibly have been the perpetrator of this crime." We have, on occasion, disagreed with Larry about particulars in this investigation, but we have to agree with his latest observation of Timothy McVeigh's persona.

Recently some home videos and still pictures of McVeigh have surfaced. They were taken when Tim went down to Waco to witness for himself what was really going on down there. He was selling politically incorrect bumper stickers some of which asked, "Is your church BATF approved?" The man who took the videos never realized that he had taken home movies of Timothy James McVeigh, the mad terrorist, because the young man he video taped didn't seem angry or unusually upset about what was happening there.

Paula Zahn aired a segment on *This Morning*, a CBS news program, in which she interviewed the man with the home video of Tim and a young reporter named Michelle Rauch from KXII-TV in Sherman, Texas, who interviewed Tim and who also took still pictures of him. Michelle never realized that the polite, young man she talked to was "the" Timothy McVeigh who was accused in the Oklahoma City bombing until she saw me on an interview with Dan Rather talking about McVeigh going down to Waco during the siege and selling bumper stickers.

Even though she had seen Tim's face hundreds of times on TV, newspapers and magazines, and even though she had talked to him face to face in Waco, Texas, during a lengthy interview, she never realized that he was the same person accused in the Oklahoma City bombing.

Michelle said the young man she interviewed "was not a monster." According to authorities, the man accused in the Oklahoma City bombing was so upset about Waco he had become obsessed with revenge. She said that Tim didn't seem unusually upset or angry about what was happening at Waco. He certainly didn't like what the government agents were doing to the Christian men, women, and children members of the Mt. Carmel church and he absolutely disagreed with the BATF's tactic of illegally using the U.S. military on U.S. citizens.

I think it would be safe to assume that any rational, thinking, informed person could not disagree with Tim's opinion that what happened to the Christian citizens in the church in Waco was, at the very least, a national disgrace.

Don't you think that enough information has surfaced about the intentional lies and false accusations told by the BATF concerning drug manufacturing, illegal weapons, and child abuse at the Mt. Carmel church that we should all be more than a little upset about what happened in Waco. They told those lies so they could use the resources of the U.S. military to murder innocent U.S. citizens.

Anyone who has not been asleep for the past four years and who was not directly or indirectly responsible should be outraged about the slaughter at Waco, Ruby Ridge — and now, Oklahoma City. Even those who were directly or indirectly responsible for these slaughters should be outraged by their own actions and they should be begging God for forgiveness. America cannot and will not forgive you for your evil deeds. We can only hold you accountable ... and we will. ♦

"What a tangled web we weave when first we practice to deceive."
— **The feds?**

CHAPTER 21: THE DECKER CONNECTION?

Time magazine explained how, back in 1988, I had talked of blowing up a federal building in Oklahoma City. They mentioned that I had even drawn pictures of the building to be destroyed. Their accusations rested entirely on a lie told to them by the FBI and on the trail to the farm in Decker, Mich., where some radical right-wing extremist farmers plotted their acts of terrorism and practiced, until perfected, their ability to turn plant food into potent explosives which would allow them to carry out their private war against the U.S. government. We did not know if the FBI just fabricated this lie all by themselves or if someone else assisted them in that fabrication, but we believed we would find out eventually.

The problem with this Decker connection was that the only thing being manufactured in Decker was the "Decker Connection." There never were any experiments with bomb manufacturing. There certainly was some goofing around. We've never denied that and there's nothing illegal about what we did on my farm.

On Aug. 10, 1995, U.S. Attorney General Janet Reno confirmed that on world-wide television when she confessed that they had no evidence against me. Just about everyone out in farm country dinks around with firecrackers, bottle bombs, spud bazookas and goes target shoot.ing We do it for fun and, quite simply, because we can. Just because someone is target shooting out on the back-40 doesn't mean they're practicing to assassinate some political leader.

Regardless of the enormous vanities they possess and no matter how important these political leaders believe they are, that's just not the case. And just because someone puts legal household chemicals in a plastic jug and watches it expand until it goes "bang" doesn't mean he's trying to duplicate a nuclear explosion or planning to violently overthrow the government. I'm not really sure, but I'd be willing to bet that most hard-working, red-blooded American guys think that doing things like blowing firecrackers and shooting guns are much more fun than sitting around with the ladies crocheting or doing something equally stimulating such as watching pencil-necks on PBS play sandbox with a variety of

50-dollar words, discussing one of their personal little issues that nobody really cares about. Not that there's anything wrong with 50-dollar words and liberal issue discussions, but that's just not a popular pastime out here in the country.

At any rate, there was never any talk in 1988 about the Murrah Building in Oklahoma City or any drawing of that building. The first time I'd ever heard of the existence of the Murrah Building was after the bombing. The FBI's "anonymous witness" who allegedly said I drew pictures of the Murrah Building and made statements about blowing it up remained a mystery until recently. I really didn't believe the person ever existed. I thought the entire story had to be a lie made up by the FBI to deceive the public into believing that they actually had incriminating evidence against me and that I had either devised or was somehow involved in the plot to destroy the Murrah Building. I didn't have the foggiest idea who might tell the feds such a tale.

If it had been true, I would have known with whom I had that particular conversation. Since it was not true, how could I determine with whom I did not have a particular conversation which never took place? Obviously, I could not. When the FBI's "302" evidence forms were finally released to the defense teams, and after some of the information started circulating in the media, a really interesting issue surfaced. The FBI told reporters that there were two witnesses who made incriminating accusations against me which, in turn, prompted them to initiate a raid on my farm and to arrest me.

That sounded convincing until the truth finally surfaced. It seems that one of their "anonymous witnesses" on whose testimony the feds based their reason for the raid and for my unlawful incarceration, didn't make his statement against me until five days after the raid! Now correct me if I'm wrong, but I was always under the impression that the "probable cause" and "oath and affirmation" came before the warrant. It would appear as if the FBI got caught in a "probable-cause lie" in this particular instance because they explained that this anonymous witness' statement constituted a legitimate excuse to raid me. They were to have used this anonymous witness against Terry and Tim as well by laying the foundation for the conspiracy on the farm in Decker.

Once the identity of their witnesses was known and after the FBI cleaned the egg off its face, it dropped at least one of their anonymous witnesses like a hot potato determining that his testimony was no longer credible. You would have thought that FBI agents would have tried to determine if their witnesses were credible before they raided my farm, put me in a federal penitentiary for a month, installed their electronic collar for almost three more months, and just generally destroyed my life and my reputation, not only locally and nationally, but world-wide as well.

Their other "anonymous informant" has a history of making false accusations against me. Had one of the FBI agents taken 10 minutes of his or her precious time to check out Kelly's track record of vengeance concerning "yours truly," it would have become obvious to all but the simplest of minds that she had a vendetta against me. The FBI had no probable cause to initiate a raid on my farm and no lawful reason to arrest me. A "lie" or a vendetta is not probable cause. The person or persons who told lies about me should be very concerned. Criminal penalties for perjury can be severe.

The FBI even leaked information to the media suggesting that an anonymous source testified before the grand jury to make those claims against me. Now, if I'm not mistaken, lying to the grand jury is felony perjury. As a matter of fact, I believe lying to the FBI is also considered a felony. You should be real worried, FBI informants.

The FBI seems to have conveniently forgotten those accusations and no longer mention the "rock-solid witnesses" they were supposed to have had.   Now that the FBI knows their informant(s) were lying wouldn't they have to charge that person or persons with felonies? I've always denied those charges because they were untrue, but I never made a big deal about it. I knew the approximate dates to which they were referring and I knew exactly what I was doing on or around those dates. We just waited for the prosecutors and anonymous witness to make the mistake of committing themselves to a specific date and that was it. They stuck their own feet in their mouths. I have absolute proof of my whereabouts on the dates in question so their allegations and accusations were proven to be completely false.

On those exact dates my ex-wife once again displayed her vindictive personality by making false accusations against me. She told lies about me and tried to get me into trouble to keep me from seeing our son. She actually accused me of molesting my own son! That seems to be a very popular and convenient way to destroy a persons reputation. It was the first time in my life that I was treated like a criminal. I took two lie detector tests and passed them both. She refused to take one! Eventually, after several months, she also agreed to take a polygraph test and guess what! The "friend of the court" refused to show me the results of her test. Gee, I wonder why.

Although the stigma of the accusations about child molestation can never be erased, I opted to not file a civil suit against Kelly to spare our son Chase the inevitable emotional turmoil he would have undoubtedly endured. Even though I had a very strong case of liable and slander against her, and even though it may have taught Kelly a hard and expensive lesson about making false accusations against someone, the pain that Chase would have endured just wasn't worth it. Apparently Kelly did not feel the same compassion or have the same consideration for Chase's emotional well-being. She couldn't have ever imagined in her wildest dreams that those lies about me in 1988 would prove to be my air-tight alibi against the allegations that she and other people may have made about me in 1995. What goes around comes around!

Anyway, so much for their anonymous witness who has yet to be prosecuted for perjury and who has never had the guts to make those accusations against me, face to face. I've been waiting two years for the FBI to bring its witness forward to accuse me in person. I'd just like the FBI to mention this witness again. Come on, guys. Inquiring minds want to see your witness. These guys and their "witnesses" get away with telling so many lies that it absolutely boggles the mind.

Which brings us around to the whole point of the Decker un-connection. The FBI's entire case hinged on the conspiracy beginning here on my farm in Decker, Mich. The fertilizer. The fuel oil. The violently radical Nichols brothers. A gun-happy Tim McVeigh. Our ties to right-wing paramilitary militia groups. Our hatred of the government and our defiance of the law.

The hinge obviously started squeaking real bad when the conspiracy accusations were proven to be false. There was no ammonium nitrate fertilizer here on the farm, only calcium nitrate which cannot be converted into an explosive. Almost everything I own runs on diesel fuel/fuel oil so I had lots on hand. Yep, Terry and I are brothers. So what? Tim's a friend who stayed here on occasion. So what, again? There are no ties to any militia groups or any other groups, except the Organic Farmers group. We have no hatred of the government, just an insistence on their compliance with the law of the land, the U.S. Constitution.

Actually, the government's hinge broke right here in Decker before they even got swinging. Do you realize how important it is to this case of conspiracy that Janet Reno confessed to the world that there was no evidence here on my farm? This is where they said it all started. Now, they admit that it didn't. This is where the feds said we gained all that knowledge and experience in ANFO bomb manufacturing which all of the experts say is necessary to get effective results from an ANFO explosion.

Now, they admit that we never made any bombs here. This is where they spent five days and millions of dollars finding bottle caps and fragments of road debris in my driveway that were supposed to be shrapnel from a bomb. Now, they admit that it wasn't. I'm the guy who they said planned it. Now, they admit that I didn't. This "Decker Connection" was what tied their whole outrageous story together and made it believable to an unknowing public. This is where they interviewed some paranoid and/or reasonably unstable people in an attempt to give their fairy tale some degree of validity. This was the link that kept their chain from falling apart. This link is broken now because it was nothing more than a paper fabrication. A well planned fabrication but, unfortunately for the planners, things didn't quite go as well as they anticipated.

"What a tangled web we weave when first we practice to deceive." That should be the new motto of our government investigators because they are getting tangled in their own web of deceit. THEY HAVE NO CASE!

You know, they particularly made an extensive search of my driveway and front yard "looking for evidence" for the sake of the media. The whole raid was staged for the media's benefit and for "show business." Our farm is on a state highway. If we were really practicing bomb manufacturing or some other illegal activity, wouldn't you think we'd be doing it out back somewhere, maybe behind the barn or something? Of course, it is somewhat of a problem getting the news camera crews and trucks back there and we are considered dumb farmers, so we probably did all of our practicing out real close to the state highway so that the thousands of motorists passing by everyday could witness us practicing our terrorist activities.

The driveway and the front yard next to the road must have been where we blew off all of those atomic bomb equivalents because that's where the FBI spent all of their time searching and, like any other government agency, they would never waste time and, consequently, taxpayer's money needlessly. •

MAY 8, 1995 $2.95

TIME

EXCLUSIVE
Yeltsin on Chechnya,
His Health and Clinton

How Dangerous Are They?

An inside look at America's antigovernment zealots

Photo courtesy *Time* magazine

One week after the famous "The Face of Terror" cover featuring the already-convicted-in-the-media Tim McVeigh, *Time* magazine, in its May 8, 1995 issue, gushed forth more propaganda by demonizing patriotic Americans with this "inside look" at "antigovernment zealots" — as if they had something to do with the Murrah Federal Building explosions.

"Government is not reason, it is not eloquence. It is force. Like fire, it is a dangerous servant and a fearsome master."

— George Washington

CHAPTER 22: MOTIVE

There's another factor in this equation that just doesn't figure. What would our motive have been for blowing up the Murrah Building?

Now, we will admit to being outraged by the slaughtering of innocent people in Waco, Texas, at the hands of over anxious bullies and murderers working for the government, creating terror in the hearts of any Americans who may defy what the government considers to be an acceptable religious belief.

We will also admit to being outraged by the murder of Randy Weaver's skinny, little 14-year-old boy, Sammy, who was shot twice in the back by a government sniper with a silencer on his rifle while little Sammy was running for his life, one of those shots nearly severing the small boy's arm.

We'll admit to being outraged by the murder of unarmed Vicki Weaver, Randy's wife, her face blown off by Lon Horiuchi, another murdering government sniper, while she stood, unarmed, in the doorway of their home holding their eight-month-old baby girl.

Yes, Lon Horiuchi, the government sharpshooter who says it was an accident but who has only recently — and finally — been charged with involuntary manslaughter and actually faces consequences for this atrocity. The government sharpshooter who can put a hole through a quarter at 200 yards. The only accident that this FBI-hired murderer had was that he didn't kill all of the Weavers. If you think these accusations are unfounded, think about this: The morning after Vicki Weaver's murder, as she lay dead on the floor in a pool of her own blood, our great, compassionate, humanitarian government agents taunted Vicki's husband and children by using a loudspeaker to ask ... "Good morning, Mrs. Weaver. We had pancakes for breakfast ... What did you have?"

Nice public servants, huh?

When Lt. Col.James "Bo" Gritz arrived on the scene at Ruby Ridge, hoping to negotiate a truce, government helicopters were hovering over the Weavers' home. Hanging from these helicopters were 55-gallon drums of flammable liquid which they were about to drop on the house with the intention of burning everything to the ground thereby destroying the evidence of their murderous crimes forever. With no one left alive to talk, the FBI's hired assassins could make up any story they wanted. These murderers are inhuman. That kind of cold brutality is unimaginable to the human mind and yes, we are as outraged by all of these murders at the hands of government assassins as we are at the senseless killing of all the innocent people in Oklahoma City. What rational, civil human being wouldn't be? Had Col. Gritz arrived an hour later we could only speculate about Ruby Ridge, and the government's crimes would have been concealed in ashes forever.

We must not forget that this entire assault and the slaughter of the Weaver family was the direct result of trumped up charges against Randy Weaver. Randy was the victim of a federal set-up and they literally murdered some of his family because he refused to be an informant on some people who the feds perceived to be bad guys. The feds had to set an example, which is not untypical for all government agencies. They love to make examples of people who protest the activity of the feds. It is their insurance that the "fear of the Fed" will continue to grow. But talk about an attitude! These government agents are the equivalent of an overgrown spoiled child who murders his parents just because he doesn't get his own way.

Tim was also outraged by the killing of all those innocent children in Waco, Texas. This absolutely ludicrous story about Tim not liking children was another fabrication by federal investigators because he had to fit the profile of a baby-killer. It's much easier to convince the public that this guy is a terrorist who murdered kids if you can first convince them that he hates kids. That was one of the first building blocks of their character assassination of Timothy McVeigh.

We know Tim McVeigh and we know just the opposite to be true. Other friends who know him will say the same thing. Tim was always little Jason's big buddy and Tim loved the heck out of him. Tim was there helping when we tried desperately to revive Jason and was pretty tore up over Jason's untimely death. Tim always got along well with my boy, Chase, also. I know Chase really liked him because he always talked about Tim.

When you apply reason, logic, and common sense to what we know about this issue, you find yourself asking: "Why would Tim try to get back at the BATF and FBI for the killing of innocent children in Waco by doing the same cowardly, dastardly deed in Oklahoma City? Why would he try to get back at the murderers of innocent little babies by killing some other innocent person's babies?"

Quite simply, he wouldn't. What we're being told just doesn't make any sense when you really think about it. Tim is a soldier, not a terrorist. Tim is the kind of guy who would face an enemy head-on. He wouldn't be sneaking around sniping unsuspecting, innocent people like many agents from all the governments in the world, including ours, are notorious for doing.

By the way, government investigators tried to cover their behinds on this preposterous lie about hating children by saying that Tim confessed to the Oklahoma City bombing to two other inmates who were being held in the same jail. Tim allegedly told them that he bombed the building, but didn't know there was a day-care center in the Murrah Building. It sounded like a feasible excuse, until it was discovered that the two inmates weren't even in the same jail or even in the same county as Tim. These guys had never laid eyes on Tim McVeigh and most definitely never had any conversation with him. And can you imagine this alleged name-rank-and-serial-number, hard-core-prisoner-of-war type guy confessing to two total strangers? It seems as if the propagandists always try to leave an opening for escape after spreading their disinformation and FLEXIBLE FACTS!. Really, all they are doing is trying to lie their way out of a lie, and they will eventually have to lie their way out of that lie and so on and so on. That's why they're getting caught again and again and again.

And if McVeigh was trying to get back at the FBI for their burning of the church in Waco, why didn't he? There were no FBI offices in the Murrah Building. The FBI offices are about five miles away. Why wasn't that office bombed if it really was revenge for Waco? Bob Ricks, the FBI chief who was in charge of the murdering, gassing, burning, and bulldozing of those innocent men, women, and babies in Waco worked in that office five miles away when the bombing of the Murrah Building took place. He was in charge of the total destruction of evidence by completely destroying and burning the Branch Davidian church in an attempt to keep the truth about the Waco massacre from ever being discovered — which brings us to another point not often reported by mainstream media.

It has been reported that most of the records concerning the Waco massacre were housed in the Murrah Building. Needless to say, those records were destroyed in the explosions. Shouldn't we at least consider who might benefit by the destruction of the records on the Waco assault? WHO BENEFITS by destroying the records that would prove the BATF was lying about the alleged drug laboratory, illegal weapons, and child abuse at the Mt. Carmel Church in Waco, Texas? WHO BENEFITS from the burning and bulldozing of the evidence in the wooden clapboard, simple frame church so preposterously labeled a "compound"? Do you think David Koresh and the members of the Mt. Carmel Church might have benefitted by the lies, the cover-up, or the destruction of evidence which would prove that there was no drug lab or illegal weapons? Do you think they benefitted by being brutally murdered? Do you think Tim McVeigh's alleged "cause" may have benefitted by the destruction of records that would incriminate government agents responsible for the Waco murders?

These are all legitimate questions which need to be addressed if government prosecutors really believe that McVeigh's motive for this act of terrorism was revenge for their murders at the Branch Davidian church in Waco, Texas.

We also have to consider the excuse we have been handed explaining that Tim didn't know that the FBI offices were not in that building. They say he didn't know there was a day-care center in the building. He didn't know there were no BATF agents there that were involved in the Waco massacre. He didn't know that the Waco records may have been stored there. He didn't know that the Gulf War Syndrome records may have been stored there. He sure didn't know very much for knowing so much did he?

Considering the amount of research he was supposed to have done on his alleged target, he sure didn't know very much about his alleged target, did he? If the FBI's allegations were true about McVeigh, he could have answered the most important of these unknowns simply by looking in an Oklahoma City phone book. Of course, no terrorist who was going to such extremes planning his act of terrorism down to the very last detail would ever think to look in the phonebook making certain that his target was really, his target, would he?

Getting back at the BATF for Waco is a really stupid argument. There were few BATF agents stationed in the Murrah Building, and it has been reported that none were inside at the time of the bombing, although there may have been a few BATF employees. Not one of the BATF agents who should have been in the Murrah Building was involved in the slaughter at Waco, so what was the point? It sure sounded good to the press and, ultimately, to a vengeful public. But when you evaluate the entire situation objectively, bringing revenge for Waco into the equation, it makes no sense at all.

Again, it has been reported that the bombing actually destroyed pertinent, incriminating records concerning the Waco massacre, possibly keeping much of the truth from ever being widely known, which would lead one to suspect that the beneficiaries of the bombing could have been the FBI (Bob Ricks) and the BATF and not some independent terrorists trying to get back at an abusive government. When you apply common sense, this bombing did more to enhance the abusive and intrusive powers of government than any other single incident in the history of this country, particularly when you consider that this bombing took place on the second anniversary of the burning of Waco allowing the feds to point the finger at the militia and other "home-grown" right-wing Christian extremists.

And, since it happened on April 19, it would certainly appear to the thinking person that whoever planned this act of terrorism wanted us to believe that it was in retaliation for the murders at Waco. Who might that someone be? An act of retaliation is almost always claimed by some kind of group. Otherwise, the act would be senseless and would have accomplished nothing in the mind of the terrorist. A true terrorist with a cause wants his victims to know why they've been targeted.

If you really want to find people who are capable of murdering children with no remorse and no accountability, then let's take a good long look at people who are known to have murdered children.

Do Sammy Weaver and the children and babies at Waco ring a bell? Do you remember seeing Janet Reno shed a tear for the innocent children at Waco? We sure don't. Any civilized person with an ounce of decency would've been angry and appalled at what happened to the people at the Mt. Carmel Christian church. She said she would take full responsibility for Waco, but did she? They have the death penalty in Texas, don't they? She confessed by accepting full responsibility. Considering that Ms. Reno has confessed, do we need a trial, or just a sentencing? Has she been sentenced? Has she even been charged? Did Janet Reno seem angry or appalled at the murder of the children in Waco? Any rational or civil human being with a conscience or even a touch of compassion would have been.

If Reno or Ricks ever expressed any remorse over the murders of the children at the Mt. Carmel Church, we sure haven't heard those expressions of remorse. In reality, just the opposite is true. They have lied, destroyed evidence and promoted the subhumans who actually carried out their murderous, unlawful orders.

Did the FBI or Lon Horiuchi shed a tear for Vicki and Sammy Weaver? Has Lon Horiuchi been charged? He's probably been promoted considering that many of the agents involved in the terrorist attack on Ruby Ridge have been given medals or promotions. Has he ever apologized to Randy and his daughters or even expressed any remorse for murdering their wife and mother? Has the FBI apologized for murdering their son and brother? Oh, yes, I forgot that Louis Freeh expressed his apologies to the Weavers by promoting Larry Potts to No. 2 man in the FBI as his reward for being in charge of the murderous raid on the Weaver family. Freeh must have considered these murders and Larry's "shoot on sight" order to be a job well done. Why else would Potts and the rest of his murderous clan have gotten medals and promotions?

When the Weaver case finally received national and Congressional attention, Freeh had to "withdraw" the promotion — pretend publicly to be displeased with Potts' aggressive actions, and then suspend him without pay. In reality he approved of Potts' handling of the slaughter at Ruby Ridge. Freeh knew what the particulars were when he promoted Potts and that promotion showed Louis Freeh's true colors. He obviously has a viciousness that we civil humans do not understand. Only after Potts became politically unpopular did Louis rear his hypocritical head and suspend his bosom buddy.

Recently, FBI Special Agent Michael Kahoe has pled guilty to obstructing justice by destroying documents that would have been incriminating to the FBI and that may have helped Randy Weaver's attorneys prove him innocent. (He was found innocent even without this evidence.) This is obviously another case of withholding and destroying evidence in a criminal trial with the intention of convicting an innocent person.

Four other FBI officials who were involved in this case have been suspended and may yet face indictment if Kahoe survives to testify against them. None of these incidents involve only one rogue special agent. Considering that there may be five or more "officials" involved in this one crime, there also had to be numerous field agents who actually perpetrated the physical crime against our Citizens and then many other agents who either looked the other way or were willing to lie about what they saw to protect the Company's butt.

If there were five known officials involved, you can bet your bottom dollar that there are many other higher officials in the agency for whom those five will be sacrificed. In light of this most recent "confession," that the Feds routinely participate in this kind of criminal activity is no longer an arguable issue for anyone who is not incurrably ignorant. The one thing we do not know is just how many of them will eventually be caught and brought to trial for their crimes against the citizens of this nation.

After learning these facts can anyone even pretend to believe that Louis Freeh put Larry Potts on the chopping block because of Louis' high moral or ethical standards? One could easily conclude that Freeh, the Director of the FBI, promoted his buddy Larry Potts because he violated peoples Rights and had them murdered. Freeh knew what had transpired during the raid on the Weavers. The FBI concealed the evidence from the people and from Congress, not from their Director. The only reasons Louis eventually dumped his friend Larry was to cover his own rear end and to put on a phony front. Larry was just another victim of a government superior following the CYOA code. Because of the Weaver trial and lawsuit some of this cover-up was made public and the pressure was on to pass the buck.

This kind of mentality is downright dangerous to any free society. They were more than willing to murder a skinny, little, 80-pound, 14-year-old boy who was trying to save his own life by running away from the gunfire of a government sniper. Another government sniper was more than willing to blow the face off of an unarmed mother holding her baby. They were preparing to burn to death Randy and his three young daughters to eliminate any witnesses and to destroy any incriminating evidence.

They were and are willing to do all of these things and more. They obviously do not have a moral bone in their bodies. Any of these wimps would sell out their own grandmothers to enhance their careers. If you don't think that statement is true just take a look at the current residents of the White House. The most dangerous thing any person can be in this decade is a "friend of Bill" or a former business partner of Hillary. It seems as if the lucky ones have a habit of ending up in court and eventually in jail. The unlucky ones? Well, we all know what happens to them.

Has anyone else in government apologized to the Weavers or to the survivors of the Waco massacre? Has anyone in our great, compassionate government told any of these people that they were sorry for lying to them, assassinating their characters, entrapping them, assaulting them, attempting to murder them, murdering their friends and families, burning and smashing their properties and belongings, destroying their lives, and then trying to "railroad" them in a "kangaroo court," denying them what little remnants of their Constitutional rights they were trying desperately to retain?

The survivors of the Waco massacre were tried and found not guilty by a jury of their peers. The judge then, violating his oath to uphold the Constitution, took it upon himself to find them guilty of another crime for the sake of the media. After all, someone certainly murdered those 80-plus people at the Branch Davidian church in Waco, Texas. If it wasn't the Branch Davidians, then who murdered all of those innocent men, women, and children?

All we heard on the news is that they were found guilty. Guilty of what? Guilty of assuming that they had a right to exercise their religious beliefs? Guilty of being assaulted and swarmed on by armed, masked terrorists? Guilty of being shot through the top of the head from helicopters while they sat eating their breakfasts? Maybe they were guilty of having their friends and families murdered before their very eyes or having their homes and their belongings crushed and burned by government tanks.

Perhaps they were guilty of having a phony government-sanctioned movie produced about them which aired immediately after the raid. The movie was nothing more than government propaganda and was obviously produced before the fact which indicates that the purpose of the movie was to sway public opinion against the Christian congregation of the church in Waco. We lost all respect for the actors in that phony movie. In our opinion, their actions were just another example of selling your integrity for a paycheck, if they ever had any to sell.

Were the Branch Davidians guilty of being the victims of intentional false accusations of drug manufacturing which, had it been true, would've made it "legal" to use military advisors, weapons, and finances to assist the BATF and FBI in their acts of terrorism on the Mt. Carmel church? (These accusations were not true, but the Feds used the military anyway.)

Were they guilty of being gunned down by FBI sharpshooters while trying to escape the blazing inferno? Were the children and babies in Mt. Carmel guilty of being tortured by the feds because they experienced excruciating pain for many hours from suffocation and cyanide poisoning resulting from the CS gas that the Feds pumped into their dwellings for six hours or more? The use of that same gas against our enemies in WAR is a direct violation of international law. Were these people and their children guilty of being psychologically tortured by the Feds who used loud noises, bright lights and annoying chants which were directed at the Mt. Carmel Church 24 hours a day for days on end

These people were actually guilty of all these things. They were terrorized and murdered by terrorists! They were depicted by a phony made-for-TV movie as ambushing (?) the BATF. Is anyone in charge of these national "police" agencies rational, civil — or even human? We really have our doubts. Under these circumstances, we should all have some very serious doubts about how much longer we, as a nation, can tollerate this kind of inhumane treatment of our citizens by *de facto* government assassins.

You know, the President even lied on national television about the people in the Mt. Carmel Church ambushing the BATF. Just give that "ambush" accusation some serious thought. These people were living in a clapboard, wood frame structure. Anyone who has ever fired a high-powered rifle, particularly with military ammo, knows that a bullet from a high-powered rifle would go completely through those buildings without even slowing down, and a military assault weapon could also go through a few people on the way.

Many of the people inside the church buildings were shot through the walls and through the roof from helicopters. Please tell us Mr. President, how could civilians, living in a clapboard structure which would provide no protection whatsoever from even a small caliber military assault rifle, initiate an ambush while they were completely surrounded by a hundred Ninja-suited BATF agents, dressed in full battle gear and armed with state-of-the-art fully automatic military assault weapons and helicopters?

Obviously, Mr. President knows nothing about doing battle. If the people in the Mt. Carmel church actually ambushed the BATF, there would have been 50 dead agents within the first ten seconds of the battle and the rest would've been killed while trying to retreat. That's what happens in an ambush, Mr. President. It's a turkey shoot. Just think about it. The suggestion that the Branch Davidians ambushed the BATF is absolutely ignorant, Mr. President, if you just apply some logic.

Of course, Mr. President wouldn't know that because his lack of courage forced him to run away and save his pathetic hide while other courageous young men accepted their responsibility and tried to defend the South Vietnamese citizens from communist aggression. And of course, Mr. President was very serious and appeared extremely sincere when he told this preposterous lie. He was much better than the actors in the made-for-TV movie about Waco.

Just think about this ambush lie. Please, just think about it. When viewing the *Waco: The Big Lie* videos or even a news video of the assault on Waco, you can plainly see the BATF agents getting their jollies off poppin' shots at the buildings whenever and wherever they want, but you can't see anything coming back at them. The BATF didn't knock on the door to serve a warrant. They could have done that with two guys in suits. With well-armed terrorists they assaulted a church in the [u]nited States of America and just started shooting. There is no doubt about it. It is a matter of record. There was an ambush all right, and then there was a turkey shoot. More than 80 dead Branch Davidians can attest to that.

Looking at this Oklahoma bombing situation from a common-sense approach, let's draw some analogies. If you have a known rapist living in your neighborhood and the woman three doors down got raped, whose door would the police knock on first? If you had a person living on your street with a long record of breaking and entering, and there was a string of B&Es on your street, whose house should the police go to first? If you had a known child molester living down the block and, God forbid, your child got molested, whom would you think may be responsible? If you had known terrorists in your midst, and an unconscionable act of terrorism was committed on innocent people, would you start investigating those terrorists, or would you go and round up a young, clean cut, highly decorated war veteran with *no record*, a 40-year-old husband and father with *no record*, and a farmer with cow poop on his boots and *no record?*

It may even be a good idea to have the terrorists carry out the investigation, but then again, maybe they are. We could go on and on with these morbid analogies, but we think that we've made our point. All we ask is that you objectively evaluate the information we're passing along to you. OBSTRUCTION OF JUSTICE! DESTRUCTION OF EVIDENCE! WHO BENEFITS?

Another preposterous motive for McVeigh allegedly blowing up the Murrah Building which has been presented to an eager media by our agents of deceit is that it was an act of revenge for the execution of Richard Snell. Before his murder conviction, Snell was a resident of Elohim City, a religious separatist community in eastern Oklahoma. He was executed on the evening of April 19, 1995, about a dozen hours after the Oklahoma City bombing. Many rumors circulated alleging that Snell, during his final hours of life, said that the bombing in Oklahoma City was done in retalliation for his execution. Strangely enough, everyone present with Richard Snell on his final day said that he made no such statement. And to suggest that Tim McVeigh would set off a bomb that had the potential of murdering hundreds of innocent men, women and children to get back for the execution of a man who, in all likelyhood, he had hardly if ever heard of is even more ridiculous than the story about his getting back at the BATF for Waco.

Keep in mind that when the Snell ordeal began in the '80s Tim was just a teen-ager. Richard Snell would not have been someone who Tim had even heard about and he certainly wouldn't have considered him a martyr if he had heard about him. During the entire time that Tim lived here and hung around here at the farm, he never mentioned Richard Snell or Elohim City. The first time we heard about Elohim City was from independent journalist J.D. Cash in the months after the bombing.

There is another thing that has always bothered us about this story. Tim was born, raised and confirmed Catholic. Would someone please explain to us just exactly what the religious doctrine of Catholocism has in common with the religious doctrine of Richard Snell and the religious separatists at Elohim City? What would have changed Tim's religious beliefs so drastically in such a short time? Would you care to answer that question Mr. or Mrs. Prosecutor?

It has been suggested by Morris Dees of the Southern Poverty Law Center and many other uninformed, do-gooder, talking heads in the media that, because of the way they dress and train and because of their appreciation for the Constitution, specifically the Second Amendment, the militia have a propensity to commit violence and acts of terrorism.

Let's give that some thought. On one hand, we have small groups of mostly middle-age, patriotic Citizens who train a little and talk a bunch, taking somewhat seriously their Constitutional responsibility to be a part of a militia established to defend the citizens of this Country. As a group, none of them have ever committed an act of aggression against the government or anyone else. They have legal weapons only stored in their homes and at the target range. They only carry and use weapons when they are training with other militia members. Most of the weapons owned by these militia members would fall into the category of hunting rifles and shotguns, none of which are fully automatic.

These militia groups consist of plumbers, mechanics, engineers, secretaries, electricians, accountants, housewives and include all races and nationalities in their memberships. Few are in "fighting condition."

On the other hand, we have a large group of individuals who have made it their profession to become experts in the use of weapons and explosives. They can show us no Constitutional provision for their existence. They routinely take part in assaulting unsuspecting citizens, often times resulting in the deaths of those citizens. They all wear black ninja suits and many of them even wear masks to hide their identities while taking part in activities which parallel the actions of organized criminals and terrorists. They are trained to kill people and to destroy things and one could reasonably conclude that they may have a tendency to enjoy those activities since they are taking part in those activities as a resuslt of their own volition. They always carry fully automatic assault weapons, often times concealed. It has been reported that there is much racism among their ranks.

If Mr. Dees believes in his own logic, then he must consider BATF agents to be extremely radical, militant, armed and dangerous and, unquestionably, potential terrorists. Apparently Mr. Dees does not believe in his own logic because he sees nothing wrong with the uncon-stitutional activities of the BATF. He obviously harbors contempt for our Constitution because he has made a career out of trying to undermine certain Constitutional guarantees and has gone to great lengths to propagandize and discredit the militia. Just what exactly is the basis for your logic, Mr. Dees? ●

"There were at least five men [involved in the bombing] ID'd by witnesses as being on the scene the morning of the bombing."
— **Hoppy Heidelberg, grand juror**

Chapter 23: John Doe No.2 — Iraqi Connection?

Another point of interest that deserves serious consideration is John Doe No. 2 and his alleged link to Tim McVeigh. Many of the prosecution's eyewitnesses claim they saw a person who looked like McVeigh at certain locations and at certain times also claim that he was accompanied by a man who appeared to be of Middle Eastern descent, whom we now all know as John Doe No. 2.

Some eyewitnesses claim to have seen McVeigh with more than one Middle Eastern companion. At least one witness says a person matching McVeigh's description was speaking with two Middle Eastern-looking men in a foreign language. Other witnesses saw a man fitting John Doe No. 2's description driving away from the scene of the bombing. They say he was driving quite fast and that he was in a brown pickup truck. A motel manager just a mile down the road from the Dreamland Motel near Junction City, Kan., reported to the FBI that a man fitting John Doe No. 2's description had stayed there two days before the bombing. He had a foreign name, spoke broken English, and was driving a Ryder truck. He had a companion who stayed in a different room and checked in under the name of "Nichols." We know that this particular Nichols was not me, and was not Terry. Does it look like someone may have been contemplating some kind of a setup here? Has the FBI followed that lead? Why is Terry in prison?

Some investigators claim to know John Doe No. 2's identity. They say he was a soldier in Saddam Hussein's elite Republican Guard and came here as part of the Iraqi POW resettlement program that began during the Bush Administration but was actually carried out by the Clinton administration. It seems that this controversial program brought thousands of Iraqis to America over the past few years. Keep in mind that since this was a "POW" resettlement program it stands to reason that all of the "resettlers" are former Iraqi soldiers who were trying to kill American soldiers but were defeated and captured. It has been reported that the man investigators believe to be John Doe No. 2 was not only a member of the Iraqi dictator's elite Republican Guard but was specially trained in demolitions and explosives. If this information that we have about John Doe No. 2 is true, and we have no reason to believe that it isn't, it just might raise some very interesting issues for speculation and might also pose some very serious questions.

Also lending to one's curiosity concerning a possible Middle Eastern connection is a memo from the U.S. Marshall's Service dated March 22, 1995, stating in part: "There is sufficient threat potential to request that a heightened level of security awareness and caution be implemented at all Marshall's Service protected facilities nationwide."

Robert Rudolph in and article written for the *Newark* (N.J.) *Star Ledger* goes on to say: "U.S. law enforcement authorities have obtained information that Islamic terrorists may be planning suicide attacks against federal courthouses and government installations in the United States. (source: *Relevance*)."

Now that's very interesting, isn't it? The U.S. Marshall's Service said there was "sufficient threat potential" from Islamic terrorists just four weeks before the bombing of the Federal Building in Oklahoma City. From where did that "threat potential" originate?

Motel managers saw Middle Eastern men in the area with a Ryder truck. Many eyewitnesses in downtown Oklahoma City saw Middle Eastern-looking men in or around the Murrah Building. Some even saw a Middle Eastern man exiting the Ryder truck in front of the building just before the explosions. Some witnesses saw a Middle Eastern-looking man in a brown pickup truck driving away from the scene of the crime. Why is it politically incorrect to suggest that Middle Eastern terrorists may have been involved in blowing up the Murrah Building?

It seems perfectly acceptable for Bill Clinton to give the order to bomb Iraq because that nation is having trouble with a rebellious Kurdish dissident population within its borders, but we dare not imply that those same people who George Bush and Bill Clinton have ordered to be blown to pieces and killed by the thousands — many of them innocent civilians and children — are capable of terrorism as a means of retaliation against the United States government. How else might the defeated, humiliated, angry and irrational Iraqi government and Iraqi soldiers retaliate against the United States government?

Here's what we see as a brief summary of the situation. Let's just say we have an elite, dedicated, extremely loyal, Iraqi soldier otherwise known John Doe No. 2. We would have to guess that, in Iraq, he would be considered a member of some kind of Special Forces unit. We send members of our armed forces (Tim McVeigh) over there to blow the living hell out of Iraq (John Doe No. 2) because they're (John Doe No. 2) raping and pillaging the people of Kuwait. Our guys (Tim McVeigh) not only beat the snot out of Saddam Hussein's elite Republican Guard (John Doe No. 2), but embarrass them (John Doe No. 2) badly in front of their friends and family causing them (John Doe No. 2) to run and hide and eventually surrender, because it wasn't even a good fight and because their primary tactic of warfare is TERRORIZING INNOCENT PEOPLE WHO CAN'T FIGHT BACK.

After being beaten and totally humiliated in front of all of his friends and family and taken as a POW, John Doe No. 2 is then paid by the Clinton Administration to come to this country (why?) to relocate and live happily ever after, never to feel any animosity towards the vicious, evil Satans (U.S.) who totally destroyed his beloved country, humiliated him, kept him in prison, killed his friends and family and, stopped him and his terrorist buddies from raping and pillaging and having all sorts of unconscionable fun and from becoming the baddest dudes in the world. It's unimaginable that this dedicated, former, elite Iraqi soldier could harbor enough vengeance towards the U.S. to ever become a terrorist in the U.S. murdering at least 168 Americans, especially after the Iraqis (John Doe No. 2) vowed to eventually annihilate the American Satans (Timothy McVeigh) and reign victorious in front of their country-men and the whole Iraqi nation.

So, the feds have dropped their reward and aren't even pursuing the investigation against John Doe No. 2. Why should they? They've got their men — Terry Nichols and Timothy McVeigh. Terry's a 40-year-old husband and father with no record, an impeccable character, and has no training in demolitions or chemicals. Tim's a decorated American patriot and war veteran with no record and no training in demolitions or chemicals who knocked the hell out of John Doe No. 2. It's obvious. Terry and Tim are much more likely candidates to become murdering terrorists in their own country than any POW from Iraq named John Doe No. 2 who just happened to be specially trained in demolitions and explosives!

See, FBI agents are not the only smart investigators around here. We've got it all figured out. Considering Bush's and Clinton's affiliations with the CIA, and considering that since the end of the proverbial "cold war" (thanks to Ronald Reagan) the CIA has had little purpose for existing, is it unreasonable to ask if maybe, just maybe, this Iraqi POW relocation program was implemented intentionally to create an opportu-nity for potential terrorist attacks?

Understand, we're not necessarily saying that we think that's the case. We're just asking some honest questions and we'd like some honest answers for a change.

Another minor thing that's been bothering us is this alleged relationship between McVeigh and these Middle Eastern guys from Iraq. Tim is a Gulf War veteran. If he was going to take up with anyone, you would think that Iraqi soldiers would be the last guys on the planet whom he would befriend. We think that government investigators have also finally realized that mistake in their elaborate setup and are now denying John Doe No. 2's existence even though everyone in Oklahoma City and the surrounding area has seen him. Again, one of the eyewitnesses claims to have seen a McVeigh look-alike speaking in a foreign language with two Middle Eastern looking men. There are a lot of people who resemble Tim McVeigh (at least two or three were seen in or around the Murrah Building) and we know for certain that Tim speaks only one language — English.

It has been suggested by some investigators that much evidence exists indicating the possibility of McVeigh's involvement with a special government undercover group, or at least that Tim thought he was. It is suspected, because of many things Tim said and because of letters he'd sent to his sister, that he had a real problem with some of the "assignments" which were required of this special government team. Because of his "problem" with the covert and often times illegal activity in which many secret Government agencies engage, Tim wanted out. Could his refusal to take part in the more disgusting of these illegal activities have prompted his "leaders" to set him up to get rid of him?

It could well be that Tim thought he was on the inside and on the *right* side of a sting operation designed to bust potential Middle Eastern terrorists conspiring to blow up a federal building. If Tim really was seen with Middle Eastern-looking men, this would certainly explain why he may have seemingly befriended them. It would also explain many of the other inexplicable coincidences surrounding this investigation. •

FBI leaks to the media may have "compromised the integrity of the proceeding, the conclusions of the grand jurors and the legality of the indictment."
— **Stephen Jones** (Source: *Media Bypass*)

Chapter 24: The Grand Jury

Some time ago Stephen Jones, Tim's attorney, and Michael Tigar, Terry's attorney, filed motions to dismiss the indictments against their clients because of accusations by a person sitting on the federal grand jury in the Oklahoma City bombing case. There are charges of prosecutorial misconduct and of a possible cover-up. At least one of the grand jurors involved in handing down the indictments against Nichols and McVeigh, and some witnesses who testified in the case, have spoken out about numerous discrepancies in the government's case concerning the bombing suspects. Federal prosecutors refused the grand jury's request to interview witnesses and to ask questions about John Doe No. 2, according to one grand juror, during a lengthy, off-the-record telephone conversation with a reporter. OBSTRUCTION OF JUSTICE? I'm certain that most legal experts would agree that a grand jury has the power to subpoena and interview witnesses, independent of the prosecution's wishes or instructions.

Concerning this issue, Prof. Peter Tague of the Georgetown School of Law said in an interview with Lawrence Myers of *Media Bypass:* "The government cannot impinge on the independence of the grand jury. It seems to me an argument could be made that if a U.S. attorney refused to help a grand jury subpoena a witness, and instead urged jurors to consider evidence that had already been presented, one could conclude that the U.S. attorney had infringed on the protection of the grand jury."

The FBI, in their attempt to avoid the issue of John Doe No. 2, claimed that John Doe No. 2 was a soldier at Fort Riley, Kans., who had no connection to the bombing. This diversion by the prosecution to deny the existence of John Doe No. 2 aroused suspicions among some of the jurors. Not one of the witnesses who identified John Doe No. 2, and there are many, was subpoenaed by the prosecution to testify before the grand jury. John Doe No. 2 was not only identified by the people at the rental agency who dispatched the Ryder truck, but by almost every other witness who has allegedly identified McVeigh as being in the vicinity of the Murrah Building and everywhere else.

Since these same witnesses presumably would have helped solidify the prosecution's case against McVeigh, isn't it reasonable to assume that the prosecutors would use them and every other witness available to them? Since they did not use certain witnesses, that action may lead one to believe that these witnesses may know something that the prosecutors did not want revealed before the grand jury.

One of these witnesses, a survivor of the bombing named Daina Bradley, who was standing at the front window of the Murrah Building, said she saw only one person exiting the Ryder truck and it wasn't Timothy McVeigh. The man was olive-complected, with dark wavy hair, and he was wearing a baseball cap. She said that he somewhat resembled one of the composites of John Doe No. 2. He first went to the back of the truck and then he walked away just a few minutes before the explosion, she explained. Believe it or not, she wasn't called to testify before the Grand Jury! That's very interesting, isn't it? OBSTRUCTION OF JUSTICE?

Bradley stuck with this version of events for months, even years, after the bombing until suddenly changing her testimony during the McVeigh trial — stating for the first time ever that a second man who "could have been" Timothy McVeigh was also seen leaving the Ryder truck just prior to the explosion.

Some freelance journalists, including J.D. Cash, contend that federal agents who met Bradley at the airport attempted to sway her testimony in an effort to ensure she mentioned a second man leaving the Ryder truck. Cash and others have concluded that some kind of witness tampering had taken place, but the allegations never received widespread notice.

Clearly, however, Bradley was shaken on the witness stand when she finally blurted out her altered — and confusing — version of events.

Keep in mind that this young lady lost two children, her mother, and a leg in the blast, so she certainly has a personal reason for wanting the perpetrators of this crime apprehended and punished. It is unlikely that anyone has endured more suffering from this tragedy than this beautiful, courageous young woman. She had long said that she did not see Tim exiting the truck, though she did not have a clear view of the opposite side of the Ryder truck. It has been rumored that the FBI had attempted to pressure Ms. Bradley into changing her story, even long before the McVeigh trial.

The final altered testimony was considered by most observers to be the single most damaging element to McVeigh's defense.

Another potential suspect appeared in the news shortly after the bombing. Enter Steven Colbern, a stocky built man who somewhat resembles the descriptions given of John Doe No. 2. According to reports, Colbern's truck was photographed by chance by the video camera in Oklahoma State Trooper Charlie Hanger's police car when he pulled McVeigh over for not having a license plate. The automatic camera filmed Colbern's truck in the background while it was filming the incident with McVeigh.

This particular brown pickup pulled over and stopped along the side of the road a good distance back while McVeigh was being questioned, stayed for a moment and then drove off. It was reported in the *Detroit News* that the plate on the truck was registered to Colbern, and that the truck contained traces of ammonium nitrate when the police located it. It was later established that the brown pickup which was legally regis-tered to Colbern was in his father's backyard and had not been moved recently. However, it was not established that Colbern's license plate was not on the brown pickup which appeared in Charlie Hanger's video recording while he had McVeigh pulled over.

Since it had first been reported that the truck in Trooper Hanger's video was registered to Colbern, it is not unreasonable to assume that Colbern's plate was used on that truck. By what other method would the authorities conclude that the truck in the video was registered to a Steven Colbern, and how else would his name surface so soon after the bomb-ing?

It was also reported that Steven Colbern earned a degree in chemistry at U.C.L.A., has no known address, has given at least 10 different birth dates over the years, and was wanted on a federal firearms charge. According to authorities, he was arrested sometime during the summer of 1994 in San Bernardino, Calif., for carrying a gun with a silencer. He posted bail and skipped town. Do you recall the article in *Time* magazine which stated that to have carried out this act of terrorism would require that the terrorists have a basic understanding of chemistry?

Now let's see if we have this one figured out. Steven Colbern earned a degree in chemistry at U.C.L.A., was seen in a brown pickup truck which may have been seen at the scene of the crime and which also showed traces of ammonium nitrate. He resembles John Doe No. 2, has a tattoo, has jumped bail for a charge of carrying a gun with a silencer (we thought only government agents used silencers?) and was recorded pulling off the road in Trooper Hanger's video when McVeigh was arrested for a missing license plate and carrying a gun for which he had a permit (not for Oklahoma). It has been reported that the government wanted to make a deal with Colbern (?) for his testimony against McVeigh who was pulled over for a missing license plate, has no record, has never skipped bail, is a decorated war veteran, had no traces of bomb material on his clothing when tested by Frederick Whitehurst, an honest top FBI scientist (his clothing mysteriously showed traces after being in the FBI's possession), doesn't even vaguely resemble the original description of John Doe No. 1, has no degree in chemistry, has no experience in demolitions and has no experience in ANFO bomb manufacturing. Why is Terry in prison, and why isn't Steve Colbern? I guess we don't have this one figured out!

Another issue which raised suspicions among the grand jurors was that the FBI told them that surveillance cameras took pictures of the Ryder truck and occupants inside and outside the truck. The pictures shown to the grand jury only identified the Ryder truck and showed no one in or around the truck. There's really no absolute proof that those pictures of the truck shown to the grand jury were even taken at that location moments before the bombing. They may have been, but common sense would dictate that if they had video tapes of the truck before the bombing, they would also have videos of the persons lighting the fuse (if that ever happened) and pictures of the actual explosions. Where are those pictures?

That some bomb-related video exists is probably true. In some of the photos taken in the area after the bombing, video cameras are still visible. Don't you think it's rather peculiar that the FBI has confiscated all of the evidence from all of these recordings and has jealously guarded it? Was there something in those recordings that the FBI did not want us to see? Could it just be another part of THE GRAND COVER-UP?

Which brings us around to something that's really bothered us about the FBI claiming that they have these real live pictures. If they had real live pictures, why did they have to go around with an artist and make up a composite sketch of John Doe No. 1 and John Doe No. 2 from eyewitness descriptions? These alleged pictures are from modern surveillance camcorders so developing wouldn't be necessary. They would've had the pictures of the suspects immediately. If they really had those pictures immediately, they would have flashed them over every TV station and newspaper in the whole world and composite drawings would not have been necessary.

Of course, the real live pictures may not be of Timothy McVeigh. If they were of someone who resembled McVeigh, that could have been easily detected with modern technology. The original pictures could have been enhanced to show exactly who was exiting the Ryder truck.

Could it be that the original pictures are of someone the government would rather not identify? If that's the case, the original pictures could also be altered to show Tim McVeigh getting out of the truck. Does anyone know how long it would take to fabricate pictures to show whomever they wanted to show getting out of the truck?

Can anyone tell us if fake pictures can be positively identified or proven to be fake? We really don't know the answers to those questions. We do know that they have the technology to show anything they want to show on moving or still pictures and we have been told by people who are very knowledgeable about the subject that the technological capability exists to fabricate pictures or movies that could not be detected as fake and could pass any examination. Just look at some of the amazing special effects coming out of Hollywood recently. We personally do not know if a fake could or would go undetected. But we'd have to believe that if the technology does exist, the government has it, is using it, and will use it to prove their charges and to conceal the real evidence in this investigation.

Grand jurors openly stated on the record during court proceedings that they had suspicions about the existence of other conspirators and that government prosecutors were deliberately withholding important information that would confirm their suspicions. Why wouldn't government prosecutors want to find everyone responsible for this horrendous crime of terror and punish all of those involved to the full extent of the law? And, if it is established that they wouldn't, and apparently their questionable actions before the grand jury have established that fact, then isn't it reasonable to conclude that truth and justice are not necessarily their ultimate goal? Now that we've come to the realization that truth and justice are not their goal, then the next question we have to ask ourselves is: "What is their ultimate goal?"

When the prosecution knowingly and willingly conceals evidence from the grand jury, thereby proving that they do not want to apprehend all of the people who may have been conspirators in this crime, those actions definitely have a tendency to lead one to believe that there's something about this bombing that the FBI doesn't want the public to know. This very important fact does more to prove our suspicions of a government GRAND COVER-UP than any other single incident in this entire case with the exceptions of the premature implosion of the Murrah Building, the filling in of the crater which disallowed the defense investigators any physical evidence and the FBI's failure to disclose any of the physical evidence until after they had ample time to alter it.

Their rush to destroy the Murrah Building and bury the remaining evidence forever raised suspicions and speculations among many alert citizens. The government, via the news media, justified the premature demolition with emotional but specious arguments. The fact that defense investigators weren't allowed to remove one single speck of rubble from the bombing site for private laboratory inspection raised few eyebrows because that information was kept from the American citizens. When citizens are told about that particular aspect of the "investigation," they are appalled and shocked, to say the least, and some refuse to believe it even though it is absolutely true. Each of these actions by government prosecutors and investigators does not in itself prove a conspiracy or cover-up within their ranks.

But when we are made aware of this combined information and take the time to objectively analyze all that we know to be true, we can only conclude that something has happened here of which many people in positions of high authority are aware but do not want the public to know about. When we have demonstrated that prosecutors and investigators have, in fact, been lying, denying the existence of numerous John Does including McVeigh lookalikes, denying the existence of two other Ryder trucks, concealing evidence, destroying evidence and falsifying evidence, how on God's earth can you believe any of their accusations against Tim and Terry?

Some people investigating the bombing of the Alfred P. Murrah Federal Building have been told by employees and lab technicians at the State Medical Examiner's office that official reports being generated by their agency are being altered by the government in many different ways before these reports are released to the defense teams and before they are made public. FLEXIBLE FACTS? How can the teams of Michael Tigar and Stephen Jones possibly defend their clients if the evidence they have received has been altered by the government? If the prosecutors had any real evidence that was incriminating to Tim and Terry, then they wouldn't need to alter the evidence and the reports to help their case. Could this just be another part of THE GRAND COVER-UP? Those who are willing to go to any lengths to "win" most certainly have little, if any, integrity and do not belong in law enforcement. WHO BENEFITS by their actions? They do violence to our justice system and to our Constitution. We don't think anyone would disagree with the fact that the person holding the winning cards does not need to cheat. LOOK WHO'S CHEATING!

If the evidence indicates that prosecutors don't want all of those responsible for this crime punished, and we know they are doing everything in their power to protect some of those who are responsible and to conceal what really happened in the Murrah Building bombing, then is it unreasonable to conclude that they wouldn't care if they prosecuted and punished the wrong people? Is it too far fetched to believe that they would intentionally prosecute and punish the wrong people? Who are they trying to protect, and why are they trying to protect them?

We just can't imagine why the Justice Department would want to drop the investigation on John Does No. 2, No. 3, No. 4, No. 5 — and the John Doe No. 1 who is 5'-10" tall, weighs 185 pounds, has brownish green eyes, acne and a misshapen jaw. Can you?

Might these suspects create an embarrassing situation for the Clinton administration? Could the Clintons have inadvertently invited into this country certain men whose only focus was to create terror and mayhem in the United States? Can the government really use U. S. tax dollars to relocate our enemies into our neighborhoods? Obviously, they can. Apparently, they did. There has been some speculation that all of the John Does are really government agents. To be honest, we are no longer surprised by any factual information that surfaces about by whom this crime was actually planned or concerning the "anti-investigation" surrounding this case.

Apparently, some of these questions weighed so heavily on one grand juror's mind that he was willing to risk prosecution for breaching the secrecy of the grand jury. His name is Hoppy Heidelberg of Blanchard, Okla. This is obviously a man of admirable integrity and courage, willing to risk his own freedom, and perhaps more, to take that which his conscience tells him is the morally proper course of action. Our hats goes off to you, sir, and our hearts go out to you. We've experienced some of the obstacles you are about to face. Brace yourself for the wrath of the federal government for bucking the system, demanding your Rights, and for trying to do that which is proper and just. These actions are, unfortunately, unforgivable modern-day sins. We can assure you that we will assist you and your attorney, John DeCamp of Lincoln, Neb., with any legal means at our disposal. Your goal is our goal. We are all determined to discover the truth.

By the way, this particular juror had in his possession and used for reference, a pocket copy of the *Juror's Handbook*. This handbook is supplied by the court and it explains, without getting into a lot of details, the juror's basic rights, responsibilities, and powers. We're sure that this handbook is provided for potential Jurors to inform them of their duties as jurors thereby making it easier to fulfill their judicial obligations.

A similar *Citizens' Handbook*, one of millions in circulation, was confiscated from Jennifer McVeigh during a search of her belongings.

Within this handbook is the U.S. Constitution which includes the Declaration of Independence, the Bill of Rights, and the *Juror's Handbook* which does go into great detail properly instructing you as to your legal rights and powers while sitting on a Jury.

According to reports, the FBI identified this pocket guide to our Constitutional rights as an "extremist tract" when they confiscated it from Jennifer McVeigh! Doesn't that show us exactly what they think of our Constitutional rights? It really makes us wonder ... Did any of the FBI agents ever read it? ♦

"We have three witnesses who say that they saw a Ryder truck out at Geary Lake on [April] the 10th, 11th and 12th with a brown pickup truck and a white sedan."
> — **Independent journalist/investigator J.D. Cash confirmed later by a six-month *Denver Post* investigation**

CHAPTER 25: WITNESSES

We believe it is worth mentioning that the feds do have one solid suspect in this case. This particular suspect is the only person who has actually admitted to being involved in the conspiracy to bomb the Alfred P. Murrah Federal Building.

His name is Michael Fortier and it is reported that he claims to have cased the Murrah Building on several occasions. On one of those occasions, he and McVeigh allegedly asked for job applications while "casing" the Federal Building. It has been reported that Fortier testified before the grand jury, saying: "Me and Tim went floor to floor asking for work and picking up job applications." The media claims that this statement was leaked to them by an unnamed federal official.

Hoppy Heidelberg, the grand juror whom the prosecution tried to keep quiet, has indicated that Fortier made no such statement before the grand jury during the indictment hearings. Obviously, this appeared to be just more disinformation leaked by the feds in their attempt to sway public opinion.

There are several problems with Fortier's statements if any of them are, in fact, Fortier's statements. The first discrepancy that we will bring to your attention is the most obvious and will expose Michael Fortier's ignorance as well as his lies. The FBI realized those potential flaws in his character and that is precisely why it were so intent on using him. Fortier's having a wife and child was simply the icing on the cake for the feds. The FBI knew that having a family would make him more vulnerable, and it seized the opportunity to take advantage of what they perceived to be a weakness. The plan appears to have worked, especially with regard to Fortier's testimony at the McVeigh trial. But when you take the time to evaluate the information that Fortier allegedly gave to the FBI and compare it to all of the other evidence we have discovered, the FBI's plan kind of evaporates out of the world of logic. It is a travesty that

Fortier's testimony was taken so seriously by the jury in the McVeigh trial. Fortier's claims that he and McVeigh cased the Murrah Building prior to the bombing start falling apart when you look at other eye witness testimony that the prosecution has ignored in their attempt to incriminate Tim and Terry.

Mike Moroz, an eyewitness working at Johnny's Tire Center on 10th and Hudson in Oklahoma City approximately six blocks from the Murrah Building, said that on April 19 just a few minutes past 8:30 a.m. a man who looked like McVeigh who was driving a yellow Ryder truck approaching from the WEST pulled into the tire center asking for directions to 5th and Harvey, which is the cross-street at the northwest corner of the Murrah Building.

The employee at Johnny's said there was also a passenger in the truck who looked much like John Doe No. 2. He said that McVeigh got out of the truck to talk to him and that Tim was wearing a baseball cap backwards. The owner of Johnny's Tire Service said he remembers that the truck stayed parked in his lot for about ten minutes after asking directions which would place the Ryder truck in his lot until approximately 8:42 a.m.

This time frame is very important. It doesn't appear as if the employee at the tire center or the owner has any vested interest one way or another ,so we have no reason to doubt that they believe they are telling the truth. Brian Marshall, another employee at Johnny's Tire, stated that he thought the truck had an extension over the cab and definitely did not have any doors on the sides of the box.

Chuck Allen, a close friend, fellow patriot and producer of the video, *Oklahoma City: What Really Happened?*, recently discovered another eyewitness named David Snider. Dave works in "Bricktown," an older section of the city EAST of the Murrah Building. This eyewitness claims to have seen a Ryder truck east of the crime scene at approximately the same time as Mike Moroz saw his Ryder truck northwest of the Murrah Building. He claims that a man with medium-length, dark hair, parted in the middle, and possibly slightly wavy or curly, was driving. The man could have been Mexican or Middle Eastern, but Dave said that it was definitely not John Doe No. 2. He also said that Tim McVeigh was the passenger. Snider said that the truck definitely did not have an extension over the cab, had a 20-to-24-foot box, and he was absolutely positive that it had a side door.

It has been suggested that one or more of these witnesses had to be mistaken about the exact time, and that is always a possibility. One or more of them could have been mistaken by a few minutes. But when you are aware that the Ryder truck approached Johnny's Tire from the west, and Bricktown is east of Johnny's and east of the Murrah Building, and when you are aware of the time frame and that Tim was identified as the passenger and not the driver, the chance that these different sightings were actually the same truck is highly unlikely. Again, you could blow this one off by saying that one of these guys must be mistaken, but that's not the end of the story.

Dave Snider also said that he had been interviewed by FBI agents and he gave them the same information, but they never came back. That's not the end of the story either. For this witness to have been interviewed by FBI field agents who never followed up on the lead would not necessarily be that unusual, particularly in this case. I'm sure there are hundreds, if not thousands, of people who would tell you the same story about being interviewed one time only. This particular man's situation is very unique because he actually saw a Ryder truck and got a close look at the occupants and claims that he can positively identify them.

His situation becomes even more suspicious when you realize that he was not interviewed by field agents from the FBI but by two FBI "generals." One of the generals was none other than Bob Ricks, head of the FBI in Oklahoma at the time. The other "general" was the special agent in charge of the investigation into the Oklahoma City bombing, Weldon Kennedy, who has since been promoted to assistant director of the FBI under Louis Freeh. Kennedy was also the FBI's spokesman to the press during the first few weeks after the bombing, effectively controlling the information to which the media had access. Keep in mind that Mr. Ricks was also in charge of the murder, lies and cover-up in Waco, Texas, so he is not without experience in these matters.

If you apply common sense to this story, you have to come to the realization that the odds of a couple of generals going out into the field and doing the work of sergeants has to be about a thousand to one. And if this was that thousand-in-one situation where the generals just happened to go into the field to "get their boots dirty," what are the odds that these two commanders just happened upon the only person in half-a-million who could positively identify the second Ryder truck with John Doe No. 3 driving and Tim McVeigh or a lookalike as the passenger on the opposite side of town from Johnny's Tire?

That computes to about 500 million to one, give or take a few million. Your chances of hitting the lotto are at least a hundred times as good. It makes us wonder just how Bob Ricks happened upon this witness. Could he have known that this witness saw the second Ryder truck before he talked to him? It would seem to us that there is no other logical explanation. Remember that David Snider, the eyewitness from Bricktown, said he had only been interviewed once, and that interview was done by Bob Ricks and Weldon Kennedy. That would obviously suggest that an FBI field agent hadn't given this information to Ricks and Kennedy after an initial interview.

So why would the "main men" in charge of the Oklahoma FBI pick this man out of a crowd of 500,000? If this was not that one coincidental chance in 500 million, there is only one other way they could have possibly found this witness. They had to have been told who this witness was and where he was before the interview.

You can draw your own conclusions as to who may have told Mr. Ricks and Mr. Kennedy about this witness. The reason they had to pacify Dave Snider is that he made eye contact with both occupants of the Ryder truck which was moving very slowly because of traffic and road conditions. It was also moving straight at him from a distance of no more than 20 feet when it turned following the curve in the street. Snider thought it was a delivery truck that he was waiting for, tried to flag it down, and became very upset when the truck did not stop. That's why Snider remembered the incident in so much detail. It wasn't just a passing truck at which he just momentarily glanced like many of the other eyewitnesses. Like Mike Moroz, something happened that made this incident stick in his mind.

Ricks had to go interview the man to pacify him. Had Bob Ricks sent a dedicated field agent to interview Snider, that particular field agent may have stirred up a can of worms that Ricks and the other insider bosses wanted to avoid completely. It was just assumed that after the interview, the witness would be satisfied that he had done his civic duty by reporting what he had seen to the great and glorious F-B-I. But David Snider was not satisfied. He knew that he had witnessed something that could prove to be very important in discovering the truth about this tragedy and, like many concerned citizens in Oklahoma City, he wanted to help. He just wasn't sure who to contact to offer that help.

The scam would have worked if not for our friend Chuck Allen who just coincidentally got into a conversation with David Snider's wife. David did not realize that what he saw would be swept under the carpet by the feds. If Mr. Ricks or Mr. Kennedy has a reasonable explanation for this phenomenon, we're all ears. And if there are any other witnesses out there who were originally questioned by Bob Ricks and Weldon Kennedy before this was written, which may have a tendency to indicate that generals Ricks and Kennedy typically do the work of privates and sergeants, please step forward. (government agents excluded.)

Of course, Ricks and Kennedy having interviewed other people in Bricktown may just lend credibility to Snider's statements and to our suspicions. There may have been some concern that other witnesses could place the Ryder truck in Bricktown at precisely the same time Mike Moroz says the Ryder truck was parked at Johnny's Tire. These two locations where two different Ryder trucks were seen and two different Tim McVeighs were seen at the same time are approximately eight minutes apart driving a car, and maybe a little longer by truck. If you drove to Johnny's Tire from Bricktown, which is east of Johnny's, and drove far enough out of your way to approach Johnny's from the west, it would take even longer. Considering these facts, it is very unlikely that all of these witness are incorrect about the time.

It may also be worthwhile noting that Mr. Ricks is no longer the head of the Oklahoma FBI. He now works directly for Gov. Keating in charge of public safety for the State of Oklahoma. The people of Oklahoma must feel about as safe now as the Branch Davidians did when Bob Ricks was in charge down there. It seems as if all the pieces of this puzzle are slowly but surely falling into place. The promotions of Ricks and Kennedy bring to mind an old saying: "In government, the scum always rises to the top." Amen!

Another witness, Dr. Paul Heath, claims that he had a conversation with Tim McVeigh inside the Murrah Building the Friday before the bombing. He said that Tim, wearing a baseball cap backward, was accompanied by two companions, one resembling John Doe No. 2. They were allegedly looking for job applications and Dr. Heath and Tim struck up a conversation. Dr. Heath asked Tim's name and he told him his name was Timothy McVeigh. Dr. Heath then responded that he knew some "McVeys" in the area and that Tim came from a good family. Tim asked for the spelling of the McVeys whom the doctor knew which turned out to be different from his. Tim then allegedly responded by saying that he was not related to that particular McVey family. He also said, "My name is Timothy McVeigh, spelled M-C-V-E-I-G-H. Remember that name, Timothy McVeigh."

That certainly sounds like something a bright, young terrorist would say to keep from being positively identified while casing the building he was getting ready to blow up, doesn't it? There's just nothing like keeping a low profile. Remember that this alleged conversation took place inside the Murrah Building on Friday, April 14, 1995.

Another issue that raises some suspicions, at least in our mind knowing Tim as well as we do, is this baseball cap. We've never known him to wear a baseball cap. He wears an Army-issue cap or a camouflage cap and we've never seen him wear it backward. It would seem that by wearing a baseball cap backward the wearer would be certain that no shadow would be cast on his face which could possibly interfere with a positive identification. We realize that this is just speculation on our part, but common sense tells us that the Tim McVeigh lookalike who was wearing his cap backwards inside the Murrah Building and five days later at Johnny's Tire wanted to make sure his face would be clearly seen.

And speaking of positive identifications, we feel it's worth mentioning that when Mike Moroz from Johnny's Tire Center went to the police station to pick John Doe No. 1 out of a line-up, Tim McVeigh was not necessarily his first choice.

"I've never heard that reported in the national media," you say. Funny, we haven't either. "Who was his first choice?" you ask. Funny, we asked the same question. "Did the FBI investigate his first choice?" you ask. Funny, that question also occurred to us. We've never been asked to pick someone out of a line-up but we have seen it done in the movies.

If the witness doesn't pick the bad guy out the first time, then that's it. Apparently in real life if the witness doesn't pick out the guy that the cops want then they just tell the witness, "Wrong guy, try again," until the witness chooses the one they want. That way the system works every time, without failure. They always get their man. Actually, Mike picked out two guys, numbers one and eight, with the emphasis on number eight. They never told him which one of the eight men in the lineup was Tim. They just told him that one of the men he picked out was Tim McVeigh and it stands to reason, if Mike had picked out Tim the first time, they wouldn't have given him a second chance to pick out their choice. Mike, being a very bright young man, also realized the significance of that apparent logic. Actually, Mike said that all of these guys in the lineup looked so much alike it was difficult to tell them apart which might have a tendency to indicate to the suspicious mind that the Feds did have several Tim McVeigh lookalikes.

Maybe the FBI knows what it's doing, and we certainly don't have any experience at this stuff, but wouldn't you think that the FBI would have at least checked out both of Mike Moroz's choices, especially his first choice? But then again, who are we to question the omnipotent F-B-I ?

Not that we need to, but we are going to submit even more evidence to prove that government investigators have "overdunit" in their attempt to implicate McVeigh. It has been reported to the grand jury that witnesses saw the yellow Mercury Marquis on April 16 in the parking lot of the YMCA just a block or two away from the Murrah Building. It was sporting a note of breakdown that said the owner would remove the auto on April 19 and it was still wearing the license plate. We are supposed to believe that this was Tim's getaway car placed into position three days before the bombing and it sounds like everything was very well-planned.

Now here's what the FBI expects us to believe: According to Fortier's testimony, McVeigh had cased the Murrah Building on several occasions in the months just prior to the bombing. Then, only three days before the bombing, he visited the scene of the crime-to-be to drop off the getaway car. According to Dr. Heath, Tim and John Does No. 2 and maybe No. 3 visited the Murrah Building on Friday, April 14. Tim would have most certainly known exactly where his alleged target was located. This extremely bright young man was about to carry out the most precisely planned and most vicious act of terrorism in the history of this country. On the day of the bombing, six blocks from the target, which he had visited many times, he had to stop and ask directions?

The Murrah Building was a very large, nine-story structure. If Tim was driving that Ryder truck and he had already frequented the proposed target on several occasions, including the visit just a few days before, and he was already close enough to actually see the Murrah Building, why would he have to ask for directions? The logical answer is that he would not.

If you had ever driven in downtown Oklahoma City you would realize that this scenario is impossible. It is a country-type city, all sprawled out over a large area. It's not like New York or Chicago, with vast areas of tall buildings. The tall-building part of Oklahoma City is very small. If you were a few miles from the downtown area you might not be able to find the Murrah Building if you were a directionally impaired person. Once you drive within a mile of the downtown area in any direction, you can't possibly miss it by accident and once you're downtown you can't possibly miss the Murrah Building. It would be the equivalent of not noticing a shrub in the middle of a football field, which leads us to conclude that, either Michael Fortier is lying, or the Feds are lying to the media about what Michael Fortier is lying about, or both.

This little introduction into the realm of common sense totally eliminates the government's only witness who links Tim and Terry to a conspiracy. It also brings up the possibility that someone other than Tim McVeigh was driving the Ryder truck and making sure that a McVeigh look-alike could be positively identified asking directions to one of the cross streets by the Murrah Building. Is it safe to assume that we can call this guy "Tim No. 2?" Maybe we should call the guy in Bricktown "Tim No. 3." The federal investigators have, in their haste to fabricate an air-tight case, obviously created conflicting evidence when that evidence is closely scrutinized. FLEXIBLE FACTS?

When you also take into consideration the testimony of other eye witnesses who were in the immediate area just moments before the explosion, a very alarming pattern begins to materialize. At approximately 20 minutes before the blast (8:42 a.m.), another witness observed a Ryder truck parked about a block away from the Murrah Building. Seated in the truck was a man bearing a keen resemblance to John Doe No. 2 and a man who looked like McVeigh (Tim No. 2 or No. 4 ?) was standing at the back of the truck with a third man (John Doe No. 3 or No. 4 ?). Parked in front of the Ryder truck was a yellow Mercury Marquis, matching the description of Timothy McVeigh's vehicle. Five minutes later, according to the same witness, the yellow Mercury and the Ryder truck had moved. The Ryder truck had crossed the intersection and was parked in front of the Murrah Building and a man who looked like McVeigh (Tim No. 2 or No. 4) was walking across 5th Street away from the truck.

Another witness claims that around 8:55 a.m., he saw a yellow Mercury parked in the parking lot next to the *Journal Record* building across from the Murrah Building. As he walked down the alley, the yellow Mercury Marquis raced recklessly toward him forcing him to hastily get out of the path of the oncoming car. He testified that the driver could have been McVeigh (Tim No. 3, No. 4 or No. 5 ?). He didn't get a good look at the passenger in the car because he was preoccupied with self-preservation but he did see a man resembling the sketch of John Doe No. 2 approach the car and enter the car on the passengers side. As the yellow Mercury sped away causing even more commotion by jumping a couple of parking lot curbs, the witness noticed a dangling license plate.

Another man, James Linehan, an Oklahoma attorney, saw a yellow Mercury Marquis circle the Murrah Building at a high rate of speed and then drive into the parking lot under the Federal Building. He said the driver fit the profile of McVeigh (Tim No. 4, No. 5 or No. 6 ?) but he could not see the persons face because it appeared as if the driver was wearing a hooded jacket or had long hair. He also remembers looking at the clock in his car and it was exactly 8:38 a.m., the same time that McVeigh (Tim No. 2) was seated in the driver's seat of the Ryder truck at Johnny's Tire and the passenger's seat of the Ryder truck seen by David Snider in Bricktown (Tim No. 3). As the yellow Mercury accelerated ahead of Mr. Linehan, he noticed that the car had no license plate.

We can't predict how you might view this situation but when all of these alarming and very incriminating eyewitness reports came to our attention, the first thought that occurred to us was: "If you were going to commit a crime, wouldn't you at least make an attempt to keep a low profile or would you go out of your way to make sure that you could be positively identified by several people in the area at exactly the right time?" Again, when you look at this sequence of events objectively, it becomes apparent that whoever was driving the Ryder trucks and the yellow Mercurys identical to Tim McVeigh's Mercury went out of their way to be noticed and positively identified in the area just before the bombs went off.

We also have to wonder, just how many 1977 yellow Mercury Marquis might be in downtown Oklahoma City at any given time? Realistically, we'd have to guess that there would be zero. What's the chance that there would be two of these "unusual" automobiles in downtown Oklahoma City just 30 minutes before the blast, and then that both of the rusty yellow Mercurys would fit the profile of McVeigh's "missing license plate Mercury?" Ignoring this plethora of unusual circumstances, all of these separate eyewitness reports could each, individually, be rationally accepted as very incriminating circumstantial evidence with a few exceptions.

One exception is Mike Moroz, the eyewitness at Johnny's Tire Center. This appears to be an intentional and successful attempt to have McVeigh positively identified as the driver of the Ryder truck and as a person asking directions to one of the cross streets at the Murrah Building. Anyone in the process of committing a crime who had an IQ above 60 would never have done such a foolish thing accidentally.

Actually, the eyewitnesses at Johnny's could be considered two exceptions because in Bricktown, eight minutes away by car and at exactly the same time, we have Dave Snider who witnessed the presence of a Ryder truck with McVeigh as the passenger. At precisely the same time a Ryder truck was parked in Johnny's Tire parking lot, another look-alike was driving a look-alike yellow Mercury into the Murrah Building basement parking garage. And a matching yellow Mercury nearly ran over a man walking down the alley at the same time Tim was allegedly walking across the street away from the Ryder truck although those two could've been the same Tim (No. 2 or No. 4).

It seems as if Tim has this uncanny ability to be in more than one place at exactly the same time, and on more than one occasion. Kind of like Terry being in Fort Riley, Kan., and at a convenience gas stop 200 miles away at the same time. And kind of like me being at the gas station in Oklahoma and in Michigan at the same time. Another exception is the identification by Dr. Heath inside the Murrah Building, obviously another attempt at making certain there would be a positive identification, not only on the appearance of McVeigh, but on the exact name as well, right down to the proper spelling.

On Friday, April 14, 1995 Timothy McVeigh, on his way from Kingman, Ariz., drove his dying blue Pontiac 2000 station wagon to a Firestone dealership in Junction City, Kan., and traded it and $250 for a 1977 yellow Mercury Marquis. The transaction took place at the Firestone dealership with a Mr. Thomas Manning, and to our knowledge nobody is disputing that this meeting of McVeigh and Manning took place and that it happened on April 14, 1995. The Firestone dealership in Junction City, Kansas is approximately 260 miles from downtown Oklahoma City. There is no doubt that McVeigh was in Junction City, Kan., on April 14. There is no doubt that Dr. Heath talked to a man who resembled and claimed to be Timothy McVeigh. Since Tim McVeigh couldn't possibly be in both of these places at the same time, is it unreasonable to conclude that there was, in fact, at least one Tim McVeigh lookalike who made it an issue to be positively identified in and around the scene of the crime-to-be?

There are numerous witnesses who saw a McVeigh lookalike in the area on the days before the bombing. Many of these witnesses say that Tim was rather loud, drinking and partying with a "babe" hanging with him. This noisy look-alike was definitely noticed and he was definitely not Tim. Tim is just the opposite of this planted impostor. Quite, polite, soft-spoken, and he doesn't frequent bars. Like we have said, each of these accounts alone appears to be incriminating to the extent that they place Tim in the area. But when you become aware of all of these sightings, they defy logic and also indicate that our suspicions of a setup may be a little more than just paranoid speculation.

This is just another example of conspirators so arrogant that they have, in their attempt to absolutely convince us of Tim's guilt, over-whelmed us with so many accounts of conflicting (time and location) eyewitness testimony that it borders on ridiculous. Keeping all of this in mind, consider also that there have been some reports that whoever actually rented the alleged Ryder truck used a phony name (Bob Kling) and possibly even Tim's social security number. Now, using your own social security number in the process of a crime sounds like something a smart criminal would do to make sure nobody could track him down. This compilation of evidence almost seems too good to be true. You know what they say, "If it seems too good to be true, it probably is."

Keep in mind also that the feds never expected Tim to survive the angry mob in Perry, Okla., so they never imagined that they would have to explain all of these conflicting eyewitness reports to anyone. If McVeigh had been assassinated would anyone have cared if Dr. Paul Heath and Thomas Manning talked to McVeigh at about the same time in different states on the exact same day more than 260 miles apart? Would anyone have paid any attention to Mike Moroz or David Snider who saw McVeigh in a Ryder truck on opposite ends of town and at exactly the same time? Would anyone on network news bother to report that it was not Tim McVeigh who rented the notorious Ryder truck and that not one piece of physical evidence nor one witness exists who can link Tim to the truck that allegedly carried a bomb to the front door of the Murrah Building?

But Timothy McVeigh did not get assassinated. All of this information proves beyond any reasonable doubt that there was one or more McVeigh lookalikes and yet nobody in network news seems to care. Nobody in the FBI or on network news seems to be interested in the facts because their minds are already made up. Like the federal prosecutors always say: "Don't confuse me with the facts. I'm arguing!"

The feds have presented evidence that seems to incriminate Tim and Terry when that evidence is selectively taken into consideration. But we must consider all of the evidence available to realize what is really going on here.

If all of the evidence is compiled and that compilation indicates that certain allegations are true, then one may conclude that those allegations are true and convincing. If a person, in the course of an honest card game is dealt a pat hand royal flush, that natural royal flush is very impressive. If the dealer turned a shuffled deck face up and spread the cards out on the table, for a person to say that there were four royal flushes within that deck would be extremely inaccurate. In reality, there are no royal flushes within the deck of cards. There are only cards that could create royal flushes when you eliminate all of the other cards. To draw a royal flush from a spread-out, face-up deck of cards would not impress anyone.

That's basically what the prosecution has done in this case. The feds have ignored, altered or discarded all of the evidence which would prove their allegations wrong. They have selectively picked out just the right cards, pretending to have a royal flush, ignoring all of the cards in between. They have, again, effectively dealt from the bottom of the deck. That turned out to be clearly obvious in the actual McVeigh trial proceedings, and Judge Richard Matsch certainly helped the cause by blocking any exculpatory evidence from being entered by McVeigh's defense team. There was one thing that Mike Moroz, the witness at Johnny's Tire, wanted to know. He asked: Why did the feds have Terry in jail? He hadn't seen or identified Terry and neither had anyone else. We told him that we didn't know why Terry was in jail, but we did know that TERRY WASN'T THERE ! Mike Moroz agreed.

Getting back to Michael Fortier's allegations, we need to examine his "Factual Statement In Support of Plea Petition." His statement that he sold guns that Tim and Terry stole stems from the alleged gun robbery of an unlicensed Arkansas gun dealer named Roger Moore. There are so many rumors floating around about this Arkansas gun dealer that it's hard to determine just which ones to believe.

It has been reported that Moore has CIA affiliations. We can't say for sure that those reports are absolutely true, but investigators have confirmed his previous involvement in government contracts and in some sort of informational cooperation with government agencies. This man seems to be very well connected with intelligence agencies within the government and may have been used in the past by these agencies. It has also been rumored that he was in some way involved in the Iran-Contra affair, perhaps as a supplier of either arms or some sort of water-craft, but at this time we cannot prove this story.

It can be shown how government investigators totally fabricated a story about Tim and Terry concerning this alleged robbery. They originally said that Moore claimed that Tim McVeigh, with the help of Terry Nichols, came to his residence in November of 1994 under the guise of purchasing guns from him, only to check out the collection of guns in his possession and to familiarize themselves with his house and the area in general. He is alleged to have said that they returned at a later date with masks on and held him at gunpoint and robbed him of $60,000 worth of cash, coins and guns and he was pretty sure it was Tim McVeigh. That seemed to be exactly what the FBI wanted him to say.

The first thing that comes to mind when trying to determine if this Arkansas gun dealer is telling the truth is: If he really thought it was Tim McVeigh and Terry Nichols who ripped him off, why did he wait until April of 1995 to implicate them? He allegedly reported the robbery in November of 1994. If he had any suspicions about Tim and Terry, why didn't he express those suspicions to the police when the robbery was first reported so the police could check out his allegations?

The FBI charged Tim and Terry in the Oklahoma City bombing and then, all of a sudden, five months after the fact, this gun dealer allegedly came forward and said they also robbed him in November of '94. We have been told by investigators who have gone to Arkansas to check out Moore's story that the local police there harbor some suspicions that the robbery may have been staged. They have no hard evidence to that effect but they have said that there was some evidence concerning tire tracks and other things that just didn't add up, suggesting the possibility of fraud. (Be reminded, too, that the government dropped this portion of the charges against Tim McVeigh and Terry Nichols in an "amended" indictment as the McVeigh trial was coming to a close. Wonder why?)

Wasn't it convenient for the FBI that this "good Samaritan" came forward just at the right time to further implicate Tim and Terry and to contradict their squeaky clean records by showing their potential for criminal activity? It also showed how they allegedly financed this terrorist plot. This gun dealer actually put three links in their chain to connect Tim and Terry to the bombing. But again, when you examine this story, those links are very weak. Not only did Moore wait five months to accuse McVeigh and Nichols in the robbery, when he first made his allegations it was reported that he didn't even have any serial numbers for the guns that were allegedly stolen. There's really no proof that a robbery ever took place.

Now correct us if we're wrong, but if you wanted to fake a gun robbery and you hadn't recorded any serial numbers, nobody could prove that you hadn't been robbed, right? You can't prove a negative. If you made up some serial numbers, you would probably get busted for fraud because it wouldn't take the police investigators long to find out they were phony, right? It's also very convenient that this guy isn't licensed. Had he been licensed, there would've been a record of all of his purchases and a record of the serial numbers. If they don't have serial numbers for the guns that were allegedly stolen, how in the world can the FBI take this giant leap into dreamland and report that the legal guns in the possession of McVeigh and Nichols were the guns that were supposed to have been stolen?

Whatever "type" of guns Terry had in his possession are supposed to be the same "type" of guns that were stolen in the robbery. If Mr. Moore's guns were all originals and were the only ones of those particular types in existence and those descriptions matched Terry's guns, it would certainly be significant and an explanation would be necessary. In fact, there are at least hundreds of thousands of similar guns in circulation so these accusations are really meaningless. It seems as if the FBI's entire case is based upon one giant leap after another, each leap taking us farther and farther from reality. THEY HAVE NO CASE!

Let's see if we have this one right. The FBI was attempting to hang Tim and Terry using evidence stemming from some guns that may or may not have existed and that may or may not have been stolen from this guy who may or may not be an Arkansas gun dealer who, most certainly, is not telling the truth. Had the FBI been sharp enough to have this guy report the robbery on April 22, it could have supplied him with the serial numbers from Tim's and Terry's guns and they would have had a much more solid case. We have heard rumors from some reporters that Moore does have serial numbers for the guns, long after the fact, so maybe the FBI has simply supplied him with the numbers of the guns in Terry's possession. Time will tell.

Another problem with this alleged gun robbery is the date that it was supposed to have taken place. Unfortunately for the FBI, Tim McVeigh has an airtight alibi as to his whereabouts on the date in question. And, unfortunately for the FBI, so does Terry.

We are hopeful that you realize the importance of this information. Most of the FBI's case rests upon the testimony of Michael Fortier and the alleged Arkansas gun dealer. This alleged robbery and the passing of stolen guns to Fortier by McVeigh is a large part of Fortier's statement and it also helps tie the FBI's story all together. This is the major link in the FBI's chain and it also puts Tim and Terry in a bad light because it portrays them as part of the criminal element who would pull an armed robbery, thereby showing their potentially violent tendencies. This appears to be another weak but nearly successful attempt at character assassination. When you are made aware of the facts surrounding this story and realize that it is a total fabrication, some very important links in their chain completely disintegrate.

Obviously, the Arkansas gun dealer is not being completely forthright about who committed the alleged robbery or if the alleged robbery ever really happened. Doesn't it make you wonder why? Why would he make up a story about McVeigh and Nichols? Did he come forward on his own or did he, in collusion with the FBI, fabricate this story?

They are the only two choices if he really made those potentially incriminating accusations. It has to be one of them because we now have absolute proof positive that his alleged story about Tim and Terry pulling a robbery was made up. TIM AND TERRY WERE NOT THERE! If the gun dealer did conspire with agents from the FBI to implicate Tim and Terry, we again have to ask some questions.

Whose idea was it to make up this story and why was it necessary? Whose idea was it for Michael Fortier to make up his story about Tim and Terry committing this alleged robbery? Do you think Fortier could have made up that kind of story on his own? Did you notice the coincidence of the magic number, $60,000? How did the FBI come up with that magic number when they raided my farm? They asked why I had $60,000 cash. I didn't have $60,000. I only had $2,000 so where did they get that exact number before Roger Moore got involved? Did they know Moore was going to accuse us before he accused us? When you really think about these facts the coincidences are, at the least, very alarming.

We have recently been told by an investigator who interviewed the Arkansas gun dealer that he said he never told the FBI that McVeigh robbed him. It seems that whenever the government investigators give an account of an eyewitness testimony to the media, which some members of the lapdog media loyally report without question, the eyewitness always says those things that make the case seem much stronger for the prosecution. Unfortunately for the FBI, when these same eyewitnesses are interviewed by independent investigators, their story seldom matches the version that the federal investigators leaked to the media. Do we detect another pattern materializing here? Alarmingly contradicting information seems to be the norm in this case of FLEXIBLE FACTS, doesn't it?

It has recently been reported (rumored?) that Kevin Nicholas and I went down to Arkansas to take part in the alleged gun robbery. Once it was known that TIM AND TERRY WEREN'T THERE, they needed some other patsies to stick with this robbery because many of their accusations and much of their fabricated case rested upon the alleged stolen guns and money. Of course, the FBI has never told me that it thought I was involved. It has already wasted millions of taxpayer dollars investigating me and searching my farm with a fine-tooth comb.

They even vacuumed the dirt off the floors of my pickup and tractors and had it lab tested. I wonder how much it cost the taxpayers for the FBI to discover that which I could have told them for free? There was some dirt, cow poop, maybe some straw, some remnants of whatever grains I've grown for the past decade, and maybe a cigarette butt or two from my buddy, Paul, when he rides with me. I would've told them that for nothin', but I'm just a dumb farmer. What do I know? They had real, live, high paid scientists checking this stuff out in a high-tech, state-of-the-art FBI laboratory at a cost to the taxpayers of probably tens of thousands of dollars. I'd be willing to bet that after extensive scientific inspection, testing and evaluation, they probably found some dirt, cow poop, maybe some straw, some remnants of whatever grains I've grown for the past decade, and maybe a cigarette butt or two from my buddy, Paul, when he rides with me. Great job, guys!

What would we do without you? Believe it or not, I did get the floor dirt back from the FBI in neat little marked, plastic bags, complete with cow poop, maybe some straw, some remnants of whatever grains I've grown for the past decade, and maybe a cigarette butt or two from my buddy, Paul, when he rides with me. Tax money very well spent.

Some investigators claim to have uncovered evidence suggesting that Tim McVeigh and Roger Moore were friends and may have even done a few gun shows together. It has been alleged that Roger Moore may have given Tim the guns on consignment to sell for him and then, unbeknownst to Tim, said that he was robbed so he could collect on an insurance claim. The problem is that nobody has come up with any evidence of an insurance claim yet, but at this time, in our educated opinion, we would suggest that the thinking Citizen should not rule out the consignment theory.

If any of these allegations were true, it would certainly do more to fuel the suspicions of a very elaborate setup intended on making Tim a patsy to take the blame for the real perpetrators of this crime than to add credibility to the prosecution's allegations of guilt. Tim did have some guns and possibly some other things that may have been given to him on consignment. If it was Roger Moore's merchandise that Tim and Terry had in their possession, it might suggest that Moore was involved in setting them up from the very beginning. It does not necessarily imply that Moore had any idea why Tim was being "planted" with evidence or that Moore knew what was going to happen on April 19, 1995, in Oklahoma City, but it sure opens the door for many speculative possibilities. (Don't tell anyone, but the feds are now suggesting that my cousin, Tim, and I "pulled off" this alleged Arkansas dream robbery.)

Another point worth mentioning is the fact that Terry possessed considerable cash assets. If he was involved in this conspiracy, he certainly wouldn't need to steal guns to finance it. And if Terry was going to be involved in this conspiracy, why didn't he leave provisions for Tim to receive a loan even if he didn't return from the Philippines? And if Tim was involved in the alleged Arkansas gun robbery that would've netted the thieves $60,000, why would he need a loan from Terry? These are all questions that we have to ask when we evaluate the FBI's story as to how Tim and Terry were involved in this tragedy. These are all questions that the feds didn't think they would ever have to answer because DEAD MEN DON'T TESTIFY. Inquiring minds are waiting for rational answers to all of these questions.

We must also bring to your attention another major flaw in the FBI's allegations against McVeigh. We all know that Tim was driving a big yellow tank that was about 18 years old, a typical "$100 flyer." Prior to that he wore out a $100 flyer which he had purchased from me.

Let's assume that Michael Fortier is telling the truth. Let us assume, very temporarily, that the FBI is correct in its allegations. Put yourself in

McVeigh's situation. You have recently pulled off a robbery netting, at the very least, tens of thousands of dollars. You are very well-financed. You have a close friend with substantial assets who will also give you whatever financial assistance you may need. You are in the process of almost single-handedly planning the biggest crime in the history of this country — crime that has the potential of taking hundreds of lives and costing hundreds of millions of dollars in property damage.

This is going to be the biggest, costliest crime against the government of this country that any person or group of persons has ever planned. Everything has to be just right. The size and type of explosives have been very carefully calculated. The exact size and type of vehicle and its weight capabilities have been precisely determined. The target has been selected and, after much consideration, the exact location of the bomb has been chosen to cause the most destruction possible under the circumstances. Everything has been meticulously planned. Your months of research is finally finished. Everything is ready. Every little detail is just right.

Now you need a dependable, inconspicuous getaway car because your little, blue Pontiac station wagon is ready to puke. Wow, you've really lucked out! Boy what a find! The perfect getaway car. A BIG, YELLOW, RUSTY, MERCURY TANK, and it's only 18 years old! What could be better? Nobody will ever notice this car. It'll blend right in and look just like all of the other BIG, YELLOW, RUSTY, 18-YEAR OLD MERCURY TANKS in downtown Oklahoma City.

It might not start but you never know, it might start and then break down. But then again, it might not break down, maybe. But hey, that's the chance you have to take when you have been so meticulous in your planning and when you only have 40 or 50 grand with which to work and, you're about to single-handedly commit the crime of the century!

The alleged Arkansas gun robbery also paved the way to help convince people that Terry and Tim were capable of robbing the construction site in Marion, Kan., of explosives, including blasting caps and dynamite. The FBI has attempted to show that these two men, each with an absolutely spotless record, had an inclination to participate in criminal activity. Again, the stories told by the FBI all seem to fit together to prove a trail of conspiracy until you take the time to evaluate all the propaganda it is spreading.

Remember that Terry got out of insurance sales because he thought his job often consisted of selling insurance to people who didn't really need it even though they wanted it. His moral code somehow dictated that continuing in that profession was the equivalent of stealing, even though most would consider it, at the very least, an honorable profession and a much needed service. To suggest that a man with a moral code of ethics which would not allow him to extract voluntary payments from customers for a requested service would be capable of armed robbery or breaking and entering for the purpose of stealing to support an act of terrorism and mass murder is absolutely ridiculous!

They say that Tim and Terry committed this robbery and then rented a storage shed in or near Kingman, Ariz., to store their stolen goods until it was time to carry out their act of terrorism. According to FBI accounts, and we're sure that Michael Fortier will confirm this allegation or any other allegation that the FBI cares to make, Tim and Terry then drove out to Kingman to retrieve their stolen explosives and then drove, with the explosives, back to Herington, Kan., where they proceeded to assemble the "monster bomb."

This all sounds very feasible, doesn't it? Have you ever taken a look at a map of that section of the United States? Do you realize just how far it is from Herington, Kan., to Kingman, Ariz.? The shortest route that we can find appears to be over 1,200 miles. The so-called "Thumb of Michigan" where we live is much closer to Herington than Kingman is to Herington. But the FBI had a problem in Michigan. Their entire fairy tale was based upon the farm in Decker being the home-base, the proving grounds where the "experiments" were conducted, and where the explosives were stored. When that fairy tale disappeared back into federal dreamland from where it came, a "new" home-base had to be created.

Again, here's what the FBI expects us to believe: Terry and Tim steal some explosives in Marion, Kan. To stash these allegedly stolen explosives, do they use any of the convenient storage sheds that they already have rented in Junction City, Kan., which is only 30 miles from Marion? No. Do they rent some other storage rooms at some other convenient location a short distance away so they don't have to spend any more time than absolutely necessary on the road with their stolen and very illegal merchandise? No.

The FBI would have you believe these guys were so stupid that they would drive 2,500 miles, round trip, just to store some dynamite? Over 1,200 of those miles would have exposed them to the possibility of getting caught with stolen explosives, including crossing state boundaries which undoubtedly would have been a federal offense. There couldn't have been an enormous amount of dynamite since it would have been transported in Terry's pickup or Tim's car. Later they would have driven another 2,500 miles to retrieve their stash to carry on with the plot. Why in the world would they drive 5,000 miles just to store a small quantity of explosives when it could have been stored more conveniently near their residence? Obviously, they would not.

By the time they made two round trips they would have driven 5,000 miles, half of which would've been driven while carrying the illegal merchandise. And there is no way ol' cheap Terry would spend the money on fuel to drive 5,000 miles if he could've accomplished the same thing driving only 120 miles. No way.

Of course, the FBI has another story which makes the transportation of these explosives believable. The FBI claims that Tim and Terry wrapped their contraband in Christmas paper thereby making certain they would not get busted for carrying illegal explosives interstate. Right guys. It sounds real good until you generate some very, very minute electrical impulses within the gray matter between your ears. People try to smuggle tiny packages of contraband inside body cavities and get caught but Christmas wrap, now that's a sure thing! No law enforcement officers would ever violate large packages hiding behind Christmas wrap, would they? But then we also have to consider the transportation of these explosives back to Kansas. We're not sure when that trip was supposed to have taken place but it allegedly happened sometime between February and early April. It was just a little late for Christmas wrap, wasn't it? Not that there's anything wrong with Christmas wrap in March or April.

This story had to be fabricated by the FBI to bring Michael Fortier into the picture as a witness against Tim and Terry. Fortier's testimony is much more believable if you can first convince people that Tim and Terry robbed the construction site in Marion of explosives, and then included Fortier in the scheme by storing their "score" near his residence.

It's very convenient for Fortier, also. Now the only person who has confessed to the bombing has a way out. A way to survive. We really have our doubts that Fortier had anything to do with the bombing or anything else for that matter, including the manufacture of the slightest brain wave. This guy appears to be a real flatliner. We believe the FBI had him so convinced that his buddy, Tim, would be convicted and that he, and maybe even his wife, would "fry" along with Tim that he would have said anything they wanted him to say. He probably would have confessed to being responsible for the last solar eclipse if the FBI wanted his confession for that event, and with the blessings of his attorney, possibly another flatliner.

When commenting to the FBI on McVeigh's alleged involvement in the bombing of the Murrah Building, Michael Fortier said: "I do not believe that Tim blew up any building in Oklahoma. There's nothing for me to look back upon and say, 'Yeah, that might have been. I should have seen it back then.' There's nothing like that. I know my friend Tim McVeigh is not the 'Face of Terror' as reported in *Time* magazine."

Considering Fortier's original statements about this bombing, is it unreasonable to conclude that the first half of Michael Fortier's "Factual Statement In Support of Plea Petition" is an absolute lie and a total fabrication? Since we are reasonably certain that the first half is a lie, and Fortier admits to having told numerous lies in the second half of the petition, can anyone believe anything this man says? He has admitted to telling many previous lies, and has even admitted to lying in his "Factual Statement." Not exactly what one might consider "factual," is it? Apparently, the FBI thinks that we should execute two men on the testimony of a habitual liar who's trying to save his own rear end, and who just happens to be the only guy whom the FBI has in custody and has confessed to being involved in the bombing.

There is another extremely interesting point in Michael Fortier's not so Factual Statement that has been brought to our attention by our friend and founder of Citizens for a Constitutional Republic, Karl Granse. We will quote a sentence from Michael's statement. "I did not as soon as possible make known my knowledge of the McVeigh and Nichols plot to any JUDGE OR OTHER PERSON IN CIVIL AUTHORITY."

The emphasis is ours, actually Karl's. Can you picture a Michael Fortier using that language? Would you know that you had to report a crime to a "judge or other person in civil authority?" Neither would we, and neither would Michael Fortier. This statement was obviously dictated to Fortier by government agents. They had him write it with his own hand so that it would appear as if these were his words and his words alone. It's just another attempt at deception by the Professional Deceivers. If they had just typed it out and had Fortier sign it, the deception would not have been so obvious and the use of those particular words wouldn't really have been important.

The feds think that they have to thoroughly convince everyone that they aren't influencing or intimidating any witnesses and, again, their deceiving habits have exposed their deceiving habits. When you really look at Michael Fortier's "Factual Statement" and are aware of all the lies in that statement, the only thing that he really accomplishes is self-incrimination. Bright move, Mikey! Do you see why we express serious doubts about Fortier's ability to come up with the phrase "judge or other person in civil authority"? Bright move, FBI interrogators! These guys sure are lucky that their promotions are based upon their criminal activities and not their successes concerning HONEST law enforcement.

When you come right down to it, we really feel sorry for Michael Fortier. From what we can gather, the feds had no evidence against him that would have convicted him in any court for any criminal offense. He's probably going to spend somewhere between 10 and 20 years in a federal penitentiary, basically for just being paranoid and very, very stupid. If there's a federal law against being stupid, then Fortier's attorney should be his cellmate for the duration. We have to get this guy's name because if he's not an FBI plant, then he has to be the dumbest guy on the planet, after Mikey of course.

Here's what Hoppy Heidelberg had to say about Michael Fortier: "They brought 24-hour-a-day pressure on him for several months. They were on him at his job in Kingman so much that he got fired. He had no attorney for that whole period and he wasn't under arrest. They didn't want to arrest him because if they did, they'd have to appoint a lawyer for him. He got conned. If I had been Fortier's attorney, he wouldn't have given a statement and he would've walked. They stayed on him so long because they had nothing better."

Remember, this is a grand juror making this statement. A man who was on the grand jury that indicted Tim and Terry. A man who listened to Fortier's testimony and to all of the other testimony the prosecution had to offer. A grand juror who said that the prosecution "had nothing better." Nothing better than what? Nothing better than Michael Fortier? We know that Michael Fortier's testimony was nothing more than lies dictated to him by the FBI. Michael Fortier should sue his attorney for either conspiring with the government against him or for extreme malpractice. Maybe for both. Wasn't Fortier's attorney supposed to represent Michael Fortier's best interests?

Hoppy's description of Fortier's dilemma was somewhat confirmed by Jim Rosencrans, a former neighbor of Michael Fortier, in an interview with Lawrence Myers of *Media Bypass*. Rosencrans said: "The guy (Fortier) has a wife with a child on the way. These agents kept after him for weeks and made him believe his wife would be charged along with him if they did not cooperate. The government is very good at intimidating people."

For all the guys reading this, if you put yourself in Michael Fortier's position it's not hard to imagine sacrificing your own skin or anyone else's for that matter to save your wife. "You can do it to me but you damn well better not do it to my wife" is not an untypical attitude for a man to have. It's in our nature as males. You can call it "macho" or a "double standard" or anything you want, but it is a fact of life. It is, in a word, "chivalry." In some ways you could look upon Michael Fortier's actions as an attempt to protect the dignity and perhaps the life of his wife by sacrificing 20 years of his life and, perhaps literally, his buddy's life. Certainly a brave gesture and for that we must give him some credit. Unfortunately for Michael and his family, no sacrifice was necessary. For that, we can only give him and his family our sympathy.

For those who still believe that Michael Fortier's statements are really Michael Fortier's statements, consider this: Michael Fortier has had in excess of 100 hours of private conversation with lead prosecutor Joseph Hartzler. One might wonder what these two men, a U.S. prosecutor and a confessed felon, liar and drug abuser, could possibly have in common which would allow them to keep each other entertained in private conversation for 100 hours! It has been suggested that Michael and Lori Fortier's testimonies are very well rehearsed. We can't imagine having to practice 100 hours to tell the truth about something that you have personally experienced. An hour or two should be more than adequate to refresh your memory and allow you to tell the truth, the whole truth and nothing but the truth. One might speculate that 100 hours of practice would adequately prepare an individual to repeat, verbatim, a script written by someone else. 100 hours of practice would also seemingly be enough to prepare an individual to hold up under intense cross-examination.

We would suggest to Michael that he conduct his own research concerning coerced testimony. His attorney, if you could call him that, apparently never informed him that coerced testimony has no validity in law and cannot be held against you or anyone else. Any reasonable person would confess to anything if a gun was held to their head. Likewise, any rational man would confess to anything if his wife was threatened with a long jail term or a death sentence. Common sense dictates that the coerced confession would mean nothing and that's why it's not considered valid in America's system of justice.

We're not supposed to beat or torture confessions out of people here in America. Those activities are supposed to be reserved for communists, Nazis, and other dictatorial tyrannies. You know, it's kind of ironic that the feds have tried so hard to prove some kind of relationship between McVeigh and Nazi-type people or groups when, in fact, federal investigators obviously harbor much contempt for our Constitutional rights and when their own activities so closely parallel those of the Nazis when the are reasonably certain they can get away with it.

Michael Fortier has pled guilty to crimes for which he could serve 23 years in a federal prison. Did you know that Fortier has yet to be sentenced? Have you wondered why he has not been sentenced even though he has pled guilty? The reason is blackmail. The feds have Michael Fortier exactly where they want him. They tell him what they want him to say and he says it. If he doesn't give the testimony they want him to give, the 23 years stick.

If Fortier complies, which he did admirably in the McVeigh trial, his sentence will probably be reduced and may well be reduced considerably if his testimony is a mirror reflection of the allegations made by the prosecutors in this case. One thing that we must mention is that not one single statement that Michael Fortier has made which may have a tendency to incriminate Tim McVeigh or Terry Nichols originated from Michael Fortier. Everything Fortier has said has been alleged, theorized or suggested to the media by FBI investigators or prosecutors long before Fortier made any incriminating statements.

And from some of Michael's own conversations with friends it has been reported that the lure of financial gain from book and movie deals had some impact on Fortier's decision to change his story. Michael Fortier probably doesn't realize it but he still has an opportunity to walk away from this tragedy as a free, innocent man, and we would be more than happy to inform him of his Rights if he wants to understand just how he can be free again. Just remember Lori and Michael, the truth could and would set Michael free.

Another observant eyewitness has passed along some very interesting information that the FBI seems to have swept under the carpet for one reason or another. Do you remember the reasonably isolated site at Geary Lake State Park where the prosecution claims that Tim and Terry mixed the alleged truck bomb? Well, this particular eyewitness remembers seeing a yellow Ryder truck parked at that exact spot for a couple of days. He said that he thought it was rather peculiar because it seemed like a very expensive rig to be leaving out there unattended. He also said that he observed several men around the truck at different times, some with suits, some in Army camo fatigues. A white, four-door sedan was there some of the time, too. Now you could say that the white sedan and guys in suits could indicate the possibility of government agents, but it certainly wouldn't prove anything. After all, government agents don't have a corner on the suit-and-white-four-door-sedan markets. Non-Government terrorists can wear suits and drive white four-door sedans too. Anyway, this particular witness saw all of this from a small boat out in Geary Lake while he was fishing.

The really peculiar thing about this story is that the fisherman saw the Ryder truck, the white sedan, and the men in suits several days before the

FBI alleges that the site was used to mix the ammonium nitrate and fuel oil to create the massive bomb which they say destroyed the Murrah Building. In fact, it was several days before Tim McVeigh allegedly rented any Ryder truck! There's no doubt about the date because this eyewitness was on vacation fishing. He knows exactly when he was there and exactly when he saw the truck, car, and men in suits.

Other witnesses saw the Ryder truck on that spot at Geary Lake also and, like the vacationer, saw it days before McVeigh allegedly rented his rig at Elliott's in Junction City. One of those other witnesses was James Sargent. He saw a Ryder truck parked at the Geary Lake bomb mixing site on the 10th, 11th and 12th of April, 1995. Mr. Sargent also said that the truck was accompanied by a brown pickup and a white four-door sedan. Since we know that McVeigh was still in Arizona and Terry was on his way back to Kansas from a visit in Michigan when the three vehicles were first seen at Geary Lake, it was obviously not Terry and Tim who were responsible for those three vehicles at that location on those dates.

The timing of these sightings makes sense when you realize what Lea McGowan from the Dreamland Motel also witnessed. It seems as if the Feds have been keeping some of this information "confidential" because it didn't quite fit in to the setup, uh, program. In addition to the earlier sightings at Geary Lake, Ms. McGowan saw two different Ryder trucks at the Dreamland. One was driven by John Doe No. 2 and another person, whom she could not identify, was present also. Lea McGowan also said that she saw Tim McVeigh with a Ryder truck. The problem is that Ms. McGowan is absolutely positive that McVeigh had his Ryder truck on Sunday, the day before the notorious Ryder truck was rented that allegedly blew up the Murrah Building.

It seems as if we have another contradiction here. The feds say that Tim rented the Ryder truck on Monday, April 17. Lea McGowan says Tim had a Ryder truck on Sunday, April 16. The feds say that Tim and Terry mixed their 5,000-pound bomb by hand at the Geary Lake State Park site on Tuesday, April 18. (Disregard the fact that TERRY WASN'T THERE!.) Lea McGowan says John Doe No. 2 had his Ryder truck in the area on Monday, which is confirmed by the manager of the Great Western Inn just down the road from the Dreamland Motel.

Is there something going on here? Could someone at Elliott's be mistaken about which day McVeigh was there renting a Ryder truck? The prosecution claims that the witnesses at Elliott's were mistaken about which day they saw John Doe No. 2 and that No. 2 was not really there with No. 1, disregard the fact that dozens of others have seen John

Does No. 1 and No. 2 together. Could there really have been three Ryder trucks? Witnesses say they saw a Ryder truck and men in military type uniforms parked at the Geary Lake site at least six days before Tim allegedly rented a Ryder truck on the 16th.

They also saw men in suits and a white, four-door sedan at that location at the same time. Independent journalist J.D. Cash's witnesses said they saw a Ryder truck at Geary Lake six days before Tim allegedly rented a truck and seven days before John Doe No. 2 had his truck and John's witnesses also saw a brown pickup (not Terry's blue pickup) and a white four door sedan. The truck at Geary Lake on the 10th, 11th and 12th, the truck that Lea McGowan saw at the Dreamland Motel on the 16th, and the truck that was rented by John Does No. 1 and No. 2 on the 17th which was seen by Ms. McGowan and the manager of the Great Western Inn certainly proves to us that witnesses actually saw three different Ryder trucks.

ABC news anchor Peter Jennings aired a special during the fall of '95 which, to the informed observer, was nothing more than a mind manipulator. Georgia Rucker, a real estate woman who knew Terry, was interviewed. As a matter of fact, she may have sold Terry the house in Herington, Kan. She stated that the man she knew and with whom she had real estate dealings certainly didn't seem like he was capable of anything like the Oklahoma City bombing. That one statement got the producers off the hook concerning the intentional incrimination of Terry.

But, we have to look more closely at the entire interview and really, at the entire program including all of the subtle suggestions. Just coincidentally, this same real estate person just happened to be driving past Geary Lake while taking her child to school when she noticed a Ryder truck parked at the notorious bomb-mixing location. When you really think about this, an attempt was made to negatively influence the uninformed mind against Terry. The woman knows Terry and this same woman saw the Ryder truck parked at Geary Lake. The subconscious connection was made. We are certain of the intent of the program because we had numerous conversations with two of the shows producers before and after it aired. Their obvious goal was to dig up any dirt available and if none was available then to try and put a muddy twist on whatever information they could get.

We should all be wondering why the producers of this "special" didn't interview any of the witnesses who saw a Ryder truck, men in suits, a white four-door sedan, a brown pickup and men in camos several days before the fact. Of all of the witnesses who saw the Ryder truck and other vehicles on the 10th, 11th and 12th of April, they only interviewed

Georgia Rucker, the witness who knew Terry. She didn't see Terry there but again, the subconscious connection was made. Are we to believe that the Ryder truck accompanied by a brown pickup, white four-door sedan, men in suits and men in Army camouflage uniforms nearly a week before the fact is not more significant than just seeing a Ryder truck and having known Terry from a real estate deal? An observant, informed person might conclude that these network news specials reflect the preconceived notions of the producers and are designed specifically to advance the agenda of the government instead of presenting objective, honest information to the viewers.

This idea of subtle suggestions or hidden persuaders resulting in subconscious influence is not exactly an "idea of the 90's." Socialist philosopher Bertram Russell once said of mass psychology, "Although this science will be diligently studied, it will be rigidly confined to the governing class. The populace will not be allowed to know how its convictions were generated (source: *Media Bypass*)."

Perhaps the FBI is absolutely correct about the site at Geary Lake. Maybe Geary Lake was the location used by terrorists to mix the fuel oil and fertilizer. Maybe the terrorists did leave evidence at the site that proves something definitely happened there. Maybe they did use a Ryder truck to assist in carrying out their conspiracy to destroy and kill innocent Americans and to undermine our Constitution. Of one thing we can be sure: If the site at Geary Lake State Park was used by terrorists to mix an ANFO bomb, or at least to make it appear as if an ANFO bomb had been mixed there, the persons involved were not Terry Lynn Nichols and Timothy James McVeigh.

Tom Kessinger, one of the employees at Elliott's Body Shop where the Ryder truck was rented, described the man who rented the truck (John Doe No. 1) as being 5'10" tall, 185 lbs., brownish green eyes and a rough complexion with acne. Vicki Beemer, another employee at Elliott's, said that the man who rented the truck was Robert Kling and that he had a misshapen or deformed chin. Kessinger also saw John Doe No. 2 and for 18 months the FBI has tried unsuccessfully to convince him that John Doe No. 2 was actually Todd Bunting, a soldier from Fort Riley, Kan. In a conversation with Glenn Wilburn, Kessinger said, "I don't know where they came up with that idea."

Kessinger has expressed to many others the absurdity in the FBI's suggestion that John Doe No. 2 was actually Todd Bunting, a Fort Riley soldier who had absolutely nothing to do with this bombing. Even Hoppy Heidelberg said that those allegations by the prosecutors were "absolutely ridiculous." There was no resemblance whatsoever between

Bunting and John Doe No. 2.

The feds eventually dropped the "Todd Bunting Tale" after it became apparent they weren't going to fool anyone with this scam. But, lo and behold, since they didn't have any other irrational information to pass along to an unsuspecting public by way of an ever-willing media, the Todd Bunting saga surfaces again.

During an exhibition of remarkable persistence, is it possible that Patrick Ryan and Joseph Hartzler, the two lead prosecutors in this case have, by hook or by crook, by threat, duress, coercion, the suggestion of financial gain, or by some other means that has somehow eluded us, convinced Mr. Kessinger to change his story? Doesn't it seem rather suspicious that within days after the fact Tom Kessinger could be so certain of what he saw, holding absolutely firm to his statements for 1 1/2 years and then, suddenly change his story to comply with what Ryan and Hartzler wanted him to say? Isn't that called "witness tampering" Mr. Ryan and Mr. Hartzler?

If defense-team investigators hounded Mr. Kessinger and somehow coerced him into changing his testimony they would be brought up on charges so fast their heads would be spinning. They would, undoubtedly, lose their jobs, would never again be allowed to practice in that profession, and would, more than likely, exhaust most of their energies just trying to stay out of prison. If witness tampering is considered a criminal offense for the defense, why isn't it a criminal offense for the prosecution, Mr. Ryan and Mr. Hartzler?

This is not an isolated incident. Throughout this investigation an attempt has been made by the prosecution to prod or intimidate a change of testimony from many witnesses — including bombing victim Daina Bradley — and, to the witnesses' credit, some have refused to be intimidated into lying and/or have refused to be intimidated into silence. Unfortunately, many others, such as Daina Bradley and Michael Fortier, have not.

As we have pointed out many times before, lying is just second nature for government prosecutors. Because lying is as natural for them as breathing it is extremely difficult for them to relate to someone whose integrity will not allow them to lie to accomplish "the mission."

One of America's most brilliant defense attorneys, Leslie Abramson, while commenting on prosecutors in general, stated that "they are trained to lie" from the first day on the job. She also said that "they don't care about guilt or innocence. They only care about a conviction."

When asked by the interviewer if perhaps there were "a few bad apples" among the many prosecutors with whom she's had contact, Ms.

Abramson stated that in her 27 years experience in the legal profession she has discovered that, in reality, there are only "a few good apples." We certainly don't have the courtroom experience of Leslie Abramson, but in the past two years we have made the exact same observations. Nearly everyone with any gumption and with some courtroom experience, with the exception of prosecutors and some judges, will tell you the same thing. We have seen Ms. Abramson in many discussions and debates and she is always the foremost defender of our Constitution. She is also consistently the voice of reason, logic and common sense.

We're certain that there are many people reading this who believe that all of the discrepancies in the testimony coming from the witnesses at Elliott's and elsewhere are not really discrepancies at all but, in fact, just people who may have been confused or mistaken about what they think they saw. Have many of these witnesses finally seen the light of day on their own or is the FBI still using the tactics of J. Edgar Hoover? Intimidation, coercion and blackmail against anyone and everyone were Hoover's methods of extracting the required performance from his witnesses and victims, many of whom were political leaders. Placing agents in certain positions of employment to keep an eye on key people was one way Hoover effectively controlled his victims. It would seem as if Hoover's perverted, disgusting methods of operation are as common in today's FBI as they were when he was the FBI chief.

Two investigators from the defense team of Timothy McVeigh attempted to get statements from witnesses at Elliott's. Eldon Elliott told them that he and his employees had been instructed not to talk to anyone about the case because the feds did not want their statements taken out of context and did not want the witnesses to get confused about what they saw.

Shouldn't we wonder, if that was really the case then why does the FBI try to get everyone to change their testimony if their story does not correspond with the prosecutions allegations? Anyway, Mr. Elliott told the two defense investigators to talk to an "employee" working "indirectly for Ryder" who identified himself as Joseph Pole.

Mr. Pole also conveniently refused to be interviewed, and used the "I-have-to-make-a-phone-call" excuse to part company with the investigators. Before the investigators drove away from Elliott's they noticed that there was a government car parked outside in the lot. When they returned the following day they noticed that the government car was still there which prompted them to ask some of the employees why the car was parked in the lot. They were told that the car was being worked on, but when they looked the car over the investigators could detect no sign of any damage. The next time they returned, and each time thereafter, the government car was parked between or behind larger vehicles in an apparent attempt to hide it from the investigators. They visited Elliott's on five different occasions and each time the government vehicle was parked somewhere around Elliott's Body Shop and the employee who worked "indirectly for Ryder" was still there.

Obviously, the feds wanted to make certain that no investigators and absolutely no reporters would be able to extract the truth from the employees at Elliott's because, if and when the real truth surfaces, it will be obvious to everyone that Timothy McVeigh did not rent the Ryder truck that allegedly exploded in front of the Murrah Building and the FBI has gone to great extremes to conceal that fact by tampering with witnesses. Information has recently surfaced which indicates that Tom Kessinger, one of the witnesses at Elliott's, has a criminal record. Shouldn't this latest news release raise some questions about why Mr. Kessinger has changed his testimony after 18 months?

Apparently the ghost of J. Edgar Hoover is alive and doing very well in the FBI, and at Elliott's Body Shop.

For a short time Connie Hood lived with her husband at the Dreamland Motel. Arriving at their room very late one evening, a man in the next room flung his door open as if he was expecting someone. Though startled, Connie Hood got a good look at the man and she described the man to the FBI. She says he closely resembled the sketch of John Doe No. 2. He was 5'-8" tall, hair brushed straight back, olive complected, and with fuller or more pronounced facial features than the John Doe No. 2 sketch.

After numerous interviews and even some polygraph tests which proved that Mrs. Hood was telling the federal agents the truth about what she saw, they finally resorted to intimidation by yelling at her, "You've never seen John Doe! John Doe No. 2 never existed!" Needless to say, Connie Hood was extremely upset with the tactics used by the FBI and to this day she refuses to change her story because she was and is telling the truth. Like Hoppy Heidelberg said, "They went through a whole lot of trouble to make John Doe No. 2 go away." Hoppy also said that the FBI sizes people up to determine what type of coercion will work on any given witness. They obviously underestimated Connie Hood and were incorrect in their assumption that they could get her to lie by using the intimidation tactic.

It has been reported that "new and incriminating evidence" has been released which puts Timothy McVeigh in the vicinity of Elliott's Body Shop at the exact time that the notorious Ryder truck was rented. A video recording of McVeigh was taken in a McDonald's restaurant less than 20 minutes before the Ryder truck was rented and this particular McDonald's is only a little more than 1.25 miles away from Elliott's.

The report sounded sensationally incriminating just like it was supposed to sound. These little "sound bites" are obviously designed to negatively influence an unsuspecting audience. What the news report did not tell you is that the Dreamland Motel where McVeigh allegedly stayed from the 14th through the 18th of April, without leaving any fingerprints anywhere in the motel, the motel room or on the rental register, is also just a little over a mile down the road from Elliott's. So what's new? It had already been established, at least in the media, that McVeigh was in the area. There was nothing new, and certainly nothing incriminating. But if you begin the story with "new and incriminating," it is assumed by the average viewer that the story really is new and incriminating.

Now we're going to give you all of the facts about this incident, including the unreported facts, and you will see that the new and incriminating evidence, when reported in its entirety, proves beyond any doubt that Timothy McVeigh was not the Robert Kling who rented the notorious Ryder truck from Elliott's on April 17, 1995.

David Ferris, a cab driver working in and around Junction City, Kansas, said that he dropped off a passenger at that McDonald's location about 30 minutes before the Ryder truck was rented. Ferris said that his passenger looked like Timothy McVeigh and that he was wearing jeans and a white shirt. The witnesses at Elliott's say the man who rented the Ryder truck was wearing camos. A very interesting thing about this story, the "thing" which went virtually unnoticed by the media, is that the McDonald's video showed McVeigh wearing civilian clothes, but not jeans and a white shirt and definitely not camos. This information could indicate that Timothy McVeigh may not have been the only person at that particular McDonald's on that particular day and at that exact time who closely resembled Timothy McVeigh, but this is by no means the most significant unreported aspect of this story.

We must examine all of this information and put it in the proper perspective. On Monday, April 17, 1995 a video camera in a McDonald's restaurant in Junction City, Kansas video taped a man who was positively identified as Timothy McVeigh. The man caught by the video camera was 6'-2" tall, weighed 150-160 lbs., had short, light brown hair, blue eyes, a perfect complexion, a straight jaw, was dressed in civilian clothes and he appeared to be alone

More than 1.25 miles up the road and less than 20 minutes later, a man was identified at Elliott's Body Shop as the renter of the Ryder truck that allegedly exploded in front of the Murrah Building. The renter of the truck was identified as Robert Kling. He was described as being 5'-10" tall, weighing 180 -185 lbs., having a crew cut, brownish-green eyes, a rough complexion with acne, a crooked or deformed jaw and he was wearing camouflage fatigues.

He was not alone. His companion was, according to the original eyewitness statements, John Doe No. 2. Now, unless Timothy McVeigh, who was positively identified in a video recording at the McDonald's restaurant in Junction City, Kan., could shrink 4", gain 30 pounds, change the color of his eyes, develop a severe case of acne, screw up his jaw, change his clothes, eat a Happy Meal, recruit a companion and, with that companion, jog uphill to Elliott's in the rain, which is more than 1.25 miles away, without getting wet and still accomplish all of this in just a little more than 15 minutes, it seems very clear to us that this "new and incriminating evidence" against Timothy McVeigh actually proves beyond any doubt whatsoever that Tim McVeigh was not the renter of the Ryder truck that allegedly destroyed the Murrah Building.

Further, contrary to the news reports, this is compelling evidence for McVeigh's defense, not for the prosecution. Equally alarming is the fact that Tim's finger prints could not be found anywhere in Elliott's Body Shop or anywhere on the rental receipts and the Robert Kling who rented the truck was not wearing gloves. If Timothy James McVeigh did rent the notorious Ryder truck, perhaps it would be appropriate to change his nickname from Lee Harvey McVeigh to Timothy James Houdini!

The public's belief that an accused person is guilty or innocent can often times be manipulated by only reporting a small piece of information through a controlled media instead of reporting the whole story. This recent incident is not untypical of the way network news has reported the information surrounding this investigation from the very beginning. Is anyone asking just whose fingerprints they did find at Elliott's and on the rental receipts signed by Robert Kling? Now that you've been told "the rest of the story" could any reasonable person conclude that this evidence is new or incriminating against Timothy McVeigh?

Some of the most recent information being "leaked" to the media by the government's damage control agents had to do with an alleged confession by Tim to members of his defense team. The *Dallas Morning News* reported just prior to the McVeigh trial that an anonymous member of McVeigh's defense has given them a copy of a document consisting of notes taken during a conversation with McVeigh in 1995.

It is alleged by *Morning News* that Tim said he picked that particular time of the day so the explosion would result "in a high body count" making sure that "the government would get the point." That statement would make certain that no potential juror would ever feel any mercy for the accused. It was also "reported," and we use that term very loosely, that McVeigh said he delivered the Ryder truck alone and that Terry was an accomplice in the conspiracy but not involved in the actual bombing.

We must admit that those exact words couldn't have been better stated for the prosecution's case if the prosecution had typed them and sent the documents to the *Morning News*. And this new, alarming, incriminating "evidence" couldn't have come at a more opportune time for the prosecutors. Just when it was finally becoming obvious to many of the more enlightened journalists across this country that the government's case against McVeigh was, at the very best, weak. And just when it became apparent to those same journalists and many millions of their readers that most of the accusations against McVeigh were nothing more than lies fabricated by the feds and, conveniently, just a month before jury selection was about to begin, splashed across the news all over the whole world, "MCVEIGH CONFESSES!" The timing couldn't have been better for the prosecution.

We're certain you remember that, "trying to squash a rumor is like trying to unring a bell." In our opinion a more accurate observation has never been put into words. Although we realize that we cannot unring the bell and we cannot completely undo the intentional damage that has been done, we will place the hand of reason, logic and common sense on that bell in an attempt to silence the ringing for those who are willing to exercise their minds instead of their emotions.

The first thing about this alleged confession that we have to examine is the claim that Tim said he delivered the Ryder truck alone. That's easy to believe if you want to disregard all of the eyewitness testimony. We have to ignore the dozens of eyewitnesses who saw a variety of John Does. We have to choose not to believe several eyewitnesses who identified John Doe No. 2 in Junction City, Kan., with a Ryder truck, especially those eyewitnesses at Elliott's Body Shop. We have to choose not to believe Lea McGowan at the Dreamland Motel. We have to choose not to believe those witnesses who saw the Ryder truck and a white four door sedan, etc. parked at Geary Lake while Tim was more than a thousand miles away. We have to choose not to believe Mike Moroz and Dave Snider.

We have to choose not to believe dozens of eyewitnesses who saw John Doe No. 2 at the Dreamland Motel, the Great Western Inn, and at the scene of the crime. And we have to choose not to believe Daina Bradley, the only person who actually witnessed the delivery of the Ryder truck and the explosion from a "front-row seat." Ms. Bradley was standing inside the Murrah Building not more than 20 feet from the Ryder truck when she saw John Doe No. 2 exit the truck just moments before the explosion. She did not see Timothy McVeigh even though the prosecutors tried to get her to say that she saw McVeigh instead of John Doe No. 2. She ended up saying that she saw someone that "might have been" McVeigh in addition to John Doe No. 2. It was enough to convince the jury.

Ms. Bradley, like many others severely impacted by this tragedy, wants to know who was really responsible for this unspeakable horror against her and her family. If Timothy McVeigh, all by himself, delivered any Ryder truck anywhere on April 19, 1995, it was definitely not in front of the Murrah Building. That was the most obvious lie.

This most recent earth-shattering news release also said that McVeigh implicated his friend Terry Nichols in the plot to blow up the Murrah Building. Needless to say, when this story hit the Internet, reporters from across the country began calling us immediately to find out what we thought about Tim's confession and that he had allegedly implicated Terry.

The first question we asked them was: If we assume that Tim is guilty, and if he was going to confess, why would he implicate Terry? We were told that Tim would probably receive a reduced sentence for his testimony against Terry. Interesting. We felt compelled to ask those journalists, exactly how they might reduce Tim's sentence? Will they sentence him for 150 murders instead of 168? Perhaps he will only receive punishment for 100 murders.

Given that Oklahoma is a death penalty state that would be a great reward for a false confession and for implicating an innocent man. Maybe the prosecutors would reduce the electricity by a couple of hundred volts during the electrocution. Maybe they will reduce the lethal injection to cause death in eight minutes instead of six minutes. As you can plainly see, these are all viable options which Tim could consider as a reward for implicating Terry. Just a little thought using common sense is all a person needs to realize that the *Dallas Morning News* report of McVeigh's confession was nothing more than blatant sensationalism on the newspaper's part and a total fabrication by the source.

The reason for making public this phony confession was to do that which prosecutors know they would have been unable to do in court. Their intention is to convince potential jurors of McVeigh's guilt before they go to court and before they are exposed to the truth. If a juror's mind is made up before trial, a conviction is assured regardless of the evidence. Guilt or innocence has nothing to do with it as far as the prosecution is concerned. Conviction at any cost is their goal and is all that really matters to the prosecutors.

We must admit, when we first heard the report about McVeigh's alleged quote concerning the time of day to get the highest body count and about getting the government's attention, we knew from whom it came, and that "whom" was not Timothy McVeigh. Those exact words were expressed to us as suggestive speculation by a certain person long before that certain person could have had an opportunity to talk to McVeigh. Shortly after we met this individual, after several hours of conversation, we shared in private our suspicions that this individual was a damage control agent for the government. As time went by our suspicions were confirmed. We are certainly not alone in our knowledge about this individual or about the intentions of the individual's companion(s).

It has been stated publicly by Stephen Jones that these documents were fabricated by the defense team to "flush out" a certain suspect and we can confirm that there is a strong probability that Mr. Jones' explanation for the existence of these documents is true to some extent. The information within the alleged confession by McVeigh is absolutely erroneous. Other than the confession itself there are some things that he wouldn't have said simply because they are inaccurate. We know and Tim would certainly know that these things are incorrect, but a person fabricating a document and making up a story would not be aware of the subtle inaccuracies, and we have no intention on pointing them out until the appropriate time during trial if it becomes necessary.

There is another aspect of this alleged confession that a thinking person should consider. In our brief career as investigative journalists, we have come to the realization that government "moles" have infiltrated every nook and cranny of our society. Government denies it, naturally. Well-meaning people scoff at the suggestion of government infiltrators among us and ridicule those who believe it to be true, labeling them as "conspiracy wackos" and many other derogatory names.

But, as we have said before, what we want to believe does not change reality. Government moles among us are a fact of life whether you want to believe it or not. After a few months into this investigation that reality hit us square in the face and that reality has been reconfirmed time and time again over the past two years. Keeping in mind that we have had little experience in this field, and considering that Mr. Jones and team have had much experience with high profile cases and government investigations, is it unreasonable to assume that Mr. Jones and team have known for many years what we have learned recently? Is it unreasonable to assume that Stephen Jones realized the likelihood that there would be government moles on his defense team and offered some bait to flush out any potential moles? Is it unreasonable to assume that the mole(s) took the bait and passed that planted bait along to another government mole who was and is posing as a journalist? These are certainly possibilities which we must consider once we are made aware of the inconsistencies in "The Confession."

Immediately after the reports emanating from Dallas attempted to convince all of the non-thinkers in the media to consider Tim and Terry guilty beyond any reasonable doubt, I made a prediction on talk radio. My prediction was that before Tim's trial and before jury selection began there would be many more stories surfacing concerning other defense documents allegedly bootlegged by a mole who felt it was his duty to pass the information along to his journalist buddy, although these stories would not necessarily come from the *Dallas Morning News*.

Somebody would have to make up excuses for the discrepancies in the first confession and somebody did. Waiting in the wings was writer Ben Fenwick and the "patsy" he would use to pass along this "new and incriminating" information to an unsuspecting public was none other than *Playboy* magazine. A cover story had to be ready to explain away the discrepancies that we were pointing out about John Doe No. 2 which McVeigh allegedly made in the first confession. We must admit, Fenwick's article in *Playboy* was very convincing. After we read it (we didn't buy it for the pictures, just the article) we all agreed that, if we were not intimately involved in this investigation, the article in *Playboy* would have convinced us beyond any doubt of Tim's and Terry's guilt. And we certainly can't criticize anyone else who is not familiar with all of the evidence and all of the information for coming to that conclusion.

But, considering the importance of this alleged information and realizing the influence that these stories would have on any and all potential jurors, and knowing that the defendants, the victims, and the American people deserve a fair trial and eventual closure of this tragedy, we can criticize those members of our media who should have made certain that this information was accurate before they reported it. And contrary to what Mr. Fenwick and others have said, they did not check for accuracy. And if they did check for accuracy and still printed it, that would suggest there was something else going on here.

The errors in the *Playboy* article are so numerous we could easily devote an entire chapter to their discredit. The first obvious mistake made by the author of this fictional story concerned the alleged truck route driven by McVeigh on his way to the Murrah Building. Had McVeigh driven the route which Mr. Fenwick described, his desired destination could not possibly have been realized. You have to understand, after exiting the interstate a left turn cannot be made at any time at the exact intersection described in the alleged confession.

Disregarding the street layout of downtown Oklahoma City, Fenwick's article explains that after McVeigh exited the freeway he made a left turn onto 4th Street which would mean that he was driving to the west. Driving on 4th Street, he drove behind the Murrah Building and made a right turn on a one-way street, which would have placed him on Harvey Street traveling north. According to Fenwick's story, McVeigh drove north one block and made a right placing him on 5th Street facing east. He allegedly said that after turning the corner he pulled over in front of a tire store in that block and set the first fuse to the bomb by pulling a cord. He then drove to the next block, parked in front of the Murrah Building, pulled the cord to the primary fuse, dropped the key behind the seat, locked the truck and exited the scene.

The first and most obvious problem with this part of the story is, if you make a right onto 5th Street off Harvey you are directly in front of the Murrah Building, not one block to the west as the story suggests. If you drive one more block to the west on 4th street to put you in a potential location to retrace the alleged route you can't make a right because that street is a one-way going south. The path to the Murrah Building described in Fenwick's story is impossible to drive unless the person driving it got away with making illegal left turns and was also able to drive the wrong way down one-way streets with a big yellow Ryder truck at 9 o'clock in the morning in downtown Oklahoma City without causing an accident, without getting a ticket, and without even being noticed! What do you think the chances are of that happening, Ben? It would appear as if Mr. Fenwick has either not checked the facts, or has not exactly been forthright with his story.

Anyone familiar with the intricacies of this case would be inclined to believe that McVeigh's alleged confession made public by Mr. Fenwick read like a script written by the prosecution. That just may be a clue to Ben Fenwick's "reliable anonymous source" who some believe is Richard Reyna, a defense team investigator. If Reyna is the source, and we're not saying he is, he most certainly was not alone.

These inaccuracies were also pointed out by Dr. Paul Heath, President of the OK City Murrah Building Survivors' Association, during an interview on Court TV and CNN. Before Dr. Heath commented on the *Playboy* article, Terry Moran, the host of the show and his guests, Raymond Brown and Tim Sullivan, were absolutely convinced of the authenticity of the alleged confession and, watching their reactions after Dr. Heath's comments, it was apparent that they thought he was going to confirm the report and assist the media in adding fuel to the "burn him at the stake" fire.

Dr. Heath pointed out the inaccuracies in the document and stated that anyone familiar with the geography of downtown Oklahoma City would know immediately that the information was false. The commentators didn't quite know how to respond to Dr. Heath's statements. They appeared to be a little shocked that an informed surviving victim would claim that Ben Fenwick's story about McVeigh's alleged confession was obviously a phony. It was apparent that the "new and incriminating evidence" bubble had just burst. To their credit, Terry Moran and his guests acknowledged Dr. Heath's doubts about the authenticity of the documents in question and briefly included this new information in their discussion. In our opinion, the most upsetting thing about Dr. Heath's comments is that they went virtually unnoticed by everyone else in the media, even on other CNN news talk shows!

Another problem with "Ben Fenwick's confession" is the story about McVeigh dropping the key to the Ryder truck behind the seat. Unfortunately, when the feds helped fabricate Fenwick's story, they didn't realize that they would need to confirm Michael Fortier's story by saying they found the key near where Fortier was told to say Tim parked his yellow Mercury. The location of the key, which was in pristine condition supposedly dropped by Tim while making his getaway, was necessary to corroborate Fortier's story.

Needless to say, if the key had been dropped behind the seat as Ben Fenwick stated in his story, it would not have been perfectly clean and shiny. Having been in the center of an enormous explosion, it would have not only been unrecognizable as a key to anything, it would have literally turned into a bullet and could have ended up anywhere within a radius of a mile or more. In all likelihood, the chances of colonizing the planet Pluto in this century would've been better than finding that key. Their "facts" keep changing to conform to their allegations which keep changing to conform to their facts which keep changing. We were unaware that "facts" could change. By the way, why hasn't Mr. Fenwick challenged the prosecution's most recent story about the key? It doesn't conform to his story. Didn't Ben say that his story was absolutely accurate and that his source was absolutely reliable? If Ben's right, then the prosecution and Michael Fortier are lying. If the prosecution and Fortier are right, then Ben's lying. Take your pick! Then again, maybe they're all lying.

On *Crossfire*, another CNN talk show, we listened to a debate about Fenwick's story between Pat Buchanan and Geraldine Ferraro which was extremely disappointing. On this particular show Mr. Buchanan, typically perceived as a champion of Constitutional conservative values, decided to leave his common sense at home and use his brains for a seat cushion. All of his very vocal and very passionate opinions were based upon his assumption that McVeigh's confession was real.

We would like to know what evidence Mr. Buchanan had in his possession which would have convinced him that these documents were authentic. He apparently choose to believe Mr. Fenwick who refuses to disclose his "very reliable" source and who stood to gain considerably from this phony story, not only from the payment he received from Playboy, but from the notoriety he has received from his exposé on the most hated man on the planet. This time the voice of reason seemed to come from Geraldine Ferraro, a liberal with whom we seldom if ever agree about anything. Go figure! We would suggest that Mr. Buchanan should, from this time forward, take the time to check the facts before he decides to convict someone on his talk show without a trial.

Not much more than a week after Fenwick's article appeared in *Playboy*, *Newsweek* got its turn to throw the rope over the limb of the lynchin' tree. When you really take a look at the *Dallas Morning News* story, the *Playboy* article and then the article in *Newsweek* it's not too difficult to see what's going on here.

Remember, shortly after Pete Slover made his story public in the Dallas paper, it was stated by Leslie Abramson, famous defense attorney and outspoken defender of our Constitutional Rights, that these documents, if they were real, had to have been obtained illegally. There was absolutely no legal way Pete Slover could have gotten them, she said. Stephen Jones also said that if the *Dallas Morning News* printed one more word about it, he would file suit against them. Enter the *Playboy* article to continue on with the scam. Are we to believe that every magazine and newspaper can get away with printing one falsely incriminating story about the same person without being concerned about a law suit?

Now if Pete Slover was very close to a member of McVeigh's defense team who stole some documents, and Pete had some exclusive information that bothered his conscience so much that he just had to print it, how did Ben Fenwick get his hands on documents which, not only covered the discrepancies in Slover's scam, but went into much greater detail describing how this bombing was accomplished? We know that the details are inaccurate and that Ben's story is also a lie, but how many people will actually realize that this whole thing is nothing more than a scam, probably written by a government mole working for the prosecution? That Slover, Fenwick, *Newsweek* and whoever else could have received nearly identical disinformation definitely indicates the probability of government plants being in key positions of employment to influence us through the media in any way they so desire.

It has been stated many times that these confession documents are a matter of record. That may be true. The FBI and the defense teams have tens of thousands of documents that are recorded and are, in fact, a matter of record. The prosecution and defense teams have in their possession statements made by a seed salesman from Indiana who said that I drew pictures of the Murrah Building and talked about bombing it in 1988.

These false documents are a matter of record. Why didn't Mr. Slover and Mr. Fenwick point to other documents in the possession of the feds and in the defense team computers which prove beyond any doubt the existence of John Doe No. 2? Why didn't Mr. Slover and Mr. Fenwick point to all of those documents and all of the facts in this case which absolutely contradict their phony stories and their phony documents which now are unquestionably a matter of record?

In their articles and in their interviews, why didn't they mention the numerous eyewitnesses who saw John Doe No. 2, particularly Daina Bradley, who saw John Doe No. 2 exit the Ryder truck but did not see McVeigh? Why didn't Mr. Fenwick include in his article in *Playboy* a map of downtown Oklahoma City so all of those people who are unfamiliar with the area could trace the impossible route described by Mr. Fenwick's reliable anonymous source?

We have to pay very close attention to what we are being told, and even more important, to what we are not being told. The professional deceivers and the government's agents of deceit have put their disinformation campaign into high gear since trial time is getting close and since they still have no hard evidence and no reliable witnesses who will confirm their allegations against Tim and Terry. We must remember that just because a statement or document is a matter of record does not mean that the statement or document is a matter of truth. •

Photo courtesy *Media Bypass* magazine

Alternative media such as *Media Bypass* magazine, shown above, have avoided the propaganda parade as espoused by much of the mainstream press and has reported on developments, as they have surfaced, pertaining to the Murrah Building explosions. In so doing, it is apparent that advance knowledge of this horrific attack was evident within the confines of government investigative agencies.

"The people are the masters of both Congress and courts, not to overthrow the Constitution, but to overthrow the men who pervert it!
— **Abraham Lincoln**

CHAPTER 26: BEYOND REASONABLE DOUBT

We have presented more than enough reasonable doubt to satisfy even the most skeptical of those citizens who, prior to reading this book, might have trusted any and all actions by their government concerning this investigation without ever questioning those actions. However, we feel compelled to expand upon some of the issues we've briefly mentioned and to bring to your attention our perspectives on some other issues that we have not yet discussed publicly.

Since this chapter will take your thoughts and your understanding of the many aspects of this investigation far BEYOND REASONABLE DOUBT about the guilt of the accused and the probable complicity of rogue public servants who are in the highest positions of authority we will not concentrate on a specific issue as in previous chapters but will explain, in depth, a variety of issues and then give you an educated opinion about what some of this evidence and eyewitness testimony really means.

We're not going to insult your intelligence like the "interpreters" on national television who take two hours to explain to us in English what a politician just said in English during a ten minute speech. Make sure that you maintain a thinking mind when you contemplate this information and when you consider our conclusions. Don't just believe what we're telling you. We want you to really think about the information we're passing along to you. When you apply logic to the information in this case we are confident that your conclusions will somewhat parallel ours.

The first issue BEYOND REASONABLE DOUBT upon which we will expound has to do with the alleged ANFO bomb. According to experts in demolitions there are different qualities of ammonium nitrate. This information was repeated by Beth Wilkinson, one of the U.S. prosecutors working on this case. We must keep in mind that Gen. Partin's theoretical diagram assumed absolutely ideal conditions resulting in the maximum potential energy of the ANFO that allegedly exploded in front of the

Murrah Building. This is an unlikely scenario for many reasons. The first reason is that the general's theory assumes that the ANFO was enhanced or boosted by a more potent explosive such as C-4 or some other high explosive of equal power. We do not know that to be the case but we will continue under the assumption that that assumption is true.

The second reason that the basis for this maximum efficiency theory is unlikely is that the most efficient explosion would have been accomplished by the enhanced, demolitions-grade ammonium nitrate being held in one container and set off by one detonator. The FBI experts say that the ANFO was contained in twenty blue plastic barrels which would have also required twenty separate detonators. According to Gen. Partin, one of the top demolitions experts in this country, that type of arrangement would have counteracted itself, each explosion negating, to some extent, each other explosion even if they were all detonated at precisely the same time which doesn't seem possible unless these barrels were detonated electronically. The FBI says that's not the case. They theorize that the fuse was lit by hand. Additionally, this concoction was mixed by hand, so say the Feds.

If the mixture was measured in absolutely perfect proportion, mechanically mixed by professionals resulting in a mixture with no clumps, kept in one container, ignited by one detonator in the middle of the ANFO, enhanced by a much more potent explosive and mixed using the highest grade ammonium nitrate available, the result would have been the explosion on which Gen. Partin based his diagram.

According to the FBI's own experts this ANFO bomb was hand mixed by amateurs, mixed in twenty separate containers with 20 separate detonators, ignited with a match, may or may not have been enhanced and, to top it all off, was concocted with typical farmyard ammonium nitrate fertilizer, not demolition grade ANFO. We don't think that the FBI's description of the bomb that destroyed the Murrah Building would have anywhere near the energy of Gen. Partin's theoretical explosion and, according to Gen. Partin, even his theoretical "perfect" bomb could not possibly knock over the closest column to the truck and would have no effect whatsoever on the column that was destroyed farthest from the truck. Like he has said many times, "You can't destroy hard targets with air blast and these columns were hard targets. You need contact explosives to destroy hard targets."

During a conversation (interrogation?) by Beth Wilkinson and two other FBI agents, one of whom had 25 years experience with explosives, Gen. Benton Partin was asked how those large cement columns inside the Murrah Building could have been destroyed by contact charges without someone noticing that the charges were there. The general suggested that contact charges could have been placed against or near the columns without detection because terrorists can sometimes be pretty smart.

The FBI special agent with 25 years experience in explosives then stated in disagreement, "If you put it (explosives) on the side of the column you're not gonna be able to bring down that column. You're gonna be able to bore in to bring that column down."

He inadvertently destroyed the government's contention that the alleged Ryder truck explosion destroyed any of those columns. The closest column was around 20 feet from the Ryder truck and the furthest destroyed column was about 60 feet from the truck. The alleged truck explosion could have only created an air blast effect against any of those columns. The alleged ANFO bomb was not contacting any of the cement columns when or if it exploded and, by the FBI expert's own admission, blast pressure could not have destroyed those columns. These professional deceivers, while trying to twist Gen. Partin's words, eventually got so involved in the conversation that their mouths got ahead of their brains and the real truth finally came out. Their own expert finally admitted the truth. What they've been trying to make us believe happened could not possibly have happened.

The professional deceivers were themselves deceived by their own attempt at deception. *Touché!* Let us just state for the record that Gen. Partin's opinion about what actually destroyed the Murrah Building was not changed by the FBI's attempt at twisting his words. It was apparent that the FBI interrogators' opinions changed although they would never admit it.

One other minor issue that we should touch on concerning the ANFO bomb is the remnants of ANFO left behind after the explosion. Realizing that the FBI's description of what took place in front of the Murrah Building could not possibly have resulted in an efficient burn of the alleged ANFO, one would have to conclude that a substantial amount of ANFO crystals or prills would've been scattered around the area.

We discussed this information in depth earlier in the book. According to Beth Wilkinson, assistant U.S. attorney and one of the assistant prosecutors on this case, only one small piece of the truck was found showing traces of ammonium nitrate crystals in their original form. That one small piece of the truck, labeled "Q507" by the FBI Crime Lab, was the only piece of evidence found at the crime scene of which we know that showed any remnants of ammonium nitrate.

Could a farmer have rented that same truck some time in the past to haul fertilizer? Considering that the ammonium nitrate crystals were in their original form (fertilizer, not ANFO) proves that they were not remnants of an ANFO explosion. Considering that lab tests showed no evidence of an ANFO explosion on any of the samples we had tested, and considering that the FBI lab technicians only found ammonium nitrate crystals in their original form on one little piece of plywood allegedly from the Ryder truck, is there a possibility that this little piece of truck could have been accidentally contaminated in the FBI crime lab along with Tim McVeigh's clothing? A reasonable person might conclude that there is at least a possibility that "accidental contamination" could have taken place in the FBI crime lab.

A reasonable person might also conclude that, since there was no other evidence of an ANFO explosion, there may not have ever been an ANFO explosion. Did the prosecutors or the defense team ever check the records for that particular Ryder truck to see if it had ever been used in the past by anyone to haul fertilizer?

You must be thinking that making such a statement borders on insanity. Everyone knows that an ANFO bomb, in some shape or form, was at least responsible for destroying the Ryder truck and causing some damage to the Murrah Building and other buildings in the area. We will admit to being told over and over again that this was definitely an ANFO explosion. We will admit that it has been universally accepted that an ANFO explosion was responsible for the majority of the damage in downtown Oklahoma City. We will admit that evidence of minute traces of ammonium nitrate crystals in their original form at the bombing site could be misconstrued as circumstantial evidence against the defendants.

But, as you well know, we have this hang-up with not believing anything until we see the evidence. And, as you well know, we have never believed any of the "ANFO reports" because there was no signature of an ANFO explosion and the severity of the damage did not reflect the type of damage possible from an ANFO explosion. We have never been shown any evidence of an ANFO explosion and when we took samples from the area and had them tested in an independent laboratory no traces of any remnants or elements were found which would indicate that an ANFO explosion had occurred. Now, after nearly two years, the truth has finally surfaced. All of the skeptics who thought we were just crazy conspiracy wackos because we were suggesting that the FBI has been fabricating evidence may finally decide to at least consider what we've been trying to tell you since the beginning of this investigation.

According to a *Los Angeles Times* article written by *Times* Washington bureau reporter Richard Serrano, the inspector general's office within the Justice Department has been very critical of the FBI crime lab's conclusions in the Oklahoma City bombing case. The inspector general determined that the crime lab has made "scientifically unsound" conclusions in this case and that some supervisors approved lab reports they "cannot support." It was also reported that many analyses were "biased in favor of the prosecution." The inspector general's report concludes that FBI lab officials may not know for certain that ammonium nitrate was used, could not identify the triggering device, and that the lab may have contaminated McVeigh's clothing.

Commenting on the conclusions of David Williams, a supervisory agent in the explosives unit, the inspector general's report stated: "We are deeply troubled by Williams' report which contains several serious flaws. These errors are all tilted in favor of the prosecution's theory of the case. We conclude that Williams failed to present an objective, unbiased, competent report." The inspector general's study also said that William's identification of ammonium nitrate and fuel oil as being the cause of the explosion was "inappropriate." FBI agents found a receipt for the purchase of ammonium nitrate at Terry Nichols' home and "because of that discovery Williams slanted his conclusions to match that evidence."

It goes on to say that Williams' identification of the type of explosives used "is not based on scientific or technical grounds and appears to tailor the opinion to evidence associated with the defendants." Williams "acknowledged that he reached this conclusion, in part, because Terry Nichols purchased ammonium nitrate and diesel oil prior to the bombing. Without the evidence of these purchases, Williams admitted he would have been unable to conclude that ANFO was used."

In light of the allegations and charges against Timothy McVeigh and Terry Nichols, considering that the presumption of guilt is consistently held by almost everyone in the media even though they insist that the accused be afforded the presumption of innocence, does anyone else find this information extremely alarming?

Does anyone else wonder why this report has been kept a secret and has actually been classified SECRET to keep it from public scrutiny? Does anyone else wonder why the phrase "unable to conclude that ANFO was used" is never repeated by federal or media prosecutors? Does anyone else wonder why Nancy Grace and other media prosecutors who passionately insist that the public be told the truth, the whole truth, and nothing but the truth about the evidence in the Oklahoma City bombing investigation aren't themselves telling the public the truth, the whole truth, and nothing but the truth about this lack of evidence in the investigation?

Does anyone else wonder why the media prosecutors refuse to include in their conversations and debates any information which disproves beyond any reasonable doubt the FBI's charges against Tim and Terry? Does anyone else wonder just what was responsible for the extensive damage to the Murrah Building? Does anyone else wonder why the FBI wanted to conclude that there was an ANFO bomb even though no such evidence existed? Does anyone else wonder why it has been consistently alleged by prosecutors and by the media that ANFO was the explosive used in the bombing even though there has never been any evidence to confirm those allegations? Does anyone else wonder why the FBI would lie about this lack of evidence?

Does anyone think that this important information has been withheld to protect the innocent? Does anyone think that this information has been withheld and labeled SECRET to protect the accused? Does anyone else wonder why everyone in the media has jumped on McVeigh's alleged confession and accepted it as authentic, even though it is not only inaccurate, but makes no sense whatsoever. Does anyone wonder why those same media personalities have chosen to not report the fact that there is no evidence of an ANFO explosion which proves that the prosecutions entire case is based on a lie?

Does anyone wonder about any of these discrepancies? Does anyone care?

Considering that the inspector general's report was written in January of 1997, does anyone else notice the correlation between the timing of the report and the "new and incriminating evidence" against Timothy McVeigh and McVeigh's alleged confessions? Does anyone else suspect that maybe this report was kept a secret so the agents of deceit would have ample opportunity to disseminate their bogus information before jury selection in an attempt to pollute the jury pool? Does anyone else realize just how desperate the prosecution was before these bogus confessions surfaced? Will anyone else be surprised if the inspector general's report is not allowed into court as evidence? Will anyone be surprised if much of the evidence discussed in this book is excluded from the trial?

Another very interesting and curious piece of information has been inadvertently brought to our attention by Oliver "Buck" Revell, former deputy director of the FBI. In a debate between the authors of this book and Mr. Revell, which aired during an episode of *Hannity and Colmes* on the Fox News Channel, we discussed, among other issues, the inspector general's criticism of the FBI crime lab's conclusions.

Mr. Hannity made mention of the inspector general's conclusion that the FBI crime lab's supervisor, David Williams, based his ANFO bomb opinions, not on evidence, but on the allegations that Terry Nichols purchased ammonium nitrate and diesel oil prior to the bombing. Mr. Revell, in defense of David Williams, unwittingly and we believe innocently, further incriminated Mr. Williams.

Mr. Revell said: "It was told to me by agents that were on the scene that the day after the bombing, before there were any suspects or before there was any amount of explosives known to have been purchased, that David Williams stated it appeared to him to have been an ANFO bomb of around 4,000 to 5,000 pounds."

Oh, really? In light of the inspector general report that two years after the bombing, using all of the scientific resources of the FBI crime lab, neither Mr. Williams nor anyone else has found any evidence among the hundreds of thousands of tons of rubble which even suggests that the Murrah Building was destroyed by an ANFO bomb, how might Mr. Williams have concluded the day after the bombing that ANFO was used? How might Mr. Williams have concluded, the day after the bombing and the day before any fertilizer receipts were "discovered" that 4,000 to 5,000 pounds were used?

Did the feds already know who they were going to blame for this act of terrorism? Did they already know that Tim or Terry had purchased particular amounts of ammonium nitrate fertilizer? Did they just assume that, like many farmers, I would also have ammonium nitrate fertilizer on my farm thereby cinching the knot on their setup? When you add David Williams predictions the day after the bombing to the observations of BATF Special (ANFO) Agent Harry Everhardt, just moments after the bombing, the coincidences of their false allegations are, at the least, alarming and to a thinking mind, could easily be construed as very incriminating.

According to investigative journalist J.D. Cash, the feds were aware of and monitoring no less than six and perhaps as many as 10 co-conspirators in the Oklahoma City bombing long before the bombing took place. The first question that comes to mind when considering this information is; if the feds knew who was involved in the plot before the bombing and knew when and where it was going to take place, why didn't they stop this unspeakable act of horror?

The second thought that occurs to the thinking mind is this: Since the bombing did indeed take place why didn't the feds, immediately after the bombing, round up and arrest all of those people who they knew were involved in the plot? If they knew who the perpetrators of this crime were going to be, then it stands to reason that the feds knew who the perpetrators were after the fact and they should have apprehended all of the culprits instead of labeling them with a variety of numerical "John Doe" monikers and then, later, denying their existence. There's absolutely no excuse for the prosecutors to ask the judge to NOT order an additional search for classified data on other possible suspects in the attack. There's absolutely no excuse for dropping the $2,000,000 reward on the "John Does." There's just no excuse for any of these things unless, of course, the feds have something or someone to hide.

That some of the feds not only had prior warning but also knew the details of this scheme far in advance certainly makes sense to us. But the agents of deceit would have us believe that this was a sting operation which went bad, similar to the "excuse" they gave us concerning the World Trade Center bombing. This blown sting concept could explain why there may have been few, if any BATF agents in the building at the time of the explosions. It could also help explain why members of the bomb squad were seen around the building nearly two hours before the fact and perhaps many hours before. The blown sting operation theory also puts the suspicious mind at ease because it's always easy and often times desirable to blame it on the bungling BATF. After all, can anyone think of another agency more deserving of blame, criticism and name calling than the infamous BATF?

In addition to this "miscalculation" by the BATF, if one is to believe this theory, one first has to accept the allegations that there were munitions and possibly even explosives in the Murrah Building being stored illegally by the BATF and by the DEA. And, as anyone would guess, these allegations are emphatically denied by the feds. There were many government agents involved in concealing the fact that there were illegally stored munitions in the Murrah Building. We have seen still pictures and movies showing government agents removing these dangerous and illegal items from the rubble shortly after the explosions. More than likely most of those agents were just following orders and believed they were saving their employer from a negligence law suit the size of which would be unprecedented in American jurisprudence. In addition they would keep some of their buddies from going to prison for being partially, although accidentally, responsible for the enormous loss of life in this tragedy.

Information has circulated, and is believed by many, that these illegally stored explosives were responsible for the second massive explosion inside the Murrah Building. This is, admittedly, a believable and a necessary explanation. Too many witnesses heard two distinct explosions several seconds apart. The seismograph registered two separate explosions and the second one was definitely not the collapse of the building. After the initial explosion from the alleged truck bomb the building collapsing on the illegally stored C-4 would certainly explain why there was a second large explosion. It has even been suggested that the notorious second and third bomb scares which took place during the rescue efforts on the morning of the bombing were staged so the BATF could remove their contraband in secrecy. Most of the surviving victims and many of the families of the victims who did not survive have expressed little doubt about this story. It answers many of the questions that have been embarrassing the feds since the very beginning of the investigation. The government could be held responsible for an illegal act, an accidental tragedy, but an illegal act none-the-less. Their responsibility could and should be reflected in monetary damages into the billions of dollars.

What these damage control agents would have us believe is that there was some criminal negligence on the part of government and then some major shuffling to conceal that negligence. Even though it is believed by many that federal agents scrambled to cover it up, we believe that eventually federal damage control agents have also exposed this cover-up. At first that seems like a contradiction, doesn't it? But, when you give it some serious thought and try to understand what's really been going on here, it makes perfect sense. Quite simply, they got caught. Too much information leaked out in those first few hours after the bombing. Too many witnesses saw and heard too many things that they weren't supposed to see and hear. Many of those witnesses have been told to shut up about what they saw but no matter how hard the feds tried they could not keep a lid on it. Consequently, they had to spread disinformation to explain away all of the questions being asked by private investigators and by some of the victims' families.

The plan from the very beginning was for this case to never get into court because, as we learned from President Kennedy's assassination, DEAD MEN DON'T TESTIFY. But plan "A" just didn't happen like it was supposed to have happened so plan "B" became a necessity for the feds. The second plan was and is to continue on with the setup which would include destruction and falsification of evidence, witness coercion, leaking false, incriminating information through their agents in the media aimed at influencing the public and potential jurors, just downright lying, and any other means necessary to make up for their total lack of "real" evidence against the accused.

While plan "B" was in motion the blueprint for plan "C" began in the summer of 1995. It was created as an insurance policy to use in conjunction with plan "B" if and when it became necessary. When numerous experts provided evidence which disproved the government's story that necessity was realized.

When it became apparent that eyewitness testimony didn't correspond with the FBI's allegations, and particularly when some of the victims started doubting the media's reports about how and why this tragedy happened, plan "C" was initiated. The intent of this particular disinformation campaign was to explain why the Murrah Building sustained so much more damage than would have been possible from a fertilizer bomb.

The plan was for related cases to eventually end up in civil court if the feds got cornered and there was absolutely no other way to explain the impossible. If there was no other way out the government could inevitably admit that there was negligence on their part, but they would have to go down kicking and screaming. They certainly won't go down without a fight. They may eventually beg for forgiveness and, with large monetary "bribes," will get that forgiveness. Yes, they will be forgiven by the victims, by the media, and by the American people. After all, they already have two unsuspecting, expendable souls sitting in prison on whom we can all vent our frustrations and on whom we can all impose our vengeance.

By admitting negligence on the part of government agencies, they will have explained why there was more than one explosion. They will have explained why the Murrah Building sustained more damage than could've possibly been done by any size fertilizer bomb. They will have given the media another "beat-up-on-the-government" story which will temporarily satisfy their otherwise insatiable appetite for sensationalism. They will finally lay to rest the accusations from the skeptics and the so-called "conspiracy wackos."

What will the feds have lost — their credibility? That's never been a concern before. Since their cover-ups of the assassinations of the 1960s they haven't had any credibility with anyone who has the slightest brain wave. The worst thing that can happen is that some of our "talking heads" will give the government a tongue-lashing for not realizing that some bad agents in the BATF and DEA were storing this contraband.

We can be certain that they will find one or two dozen equally expendable "scapegoats" in these agencies on whom they can blame the enhancement of this tragedy. They always do. Fire the scapegoats. Throw them to the wolves for public humiliation and pay off the victims and their families with checks from the U.S. Treasury. The government hasn't lost anything but it has gained an enormous amount of power by hacking away many of our Constitutional rights resulting from the passage of the anti-terrorism bill, turning the public against their neighbors in the militia, attempting to place "patriot" in the four-letter-word category, inducing a public fear of terrorism and several other, more subtle infringements.

Nobody complains. They still have their villains who caused this tragedy. They will be given a media trial and executed just like the President and his attorney general promised. Everyone has their revenge. The FBI got their men and the government investigators have answered all of the unanswered questions. Everyone's satisfied. Right?

Before we accept this very believable "damage control theory" let's look objectively at the information we have and closely scrutinize this story which we are certain was fabricated by the government's agents of deceit. If this had really been a sting operation with their guy or guys on the inside would someone please explain to us how the government agents who were monitoring and watching these villains could possibly have lost track of at least six and perhaps as many as ten co-conspirators, no less than two or three slow-moving BIG YELLOW Ryder trucks, 5,000 pounds of ANFO, at least two 1977 YELLOW Mercury jalopies, a couple of extra license plates and Lord knows how many Timothy McVeigh lookalikes. Their story becomes much more difficult to swallow if you choose to believe that the feds had an informant on the inside whose objective, along with his bosses, was to assist in nipping this thing in the bud just before it happened.

It becomes considerably more unbelievable if you have even minimal understanding of the surveillance and tracking capabilities of the feds. No less than two decades ago their satellites in orbit could literally read the license plate on a car traveling down the road. At least that's all they would admit to us. But even if that was their limitation two decades ago, which common sense dictates it was not since it would not have been prudent for the government to reveal to the world their technological capabilities, they have, in this age of aerospace and computer technology, undoubtedly advanced in leaps and bounds over the past 20 years. Does anyone who is actually living in the 90s really doubt that the feds could track anyone, anytime and anywhere once they got "anyone" in their sights?

There is one exception to our conclusions that this operation could not have been botched with a government informant on the inside. That exception would have to be that the "bosses" had no intentions on nipping this thing in the bud. If the bosses were involved with other conspirators in this act of terrorism that would mean there were several other "informants" on the inside and the lone informant, whose goal was to keep the bosses informed so they could intercept the terrorists, would actually have been the patsy on whom they could place the blame.

Considering all of the John Does who witnesses have seen, all of the men in suits and in army camos with a Ryder truck at Geary Lake before anyone claims to have seen McVeigh with a Ryder truck, all of the BATF and bomb squad personnel at the scene before the fact and suspiciously missing during the fact, and a variety of others who were apparently involved, who might that well-meaning informant be? It seems as if all of the alleged John Does have disappeared from the face of the earth, with one exception. That exception, and one of his buddies, appear to be the Lee Harvey Oswalds of the '90s awaiting trial for a crime they did not commit.

Sometime during the fall of '95 a new potential co-conspirator was brought into this scenario. His name is Andreas Strassmeir, a.k.a. "Andy the German." It was originally thought by private investigators that Andy was involved in this conspiracy with McVeigh and some religious radicals from Elohim City, which is the name given to a settlement of religious separatists located in eastern Oklahoma. It was believed by many that Andy the German could be the notorious John Doe No. 2, although in our opinion Strassmeir doesn't resemble John Doe No. 2 any more than McVeigh resembles the original description of John Doe No. 1. Michael Brescia, one of Strassmeir's close friends, does bear a striking resemblance to the sketch of John Doe No. 2 as well as fitting John Doe No. 2's overall profile.

According to FBI documents, several witnesses can link Brescia with Strassmeir and it seems to have been reasonably established that they both spent considerable time in and around Elohim City where the BATF is alleged to have had an informant. J.D. Cash has reported in the *McCurtain* (Okla.) *Daily Gazette* that for two months prior to the bombing the informant, Carol Howe, reported regularly to the BATF about Strassmeir, Brescia and others who were planning to bomb a federal building in either Tulsa or Oklahoma City on April 19, 1995.

Ms. Howe has stated that Strassmeir was the chief instigator of the conspiracy and that he was a member of the Aryan Republican Army. Two days after the bombing she told the FBI that Michael Brescia was John Doe No. 2 and that Strassmeir seemed to have a great deal of influence on John Doe No. 1 (Timothy McVeigh?). Shortly after the bombing Andreas Strassmeir left the United Stated and returned to his parents home in Germany. Mission accomplished? Who knows?

Recently Michael Brescia and several other men have been arrested in

Philadelphia and Ohio by the FBI for their possible involvement in a string of bank robberies in the Midwest. One of the men arrested in Ohio in connection with those bank robberies bears an uncanny resemblance to the sketch of John Doe No. 1 and generally fits the original description of the man (Robert Kling) who rented the Ryder truck.

Could this be the same man who witnesses saw with Brescia and Strassmeir on different occasions? Could these witnesses be connecting one of the accused bank robbers to the sketch of John Doe No. 1 and then assuming that John Doe No. 1 is Timothy McVeigh because that's who the FBI has told them to identified as John Doe No. 1 and because that's who they have consistently seen portrayed as John Doe No. 1 in magazines, newspapers, and on television? Could the accused bank robber who looks like the sketch of John Doe No. 1 have successfully passed himself off as Tim McVeigh, or is John Doe No. 1 being identified as Timothy McVeigh just the result of induced confusion by the FBI?

Considering the allegations from the BATF's informant in Elohim City who said that Strassmeir was the "instigator" of this bombing, the striking similarities in appearance between Strassmeir's friend Michael Brescia and John Doe No. 2, the fact that Brescia is suspected of being involved in several bank robberies with five other accomplices, Mark Thomas, Peter Langan, Scott Stedeford, Kevin McCarthy and Richard Guthrie, and the remarkable resemblance between John Doe No. 1 and one of the other bank robbery suspects, doesn't it seem odd that the FBI would totally ignore the obvious evidence which suggests that these seven may be the real conspirators in the Oklahoma City bombing?

Doesn't it seem rather curious that Richard Guthrie, the only one of those bank robbery suspects who agreed to testify for the government, was found hanged to death in his jail cell before he could give that testimony? Of course, the official report states that Guthrie was the victim of an apparent suicide. Convenient.

Doesn't it seem rather curious that the BATF's informant at Elohim City, Carol Howe, told the agents as early as April 21, 1995, that she thought John Doe No. 2 may actually be Michael Brescia, yet they never acted on that information? That same day, April 21, 1995, instead of pursuing the lead about John Doe No. 2 given to them by their own paid informant, they came to Michigan to blame me and to accuse me of being the "guru" behind this tragedy

Even before the feds took me into "protective custody," their own paid informant told them that Strassmeir initiated the plan for this bombing. Why did they blame me if their informant had already given them the identity of the real "guru"? Even before the feds sent forth their swarms of officers to harass Terry Nichols and his family, spreading the word that he was the notorious John Doe No. 2, their own paid informant had already given them the identity of the person who she believed to be John Doe No. 2. Were they trying to protect the identity of their real inside man who actually planned this bombing? Did they successfully protect the identity of their real inside man who made certain the mission came off without a hitch and who made certain there would be a Lee Harvey McVeigh and Company carefully manipulated into a position to absorb the blame for this act of terrorism by leaving a suspiciously obvious trail of very circumstantial evidence? Wasn't their "trail" just a little too obvious?

Shortly after Carol Howe, the BATF's own paid informant, "spilled the beans" about Strassmeir and Brescia to J.D. Cash, she was suspiciously arrested, charged with complicity in some other bombings, and effectively "removed" from circulation. After spending some time in jail, Ms. Howe's story will probably change to completely conform to the prosecution's allegations in this case. Threats, duress, coercion and, if necessary, a little time in prison seems to have that effect on most potential witnesses.

Since the BATF's paid informant can't claim the reward for John Doe No. 2, and since nobody else has, let it be known that James Nichols and Bob Papovich want to claim the $2,000,000 reward for John Doe No. 2 after publicly claiming that Andreas Strassmeir may be the instigator of the bombing, that John Doe No. 2 may be Michael Brescia, that either Scott Stedeford or Kevin McCarthy, considering their ages, may be John Doe No. 1, and that the rest of the "bank robbery ring" who are either in prison or dead could have assisted directly or indirectly in the bombing.

Investigators, using phone records, linked McVeigh to Strassmeir to Elohim City, on and off, over a period of around two years. We have always had a problem with the feds, basing any of their so-called evidence on phone records. Unless you have a recording of the conversations in question, how do you know who actually made the call or who even took part in those particular conversations?

Not that an audio recording would necessarily be absolute proof, but it certainly would help. Without a recording, what would the FBI know about the content of those conversations? If someone, somehow got your calling card number that someone could make calls using your number any time they wanted. Just because your card number is used to make a call it doesn't necessarily mean that you made the call.

All of the calls among the FBI's extremely circumstantial evidence against McVeigh were made on a calling card number. And, according to investigative journalist Lawrence Myers, only one call was made from McVeigh's calling card to Elohim City, not numerous calls as the media has reported. We must mention again that there is absolutely nothing in Tim's religious background which would in any way suggest that he might share the same religious philosophy with the people of Elohim City. The suggestion that Tim was involved with those people just never made any sense to us.

Among others, members of McVeigh's defense team have interviewed and investigated Andreas Strassmeir. J.D. Cash and the late Glen Wilburn have also included in their evidence gathering an investigation of "Andy the German." They have concluded, from an apparent conversation with Andy, that he could have been the informant who the BATF had on the inside of this conspiracy. Their conclusion is not totally without merit. According to Cash and Wilburn, Andy has close ties with American intelligence agencies, has been working with the BATF and, at some time, has been on their payroll. It has been reported that Andy is a German Army officer and is also the son of a member of the German parliament which may indicate that he has been associated with intelligence operatives within our State Department. That Strassmeir is well-connected in the U.S. and in Germany has been established by many investigators.

That Andreas Strassmeir may have been on the inside in this conspiracy certainly seems within the realm of possibilities surrounding this disastrous act of terrorism. But Cash's and Wilburn's theory that Strassmeir was the "good guy" informant is based solely upon some very general statements that he made. While hypothesizing about the probability of an informant, Andy said that the person in question is, not could be, but "is" afraid to talk about the incident. Cash and Wilburn construed that one little word to be a confession by Strassmeir. That statement, along with some other very generic statements convinced these two well-meaning investigators that Strassmeir was indeed the informant.

Although J.D. Cash and Glen Wilburn have brought forth much very valuable information over the past two years, their conclusions throughout this investigation have often times defied logic. They have completely refused to even consider the issue of intentional complicity in the bombing by rogue government agents even though all of the evidence indicates that that is the case. Their conclusions are that after government agents blew their sting operation, they also assisted in covering up their negligence involving the illegally stored munitions in a federal building that, not only housed many non-law enforcement employees, but also a day-care center. It has been reported by Glen Wilburn and J.D. Cash that the feds expected this bombing would take place in the wee hours of the morning on April 19. Their report conveniently explains why so many people witnessed unusual things in and around the Murrah Building during the days and hours prior to the explosions. But there are two other witnesses, requesting anonymity, who told investigators that they saw a construction crew working on the foundation in the parking garage under the Murrah Building just a few days before the explosions.

Two more unnamed witnesses working in the Federal Courthouse across the street claim to have seen two persons with flashlights sometime between 2 a.m. and 3 a.m. on April 19 going floor-to floor-inside the Murrah Building. There were no regular maintenance or security personnel on duty and no one was supposed to be inside the building at that time. Many other witnesses saw what they thought were law enforcement agents, including BATF and bomb-squad personnel, around the Murrah Building many hours before the bombing. The eye witness accounts from people interviewed by Cash, Wilburn and other investigators are nearly endless and, at first thought, these sightings would clearly indicate that the feds were preparing for a sting operation.

According to Cash and Wilburn, the feds somewhere along the way lost track of the trucks. They were there waiting to bust the scoundrels but the trucks didn't show up as planned. The first problem that we had with this story was the visibility of the agents who were allegedly waiting to pounce on the terrorists. If you were an FBI, BATF or bomb-squad agent getting into position to initiate a sting operation would you be walking around with big letters BATF or BOMB SQUAD written on your back in plain sight for someone to see or would you be just a little less visible? If you were a terrorist driving a Ryder truck filled with explosives and upon arriving at your destination under the cover of darkness noticed BATF and bomb-squad agents kind of hangin' around your target area wouldn't you think that just maybe the "surprise" was no longer a surprise and that someone may have caught wind of what was going on? And this is not the only over-size chunk of this sting operation theory that we had a great deal of difficulty swallowing.

We had and still have a second chunk that just wouldn't go down no matter how long we chewed on it. Again, we need to put ourselves in the position of a government agent involved in a sting operation to fully understand the absurdity of this theory.

Just imagine that your are an agent of the FBI or BATF and, for quite some time, you have been intimately involved in a terrorist sting operation. Your job is to intercept a gang of terrorists just before they light the fuse to a massive bomb in front of a large, new federal building in downtown Oklahoma City. You and dozens of other agents have dedicated your every waking hour, your very souls to this project. This is precisely why you have trained so hard for so many years. This is why you have devoted your life to the "Company." This will be the chance of a lifetime, maybe your only chance to really test your training and your skills to their maximum capabilities, and perhaps beyond, far beyond.

You have been waiting months for this very moment. This is the climax that you and all of your colleagues have been anticipating. This is the bust. This is what makes it all worthwhile. Now is the time when all of those years of training and all those months of planning will finally pay off. You will actually be involved in stopping the most elaborately planned act of terrorism in the history of this country, the real crime of the century. You will be responsible for saving hundreds of lives. You will literally be a part of history.

Right now is the most important moment in your career, in your life! You're thinking to yourself: "It's 3 a.m. and they should be arriving soon. Stay alert ... Now it's 4 a.m. and they're an hour late ... It's 6 a.m. ... The building's still empty and the terrorists aren't here yet. Maybe they got a flat tire. I sure hope they get here before the streets get busy with traffic and people start going inside the Murrah Building ... It's 7:30 and they still aren't here yet? It's 8:30. The streets are loaded with traffic and the building is filling with people. The heck with it. I'm going home or maybe I'll just go to the golf course and play with Bob Ricks and the rest of the good ol' boys."

As you can see, if this theory were true, every BATF agent or any other agent assigned to this case would have had to come to the same conclusion at the same time, or at least by 8:30 a.m. They couldn't have had any concern whatsoever about the hundreds or maybe even thousands of people in and around the proposed target. They couldn't have left any agents behind, just in case the bad guys were a few hours late. The feds couldn't have left anyone standing guard, monitoring the situation for a couple of days or even a couple of hours just for safety's sake.

After giving this theory some serious thought and exposing this theory for the blatant attempt at disinformation and for the fraud that it really is, it becomes obvious that at this point we could easily rest our case, but we won't.

Some of the other things that have always bothered us about the suggestion that illegally stored explosives were responsible for the second explosion have never been successfully explained to us. First, these alleged explosives were stored on the ninth floor. A point that we have made many, many times is this: If the explosives were on the top floor and that section of the building did come down, it stands to reason that the top floor would come down last.

Now if reason controls our thought processes, which it should, what was it that came down with a force of 3,500 pounds per square inch which some experts say is necessary to explode C-4? Did the sky fall on the C-4? If the C-4 did explode, why didn't all or most of the other munitions and explosives also explode? We must mention that we have seen no evidence that C-4 was actually stored in the Murrah Building, only that munitions were stored there and if there were only munitions, what could've caused the massive explosions inside the building that blew huge chunks of concrete up and over the alleged truck bomb explosion and into the parking lot?

We will now bring to your attention a similar point of interest which we have never before talked about in public. Our intentions are certainly not to insult or anger any fellow investigators but, in our opinion, some investigators have themselves been victims of disinformation. Their theories are based upon that believable disinformation because the alternative is just too terrible to comprehend.

That government agents would take part in a cover-up is obvious to all but the most naive in our society. That agents of our own government would actually cause such a horrendous crime is something that none of us really want to believe. But keep in mind that government police and intelligence agencies are part of a system that perpetuates itself. If we have no drug trafficking, we have no need for the DEA.

Hence, we pour money into those countries whose puppet governments benefit from graft via the drug trade. Among other things, our tax money helps build better roads to move their contraband more efficiently. Consequently the size and power of the DEA keeps expanding.. If we have no "cold war" we have no need for counterintelligence or for the CIA. Hence, for pennies on the dollar, we sell the brutal communist Chinese government technology of which they have not yet dreamed for building state-of-the-art war equipment for export to maniacal dictatorships like Iran, Iraq and Libya.

Bill Clinton has given Red China the "most-favored nation" trading status even though they have consistently deceived us and lied to us about our trade "deals" and even though the Chinese people are more oppressed, violated and murdered by their own government than any other people in history. By his actions one might conclude that Mr. Clinton agrees with their political philosophy and with their total disregard for the civil and human rights of their citizens.

Considering that the Chinese have made large contributions to the Clinton re-election and defense funds, a reasonable person might conclude that they also agree with his political philosophy. And, to top it all off, we generally finance these sales by loaning them the money to buy our technology and, historically, seldom if ever get paid back for our "loans." Our own money and technology is used against us in the ongoing "cold war" and even in some "hot wars."

And the CIA keeps gaining power. If we have no acts of terrorism we have no need for the anti-terrorism bill, Bill. Since its passage we have seen more acts of terrorism than at any other time in this Country's history, with the possible exception of the decade of leftists in the '60s who are now our political and media bosses. Obviously the anti-terrorism bill is not an "anti"- terrorism bill, Bill ... and the government gets progressively more intrusive.

While considering the theory about the illegally stored explosives being responsible for the second explosion, try to imagine who may benefit by the public's belief that the second explosion was unintentional. If we can be convinced that the second explosion was an unfortunate accident as a result of negligence, but ultimately caused by the truck explosion, the blame can still rest solidly on McVeigh's shoulders, and Terry's if prosecutors can successfully stack the jury with non-thinkers.

While all of these deep thoughts are occupying our minds, realize also that Mr. Cash and Mr. Wilburn have, in public interviews and in private conversations with us and many others, stated that the second explosion from these illegal munitions was responsible for the massive damage to that area (known as the pit area) inside the Murrah Building where the C-4 allegedly detonated. They say that the second explosion blew large chunks of the building northward, over the alleged truck bomb explosion and into the parking lot between the Murrah Building and the *Journal Record* building. They have both stated that the second explosion was probably responsible for many more deaths than the first explosion. We could not agree more with their observation about the explosion inside the building blowing large chunks of rubble out and over and for creating most of the death and destruction. We have taken video pictures of just such a chunk and the only way it could have gotten there is from an explosion within the building itself. However, the theoretical source of Mr. Cash's second explosion is a point on which we totally disagree.

We will proceed to prove BEYOND ANY REASONABLE DOUBT our contention that the second explosion did not come from illegally stored munitions or explosives and that the second explosion was not and could not have been an accident.

We must first remember that it was the pit area in the building, the southeastern most part of the damaged area, which sustained the most destruction. It was also the area directly beneath the illegally stored explosives. We know from Gen. Partin's report that the explosion from the outside could not have sheared those columns and, accepting this expert of expert's opinion, we then have to realize that an explosion or explosions from the inside were responsible for bringing those columns down. Remember also that the general's opinion was inadvertently confirmed by an explosives expert within the FBI who had 25 years demolitions experience. Now in order for the illegally stored C-4 to have blown to pieces that section of the building where this alleged C-4 was stored, something very large and very heavy had to cave in on the C-4; 3,500 pounds per square inch type heavy, actually.

Since that column could not possibly have been sheared as a result of the alleged ANFO truck bomb and that part of the building did not collapse as a result of the alleged ANFO truck bomb then how did the explosives fall from the ninth floor? In other words, how did that part of the building get destroyed before the explosives fell and were crushed causing them to explode resulting in the destruction of that part of the building? That area of the building would have had to sustain the damage before the explosives that allegedly caused the damage, caused the damage.

That's hard to follow, and even harder to swallow once you've followed it. If you choose to believe Cash's theory, you have to put the cart before the horse. If there really were illegally stored explosives on the ninth floor, what caused the ninth floor to collapse if the explosions in that part of the building hadn't happened yet? The destruction would've had to happen before the explosions that caused the destruction, and that's just not reality. Even if the BATF's contraband was stored on the first floor, what caused that part of the building to collapse and detonate the C-4 if there was any C-4? We know that the truck bomb did not shear that second row column or any of the columns in the first row, according to the experts.

If you choose to believe in the "blown sting operation" theory you have to choose not to believe the witnesses who saw the Ryder truck, white four-door sedan, brown pickup, men in camos and the men in suits at Geary Lake on April 10-12.

You have to choose not to believe rescue workers at the scene who claim to have seen fulminate of mercury canisters inside the Murrah Building after the explosions. You have to choose not to believe some survivors of the bombing who felt a rumble and had time to hide under their desks before the primary charges exploded.

You have to choose to believe that the support columns were not sheared as the result of an inside job but were instead knocked over by air blast pressure. You have to choose not to believe an FBI agent with 25 years demolitions experience who said you have to "bore in to bring those columns down." You have to choose not to believe Gen. Partin and many other experts who have said that air blast pressure could not possibly have sheared those columns.

You have to choose not to believe the witnesses who saw persons with flashlights going floor to floor inside the Murrah Building in the wee hours of the morning while other witnesses saw BATF and bomb-squad personnel standing guard outside. You have to choose not to believe all of the early reports about bombs being removed from the building.

You have to choose to believe that bomb-squad professionals could not find the planted bombs inside the Murrah Building before the explosions. You have to choose to believe that bomb-squad professionals could not tell the difference between a training device and a real bomb and, because of that incompetence, allowed seriously injured victims to bleed to death while they ordered the area to evacuated because of those "non-bombs."

You have to choose not to believe numerous FBI whistle-blowers who have stated in court, under oath, that the FBI has falsified and tainted evidence in this case. You have to choose not to believe Carol Howe, the BATF's own informant, who said that Andreas Strassmeir, reportedly on the BATF's payroll, was the instigator and planner of this crime.

You have to choose to believe that the government had nothing to hide when it imploded the Murrah Building and filled in the crater. You have to choose to believe that the government had nothing to hide when they refused to allow defense investigators even one little speck of virgin rubble for independent analysis. You have to choose to believe that the government investigators had nothing to hide when they refused to turn over any evidence until the court ordered disclosure ten months after the fact, allowing ample time to "alter the evidence" in any way they so desired.

You have to choose to believe that, after months of planning, dozens of federal agents lost track of the conspirators during the final hours of the sting operation and simultaneously decided to abandon the operation and to abandon hundreds of innocent citizens in the Murrah Building simply because the bomb truck didn't show up on time! You have to choose to believe that two patriotic American citizens with absolutely spotless records, no history of criminal activity, no propensity toward violence, no experience in demolitions, no education in chemistry, no means by which they could have effectively mixed 2.5 tons of ANFO, and with no motive, would take it upon themselves to murder 168 innocent Americans and destroy the lives of thousands more.

If you choose to believe that Tim and Terry were the subjects of this "blown sting operation" you have to choose to believe in magic and much, much more. You have to choose to disregard all of the facts and all of the evidence in this investigation. You have to choose to abandon reason, logic and common sense.

"Well," you might ask, "if those illegally stored explosives weren't responsible for the massive damage to the Murrah Building, then what was responsible?"

To fully appreciate and then to understand the answer to that question we have to again review the information that we have discussed and then examine information and evidence which we have not previously covered. First, Gen. Partin says that blast pressure from the alleged ANFO bomb couldn't have destroyed any of those columns. A contact explosive would have been required to bring down those steel reinforced concrete columns. This was confirmed by an FBI demolitions expert who said that you couldn't bring that column down by putting explosives along side the column.

"You're gonna have to bore in to bring that column down," is exactly what he said. (Don't worry Agents Wilkinson, Defenbaugh, and Goldman, we won't squeal on you for your "slips of the tongue," but you are on tape.)

Both of these expert's opinions and all of our suspicions were absolutely confirmed by an engineering report sanctioned by the Pentagon and furnished by Walker Aerospace Group, Inc. The report said, in part:

"The current theory advanced by the federal government is that the total source of the damage was the result of a single truck bomb consisting of 4,800 pounds of ammonium nitrate and fuel oil combination installed in the cargo van of a rented Ryder Truck.

"This conclusion is not supported by the evidence as manifested by the building itself post explosion. The pattern of damage strongly supports that the mode of destruction is the result of a truck bomb in combination with internal explosive devices placed at major structural connection points."

Take notice that the report makes reference to "internal explosive devices PLACED at major structural connection points." Even though this is what we've been saying all along and have been severely criticized by many in the media for saying it, these are not our words. These are the words of the ultimate experts in the field in an independent study mistakenly sanctioned by the Pentagon. "Why haven't I heard about this report in the news?" you ask.

Good question. A question we've been asking (without an answer) is: Could the explosives have been "PLACED at major structural connection points" by happenstance when the illegally stored explosives(?) fell perfectly into place at the base of and contacting several different columns spanning an area of well over 120 feet? To believe the theory that this damage was the result of an accident from the illegal munitions that is precisely what had to have happened. The report goes on to say:

"It is nearly impossible to produce a mode of failure in this type of structure through air coupling (blast pressure) as has been suggested. The lack of damage to the other areas of the structure suggests that the truck bomb was not responsible for the massive structural damage to the building. Buildings on the periphery of the site which sustained damage were not of the type of construction of the Murrah building and could have sustained damage by blast pressures of 1 pound per square inch (p.s.i.) or less.

"The probable cause of the damage to the Murrah Building was a series of demolition charges placed on the columns at the interfaces of the floor structures, with the blast from the truck augmenting the demolition charges. This would produce a mode of failure which appears at the Murrah site. In using small demolition charges, the object is to disconnect the structural connections and let gravity do the work of bringing the building down. The probable placement of the charges would probably be surface mount below the drop panel in the ceiling space. Another possible placement would be satchel charges placed on the floor directly over the t-beams, thereby severing the floor connections. While a surface mount explosive would not be as effective as a drilled in charge, the direct physical coupling would produce the desired effect with a small charge. It would not be necessary for the charge to completely sever the structural connections, just merely weaken them to a point in which gravity takes over and produces the desired effect. The perceived time to an individual would be the same whether a large charge completely severing the connections were used or the smaller charge merely weakening the joint were used."

The CONCLUSION of the engineering report states:

"It is nearly impossible that a single truck bomb could produce the damage manifested at the Murrah Federal Building on April 19, 1995. All of the initial conclusions contained herein, are based upon a perfect explosive device as described by General Partin in his report. It is known that these conditions did not exist. However, even with the use of the optimum figures and yield, it is at this stage nearly impossible to reasonably predict failures in the structure that would result in the damage produced by the event. Therefore further investigation is warranted in this event as it appears that a high level of sophistication beyond that of one or two lone bombers with a truck bomb of ANFO was necessary to produce the damage.

"There are many unanswered questions relating to this event and only a thorough independent investigation can answer all of the questions. It is most unfortunate that the federal government HAS CHOSEN TO DISPOSE OF PHYSICAL EVIDENCE, AND HAS NOT MOUNTED A MORE AGGRESSIVE INVESTIGATION AND MADE ALL OF THE FACTS CONCERNING THIS CASE PUBLIC." (Amen, emphasis ours.)

We did not include this report in its entirety because it was not necessary but the report does go into great technical detail proving their conclusion. As we have already pointed out the report refers to the "explosive devices PLACED at major structural connection points." It also refers to a "series of demolition charges PLACED on the columns at the interfaces of the floor structures" just like Gen. Partin suggested in the article by William Jasper in *The New American*.

The report suggests that "small demolition charges" could have brought down those columns lending much credibility to our arguments that there is overwhelming evidence indicating that the support columns were sheared first. Some of the surviving victims stated that they felt the building rumble "like and earthquake" (small disruption of tranquillity) and that they actually had time to hide under their desks which again indicates that the columns were sheared with relatively small, strategically placed charges before the explosion outside which, we are absolutely certain, acted as a distraction for the final, larger explosions on the inside. The report even goes on to explain how and where else these charges could have been placed "below the drop panel in the ceiling space" and "at the interfaces of the floor structures."

We're certain that you remember, since we have reminded you enough times, that witnesses in the federal courthouse saw two persons with flashlights going from floor to floor inside the Murrah Building around 2 or 3 a.m. when there was supposed to be no security or maintenance personnel on duty. And you most assuredly remember that private investigators have reported that the BATF was expecting a terrorist attack which was supposed to have taken place at around 3 a.m. If the BATF was expecting a bombing to take place at 3 a.m. do you think that any or all of them would have arrived to take their positions at exactly 3 a.m. or do you think they may have gotten there just a little sooner, like maybe an hour or two sooner?

Who might that have been snooping around inside the Murrah Building between 2 a.m. and 3 a.m. in the morning while the BATF and bomb-squad agents were on duty, monitoring and watching? We think it is at least reasonable to ask how anyone could've entered that building without the BATF and bomb-squad agents knowing about it? We think it is also our responsibility to ask whether the BATF agents who were on the site were there to catch the terrorists when they arrived at their destination, or if they were there to stand guard for the terrorists planting the bombs that would virtually destroy the Murrah Building along with 168 innocent American citizens? Of course, there's always the possibility that the terrorists were just dressed up as BATF agents. If the historical record of the BATF is in any way indicative of the incidents surrounding this tragedy, that may well have been the case.

The Pentagon-sanctioned engineering report also goes into great detail explaining how the damage to the large header which supported the front of the Murrah Building does not reflect the FBI's single truck-bomb theory. If the blast from the truck bomb exerted enough pressure to shear the upright column closest to the truck it would have needed a certain amount of pounds per square inch (p.s.i.) to accomplish that destruction. Taking that p.s.i. number and multiplying it by the square inches of surface area over the large header beam on the third floor across the front of the building, Walker Aerospace calculates well over eight million pounds of pressure against that header.

They have concluded that if the truck bomb generated enough blast pressure to shear the column closest to the truck, it would have also blown that 100,000-pound header into and through the Murrah Building. The header beam fell straight down, apparently another victim of the "shear-and-drop" method, which adds considerably to the proof that the truck bomb was not responsible for the structural damage to the building. If we want to believe that this was a blown sting operation, and if we refuse to believe that this was not the result of an inside job, we have to choose not to believe the engineering experts from Walker Aerospace. We have to choose to totally ignore the facts and the evidence in this investigation. We have to close our minds to reason, logic and common sense. We have to choose to ignore the truth.

"You asked me and I told you, I don't lie for anybody. There's a lot of people who just don't want to get involved in this thing." Harvey Weathers, chief dispatcher for the Oklahoma City Fire Dept. quoted by Glen Wilburn. Dispatcher Carla Robberson and chief dispatcher Weathers disclosed to Wilburn that Assistant Fire Chief Gaines had received a call on April 14t 1995, from the FBI warning of a possible terrorist attack. Gaines alerted dispatcher Carl Purcer of the warning. When Glen asked Gaines about the warning, Gaines denied it. Weathers would not lie for Gaines. In an attempt to make further contact, Glen Wilburn, and then Relevance, were told that Gaines, Robberson, Weathers and Purcer had all gone on leave (source: *Relevance* of Birmingham, Mich. Definitely subscribe.)

In the video, *Oklahoma City: What Really Happened?* Glen Wilburn stated: "We also have been told by two different witnesses that the bomb squad was in front of the federal courthouse that morning at 7:30 and that they had already cleared the Murrah Building."

They had already cleared the Murrah Building of what? Obviously not people. Hundreds of people were injured and killed and at 7:30 in the morning there wouldn't have been many people to clear. If they didn't clear the Murrah Building of people, what was the Bomb Squad supposed to have cleared from the Murrah Building? Bombs? You'd think that would've been the job of the bomb squad, wouldn't you? To remove bombs? According to Glen's witnesses the bomb squad had already "cleared" the Murrah Building, we assume, of bombs. Yet, it is obvious that bombs inside the building caused the majority of the damage. What … might … that … tell … you? What was the bomb squad doing there before the fact if it didn't remove the bombs?

The Walker Aerospace Group engineering report clearly indicates that the extent of the destruction to the Murrah Building would have been an impossible result of a truck bomb as has been alleged by government prosecutors even if the explosive device and conditions were absolutely perfect. It suggests that a "high level of sophistication" would have been necessary to accomplish that amount of destruction with explosives and also pointed out that it was "most unfortunate that the federal government has chosen to dispose of physical evidence." You just can't help but ask, why did the federal government choose to dispose of that evidence? And who, in or around the Murrah Building on that particular day, might have possessed such a "high level of sophistication" in demolitions in addition to having unlimited access to the federal building? For demolition charges to have been placed at T-beam junctures inside the building, someone would need access to the third floor. As Gen. Partin has said, you can't just walk in off the street and place explosives on the columns on the third floor in a federal building. It was done by someone on the inside.

Here's what some witnesses had to say about the single bomb theory.

"I just had sat down when I heard this very violent rumble under the bus. It was a pushing-type motion. It actually raised the bus up on its side. About six or seven seconds later, another one which was more violent than the first pushed the bus again. I thought the second time that the bus was gonna turn over." — Michael Hinton, from *Oklahoma City: What Really Happened?*

"I had talked to a lady that worked at the Water Resources Building and she had heard the explosions and she said that she was upset about the fact that when it came over the news media that they were saying there was just one explosion when she heard two explosions that morning." — Toni Garrett, rescue nurse, *Oklahoma City: What Really Happened?*

There's another important issue that has not really been mentioned by the national news, not since the first day anyway. There were at least three bomb scares during the first few hours after the bombing. During these scares many rescuers had to leave behind some of the victims who they were trying to free from the rubble. Many of these victims lay bleeding to death and dying and begged not to be abandoned. Some of the more unfortunate victims died before the rescuers returned to continue in their efforts of saving lives after the bombs were removed.

During an interview in the video *Oklahoma City: What Really Happened?* a rescuer inside the Murrah Building said: "Just the other side of this and down, we had some survivors the first day. Half way through myself and the people from a mutual aid company went behind the rubble and there were two survivors here when we had the first bomb scare ... We had to leave the area and they asked us not to leave then and it was real trying. We had three survivors and all three begged us not to leave. We prayed and said we'd be back."

These next statements are to again bring to your attention the mentality of the sub-humans who were responsible for this tragedy.

"We've been told that the first bomb scare was not, in fact a bomb scare. It was designed that way to get the civilians back and all personnel back and the ATF went in there to get their files and also to take explosives out that they had illegally stored and their munitions on the ninth floor." — Glen Wilburn, *Oklahoma City: What Really Happened?*

"I talked to Dick Miller who's the assistant marshal for the Oklahoma City Fire Marshal's office and he, in very clear terms, readily admitted that there were explosives removed from the Murrah Building immediately after the disaster on the very same morning and it was those devices that were removed from the Murrah Building that caused the evacuation of the rescue workers on at least three different occasions. And it's important for people to understand that while they are in the process of

removing these explosives people are left bleeding to death and dying."
— J.D. Cash, *Oklahoma City: What Really Happened?*

The feds would have us believe that the bombs inside of the Murrah Building were not really bombs at all but were, in fact, training devices. Because of this explanation and because the truth is just to horrible to comprehend, the media has all but ignored what really happened during those bomb scares. But because we always give the feds the benefit of the doubt we will explore this scenario under the assumption that, for the first and only time, they are telling the truth. (Hint — this assumption will be short-lived.)

To begin, anyone who has ever been in the military or who has ever entered into any business contract supplying government with anything will have had first-hand experience with precisely what we're about to explain. We are absolutely confident that if everyone reading this took even one quick glance at the several thousand page FAR (Federal Acquisition Regulation) manuals no further explanation would be necessary.

Any military training device would be specifically marked "Military Training Device." There can be no mistaking a training device for a real bomb. Any person even unfamiliar with military demolitions could not make that kind of mistake because government "anything" is always very clearly marked and often times outrageously overmarked. Just ask someone who has manufactured something for sale to the government. Federal regulations for packaging and marking are so stringent and often times so complex that many manufacturers and would-be sales persons give up in total frustration. Many times it costs the supplier much more to package and mark an item than to manufacture the item. It would have been virtually impossible for anyone, particularly bomb-squad or BATF agents, to mistake a training device for a real bomb.

Keeping that small, generally ignored detail in mind, remember the feds claim that all of these devices which they removed were inert. If we assume that the feds are telling the truth about these "inert" devices, then why would someone have given the order for rescuers to abandon the building and leave behind those living victims who had little chance of surviving without immediate attention? Would the federal agents in charge have allowed injured people to needlessly die while they removed training devices? We do not believe the agents in charge did that. Not that it's beneath their moral character, we just don't believe that that was the case.

It is important to consider what Glen Wilburn said about the first bomb scare being staged so the BATF could remove their illegally stored munitions. What Mr. Wilburn unwittingly described is exactly how so many government agents were brought into the conspiracy as accomplices after the fact. They unintentionally assisted in the cover-up of murder and conspiracy, assuming that they were owning up to their responsibility of saving the "Company" from public ridicule and judicial reprimand.

This does not in any way excuse their actions. They are all still guilty of criminal involvement in the cover-up and are still responsible for chasing away the rescuers while people died during the bomb scares. That is precisely why so few of them are willing to talk about what they saw, and took part in, that morning. Testimony from any of the agents who assisted in removing the contraband would amount to self-incrimination and would result in considerable prison time for those agents, assuming they lived to testify and to do that time. You just have to wonder what kind of person could be so cold and calloused as to let innocent people, some of them friends, colleagues and children bleed to death while they were covering the Company's butt?

Many investigators still believe that all of the bomb scares and this whole cover-up were designed to hide the fact that there were munitions stored illegally in the Murrah Building. We have never believed that to be the case because the evidence and the eyewitness accounts disprove that theory. We know, BEYOND ANY REASONABLE DOUBT that rogue government agents used the bomb scares to actually remove some of the explosive devices placed at strategic locations inside the Murrah Building that failed to detonate and have used the illegally stored munitions excuse to hide that fact.

As you know, Gen. Partin stated that explosive devices had to be placed next to and probably contacting the cement columns. His opinion was verified by the engineering report and, inadvertently, by an FBI demolitions expert. Although we cannot discount common sense, which also dictates that there had to have been contact charges skillfully placed inside the Murrah Building, eyewitness testimony is generally given more weight in court than common sense, so we will also back our contentions with some eyewitness testimony.

Again referring to Chuck Allen's video, *Oklahoma City: What Really Happened?* rescue nurse Toni Garrett stated: "There was a period when we were bringing the bodies to the playground and that's when we had notice that we needed to evacuate the building because there was another bomb. There were at least four other people (rescuers) who told me that there was a bomb inside the building. And there were a couple of people who had actually seen them remove the bomb when the bomb squad had come down to the Murrah Building. There was a timing device on the bomb that they had secured earlier that morning that had been set to go off ten minutes after the bombs had gone off that morning which they assumed that the mechanisms of the bomb malfunctioned because of the blasts."

Question by Chuck Allen: "Did any of these people tell you that it was definitely an active bomb?"

Answer by Toni Garrett: "Yes. The bomb squad took it off." When the FBI took over, "there was a cold, calloused atmosphere. We were told by the FBI, to get out and keep our mouths shut. He was downright rude." — Earl Garrett, Toni's husband

Question by Chuck Allen: "Have people been threatened or told not to talk about what they saw on the day of the bombing?"

"I saw a lot that day I wish I hadn't. I can't talk about it. I have a family. I have a job. I've been threatened. We've been told not to talk about the devices." — J.D. Cash, quoting law enforcement employees.

It certainly makes one wonder, if these "devices" were really inert training devices and were not incriminating to any federal agency, why would those witnesses have been threatened and told not to talk about the devices in question?

We cannot ignore some of the early reports and statements regarding the unexploded bombs found inside the building immediately after the bombing. One of the experts on the scene, when asked about the importance of the bombing devices that did not explode, commented that these unexploded bombs would undoubtedly prove to be the most significant evidence surrounding this investigation because it would reveal just how this act of terrorism was carried out and, quite probably, by whom. It was also reported that the bomb squad had carted off at least one of these bombs and detonated it. Why would anyone want to remove and destroy what might prove to be the most significant evidence found at the scene of the crime? Has anyone heard the FBI prosecutors claim that they have in their possession unexploded bombs that would help incriminate the accused?

It is important that we make the distinction between explosives and bombs. Explosives can be used to make a bomb but they are not necessarily bombs. When it is said by witnesses that bombs were removed by the Bomb Squad they are not referring to packages of C-4 or boxes of munitions.

The bomb squad did, in fact, remove unexploded bombs from the inside of the Murrah Building shortly after the explosions. If you still have doubts, take the time to check the news reports that aired on the morning of April 19 for your own satisfaction. On Channel 4 television in Oklahoma City, a reporter interviewed an official who stated that the bomb squad had already defused one bomb and it was in the process of defusing another. It's a matter of record available for all to see and hear. The most important evidence in this investigation has conveniently disappeared while in the safe keeping of government agents. Who might benefit by the disappearance of evidence while in the hands of the bomb squad? Do you think that government agents might make evidence disappear to protect Tim or Terry?

An employee who worked at the *Journal Record* building told investigator J.D. Cash that just before 9 a.m. he saw a yellow Mercury backed up against the Athenian Restaurant, parked illegally. A person who resembled Timothy McVeigh was sitting in the driver's seat and another man, possibly of Middle Eastern descent, resembling the sketches of John Doe No. 2 walked up to the car and entered the car from the passenger's side. As the car sped away, jumping a couple of parking curbs, the witness noticed a dangling license plate. This same man, according to Cash, assisted the FBI in drawing the sketch of John Doe No. 2 so it would be reasonable to assume that it was, in fact, No. 2 entering the yellow Mercury on the passenger's side.

We know what you're thinking. The witness who was interviewed by J.D. Cash confirms McVeigh's connection to John Doe No. 2 and to the conspiracy to bomb the Murrah Building. That is John's interpretation also and at first thought, that certainly seems to be the case. But, when you evaluate these statements, a perceptive person may point out that the driver of the yellow Mercury made no attempt whatsoever to be inconspicuous while driving away from the about-to-be scene of the crime. As a matter of fact, according to the eyewitness' statement, it would almost seem as if the Timothy McVeigh who was driving that yellow Mercury wanted to be seen. Of course, the man did notice the dangling license plate which certainly helps prove that it really was McVeigh driving away from the scene of the crime with No. 2. Doesn't it? After all, we all know that McVeigh got pulled over for a missing license plate.

We must confess, we have held back a small tidbit of information from Cash's eyewitness, a little piece of testimony that seems to have eluded all of those concerned with really discovering the truth. It seems as if this particular eyewitness was just a little more observant than he was supposed to have been.

Unfortunately for Mr. Cash's theory, for the prosecutors, and for everyone else in government or in the government's media who are hell-bent on executing Timothy McVeigh and Terry Nichols, even if they weren't there, the license plate dangling from the yellow Mercury that sped away from the scene of the crime. ... was an OKLAHOMA license plate! That's right, an Oklahoma license plate. It has already been established BEYOND ANY REASONABLE DOUBT that the license plate on Timothy James McVeigh's yellow Mercury was an ARIZONA license plate, sporting the number, LZC646!

That was the license plate on Tim's car before it was removed making sure that he would be stopped by the police. Another yellow Mercury was seen with no license plate at 8:38 a.m. by Mr. James Linehan. That could have possibly been Tim's yellow Mercury. If Tim was actually driving it, we do not know. If he was setup to meet someone there, making certain he was in the area, we can't say for certain. We can say for certain that if Tim was actually driving that yellow Mercury with no plate, someone did not intend for him to get out of Oklahoma City before being stopped and arrested.

With no license plate on his vehicle, Tim's being pulled over was pretty much guaranteed. With no plate, no insurance, and carrying a loaded weapon, being arrested after he was stopped was an absolute guarantee. Someone in a brown pickup truck even pulled over to confirm that McVeigh was taken into custody. That someone must have been tailing McVeigh. Eyewitnesses say they saw a brown pickup at Geary Lake, a brown pickup rapidly driving away from the scene of the crime in downtown Oklahoma City, and then a brown pickup appears in Trooper Charlie Hanger's automatic camcorder video when Tim was pulled over. Just a coincidence, right?

One would suspect that Arizona license plate, No. LZC646 might have been stashed somewhere inside that brown pickup having been recently removed from McVeigh's yellow Mercury. We must also keep in mind that the yellow Mercury with no license plate was seen by Mr. Linehan at 8:38 a.m. The yellow Mercury with a dangling license plate was seen just a few minutes before 9:00 a.m. If we are to believe that these are the same vehicles we would first have to believe that a recently attached license plate fell off Tim's car all by itself. Then we would have to believe that sometime between 8:40 a.m. and 9:00 a.m. an Oklahoma license plate jumped up from nowhere and attached itself to the yellow Mercury that had lost its recently attached Arizona license plate until it was seen by the witness at the Journal Record Building and then fell off immediately thereafter.

Would the REAL Timothy James McVeigh ... PLEASE STAND UP?

Speaking of that same employee from the *Journal Record* building coming to assist in the rescue efforts just minutes after the bombing, John

Cash says: "Immediately as he joins a circle of workers he looks over just a few feet away, in the middle of all this chaos and blood and crying and screaming, here is another Middle Eastern person standing there staring at the Murrah Building with a smile on from ear to ear. He said it was the most chilling thing that he's ever seen in this whole thing, in spite of all the injuries. As he looks back over it, it's spooky, it's chilling, it's sickening. But he said the man was almost in rapture over what he was looking at, and after having interviewed forty or fifty people that were in that building and injured that day in all their experiences around there, believe me, there wasn't a single soul in downtown Oklahoma City that morning that was smiling except for this individual (source: *Oklahoma City: What Really Happened?*)."

There's obviously no Middle Eastern connection here. It just has to be home-grown terrorism. Right, Janet? Right, Louis? Right, Bill? The only home-grown terrorists of whom we know are those terrorists who are attempting to terrorize our Constitution with a phony anti-terrorism bill, and those terrorists who assault, murder and burn innocent men, women and children who are minding their own business and trying to exercise their Right to think and worship free from government interference.

Can the prosecution present a case of proof beyond a reasonable doubt when the evidence proves beyond any doubt that the prosecution has attempted to intimidate and coerce witnesses into changing their testimony? Can the prosecution present a case of proof beyond a reasonable doubt when the evidence proves beyond any doubt that the prosecution has altered, falsified and destroyed much of the evidence in this investigation? Can the prosecution present a case of proof beyond a reasonable doubt when the evidence proves beyond any doubt that the prosecution had all of the evidence from the scene of the crime in their possession for 10 months and would not allow the defense team investigators even one speck of evidence for private lab tests? Do you think the prosecution can present a case of proof beyond a reasonable doubt with so-called evidence that is based entirely upon reasonable doubt? •

"The Constitution was not written about the life and times of 1789, when the Bill of Rights was adopted. It was written about tyranny; it was written about freedom; it was written about liberty. The Framers did indeed understand what government today is all about. The challenge for us is to understand what 1776 was all about."

— **Colorado State Sen. Charles Duke (source:** *Media Bypass***)**

Terry Nichols shares a moment with his son. Joshua, in a family photo — one of only a precious few that have survived the evidence-sweeping vacuum of the FBI. Like his former U.S. Army buddy Timothy McVeigh, Terry Nichols faces conviction and a death sentence as a result of being charged with helping build the bomb that destroyed the Murrah Federal Building.

James Nichols is shown here in a 10-year-old snapshot playing with his young son Chase. James Nichols, though surviving the federal onslaught on his own person, is yet suffering through the ordeal of his accused brrother, Terry, as the aftermath of the Murrah Federal Building explosions continues to echo through the years.

"Enlighten the people generally, and tyranny and oppressions of body and mind will vanquish like evil spirits at the dawn of day."

— **Thomas Jefferson**

CHAPTER 27: THE TRUTH, THE WHOLE TRUTH AND NOTHING BUT THE TRUTH

Many new issues and questions about this investigation surface daily. Much of the information and evidence about the real facts in this case which prove that the FBI's allegations are absolutely false are virtually ignored by our mainstream media. Because of their lack of solid evidence the agents of deceit, in their desperation, are leaking new and more potentially incriminating disinformation on a regular basis.

These rumors are floating rampantly throughout the media, all of them marked "bad intentions." Even as we write, the trial of Timothy James McVeigh has taken place, and the young man, as expected, was found guilty and sentenced to die by a vengeful federal government. Unfortunately, the media trial had been in full swing since Jan., 1997, when the inspector general's exposé was written, and since BATF informant Carol Howe's very revealing interview. It is interesting to note, again, that Ms. Howe had been flown to Denver for the McVeigh trial and was to be a defense witness until Judge Richard Matsch prevented her from appearing. Again, justice was not served.

A media conviction of Tim and Terry was desperately needed before any new and alarming information was introduced to potential jurors. Regardless of the evidence revealed during the trial, every juror undoubtedly remembered hearing that McVeigh confessed and, in that confession, implicated Terry Nichols.

Because of the prosecution's total lack of real evidence, its insecurity, incompetence and total disregard for the truth, because of its goal of conviction at any cost regardless of guilt or innocence, it has found it necessary to try Tim and Terry in a media court and, by the media, they have been found "guilty as charged."

We realize that we cannot unring the prosecution's bell of disinformation, but whatever the odds against us, we can't stop trying. There's much more at stake here than the fate and perhaps the lives of two innocent young men. All of our futures hang in the balance. How many more times will we allow government agents and officials to cover up their crimes? How many more times will we allow these agents and officials to run roughshod over our Constitution? How many more assassinations and "suicides" will we allow to go unsolved? How many more innocent citizens will be murdered because their church is not "BATF APPROVED?" How many more "John Does" who have close ties to government intelligence agencies will be allowed to escape? How many more Lee Harvey McVeighs will we put in our jails and in our chambers of death? It is estimated that prosecutors convict and imprison 8,000 innocent people annually. This year, let's not increase that number to 8,002.

We hope to keep these questions fresh in your mind should you decide to ask your Congress persons or your local federal agent about some of these discrepancies and unanswered questions, although we would not suggest holding your breath while you're waiting for the answers

• **Question No. 1: Why did the FBI find it necessary to coerce Jennifer McVeigh into saying something, anything?** They lied to Jennifer, making her believe she could be charged with some sort of complicity in the Oklahoma City bombing. They picked her up at home early in the morning and interrogated her intensely until late in the evening, showing her pictures of burned babies and large posters of her picture and the charges they would impose against her, the death penalty or life in prison (for what?).

Jen said the FBI wanted her to take a lie detector test and she refused. Apparently they were only using the lie detector test as a threat because when she finally agreed to take one, they no longer wanted to give her one. We would have to conclude that the Feds knew if they gave Jennifer McVeigh a polygraph test they would no longer have anything with which to threaten her because the test would clear her of any wrong doing. The lie detector test may not hold up as an "absolute" in court, but it does carry a lot of weight in the defense of an accused and it is a difficult piece of evidence to overcome for a prosecutor. Members of the Grand Jury were upset at the way Jennifer McVeigh was mistreated by the prosecutors. If you ever met Jennifer, you'd realize what a sweet, sensitive young lady she is. We should all be upset.

There is no question that Jennifer was tortured emotionally, if not physically. Psychologists will tell you that there's not a lot of difference between physical and emotional torture and, between the two, emotional torture can arguably be worse. We were under the impression that we left torturing suspects and witnesses somewhere behind us in history, like way back in the Dark Ages. Of course, exceptions are those countries where the political systems are based upon communism, fascism, socialism and a variety of other "dictatorisms." Might that tell you something about the mentality of the people running the justice system in this country and of the U.S. government in general?

Here's what a grand juror had to say about Jennifer McVeigh. "She had more damaging evidence against the government's involvement in this case than anything damaging against her brother."

• **Question No. 2: Why did prosecutors find it necessary to force a 12-year-old boy (Joshua) to testify, seemingly, against his father, Terry Nichols?** The grand jury was very upset with the prosecution's tactics of forcing a child, against his will and against the will of his mother, to testify in court. He had already been intensely interrogated by the FBI so all of his statements were a matter of record. They did not need to have him personally repeat to the grand jury everything he had said during interrogation. Since Joshua had corroborated Terry's story, and since nothing he said could implicate his father in this conspiracy, it would seem as if the only reason the prosecutors forced him to appear in front of the grand jury is to inflict pain, not only on Josh, but on Terry as well. Think about the people who are involved in the prosecution and investigation of this case. When you are intimately aware of the facts, the actions of these "public servants" become frightening, at the very least.

Another minor thing that the government accomplished by forcing Josh to testify was to strike fear in the hearts of every man, woman, and child in this country. It was now proven that the omnipotent government could force any child to do even that which the parents disallowed. The icing on the cake was the made-for-TV movie which attempted to brainwash us into believing that forcing a minor to testify was absolutely necessary.

The movie was based upon an evil father who had committed a murder and the prosecutors were attempting to force his seven or 8-year-old son to testify against his dad. Needless to say, it was a very traumatic experience for the young boy, but I'm certain the vast majority of the audience was rooting for the prosecution to win their argument and have this man's son testify because we all knew that the accused was guilty. After all, we saw him do it on television. Being honest, the boy could not tell a lie and his testimony convicted his father. Justice was served and everyone lived happily ever after and members of the viewing audience (We The People) turned off their TV sets and went to bed, satisfied that this scenario was justified and that they could sleep safe and sound because their government would take care of the bad guys.

Coincidentally, this movie was on the air shortly after the incident about Josh was in the public's eye. The timing wasn't quite as good as the phony made-for-TV movie about the Waco "ambush," but close. Apparently just using the news media in an attempt to brainwash the public into believing their disinformation campaign isn't quite good enough for government damage-control agents. Hooray for H-o-l-l-y-w-o-o-d !!

We recently watched a made-for-TV movie (CBS) about Ruby Ridge, with actor Randy Quaid playing the part of Randy Weaver and Laura Dern cast in the role of Vicki Weaver. Much of the movie was accurate although much of it was obvious propaganda attempting to portray the Weavers as a bunch of Nazi racist criminals. Some of the government's abuses against the Weaver family were shown. Do you remember Hitler's technique for convincing people that lies are the truth? Their objective is to turn neighbor against neighbor, brother against brother, and to keep people eternally confused by keeping them totally dependent upon a spoon-fed media. Again, we can thank Big Brother for Hollywood or, Hollywood for Big Brother, which ever you prefer.

• **Question No. 3: Why did Terry drive to the Herington, Kan., police station immediately after hearing his name, or close to his name, on the radio?** If he had any prior knowledge of this tragedy, doesn't it make sense that he would have discarded anything that might have had a tendency to implicate him? The feds would have us believe that Terry and Tim planned this act of terrorism many months before the fact. If he had known that far in advance, wouldn't he have made certain long before April 19 that there was nothing at his house that could even remotely link him to anything incriminating? Even if Terry was an unwilling participant like the FBI has recently indicated, he would have been so paranoid that he wouldn't have even had a firecracker at his house. He most certainly would not have had a receipt for fertilizer with Tim's thumbprint on it (so says the FBI) or anything else that would tend to suggest his involvement in any kind of sinister conspiracy. And that thumbprint has always puzzled us. How in the world would you get only your thumbprint on a receipt?

It has even been suggested that the fertilizer receipt was planted by Terry to set up Tim! Believe it or not, many members of the media have entertained that possibility. Whoever thought of that absolutely ignorant idea most certainly has an I.Q. which precedes their age. If you wanted to set up someone else, would you leave the evidence at your house? Wouldn't that also implicate you to some extent? Wouldn't you make certain that, if you were going to plant incriminating evidence against someone else at your house, you wouldn't have anything else around that might have a tendency to incriminate you? Apparently this realism never occurred to the incurably ignorant person or persons who originated this unbelievable absurdity.

Let us assume for a moment that Terry didn't know anything about the bombing before the fact. Let us also assume that, after the fact, he had some suspicions that his buddy, Tim, was involved. Wouldn't it then be reasonable to assume that he would've discarded anything and everything that may even have the slightest tendency to incriminate him during the two days after the bombing before he drove with his pregnant wife and eighteen month old child to the police station? Wouldn't it also be reasonable to assume that if Terry knew he had stolen firearms in his possession, as the FBI claims, he would've removed them from his home before he drove to the police station?

The FBI admits that there are no serial numbers on record for the guns allegedly stolen, but Terry wouldn't have had that information. If he had any suspicions whatsoever that the guns in his possession weren't perfectly legal, or if he knew that he was involved in anything illegal, it stands to reason that the guns would've been the first to go before he drove to the police station. All of Terry's actions are quite obviously the actions of an innocent man. At least it's obvious to We The People who can still think for ourselves ... TERRY WASN'T THERE!

• **Question No. 4: Why would Terry be setting up permanent residence in Kansas early in 1995 if he was involved in the planning of the bombing since late in 1994?** Why would he have just purchased a house if he was involved in this conspiracy at any time or if he even knew about it? Realistically, if Terry even had a hint about a conspiracy that would take innocent human lives, he would've done what any decent person would do ... He would have squealed! TERRY WASN'T THERE!

• **Question No. 5: Why, if Terry had been or was going to be involved in any type of criminal activity would he write a letter to Marion County, Kansas declaring that the de facto United States government had no jurisdiction over him and also declaring his withdrawal from the voting register because he correctly believed all branches of government to be corrupt?** Why would he intentionally draw attention to himself if he was involved in anything criminal? Wouldn't a low profile have been the order of the day for a conspirator in this act of terrorism?

• **Question No. 6: Why did the FBI find it necessary to keep Marife, Terry's second wife, and Terry's and Marife's daughter Nicole in custody during five weeks of intense interrogation without an attorney present?** Why did they lie to Marife when they told her an attorney would cost her $10,000? Why didn't they advise her of her right to have an attorney present? Why wouldn't the FBI let the family know where they were hiding Marife and why wouldn't they allow us to contact her during those five weeks? Would she have something to fear from her own friends and family? If Marife really is a witness for the prosecution, why isn't the FBI protecting her?

We can tell you why. Everything Terry said during questioning was confirmed by Marife during that five week FBI interrogation. And everything Terry and Marife have said was confirmed by Josh during his FBI interrogation. We can assure you that Terry's wife will be one of, if not the best witness that the defense presents. If Marife has anyone to fear, it would have to be agents for the prosecution. We believe that they would rather she did not testify.

• **Question No. 7: Lea McGowan, manager of the Dreamland Motel said that Tim McVeigh had a Ryder truck at her motel on Sunday, April 16. What happened to the truck that Tim had on Sunday? Where's the receipt for the rental of that truck?** Considering that Tim checked into the Dreamland using his own name and drivers license, and considering that he successfully talked Lea McGowan into renting the room to him for $20 a day instead of $28, obviously bringing attention to himself, why would he bother using a phony ID when and if he allegedly rented the notorious Ryder truck on April 17? When did Tim actually rent the truck that he had at the Dreamland on Sunday?

Considering that the Ryder truck that allegedly exploded in front of the Murrah Building was rented on Monday, April 17, why is the FBI so certain that McVeigh rented that truck also? Isn't it possible that the people at Elliott's Body Shop remember Tim from the truck he rented on Sunday, the truck that did not explode in front of the Murrah Building? Isn't it possible that a McVeigh lookalike named Robert Kling rented that second truck? Isn't it possible that John Doe No. 2 rented that second truck with a person who somewhat resembled McVeigh but was four inches shorter, thirty pounds heavier, had brown-green eyes instead of blue, a rough complexion with acne, a crooked jaw and was wearing camouflage fatigues? That was the description of John Doe No. 1 given by the witnesses at Elliott's Body Shop. And according to Glen Wilburn,

Mr. Elliott at Elliott's Body Shop said, "It doesn't matter what the FBI says, I said there was a John Doe No. 2."

• **Question No. 8: What about this mysterious "Bob Kling" connection?** Jeff Davis, who works for a Chinese restaurant in Junction City, Kan., delivered food to Room No. 25 at the Dreamland Motel while McVeigh was supposed to be staying in that room. The order was phoned in by a Bob Kling. When Mr. Davis brought the order to the room, the man who answered the door and signed the receipt for the food "Bob Kling" was not Tim McVeigh, was not Terry Nichols, and was not John Doe No. 2.

Mr. Davis said that the man was six feet tall, had light brown hair, shorter on the sides and longer on the top, and appeared to be in very good condition, like a weight lifter or something. He said that there did not appear to be anyone else in the room. He said when the FBI interviewed him, they were obsessed with getting him to say that the Bob Kling in room No. 25 was Tim McVeigh. He refused to comply with their intimidation. They didn't even want to make a sketch of the man who he actually saw!

The feds were only interested in getting him to say that the guy was McVeigh. When it became obvious that he would not say what they wanted him to say, they discontinued their questioning and departed.

Why wouldn't the FBI be interested in the Bob Kling who answered the door in room No. 25? If it was Tim McVeigh who ordered the Chinese food, why didn't he use his real name? He had already registered the room under his real name. Was someone trying to establish that Tim McVeigh was also Bob Kling? Doesn't it make you wonder if just maybe the Bob Kling who ordered the Chinese food from room No. 25 might be the same Bob Kling who called about the Ryder truck from room No. 25, and then proceeded to rent the Ryder truck that allegedly exploded in front of the Murrah Building? According to all of the witnesses who the FBI would prefer to ignore, Bob Kling's description did not even come close to fitting the description of Timothy McVeigh.

• **Question No. 9: What about the confusion surrounding fertilizer purchases, and who bought what and when?** The employee at the Mid-Kansas Cooperative Association, where the feds say the fertilizer used in the bomb was purchased, says that neither of the men who bought the ammonium nitrate were Timothy McVeigh. He said that one of the men had light brown hair and the other man had darker, shorter hair and that neither man wore glasses. The taller man had longer hair than the shorter man which might suggest that one of the men who bought the fertilizer was the illusive Bob Kling who ordered Chinese food from room No. 25.

The shorter man with darker hair had shorter hair than the taller man and was not wearing glasses, which proves beyond any doubt that it was not Terry. His hair is darker than Tim's but it is also longer, and Terry always wears glasses. The employee also said the truck which the two men were driving was definitely not Terry's blue pickup and that they were towing a trailer made from a red Ford pickup truck box. Has the FBI pursued the two men who actually purchased the ammonium nitrate fertilizer? Have they, with composite drawings, made an attempt to determine if the taller of these two men matched the description of Bob Kling from Room No. 25? Have they tried to match the description of either of these two men to the Bob Kling who rented the notorious Ryder truck? If they haven't, would a representative from the FBI please tell us why they haven't?

• **Question No. 10: Why is there continued confusion over who checked into the Dreamland Motel and when?** According to statements made by the manager of the Great Western Inn on I-70 in Junction City, Kan., which is just the next exit down from the Dreamland Motel, two men checked into his motel on April 17 and one of men matched the description of John Doe No. 2. He was driving a Ryder truck, spoke with a foreign accent, appeared to be of Middle Eastern descent, and checked in using a foreign name. He stayed in room No. 107.

The manager doesn't know what name the man used because the FBI confiscated his log book. The other man checked in under the name of Nichols, but at this time we do not have a description of him. These two men stayed in separate rooms and both men checked out the next day on the 18th of April. The feds definitely got John Doe No. 2's name from the motel register. Why won't they tell us what name he used? Why do they still deny his existence?

• **Question No. 11: Where has the manager of the Junction City, Kan., Great Western Inn gone and why is he missing?** It is well-known that on the dates in question I was in Michigan, so the feds know I didn't stay at the Great Western Inn. A reasonable person would assume that the feds believe it was Terry who checked into the Great Western Inn the same time as John Doe No. 2.

The problem is that the FBI also knows that Terry was at home with Marife and Nicole on the 17th watching videos. They know where he rented the videos, which videos he rented, and even that he watched *The*

Lion King with Nicole. It looks like somebody wanted it to appear as if Terry checked in with John Doe No. 2 thereby suggesting some complicity in the conspiracy.

The manager of the Great Western Inn also said that on April 7, 1995, someone signed in under the name of James Nichols. That would also tend to implicate me by placing me in the area 12 days before the bombing except for the fact that I wasn't there and I can prove it. Of course, if things had gone as planned we wouldn't be around to prove that we weren't there because ... DEAD MEN DON'T TESTIFY.

By the way, has anybody seen the manager of the Great Western Inn lately? It seems as if nobody has heard from this guy for a long time. This man can positively I.D. John Doe No. 2, whoever it was that was passing himself off as Terry and whoever it was that checked in under the name of James Nichols.

Asking about this manager's whereabouts, and suggesting that he may have disappeared, was one of the issues raised by Hoppy Heidelberg in a letter to Judge David Russell who immediately dismissed Hoppy from the grand jury. Where is this key eyewitness? Hoppy Heidelberg would like to know and so would we. Apparently Judge Russell, along with the FBI, would prefer to ignore this information. Historically, any witnesses who see anything that the feds want to conceal have a bad habit of either disappearing or succumbing to some kind of a violent death generally classified as an accident or a suicide.

The Kennedy assassination is up around 40 mysterious deaths of potential witnesses. Friends of Bill are running a close second with a score of around 30. The Oklahoma City bombing is only up to four or five, but it's still young. Give it time.

• **Question No. 12: How did an empty canister get turned into an "anti-tank weapon" by the government and its media lackeys?** Some copies of the *Arkansas Democrat Gazette* were sent to us recently by a young lady named Rachael B. from Pine Bluff, Ark. One of those papers dated April 27, 1995, contained a particularly interesting article written by Sharon Cohen concerning a request made by federal prosecutors in Wichita, Kan., to have Terry moved to Oklahoma City. To prove the point we're about to make, it is necessary to reprint a couple paragraphs from that article as follows:

"U.S. District Judge Monte Belot seemed skeptical that the 33 guns, a 60mm anti-tank rocket and blasting devices confiscated from Nichols' home could be explained by his status as a military surplus dealer.

" 'I don't believe most of the citizens of the United States have anti-tank weapons,' he said. 'I don't know that U. S. citizens have that many guns or pamphlets about Waco or literature about government warfare.'"

Apparently, members of the media no longer enjoy the exclusive honors of being lied to and manipulated by the FBI. It seems that, somewhere along the way, federal agents have determined that it wouldn't be prudent to limit their "storytelling" to members of the media only.

Considering Judge Belot's statement about the anti-tank weapon found at Terry's house, it is obvious that the judge did not know this device was only a display and incapable of being used as a weapon. Since the FBI knew the truth in this matter, and realizing that the judge was acting upon information given to him by federal prosecutors via the FBI, the only logical conclusion we can make is that the FBI and/or the prosecutors lied to a federal judge in an attempt to prejudice his decision.

When you really think about the other statements made by Judge Belot, the FBI may have "overdunnit" again. It doesn't look like they needed to lie to this particular federal, "judge?" We don't recall ever reading in the U.S. Constitution a limit on the number of guns a citizen could possess. And how could pamphlets concerning the government's slaughter of innocent citizens in a church in Waco, Texas, be misconstrued as incriminating to any citizen in this Country, except for the terrorists who carried out the slaughter? Are we not supposed to possess any literature that is critical of government activities? Has the U.S. government somehow adopted the laws of Nazi Germany while we weren't paying attention? Are they planning on burning our books or just prosecuting us for all of the literature with which Judge Belot and others who share his obvious disdain for the Bill of Rights do not agree?

Considering that they're getting all of its information from an agency (FBI) that has labeled the Constitution an "extremist tract," none of the government's remarks or opinions should surprise us.

Perhaps the "judge" should rethink his position on "literature about government warfare." If possessing that kind of literature is a crime, then the CIA, FBI, DEA, BATF, SS, IRS, Dept. of Defense and the Pentagon are all involved in criminal activity. Of course, we all probably knew that anyway.

By the way, after reading the transcripts from that hearing we realized that later in the hearing Judge Belot was informed by Terry's temporary counsel that the "anti-tank bazooka" was nothing more than an empty canister used for displays only. The truth obviously had no impact on his opinion so our suggestion that Judge Belot harbors utter contempt for, at the very least, our First and Second Amendment rights has really been confirmed by his actions. Like we said, the FBI "overdunnit" again. Why haven't the FBI agent or agents been brought up on charges of lying to a federal judge?? We would like to thank Rachael B. for bringing to our attention this, and much more, very enlightening information.

• **Question No. 13: Why did government agents find it necessary to lie about how they orchestrated a raid on my farm so quickly after they located Tim?** First, it was Trooper Charlie Hanger who noticed Tim's resemblance to John Doe No. 1. He then notified the FBI and they checked it out and, by the grace of God, just in the nick of time, moments before Tim's release, the FBI contacted the Sheriff in Perry, Okla., and saved the world from the mad bomber. They played our emotions to the hilt on that one suggesting that fate played a hand in capturing all of those vicious terrorists.

Unfortunately for the feds, before they could "brief" local officials in Perry, Mark Gibson, Noble County assistant district attorney, admitted in an interview with Ted Koppel on ABC's *Nightline* that neither he nor Trooper Hanger ever noticed that Tim McVeigh resembled the composite of John Doe No. 1. That admission on national television made a second lie necessary to cover their lyin' behinds. The second story from the "professional deceivers" in the FBI's Damage Control Department suggested that they got an anonymous tip that John Doe No. 1 resembled a guy named Timothy McVeigh.

They then had to revise that story slightly because they didn't actually call the Sheriff in Perry until April 21, 10:30 a. m. Oklahoma time and they were already descending upon Lana (Why did her name come up before they allegedly found Tim?) in Las Vegas at exactly the same time and assaulting my farm with a small, well-armed army two and one half hours later. They claimed to have gained the information about me from Tim's driver's license and it didn't take long to figure that there just wasn't enough time to have organized this enormous raid complete with satellite TV dishes; many satellite TV dishes. I've often wondered how and why they went to Lana's in Las Vegas several hours before they came to Terry's house or to my farm?

Their third claim was that they actually called the prosecutor in Perry earlier that morning which gave them a "cushion" of a couple of extra hours. Then the information began circulating that the *Sanilac News*, a local paper here in Michigan, reported that the feds had contacted the sheriff's department at approximately 11 p.m. the night before the raid and set up shop in a county building at 5 a.m., the morning of the raid.

They also set up communications between themselves, Washington

D. C. and the FBI in Oklahoma City at 5 o'clock that morning and started watching my farm at approximately the same time. Since the information was out that they made their first call to our local sheriff at least 11 hours before their latest lie about locating McVeigh, they had to change their story again.

This time, it was the vehicle identification number on the axle. In their fourth story, they claimed to have traced the VIN down to the rental location in Junction City, Kan., which allowed them to eventually locate Tim in the Perry, Okla., jail by carrying out a very thorough FBI computer investigation. The problem still existed in that, by their own admission, they had not called the Perry authorities until Friday morning on April 21. Oops. They had to rethink that one. It took them almost seven months but rethink they did.

Fortunately, they're not very good rethinkers. As we told you earlier, their fifth and, we would assume, final lie doesn't make any more sense than their first four lies. Now they're saying that they had already identified and located Mr. McVeigh on April 19, the day of the bombing, and were patiently waiting for the judge in Perry to release Tim on bail. According to reports the judge's schedule was loaded down with divorce cases and other local problems and Tim's release was postponed for more than a day while the FBI waited, without intervening.

Of course, while they were waiting, all of the John Does flew back to D.C., Iran, Iraq, D.C, Libya, New York, L.A., D.C. or some other terrorist haven without fear of being caught because all of the brilliant FBI investigators in the whole country were monitoring the jail in Perry and the thought never occurred to even one of the thousands of these federal crime-fighters to tell the judge in Perry to let Tim go so they could follow him!?

The scam gets worse when you apply a little more simple logic. If this fifth and final lie was the truth, then why didn't they say so from the very beginning? We don't see any sort of national security reason for not telling that fifth lie first, do you? We believe, if the FBI had never been challenged on the first story, they would've never made up the second story and if they hadn't been caught in the second lie, there would've never been a third and so on and so on. How could anyone believe anything these liars leak to the media? We've yet to hear them tell the truth about anything in this case. Again, why did the feds find it necessary to tell the original lie? What exactly were they trying to hide?

• **Question No. 14: Why did law-enforcement officers march Lee Harvey McVeigh out in front of an angry Oklahoma mob without a** bullet-proof vest even after he had asked for one several times? Tim also asked to be escorted out the back door but to no avail. Why didn't they sneak him out the back door making certain they could exit with some degree of safety? Who leaked the information to the public that a bombing suspect was being held six hours before they openly escorted McVeigh out to face potential executioners?

• **Question No. 15: Why does the stocky-built, olive complected, dark-haired law enforcement agent standing in the line of police guarding McVeigh as he's being escorted from the Noble County courthouse, bear such a striking resemblance to John Doe No. 2?** If his face was interchanged with the composite sketch of John Doe No. 2 you could not tell the difference, which proves that you don't need to look very far to find people who resemble the sketches of John Does No. 1 and No. 2.

• **Question No. 16: Is it a coincidence that Floyd Zimms, the bald agent with a beard who assisted in escorting McVeigh from the Noble County courthouse, is one of the FBI's top specialist in disguises and sting operations?** Is it really just a coincidence that his overall appearance and stature resembles me? Doesn't it seem rather curious that the FBI's top expert in disguises, who just happens to look like James Nichols, was immediately involved in this investigation and that he was with the first wave of federal agents on the scene at the courthouse in Perry, Okla., to interrogate and to escort McVeigh? Is it a coincidence that during the walk from the courthouse, Agent Zimms stepped just far enough to the left of the bright orange target to provide an opportunity for a clear shot at McVeigh?

Looking at the video of their march from the courthouse it would appear as if a kid could have hit Tim between the eyes with a peashooter from 30 yards. It's hard to imagine that the conspirators in this crime would not have a man in position to "take out" the patsy. Is it possible that some unsuspecting citizen who was coming to see what the commotion was all about could've been in the right or wrong place at the right or wrong time to unwittingly foil the plan to "solve" this case and lay it to rest with one little squeeze on the trigger?

• **Question No. 17: Why did the BATF try to set me up in my house by encouraging me to pick up and move my loaded pistol so I could get some money to take with me while I was being taken into "protective custody?"** Is it standard operating procedure for the BATF to offer the most wanted man on the planet an opportunity to get his hands on a loaded 44 Magnum?

• **Question No. 18: Why was the $60,000 figure, pertaining to the amount of cash I was supposed to have stashed under my mattress, suddenly on the lips of officers who raided my farm?** On April 21, 1995, the day of the raid on my farm, the FBI asked me why I had $60,000 cash. Actually, I only had about $2,000 cash hidden under my mattress. From where did the FBI get that $60,000 figure? Is it just a coincidence that it was the exact same dollar amount of guns, coins and cash that Roger Moore claimed was stolen from his Arkansas home?

Considering that considerable time had passed after the raid before Moore made any allegations against Tim, that magic $60,000 figure just had to be a coincidence before the fact, right? It must have been the same kind of coincidence that occurred when, 20 minutes after the bombing, BATF ANFO expert Harry Everhardt declared to the world that the Murrah Building had just been destroyed by an ANFO bomb even though, two years after the fact, all of the scientists and resources in the FBI's crime lab have been unable to provide any evidence confirming Agent Everhardt's declaration.

It must have been the same kind of coincidence that occurred when, the day after the bombing, David Williams, a supervisory scientist in the FBI's crime lab, stated that it appeared to him to have been an ANFO bomb of around 4,000 to 5,000 pounds even though, two years after the fact, Mr. Williams and all of the other scientists using all of the resources in the FBI's crime lab have been unable to provide any evidence confirming Agent Williams coincidental "opinions" the day after the bombing. These are some very remarkable coincidences.

• **Question No. 19: Why did the FBI contradict their own testimony on four occasions when my attorney, Robert Elsey, cross-examined their Special Agent on the witness stand at my bail bond hearing?** Why did they find it necessary to lie and to discredit me in court by presenting what proved to be false evidence? Isn't it their job to convict the guilty and not to fabricate evidence and lie in court in an obvious attempt to railroad the innocent? Why haven't those agents been charged with perjury?

• **Question No. 20: When the feds assaulted my farm, why did they spend so much time searching the fields and driveway close to the main road?** Why didn't they search behind the barn and out on the "back

40," far from the road in areas that anyone with an ounce of common sense would realize would've probably been used if there had been any experiments in bomb manufacturing? Did they search more extensively close to the highway just to put on a show for the world to see via media satellites and to strike the "Fear of the Feds" into the hearts of all honest, hard-working Americans?

• **Question No. 21: Why did the FBI confiscate all of the seismograph readings from the area shortly after the bombing?** Fortunately, before the feds got there to confiscate the evidence, someone had the insight to make copies of the readings and that's why we have proof that there were at least two blasts of near equal force approximately 10 seconds apart confirming the testimony of numerous eyewitnesses. Of course the feds deny that there were two distinct blasts even though the seismic reports prove it. Should we be surprised?

• **Question No. 22: Why did the FBI jealously guard all of the video information that was confiscated from the area on the morning of the bombing?** Confiscation of this evidence by the feds was proper procedure and shouldn't alarm anyone. But not making public, at the very least, a still photo of the suspects exiting the truck, particularly John Doe No. 2 who was seen by many eyewitnesses and victims, should raise a red flag in everyone's mind.

Was there someone in those original photos that the FBI did not want identified? Did something happen in front of or inside of that building that the feds didn't want us to see? If any of those cameras remained operational during the explosions, then multiple explosions would've been recorded on film and the feds would have had some major explaining to do.

Even though seismograph readings and eyewitness testimony prove beyond any doubt to any rational, thinking person that there were multiple explosions, the feds still lie and deny. Even though we all know beyond any doubt, we cannot prove beyond any doubt that there were multiple explosions because the feds have confiscated all of the physical evidence. An on-the-scene video might prove beyond any doubt that which we already know and that could be why the FBI has guarded and either altered or destroyed the original, potentially self-incriminating photos.

• **Question No. 23: Why did they find it necessary to destroy the Murrah Building with demolitions a month after the fact?** They had a several-square-block area completely fenced in and closely guarded, so there was obviously no risk to the public from this "dangerous" structure. The public couldn't even get close to the area. By the time they dropped the Murrah Building, most of the mess and dangling, dangerous debris had already been cleaned up and trucked away to a well-guarded landfill. The architect who designed the building considered it solid enough to rebuild. As late as February, 1996, the Athenian Restaurant directly across the street from the Murrah Building was still standing. The front of that building was blown off with chunks of debris dangling out all over the place and the back of the building was wide open and easily accessible to anyone, including any child, who might want to "enter at their own risk."

As a matter of fact, there were several buildings in the area that were not behind a fence, were easily accessible, and appeared to be quite dangerous. It didn't appear to us that the people in charge considered public safety a top priority or even a secondary concern.

• **Question No. 24: Why were the feds in such a hurry to bury the evidence in an ongoing criminal investigation?** As a matter of fact, this is the biggest criminal investigation in the history of this country. Not only did they destroy this evidence but, under closely guarded conditions, carted off many thousands of tons of the evidence and buried it at another fenced and guarded location and then sodded over the area where the Murrah Building once stood.

And now that the safety hazard has been eliminated, have they removed the cyclone barbed-wire fence? No. They've only removed the fence around those damaged buildings that are not guarded and are still dangerous to the public. Those buildings that contain no evidence which would allow We The People to find out what was really responsible for causing this tragedy.

• **Question No. 25: Why was the mammoth crater in front of the Murrah Building filled in the day before defense investigators were to have entered the crater for inspection?** Was there something in that crater that the feds didn't want found? Why isn't anyone taking credit for giving the order to fill the bombed out hole before any information could be gathered by the defense teams and why hasn't anyone in the media reported this alarming information about the obvious destruction of evidence and OBSTRUCTION OF JUSTICE by the feds? WHO BENEFITS by the destruction of that evidence? WHO BENEFITS by keeping this specific information from the public?

• **Question No. 26: How did an ANFO bomb sitting above the ground, inside a truck, sand-bagged and directed toward the Murrah Building, still manage to blow an 8'x30' hole into the ground through the asphalt and hardpan in the street?** And, if the "ANFO bomb" could have blown that huge crater while sitting above the ground, shouldn't the crater in the road have contained many pieces of the truck that were under the bomb when it went off? Maybe some parts of the undercarriage, not limited to but including the rear axle?

• **Question No. 27: How did the rear axle housing from the Ryder truck get blown up and away through the explosion and then land several hundred feet away in clear view to be easily found by either the governor of Oklahoma or a bomb-squad cop depending on who's story you want to believe?** And nobody saw this thing flying through the air and bouncing down the street? The laws of physics dictate that this very heavy rear axle housing would have been blown down into the crater away from the center of the explosion along with many other pieces of this truck which were under the alleged bomb.

A thinking person might conclude that to create such a large crater through the asphalt and hardpan and to blow that heavy rear axle housing up and away there would almost have to be some kind of an explosion from underneath the truck, but then again, just who do we think we are pointing out these holes in the government's story which defy common sense, logic, and the laws of physics? The feds write the laws so if they want to re-write the laws of physics and create their own reality where "A" is actually "B" and down is really up, then maybe they can. Apparently, they have.

• **Question No. 28: Why weren't the defense investigators allowed to remove and inspect one little speck of rubble from the bombing site?** What in the world are these federal investigators trying to hide? How can they get away with hoarding all of the evidence, and destroying much of the evidence, in a criminal investigation, particularly concerning capital crimes?

• **Question No. 29: How can it be possible that federal authorities have simply given up on John Doe No. 2?** It has been reported that Janet Reno dropped the $2 million reward for John Doe No. 2. If this information is true, do the feds no longer consider John Doe No. 2's obvious involvement the crime, or are they just completely denying his existence in spite of dozens of eyewitnesses, including victims, who have confirmed his presence in and around the Ryder truck and in or around the Murrah Building? Can the feds just assume that all of these eyewitnesses will change their testimony for the trials or before they can actually identify John Doe No. 2?

• **Question No. 30: Why did BATF supervisor Alex McCauley try to gain sympathy by making up the story about "free-falling" five or six stories in an elevator?** The elevators were all checked out by experts and it was confirmed that none of the elevators showed any evidence of a free-fall. As a matter of fact, according to independent journalist J.D. Cash, the experts said that because of inherent safety devices none of the elevators in the building could free-fall.

Why did McCauley find it necessary to fabricate this story? J.D. Cash has exposed the myth about McCauley and a DEA. agent narrowly escaping death after their elevator fell six floors. As a matter of fact, this particular DEA. agent, Dave Schickendanz, was honored in *Parade* magazine with a 1996 Police Officer of the Year Award for the bravery and heroism that he displayed during the rescue efforts immediately after the bombing.

At this time, we are not disputing the bravery and heroism allegedly displayed by Agent Schickendanz. But since it has been proven to any reasonable person that someone is not exactly being forthright about the elevator in which Agents McCauley and Schickendanz were riding, is it not our responsibility to ask if and why Agent Schickendanz may have taken part in this apparent lie?

And, please, apply some common sense to this scenario — even if journalist J.D. Cash had not exposed this fabricated story, even if the experts had never inspected all of the elevators and determined that they never free-fell any floors. Imagine standing inside a metal box and it suddenly got dropped off a six-story building crashing to the ground. The result would be the same if you were dropped from a six-story building with no metal box. You would probably be killed instantly and/or most of the bones in your body would be crushed.

These two agents claim to have fallen six stories, and yet they both escaped relatively unscathed? Cash's conclusions were drawn after thoroughly investigating this matter and those conclusions certainly seem much more believable to a rational, thinking person than the accounts by the two government agents who are being praised by the news media as "heroes." To quote J.D. Cash: "The bottom line is this: No elevator free-fell that day."

• **Question No. 31: What really happened to one of the high-ranking BATF officials at the scene?** BATF chief Luke Franey claims to have been inside the Murrah Building at the time of the explosion. It has been reported that he was trapped under debris inside the building for an hour or more and that he used his martial arts skills to kick and chop his way to safety. It has also been reported that pictures taken the day after the bombing showing Agent Franey wearing a cast on his arm somewhat verify this very dramatic accounting of his experiences.

We have been told by independent investigators that pictures exist of Agent Franey standing in front of the Murrah Building at approximately 9:30 a.m., a half-hour before he escaped certain doom while he was trapped inside the building. The investigators can determine the exact time because of the equipment pictured in the background. They say that Agent Franey appears to be very clean, as if he had just arrived on the scene, and that he was shaking hands with another man using the hand that he had allegedly broken during the bombing or as a result of his escape.

If Agent Franey was trapped inside the damaged Murrah Building until well past 10 a.m., how did he appear in pictures taken in front of the building at 9:30 a.m.? How did he get so clean 30 minutes before he emerged from the building? How could he shake hands with a broken hand or arm? If he was in the building at any time immediately after the explosions, what was he doing in there?

• **Question No. 32: Was Dr. Howard Chumley asked to file false reports about the bombing by government investigators?** Dr. Chumley was one of the first doctors on the scene to assist in the life saving rescue efforts. It has been rumored that the BATF ask Dr. Chumley to fill out false medical reports immediately after the bombing? If these rumors are true, why would they ask him to lie saying that he had treated seriously injured BATF agents who, in reality, had no injuries?

It has been reported that when Dr. Chumley refused to cooperate, the BATF approached another doctor on the scene who agreed to go along with their scam. Dr. Chumley told the other doctor, whom he knew, that he would expose him if he falsified medical records or lied about treating BATF agents.

• **Question No. 33: What really caused Dr. Chumley's airplane to crash?** Dr. Chumley was an honest, moral man, admired and held in high esteem by all who knew him. Those who knew him also said that he was the most careful and meticulous person they had ever met. Dr. Chumley's private plane had just undergone a very thorough, professional inspection. During one of his first flights after the inspection, Dr. Chumley's plane just fell out of the sky, according to witnesses, crashing and killing him.

Dr. Chumley's death was ruled an accident, even though the entire incident seems extremely suspicious. Dr. Chumley was a very experienced pilot and his plane was in excellent condition. There was no apparent reason for his recently inspected Cessna 210 to just fall from the sky. It would seem reasonable to assume that we can rule out the "wear and tear" explanation expressed by some investigators and, considering Dr. Chumley's abilities as a pilot, we can all but rule out the "pilot error" explanation expressed by other investigators.

• **Question No. 34: Did Oklahoma City police officer Terrence Yeakey really commit suicide, and if he did, what caused him to do it?** It has been reported that Officer Yeakey, who worked in the rescue efforts in the Murrah Building, committed suicide. Why do all of his friends say that he was absolutely not suicidal? We have been told by private investigators from Oklahoma that Officer Yeakey had been in contact with Dr. Chumley, sharing information about their suspicions of a cover-up by the BATF.

Is it a coincidence that both of these men, who may have had some very incriminating information against the feds, have some very questionable circumstances surrounding their deaths? Is it a coincidence that Bob Ricks, former head of the FBI in Oklahoma, has now been put in charge of STATE law enforcement (public safety) enabling him to be in a position to know about and to effectively keep a lid on incriminating information that may be leaked to the public by state employees (i.e., Terrence Yeakey)?

• **Question No. 35: Is it a coincidence that Weldon Kennedy, Special-Agent-In-Charge of the Oklahoma City bombing investigation has been promoted to the number two slot in the FBI?** It's still rising to the top, isn't it?

• **Question No. 36: What really happened to Rebecca Anderson, a brave nurse who immediately was on the scene attempting to save lives?** It was reported that she was struck by falling debris before she came staggering out of the Murrah Building rubble and collapsed into a coma and died. The problem is that she had no physical signs of being struck by a chunk of anything. They then reported that she may have had an aneurysm, but her actions indicated that she had not. She had obviously suffered from some kind of blunt trauma and, to our knowledge, that was the finding of the final report on her unfortunate death.

Had Rebecca been struck by any kind of hard construction material that fell on her, there would have been some evidence proving that that was the case. As far as we know, there was nothing indicating that she had been struck by falling debris. The type of blow that killed Rebecca Anderson came from a softer, duller object than a chunk of cement. The type of object that might be found on the end of a martial artists arm. Did Rebecca Anderson die needlessly because of her compassion and because of her desire to help others? Did Rebecca Anderson die because she was one of the first courageous people to ignore potential hazards to her own safety placing above all else her concern for the well-being of others?

Did Rebecca Anderson see something inside that bombed out building that she was not supposed to have seen? Did she needlessly pay with her own life for her deep concern about others?

• **Question No. 37: Why did witnesses see the bomb squad outside the Murrah Building several hours before the explosions?** Did the feds have prior knowledge and if they did, why didn't they warn everyone else?

• **Question No. 38: What about the widespread belief that BATF personnel were told to stay home on April 19, 1995?** It has been widely reported that BATF agents who normally work in the Murrah Building were told not to come in to work on the morning of the bombing. The BATF vehemently denies these reports.

Oklahoma State Rep. Charles Key said that "they [BATF] were mysteriously, uncharacteristically absent from the building that morning." It has been suggested, and universally believed by all of those who are skeptical of the government's story, that the BATF agents who normally work in the Murrah Building had prior warning so their lives would not be put in jeopardy. We have a different perspective on this issue and one that we believe will eventually surface as the real truth about the BATF's prior knowledge.

If the objective was to catch the bad guys one might conclude that the good guys would want as many BATF agents on the scene as possible. But, if too many uninvolved, honest, hard working BATF agents had gone to work that day, is it possible that they may have been experienced enough in anti-terrorism training and alert enough to really catch the bad guys?

We do not believe that saving the lives of those agents had anything to do with their "day off." We believe some of those agents may have detected the bombs planted inside the building and may well have exposed and spoiled the entire plot and, consequently, the anti-terrorism bill, Bill. There was certainly something "uncharacteristic" going on but we have to believe that most of these BATF agents are well-meaning citizens, albeit a little confused.

• **Question No. 39: Did two witnesses working in the federal courthouse across the street from the Murrah Building see two persons with flashlights inside the Murrah Building sometime between 2 a.m. and 3 a.m. on the morning of April 19, and if so, who were these people?** There were no security personnel scheduled for duty in the Murrah Building that night. If the people who were reportedly seen in the building at that time were supposed to be there, then why were they sneaking around with flashlights instead of just turning on the regular lights?

We have heard the suggestion that they may have been searching for bombs. If that was the case why didn't they just, turn on the lights? It seems more likely that someone sneaking around in the dark with flashlights while no security personnel were on duty may well have been a part of the "team" of government agents that many witnesses claim to have seen hanging around outside of the building also.

Evidence dictates and witnesses have stated that bombs were planted inside the Murrah Building. It seems as if April 19, around 2 or 3 a.m., would have been an ideal time for two people with flashlights to place the bombs in an unguarded Murrah Building. Oh, we forgot! According to witnesses, the Murrah Building was heavily guarded at the time — by government agents! Now what might that suggest?

• **Question No. 40: What was the real reason that Judge Wayne Alley was forced to step down as the presiding judge over this case?** The reason the Justice Department gave to the press, and ultimately reported to the people, was that Judge Alley's offices were damaged in the bombing and that he knew some people who were injured and killed in the blasts, a circumstance that could prejudice the judge.

If those were the real reasons, then why did the Justice Department wait until December to relieve Judge Alley of his position as presiding judge? Didn't the same circumstances apply from April through November? If he was really relieved for those reasons, why wasn't he relieved back in April or May? We would like to know why he was appointed in the first place if it was determined that he could not be impartial?

Fortunately, in December our friend and video producer, Chuck Allen, received some information from Jim Redden, a patriot in Oregon, concerning an article that appeared in *The Oregonian* on April 20, 1995. The article was written by Dave Hogan who did a telephone interview with Judge Alley shortly after the bombing.

In part of his conversation with Dave Hogan, Judge Alley stated: "Let me just say that within the past two or three weeks, information has been disseminated ... that indicated concerns on the part of people who ought to know that we ought to be a little bit more careful ... there has been an increased vigilance."

He pointed out, "Of all the days for this to happen, it's absolutely an amazing coincidence."

Judge Alley also commented that his son and daughter-in-law had considered using the Murrah Building day-care center for their baby but chose another facility instead. "The thought that our grandchild might have been in there was the thing that was the most chilling about all of this," Alley said.

Chuck Allen relayed this information to J.D. Cash ,who relayed it to Edye Smith who, on a talk-radio program, questioned the fact that the judge did not reveal this information about prior warnings to everyone else so they may have had the same options that he and his family enjoyed. The Justice Department immediately relieved Judge Alley and replaced him with Judge Matsch.

Now a suspicious person may think that Alley was fired because of this alarming information that finally surfaced. We personally wouldn't think that because the feds already gave us the reason for relieving Alley and that reason didn't include prior warnings of a potential bombing. And we all know that the feds wouldn't lie, right?

There's one thing really bothers us about this incident. Why didn't anyone else in the national media, aside from *The Oregonian*, pick up on this extremely important information about Judge Alley? If not for a very concerned patriot in Oregon who was aware that this interview had appeared in *The Oregonian*, if not for the tenacity of Edye Smith, and if not for some other concerned citizens in Oklahoma, Judge Wayne Alley would probably still be presiding over this case.

Many people do not believe that the Justice Department would've relieved Judge Alley if not for their fear of the public's perception of intentional wrongdoing on their part. It has been suggested that they could not risk the open challenge in court about Alley's possible prejudices against the defendants because much of the information about prior warnings would've been made public. When all of this alarming information is brought out into the light of day a suspicious person might conclude that Judge Alley was picked to judge this case because of the particular prejudices he may harbor, or perhaps for some other reasons which we may be unaware of at this time.

• **Question No. 41: Why didn't the prosecution offer witnesses before the grand jury who had seen and could identify John Does No. 2, No. 3, No. 4 and No. 5 and the real John Doe No. 1?** The prosecution claims, and even Judge Richard Matsch indicated during hearings to dismiss the indictments, that this "withholding of evidence" from the grand jury had no influence on the grand jury's decision to indict Tim and Terry.

How they may have arrived at that conclusion is beyond us, particularly when you consider that it has been reported that the Justice Department has dropped the reward for John Doe No. 2 and is basically denying the existence of John Doe No. 2 in spite of dozens of eyewitnesses. They even went so far as to suggest that John Doe No. 2 was a soldier from Fort Riley, Kan., who doesn't even remotely resemble the composite drawings, suggesting that the witnesses at Elliott's Body Shop didn't really see who they claim to have seen.

The feds say that this soldier had been there a day or so earlier and all of the witnesses at the Ryder truck rental location were mistaken. Actually, sayeth the feds, they all just thought they saw him there with John Doe No. 1. Even though the truck rentals had only happened a few days before the questioning by the FBI, none of the eyewitnesses could have possibly known what they had seen. The FBI was not there, yet they knew what the actual eyewitnesses didn't see. Or did see? Or thought they saw? Or thought they didn't see or ... anyway, if you can understand all of this, you're either in the FBI or you're a federal judge.

• **Question No. 42: During Tim's and Terry's indictments, why wouldn't the prosecution allow the grand jury to question witnesses?** Why couldn't the grand jury subpoena witnesses? Why did the prosecution withhold (suppress) evidence from the grand jury? What was it that they did not want the grand jury to investigate? Technically, the grand jury has the power to question, to subpoena and to carry on its own investigation. Why would the feds OBSTRUCT JUSTICE by stifling the grand jury?

• **Question No. 43: Why did the prosecutor lie to the grand jury?** Why did a federal judge allow the prosecutor to lie in his courtroom? It would seem that the grand jury should have had the prosecutor arrested immediately for OBSTRUCTION OF JUSTICE, and perhaps the federal judge who allowed the prosecutor to lie and obstruct justice in his courtroom should have shared a bunked in Club Fed with the prosecutor. It's not too late.

• **Question No. 44: Why did Hoppy Heidelberg, an outspoken member of the grand jury, have to hire an attorney to defend himself against charges from the prosecutor?** Doesn't the grand jury have the final say-so in this country's justice system? That was certainly the original intent of the Framers of our Constitution. The grand jury and, finally, the petite jury exist specifically to be the final "check" in our checks and balance system of government. When this pathetic excuse for a prosecutor stopped the grand jury from exercising its powers, he violated his oath and, with the assistance of the judge, literally undermined the foundation of our justice system. The prosecution claims that Hoppy violated the secrecy of the grand jury because he talked to members of the press and, therefore, he should face charges. This brings us to our next question ...

• **Question No. 45: How did the identity of Hoppy Heidelberg — the breakaway grand juror who challenged the prosecutors to allow more witnesses to testify in the grand jury hearings against Tim and Terry — become known to the press?** The prosecution would have us believe that Hoppy sought out a journalist to tell his story, but that is not the case. Apparently, Hoppy was the only member of the grand jury who actually read his government-issue *Grand Juror's Handbook* and had at least some understanding of his rights and powers as a juror.

From the beginning, he realized that something was seriously wrong with the prosecution's presentation of evidence and witnesses, or lack thereof, and started speaking up and asking questions. Lord knows that in today's "Just-Us" System, challenging an officer of the court is an unforgivable sin. Hoppy made many challenges to the prosecution's tactics which apparently put a few bumps on the tracks of the government's "railroad."

The secrecy of the identity of the grand jurors was obviously a very important matter. Each morning the jurors were brought into the federal courthouse secretly through an entrance which would not allow them to be seen by any members of the press. One day, after the prosecution realized that Hoppy had a thinking mind and might present an obstacle which they could not overcome, the prosecutor brought the jurors into the courthouse through the front door — taking the grand jury out in the open for all the members of the press to see.

Hoppy is recognizable to some local reporters because of his affiliation with the Horse Breeders Association in Oklahoma. As expected, he was recognized and was later contacted by at least one of those reporters. His identity was eventually discovered by Lawrence Myers from *Media Bypass* who did and informal interview with Hoppy on the phone and, afterward, the proverbial s - - t hit the fan!

Now the prosecution had, or thought they had, the ammunition to eliminate an intelligent, observant and gutsy thorn in their side. When you are aware of what really happened to Hoppy, it doesn't take a rocket scientist to figure out that the U.S. attorney set him up to be identified so he would be approached by members of the media allowing the prosecution to kick this "troublemaker" off the grand jury.

One thing prosecutors cannot and will not tolerate in OUR current martial-law judicial system is "informed" jurors. The session of this grand jury was supposed to have ended Dec. 31, 1995. The end of that session would have allowed Hoppy and other members of the grand jury to speak openly about the moral and perhaps legal transgressions of some of the prosecutors which would have really opened up a can of worms. The court curiously extended the grand jury's session by six months. Doesn't it make you wonder if maybe, just maybe, they might have extended the grand jury's session to protect the worms?

We must also consider an aspect of Hoppy's predicament which has really never been mentioned by the media. If a citizen sees a crime being committed and says or does nothing, doesn't that citizen become a lawbreaker too? Is it not a citizen's moral, civil and legal responsibility to report criminal activity?

We're not talking about kid stuff or simple misdemeanors, we're talking about crimes. If you witness a government servant violating his OATH to uphold the Constitution, violating the principles of the Constitution, lying to a grand jury or OBSTRUCTING JUSTICE, isn't it your responsibility as a citizen to report such felonious criminal behavior? Believe it or not, Hoppy Heidelberg was the only one of 23 citizens on that grand jury who had the gumption to accept that responsibility. Perhaps the other 22 grand jurors are actually just mere citizens.

• **Question No. 46: Why did witnesses inside the Murrah Building feel the building rumbling as if there was an earthquake, some seconds**

before the open-air bomb exploded? Seconds elapsed before a large explosion outside occurred. What caused the first "disruption of tranquility" inside the Murrah Building that caused these survivors to dive for safety? Considering that the speed of a low velocity explosive is 8,000 feet per second, it is obvious that the first tremor occurred a few seconds before the first large explosion. Can any government agent or investigator explain this sequence of events to us? And another issue of equal importance is: What caused the second series of large explosions from inside the building several seconds after the first large explosion from the outside?

Clearly, this was evidence that internal explosions took place to sever support columns in the building before the much larger sound of the outside bomb was heard. This was clearly obvious to people in the courtroom of the McVeigh trial when an audio tape recording of the explosion was played back before the jury — and later heard by the rest of the world as the international news media also played the tape.

The tape is of a woman's voice. She was lecturing in a meeting room in a building across the street from the Murrah Building. A low, rolling rumble is heard, as if some kind of muffled explosions were taking place underground. The woman senses these rumblings, and as they subside, she stops talking.

Then, *BBLLLLLLAAAAAAAAAAAM!* The large outside detonation takes place, triggering pandemonium. Make no mistake. Multiple explosions brought down the Murrah Building. People heard it. People sensed it. Tape recordings prove it. Seismic readings prove it. There is no denying it.

• **Question No. 47: Why did four main columns of steel-reinforced concrete two feet thick show evidence of contact-charge damage?** (See *The New American*, Aug. 7, 1995, by William Jasper, "Special Report Concerning Gen. Partin's Findings.") How could an open-air explosion such as a truck bomb shear these concrete columns?

All of the experts say, "it couldn't." According to Gen. Partin, a separate contact charge was necessary to shear every other column. According to the prosecution's FBI expert with 25 years demolition experience "you have to bore in to bring those columns down." According to the engineering report, strategically placed charges in several locations would've been necessary to achieve the end result.

Why would the explosion from outside take out a center-row column near the east end of the building — and not destroy columns much closer to the explosion? How could the blast destroy that center-row column and not even blow the drywall off columns closer to the blast? Why didn't the rest of the building sustain structural damage if an open air blast was capable of causing structural damage to areas of the building that were much farther from the blast than some areas which had no structural damage?

According to all of the experts, "it couldn't." Period!

• Question No. 48: Why wasn't the damage to the Murrah Building symmetrical or at least somewhat circular? Why was the least damaged area closest to the crater in the street and the most damaged areas farthest from the crater? Why did there appear to be three circular patterns of destruction, again, the least of which is closest to the crater? Why is the most severe damage actually "around the corner" from the truck-bomb area?

• Question No. 49: Why was Bob Ricks seen at the bombing site by several witnesses just moments after the explosions? It has been alleged that many government agents, including Bob Ricks, were on a golf outing when the bombing occurred. This particular golf course is about 45 minutes away from downtown Oklahoma City. That, they say, is why so many high ranking government agents were absent during the explosions. We have been told by investigators that a private citizen has a picture of Mr. Ricks proving what several witnesses claim to have seen, but we have not yet seen the picture ourselves.

Needless to say, it might not be in the best interests of these witnesses' ability to enjoy their retirement programs or to appreciate the possibility of reasonably average longevity if their names were known to the feds.

• Question No. 50: Who is Dr. Louis Jolyan West and what does he have to do with this tragedy? His résumé includes involvement in the botched LSD experiments with military personnel in the 1950s and he is considered one of the government's top psychologists in the area of mind control. The key word here is "botched." To remain the government's top anything it would appear as if one would have to consistently botch everything. He has been involved with terrorist mind-control research for years and testified for the defense in the Patricia Hearst bank-robbery trial in 1976. Why did his name come to the attention of informed patriots just weeks after the bombing? More on Dr. West later.

• Question No. 51: Who is Gary Hunt and why did his name surface with Dr. West's name and two others who we cannot mention at this

time? More on this later, too.

• **Question No. 52: Why were people left bleeding to death and dying during the first, second and third "bomb scares" if there really were no bombs?** The feds have claimed that the alleged bombs were not really bombs at all but were, in fact, just training devices. Could all of the bomb experts in the bomb squad really be so incompetent that they could not distinguish a training device from a real bomb even though all training devices are specifically marked as such?

• **Question No. 53: What happened to the bombs that the bomb squad removed?** It was reported that one of those bombs was taken out and detonated. Why in the world would the bomb squad destroy the most important evidence in this entire investigation? What about the other bombs that were defused and removed? Witnesses have stated that they saw canisters about the size of five gallon buckets which were plainly marked "Fulminate of Mercury," a very potent military explosive. What happened to those canisters?

• **Question No. 54: How did the FBI's crime lab in Washington, D.C., find bomb residue in Tim's clothing even after Frederick Whitehurst, who has a Ph.D. in chemistry from Duke University and was the FBI's top bomb residue analyst alleges that he found NO BOMB RESIDUE ON TIM'S CLOTHING?** He has stated on national television that some individuals in the FBI's crime lab have deliberately falsified evidence to achieve convictions at any cost. Maybe that's why he "was" the FBI's top bomb residue analyst. Apparently Dr. Whitehurst's claims, which have been vehemently denied by the FBI hierarchy, are being confirmed by 37 other witnesses.

FBI chemist Mary Tungol and FBI lab technician Brett Mills are two of the witnesses who have been questioned at pretrial hearings concerning Whitehurst's allegations of sloppy lab work, evidence contamination and slanted reports. Dr. Tungol claims that evidence taken from Tim's car was contaminated. Brett Mills claims that an area in the FBI laboratory which was used to store evidence against McVeigh was contaminated with PETN. This is the substance found in "detcord" that the feds say they found in Tim's clothes after Dr. Whitehurst examined his clothing and found no evidence against McVeigh.

Perhaps now we know why the feds "found" PETN on Tim's t-shirt. We've been saying all along that they really have no hard evidence against Tim, and less than zero against Terry. Maybe, just maybe, someone will finally listen to those of us who have really figured out what's going on here instead of those who want their 15 minutes of fame and fortune or those whose intentions and conditions of employment are to spread disinformation. And finally, the inspector general's report has confirmed that which we have been saying from the beginning. There was and is no evidence of an ANFO bomb.

• **Question No. 55: Does any video exist showing John Doe No. 1, or anyone else for that matter, exiting the Ryder truck just prior to the explosions that brought down the Murrah Building?** There is a rumor that has been floating around which originated from a reporter who is notorious for his "exaggeration of the truth." (We're trying to be kind.) He claims to have seen some video footage that shows John Doe No. 1 exiting the Ryder truck. This video tape is alleged to have been illegally copied by FBI agents suffering from an overzealous entrepreneurial spirit who wanted to make a few hundred thousand bucks on the side. Since these alleged tapes have been obtained illegally, they have somehow supposedly gained a great deal of credibility. After all, if the tapes surfaced "legally" a year after the fact, everyone would cry fake, right? But if it is claimed that they were stolen and copied illegally for payoff, then they must be real, right?

Concerning a videotape of the Ryder truck in front of the Murrah Building minutes before the explosions, the lead prosecutor for this case, U.S. Attorney Patrick Ryan said: "You can't see that there is anyone in the truck, much less who it is." Somebody's obviously lying. Maybe everybody's lying.

• **Question No. 56: Why did the federal government suddenly make it legal for intelligence operatives to pose as journalists?** Prior to 1995, there was a law on the books which forbade government agents from posing as journalists or clergy. The feds thought it was necessary to repeal this law which protected citizens from government intrusion into personal matters.

Coincidentally, the law was repealed shortly after we discovered that a journalist who had befriended us was actually working for the feds. We were not supposed to have found out, but we did have some suspicions about this particular person shortly after our first conversation. Actually, we can pick out several "journalists" who, during 1996-97, we have suspected of being agents and, to be honest, we didn't even know that posing as a journalist was against the law for government agents until we heard on the news that the law had been changed.

Before this investigation we never had any reason to give it any thought. When we heard the news report the old light bulb just kind of turned on in our heads. Apparently the feds figured that since it would be very embarrassing to admit that they had been breaking their own law they would just, change the law! Not at all untypical for the feds. Now, the fact that they had been breaking the law is a moot issue. (We still consider the person a friend, but we doubt that the feeling is mutual.)

But just think about the intrusions into our privacy because of this new "legal repeal." Now the journalist to whom the confidential informant gives his confidential information is the very person to whom the journalist did not have to reveal his confidential source. So much for confidentiality. Most average citizens wouldn't have a problem with agents posing as journalists because it would never affect us personally. But the journalist/agent is certainly not the most alarming aspect of this law.

Consider that now your priest, minister, reverend or pastor might not be the "Representative from God" who you always thought he was. Some day you may assume you are having a very private conversation with your preacher, a man of God, whom you can trust with your very soul. Some day, you will be confessing your most intimate thoughts and sins to God through your priest and then, just when you think you've been forgiven for your sins because you have opened up your heart to God during confession, the man to whom you have confessed will pull back the curtain, flip open his badge and say, "Secret agent, ma'am. You're under arrest!"

So much for the "personal and private" relationship between God and man. They no longer have respect for anyone's privacy, not even yours and God's. Just another notch on the feds' handle as a result of the Oklahoma City bombing. WHO BENEFITS?

"Necessity is the plea for every infringement of human liberty; it is the argument of tyrants; it is the creed of slaves."
— **William Pitt**

• **Question No. 57: Why were federal investigators absolutely positive so soon that McVeigh was their man?** The description from Elliott's Body Shop wasn't even close. And according to FBI Special Agent John Hersley, three witnesses who saw John Doe No. 1 near the Murrah Building on the morning of the bombing could not positively identify Timothy McVeigh! Didn't know that, did you? Now you do.

324 ♦ Freedom's End

• **Question No. 58: How could blue plastic recycling barrels inside the Murrah Building be blown to bits by an open-air explosion outside the building?** Richard Williams, manager of the Oklahoma City branch of the federal General Services Administration, has stated that approximately 80 large blue plastic barrels used for recycling bins were stored throughout the Murrah Building when the bombing occurred.

Since the FBI crime lab claims that the evidence on the pieces of blue plastic barrels found throughout the Murrah Building and in some of the bodies of the victims indicated that the barrels had been blown to bits by an explosion from inside the barrels, doesn't that raise a question as to exactly where the explosions came from?

Considering that some of these large, rubberized, hard but flexible plastic barrels were blown into little pieces, how could an explosion from outside the building have imposed that kind of destruction on the barrels? How many of these blue plastic shards have been found in the area outside the Murrah Building? If the barrels containing explosives were blown apart from inside the truck on the outside of the building, shouldn't there be more blue plastic shards scattered around outside than within the boundaries of the Murrah Building?

The "Preliminary Event Analysis" written by the Walker Aerospace Group concluded that the Murrah Building had been brought down by a "series of demolition charges placed on the columns at the interfaces of the floor structures."

Richard Williams said that there were blue plastic barrels used as recycling bins placed throughout the Murrah Building. Where might one place those large barrels for recycling materials? Would they be placed in the middle of hallways or in the middle of rooms, or might they be placed against walls or against large support columns? Might they have been placed against several of the support columns inside the Murrah Building?

Wouldn't those barrels have been convenient places to hide explosive charges at around 2 a.m. or 3 a.m. on the morning of the bombing while the BATF and bomb squad were standing guard? A terrorist wouldn't need much time or any more than a flashlight to locate the appropriately placed containers. Why hasn't the media mentioned these barrels? Their silence on these matters is deafening.

• **Question No. 59: Who really stole the explosives from the rock quarry in Marion, Kan., in October 1994?** The FBI claims that Tim and Terry broke into the sheds containing explosives and burglarized the quarry of some dynamite, detcord and other materials which were allegedly used in making the bomb.

The prosecution has an "expert" witness who will claim that the imperfection on a drill bit found at Terry's house reasonably matches the markings made on a storage shed lock that had been drilled to break into one of the sheds. The problem is that Terry's drill bit was compared to the markings in the lock six months after the fact. How many times was his drill used during that six-month period? Could Terry's drill bit have acquired a similar imperfection during that time period?

Any handyman or handywoman knows that drill bits routinely receive nicks and scars through normal usage. The pattern of markings from a drill bit can change in a matter of minutes when drilling hard objects or after resharpening. If the FBI checked out 1,000 same-size drill bits from 1,000 different workin' dudes' toolboxes, how many might also reasonably match the markings in the lock?

Examining the markings on a drill bit basically entails the same procedure as a ballistics test on a bullet. The primary difference is that the markings inside the bore of a gun barrel remain relatively consistent over time. The markings from a drill bit can change with one usage, depending upon the material being drilled. The prosecution will probably say that the drill bit had not been used since the burglary and that's why the markings on the drill nearly match those in the lock.

That certainly sounds reasonable, and it would definitely explain why, six months after the fact, the markings would match. The problem is that under microscopic examination, and after all of the FBI Crime Lab's scientific tests, the notorious drill bit shows no trace of brass from the lock. Not even microscopic traces. Under the circumstances, that would be impossible if the drill bit allegedly found at Terry's house was used to drill the lock at the quarry in Marion, Kan.

There is another issue concerning this burglary that has somehow eluded the mainstream media. The Marion, Kan., sheriff who investigated the burglary has indicated that whoever was responsible for stealing the explosives had to have been very familiar with the quarry. When the sheriff went to the quarry, he had to have a person take him back to the storage sheds through a maze of roads and cow paths through many farm fields. He said that he could have never found the sheds on his own.

The owners of the quarry gave him the names of two suspects, a former disgruntled employee who had been fired and another current employee who had been demoted. The quarry had been closed for four days during the time of the burglary, affording the would-be burglars ample time to accomplish their mission also indicating inside knowledge that the quarry would be closed.

Witnesses claim to have seen a pickup truck with a light bar on top at approximately the same time as the burglaries occurred. Neither Tim nor Terry have that kind of pickup. Even though the sheriff had the names of suspects and concluded that it had to be an inside job, unfortunately he failed to question, investigate or get a warrant to search any of those suspects. Unfortunately, the FBI hasn't pursued those obvious leads, either.

Another significant issue concerning the burglary at the Marion, Kan., quarry is the contents of the two sheds that were burglarized. One of the sheds broken into was an ANFO shed, yet no ANFO was stolen. This was commercial-grade ANFO, much more potent than the low-grade ammonium nitrate available from the local farm co-op which Terry purchased for resale at trade shows. We certainly considered this to be very important information because it would seem that a person or persons who were planning a terrorist attack using ANFO would take advantage of an opportunity to acquire unlimited quantities of commercial-grade ANFO instead of buying low-grade ammonium nitrate and then trying to mix it themselves.

But if a disgruntled former or current employee wanted to get back at the owners of the quarry by stealing explosive materials that could be sold illegally, ANFO, considering its weight and volume, would not necessarily be a "great find," would it?

• **Question No. 60: What happened to the brown pickup truck that witnesses saw leaving the scene of the crime, at the Geary Lake "bomb mixing site" and on the highway when Tim was pulled over by Trooper Charlie Hanger?** According to investigative journalist J.D. Cash, there is a witness concerning that truck's whereabouts. Within a few days after the bombing, and not too far from Oklahoma City, a woman saw a yellow pickup truck drive up and park across the street from her home. A man, possibly of Middle Eastern descent, while exiting the truck, made eye contact with the woman who was standing outside in the yard in front of her house. She said that he gave her a glaring stare as if to say, "mind your own damn business."

Apparently some time had passed and the "John Doe No. ?" did not return to retrieve his truck. Thinking the whole situation seemed rather suspicious, she contacted the FBI who came immediately and, after examining the truck, towed it away. When the FBI agent came to her house to question her, it became obvious that the questioning was directly related to the Oklahoma City bombing. Questioning the agent, she asked what this "yellow truck" had to do with the bombing. She had heard on the news that they were looking for a "brown pickup."

The agent told her that she was absolutely right. He also told her that the yellow truck which had been abandoned in front of her house had recently been repainted. It used to be brown! Where is that brown/yellow truck? Perhaps it's keeping those unexploded training devices company!

• **Question No. 61: Why have the federal agents assigned to the bombing investigation been ordered to stop sending Denver prosecutors any further information on any suspects other than Tim McVeigh and Terry Nichols (source: *McCurtain Daily Gazette*)?**

• **Question No. 62: What of inconsistencies in the story about how Timothy McVeigh acquired the infamous yellow 1977 Mercury "getaway car?"** According to FBI records, shortly after arriving in Junction City, Kan., on Friday, April 14, 1995, Tim McVeigh pulled in to the Firestone dealership because he was having problems with the Pontiac 2000 station wagon that he bought from me. The repairs were going to be too costly so Tim made a deal to buy a 1977 yellow Mercury for $250 from Thomas Manning, an employee at the tire store.

Manning has been interviewed on 11 different occasions by FBI agents and by defense investigators. There has never been a problem with any of his statements about selling McVeigh the yellow Mercury. Nobody has ever doubted the time period in question when Mr. Manning claims the automobile transactions took place. At least not until the feds discovered that two calls were made from McVeigh's calling card at exactly the same time that Mr. McVeigh was talking to Mr. Manning. Now, all of a sudden, after eight FBI interrogations, after three interviews by defense investigators, 18 months after the fact, Mr. Manning is alleged to have stated that Tim left for about 10 or 15 minutes during their conversation.

Gosh, what a stroke of luck for the FBI. Just when it appeared as if someone else had been using McVeigh's calling card number, one-and-a-half years after the fact, Mr. Manning conveniently remembers that Tim left for a few minutes during their conversation which suggests that Tim could have made those calls if he really did leave for 10 minutes during their conversation.

Whose idea was it that Mr. Manning change his statement? Could this just be another case of FLEXIBLE FACTS? Many witnesses have claimed that the feds tried to intimidate or coerce them into changing their stories.

Many witnesses have had the courage and integrity to stand by the truth. It doesn't appear as if Mr. Manning fits into that category. We may wonder if, after reading this, the feds will convince Dr. Paul Heath that he should change his statement about seeing McVeigh in the Murrah Building, approximately 260 miles from the Firestone dealer in Junction City, Kansas, with a couple of John Does looking for job applications on Friday, April 14, 1995?

• **Question No. 63:** **What happened to the two Middle Eastern-looking men who witnesses say were running toward a brown pickup just before the explosions?**

• **Question No. 64:** **Why was a cautious prison security chief suspended for simply protecting his prisoners?** During their stay at El Reno Federal Correctional Institution, a hypodermic needle and cigarette butts were slipped into Tim's and Terry's food trays. When Capt. Milnar, the officer in charge of prisoner security, tried to take measures to increase security and to make certain that Tim and Terry could appreciate a higher degree of safety, he was suspended! Why would Warden Thompson suspend Capt. Milnar for trying to do his job? Was someone trying to send the accused a message that they weren't "out of reach?"

• **Question No. 65:** **Why did prosecutors wait nearly seven weeks to show Ryder truck rental employee Eldon Elliott a photo line-up which included McVeigh?** Having seen McVeigh's picture splashed all over the news for seven weeks, Mr. Elliott had no problem picking Tim's picture from a photo line-up. When you take into consideration that the description Mr. Elliott's employees originally gave to the feds doesn't even come close to matching McVeigh, doesn't it seem a little curious that they would wait seven weeks to show their primary witness a photo line-up? A suspicious mind might conclude that the feds did not accidentally wait seven weeks for the news media to condition Mr. Elliott's memory. A suspicious person may also be inclined to believe that promise of a $2 million reward could make someone remember almost anything that the persons offering the reward wanted someone to remember.

• **Question No. 66:** **Why did Special Agent John Hersley say that recovering the trucks Florida license plate helped authorities trace down the vehicle in question?** Apparently Frank Keating forgot to tell him that he found the rear axle which led the FBI to Elliott's Body Shop which led the feds to the Dreamland Motel which led the feds to my farm, Lana's house, Terry's house, Kevin's house, my mom's house and to Tim McVeigh in the Perry, Oklahoma jail.

• **Question No. 67: If Tim really was planning this crime, why would he use my address when he checked in to the Dreamland Motel?** Why would he intentionally implicate a friend if he was up to some sort of sinister activity? If he did have the fake I.D. like the Feds claim, why didn't he just use it to rent the motel room?

• **Question No. 68: Why didn't the FBI find Tim's fingerprints anywhere in room No. 25 or anywhere else at the Dreamland Motel?** They didn't find his fingerprints on the motel register or on the receipt for the room rental. How could the real Timothy James McVeigh stay at the Dreamland Motel for four days and four nights and not leave even a single fingerprint from the real Timothy James McVeigh anywhere on the premises? It has been suggested that Tim may have worn gloves.

Neither Lea McGowan nor her son has mentioned anything about Tim wearing gloves. And, if Tim wanted to hide his real identity by wearing gloves and being careful to not leave any fingerprints, why would he use his real name and drivers license on the motel register? Whose fingerprints did the FBI find in room No. 25 and on the motel receipt? Could a lookalike actually fool people into believing he was Tim McVeigh? Is it possible for one person to so closely resemble another person that most people could not tell the difference?

Would the real Timothy James McVeigh please stand up?

• **Question No. 69: Why was there such a strong push to stop Oklahoma State Rep. Charles Key from spearheading an expanded inquiry into the Murrah Building explosions?** When Rep. Key tried to organize a state-sponsored investigation he was criticized and successfully stopped from doing so by the Speaker of the House in Oklahoma and by Oklahoma's governor, Frank Keating.

Why would any rational person want to block such an investigation? Why would the governor of any state suffering from such a tragedy do anything to block any investigation aimed at finding the truth? Why wouldn't he use every resource available to get to the bottom of this thing? Keating's response to Rep. Key's concerns: "People need to have more faith and trust in the federal government and its agencies."

Where in the heck has this guy been for the past 50 years while those federal agencies have been lying to us, deceiving us and murdering innocent citizens? Has he ever heard of Ruby or Waco? Oh, that's right. ... he's been supervising those "federal agencies."

The late Glen Wilburn — who passed away earlier in 1997 because of inoperable pancreatic cancer and who lost two grandchildren in the Murrah explosions — and Rep. Key have also petitioned the court to permit the convening of a county grand jury to investigate this crime. Oklahoma City prosecutor Robert Macy opposed their request, but assured them that he would abide by the court's decision. That was before Macy realized that the court would grant their request.

To Wilburn's and Key's surprise, Macy immediately filed an appeal. It didn't surprise us in the least. Like attorney Leslie Abramson said: "From the first day on the job, prosecutors are trained to lie." By his own actions, Robert Macy has proven that he is not an exception to Leslie Abramson's observation.

When Wilburn and Key filed the request in December of '95, the laws of the State of Oklahoma dictated that they needed 500 signatures on their petition to convene the grand jury. In 1996 the Oklahoma legislature, headed by Frank Keating, threw another stick in the spokes of Wilburn's and Key's county grand jury. The legislators took it upon themselves to change the law, so that now Wilburn and Key needed 5,000 signatures on their petition instead of 500. It's amazing what one little zero will do, isn't it? Who said there was no cover-up and conspiracy In Oklahoma?

However, despite the new law, residents racked up 13,000 signatures and, as of the summer and fall of 1997, the grand jury was convened and additional testimony taken. As of this writing, Rep. Key stated that former BATF informant Carol Howe and former leader of Elohim City, Robert Millar — himself a paid informant of the FBI — are expected to offer evidence of an expanded conspiracy to bomb the Murrah Federal Building.

• **Question No. 70: Why was Tim McVeigh's defense teams prevented from defending him during his trial?** Early on in this investigation, both defense teams filed motions before the court that would require the prosecution to convert its disclosure information onto computer-ready software. Realizing that more than 200,000 pages of information existed to sift through, Judge Matsch granted the request.

You can imagine the impossible task of trying to find a name or reference in a 200,000-plus page document with no index. The computer programs allowed the defense teams to access information at will by just typing in a name or word, or so they thought.

Stephen Jones challenged the prosecution for withholding very damaging information from the defense teams about Carol Howe and others at Elohim City. Government prosecutors defended their position, stating that, in fact, the information was there among the 211,000 pages of information disclosed to the defense more than a year ago. After some coaxing, the prosecutors provided Jones with the number on the documents in question. After locating the documents, the defense team realized that every name contained within the document concerning Elohim City had been misspelled — preventing the computer from finding the names when accurate spellings were used in database searches. For example, Elohim City was misspelled as "Elohm." Dennis Mahon, one of the men along with Andreas Strassmeir, who might have had a hand in planning the Murrah Building attack, was misspelled "Mehaun."

Strassmeir was misspelled "Strassmeyer," and the Rev. Robert Millar, founder and patriarch of Elohim City — and yet another FBI informant according to recent court testimony — was actually in the FBI files as "Bob Lamar!" And, believe it or not, Carol Howe was not even mentioned anywhere in the files pertaining to Elohim City!

One might also excuse this oversight in spelling as just another of those many hundreds of "coincidences" that all seem to favor the prosecution's side. We are a little more realistic in our opinion of these and many other coincidences. Tim's defense team has petitioned the court, claiming that these misspellings were not an accident but a deliberate doctoring of the documents by the prosecution in a successful attempt to keep this information from the defense — thereby violating the laws of disclosure by deception, and violating the defendant's right to a fair and impartial trial.

We must admit that this was obviously a very slick move by someone on the prosecution's team. It is also very underhanded, dirty, dishonest, unconscionable and downright criminal in just another of the many attempts to falsify or alter evidence. Can you understand why we have dubbed them the "professional deceivers" and the "agents of deceit?" These are both very appropriate and accurate descriptions of federal agents, prosecutors and maybe even some judges.

Why would an honest judge allow prosecutors to get away with such an obvious cover-up?

• **Question No. 71: Why did the media jump on the "new and incriminating" evidence bandwagon after it was reported that the McDonald's video placed Tim McVeigh in the vicinity of Elliott's Body Shop when the Ryder truck was rented — but totally ignored "the** rest of the story" which showed that the video actually proved beyond any doubt that Timothy McVeigh couldn't possibly have rented the notorious Ryder truck? Why did the media provide extensive coverage of McVeigh's alleged confession which appeared in Pete Slover's article in the *Dallas Morning News* but chose to totally ignore the obvious lies in that phony confession? Why did the media go into a frenzy over McVeigh's alleged confession appearing in Ben Fenwick's article in *Playboy* magazine but chose to totally ignore the obvious lies in that phony confession even after one of the surviving victims pointed out some of those lies?

Why has the mainstream media all but ignored Carol Howe, the BATF's own paid informant in Elohim City, who positively identified Andreas Strassmeir as a primary instigator of this crime, and further identified his buddy Michael Brescia as John Doe No. 2? Why did the feds put Carol Howe, their own paid informant, in jail almost immediately after she exposed Strassmeir and Brescia in an interview with a journalist?

Not a peep from the mainstream media, although *Media Bypass* and a few other alternative magazines, and independent journalist J.D. Cash, investigated this matter. Why did the media jump all over the ANFO truck bomb scenario without ever seeing any evidence, but when the "Preliminary Event Analysis" provided by Walker Aerospace showed that the building was brought down with strategically placed charges from within? Not a peep! Why does the media believe everything the FBI tells them about the evidence of an ANFO bomb but when the inspector general's office in the Department of Justice reported that there was no evidence that an ANFO bomb was responsible for the explosions in the Murrah Building, the silence was deafening?

• **Question No. 72: Why is the government, with the help of the national media and the Southern Poverty (anti-Constitution) Law Center and their ilk, trying to work the citizens of this country into a frenzy of fear over the militia and self-proclaimed patriots?** Being in the militia is not only a right as many militia members claim. When the need arises, it is a RESPONSIBILITY for all of us as citizens of this great nation.

"That whenever any Form of Government becomes destructive of these ends (unalienable rights), it is the Right of the People to alter or abolish it, and to institute new Government ..." So it says in our Declaration of Independence signed on July 4, 1776.

Could Mr. Morris Dees or any other anti-Constitutionist or non-patriot in the SPLC please tell us why they have made "patriot" a four-letter-word? Could they tell us why they are so insistent that American citizens fear the militia, many of whom are their next door neighbors? Could Mr. Dees please tell us how many citizens have been killed by patriots and Constitutionally guaranteed militia groups? Could Mr. Dees please tell us how many government agents have been killed by those same patriots and militia groups of whom he insists we are supposed to be afraid?

We don't really know the answer to those questions, but we are certain the numbers are either very small or virtually non-existent. But we do have some numbers that may cause considerable alarm among all of the concerned citizens in this country and considerable distress among the anti-Americans in the SPLC who would prefer that you were not exposed to such inexplicable information.

Since 1900, more than 175 MILLION human beings have been murdered on this planet by governments. That number does NOT include soldiers. And Morris Dees, Bill Clinton, Janet Reno, Louis Freeh, most politicians and many members of the media, etc. have made a concerted effort to convince us that we have a reason to be afraid of the militia?

When was the last time you heard about the militia kicking in a citizen's door and murdering them? When was the last time you heard about members of the militia ambushing and murdering a 14-year-old little boy? When was the last time you heard about the militia sniping and blowing the head off an unarmed mother while she stood holding her infant child? When was the last time you heard about a militia or patriot group assaulting, murdering and burning 81 members of a church? When was the last time you heard about a patriot or a member of a militia group murdering an innocent citizen and receiving an employment promotion and a commendation for a "job well done?"

When was the last time you heard about a patriot or militia person murdering unarmed citizens in cold blood and not being prosecuted for the crime? How many members or founders of patriotic groups or citizen militias are collecting a salary of $160,000 a year from donations, i.e., the fruits from the labor of working people? How many of these groups have accepted tens of millions of dollars in contributions and only used a third of those contributions on actual programs, the rest on undisclosed investments? Why did they put the word "Poverty" in the name of an organization with tens of millions of dollars in assets? Is that name an intentional deception or is it just an innocent coincidence? Has anyone else been able to raise such an enormous amount of money for what is basically a hate group?

Don't they hate the militia, the patriots, and much of the Bill of Rights, particularly the second amendment? We are waiting patiently for answers to all of these questions Mr. Dees.

• **Question No. 73: How many people were actually killed in the bombing of the Alfred P. Murrah Federal Building on April 19, 1995?** Originally it was universally accepted that there were 168 victims. After nearly four months into the investigation it was discovered that the medical examiner had a left leg that apparently did not belong to any of the known victims. The feds had been concealing this information from the public and from the defense teams because if could be shown that this leg did not belong to any of the known victims, then it had to belong to someone who was not supposed to be there at the time. That missing person's identity had gone "unclaimed" for four months suggesting the possibility that whoever might have known this person did not want to claim him or her.

The leg was wearing military clothing, a combat boot, and a blousing band. The problem was that no military personnel were unaccounted for. It was suggested that the person may have been a civilian wearing military clothing, not necessarily atypical of today's fashion trends. Had this been a case of a civilian just passing by, someone certainly would have declared the person missing after weeks or months had passed.

Then the feds said that the leg may have belonged to a homeless person who dressed in military clothing and was known to frequent the area. The problem we had with the homeless person or civilian explanation was the presence of the blousing band. Most civilians do not know what a blousing band is, and a homeless person certainly wouldn't take the time to use a blousing band even if he did know why it was used. As a matter of fact, most military personnel don't bother using blousing bands. They just tuck the ends of their pant legs into the tops of their boots and blouse their fatigues from their. At least that's what Bob said everyone did when he was in the Army, with the possible exception of some career soldiers.

The government changed their story several times as to the race and gender of the owner of the mysterious left leg. First it belonged to a white male. Then it belonged to a dark-skinned male Caucasian. A few other possibilities were tossed around and finally federal investigators claimed that the leg belonged to a young, black woman.

Just coincidentally they also claimed that a young, black military woman named Lakisha Levy, one of the victims of the bombing, had been buried in Louisiana with the wrong left leg. They even went so far as to exhume the body to prove that Lakisha Levy had been buried with the wrong left leg.

After the exhumation and investigation, the issue was dropped and has since been virtually ignored. To be honest, as closely as we have monitored this case, we thought the question about the leg had been resolved with the exhumation.

For nearly a year and a half the media has kept quiet about the mysterious leg. We have recently discovered that the leg did not match Ms. Levy, and has still not been identified.

McVeigh's lead attorney, Stephen Jones, believes the leg belongs to one of the actual bombers who was virtually disintegrated in the explosion, leaving behind only a part of his left leg. This is certainly an issue that the feds, with the help of the media, have swept under the carpet. A reasonable, thinking person might be inclined to believe that the person to whom the leg belonged was a kamikaze bomber, an accomplice of John Doe No. 2, who either decided to stay with the truck or stand next to one of the bombs placed inside the building and go out in a blaze of glory.

Or, he may have stayed behind "involuntarily," being the victim of John Doe No. 2 who did not want to leave behind any witnesses. The only way a person could have been so completely disintegrated is to have been right next to one of the bombs when it exploded. Unfortunately for the feds, when someone picks up the carpet, the dirt's still there.

One thing we must keep in mind while contemplating the existence of John Doe No. 2 and victim No. 169, the owner of the extra left leg, is the testimony of Michael and Lori Fortier. According to both Fortiers, Timothy McVeigh had no co-conspirators.

Michael Fortier outlines the following points, which were largely confirmed in his testimony at McVeigh's trial:

• Timothy McVeigh originally planned this bombing with the assistance of Mr. Fortier and Terry Nichols.

• Terry Nichols backed out of the conspiracy several weeks before the plan came to fruition.

• McVeigh then approached Mr. Fortier requesting his assistance.

• Fortier refused McVeigh's request.

• McVeigh then carried out this act of terrorism alone.

• There was no John Doe No. 2.

• There was no John Doe No. 3.

• There was no other accomplice who was literally disintegrated by his own bomb, unexpectedly leaving behind his or her signature; a left leg with a military boot and a blousing band.

• Mike Moroz was lying when he said he saw John Doe No. 2.

• David Snider was lying when he said he saw John Doe No. 3.

• Jeff Davis was lying when he said he delivered Chinese food to Bob Kling in room No. 25 at the Dreamland Motel.

• Vicki Beemer, Tom Kessinger and Eldon Elliott were all lying when they said they saw John Doe No. 2 at Elliott's Body Shop.

• Several witnesses in downtown Oklahoma City were lying when they said they saw John Doe No. 2 escaping in a brown pickup truck.

• Daina Bradley was lying when she said she saw John Doe No. 2 and another person exiting the Ryder truck in front of the Murrah Building on the morning of April 19, 1995, and neither of them was Timothy McVeigh (note that Bradley changed this testimony and stated that one of the men "could have been" Timothy McVeigh, a damaging admission with regard to McVeigh's defense).

Mr. Fortier, who has admitted to committing perjury, burglary, selling drugs, conspiracy to destroy federal property and to commit murder, is a habitual drug user and has stated in a taped telephone conversation with a friend that he was perfectly capable of making up a fable for profit and that that fable could make him millions in book deals and movie rights, everyone in the world is lying except Mr. Fortier. Would anyone argue that the prosecution's key witnesses have a major problem with credibility? Could any rational person impose a death penalty, a prison sentence or even a spanking on the testimony of Michael or Lori Fortier?

Recently our good friend, reporter Maryann Struman from the *Detroit News*, faxed us an Associated Press release wherein they apologized for reporting an erroneous confession by Terry. The prosecution said that Terry's 9.5-hour statement to the police in Herington, Kan., was tantamount to a confession. The AP ran a story which erroneously stated that Nichols had said he didn't warn authorities in advance about plans to blow up the federal building because he didn't think McVeigh was serious, and believed he couldn't carry out the plot without his help.

Just coincidentally, Michael and Lori Fortier testified that they didn't warn authorities in advance because they didn't think McVeigh was serious. They testified that McVeigh told them Nichols had backed out of the plot and they didn't believe McVeigh could carry out the plot without help. Once you are aware that the alleged statements made by Terry were, in reality, not made by Terry at all, it doesn't take a rocket scientist to realize that the prosecutors screwed up again.

When they wrote the Fortier's scripts, they mistakenly believed their own disinformation which they began spreading two years ago. Apparently old lies are the hardest to remember. It would seem that the prosecutors for the Oklahoma City bombing case could attest to that from their own very recent experiences. This further proves our contention that all of the Fortier's statements are nothing more than a script written by the prosecution.

• **Question No. 74: Why did Bill Clinton add a little "kicker" to the so-called anti-terrorism bill?** This little piece of UNCONSTITUTIONAL legislation will severely limit the power of federal judges to grant appeals in state court cases for defendants who challenge their state court conviction on Constitutional grounds. In other words, get the guy in state court to violate his Constitutional rights and then deny him his appeals process in federal court.

This paves the way for the proverbial "railroad" in a kangaroo court. Do you have any idea why Bill Clinton did this? It was a very timely and well-planned maneuver. This has been on the drawing board for quite some time and is all part of a very large package of deception.

The court system has been stacked with many extremely liberal federal judges who have allowed things to get drastically out of hand. We are constantly hearing about the thousands of frivolous law suits filed by convicted felons who are still in prison. Some of those judges have granted so many appeals to obviously guilty death-row inmates that many of these murderers will never pay for their crimes with their lives as had originally been ordered by the court. Many of our extremely liberal judges have allowed the system to be abused to a point that there has been a public outcry to do something about it.

An oft-used phrase coined by noted African-American columnist Dr. Walter Williams about the government "manufacturing a crisis" most definitely applies in this case. The plan is to do away with the double jeopardy clause in our Constitution and to receive the blessings of the uninformed citizens and of the media in the de facto socialist democracy.

You think not? Think about this. A few years ago, the Rodney King ordeal shocked the nation. Rodney was a man with a criminal record escaping from the police after committing an apparent traffic violation. When the police finally caught up with him, they beat the living hell out of him and violated his rights.

The fact that Rodney was black and the fact that some of the criminal officers who were beating him made racial remarks brought a conflict between the races into the picture. The officers were tried and found not guilty. We can't imagine how that could have happened since the whole beating was on videotape but, at any rate, they were retried in a civil court and Rodney won a considerable judgment. The civil court trial accomplished two things. It stopped a potential second race riot and it got the camel's nose in the tent on a nationally publicized case challenging the double-jeopardy clause within the 5th Amendment of the Constitution, a part of the Bill of Rights. Being that this was a civil trial and not a criminal trial, and being that it had to do with race, made it all seem justifiable and, legally speaking, it was.

The next nationally publicized "back door" challenge to the double-jeopardy clause came with the O. J. Simpson trial. Nobody could be satisfied with the verdict of a jury. The jury found O.J. not guilty. What else needs to be said? If you objectively evaluated the information in the news, it appeared as if the man may have been set up but our opinions don't really matter. The jury said "not guilty."

The opportunity again presented itself to challenge double jeopardy with the public's blessings in a civil trial. We realize that a technical argument could be made that this is not double jeopardy because the phrase "life or limb" within our Constitution applies only to criminal penalties. In all honesty, we can't disagree with that argument but we think there is a much larger picture to behold. Have you heard the old story about how to cook a frog? If you drop the frog into a pan of hot water he will immediately jump out. But if you put the frog into a pan of cool water and then slowly turn up the heat, he won't know he's being cooked until it's too late. We're the frogs, and the government is slowly turning up the heat.

What does all of this have to do with the Oklahoma City bombing? We had hoped, if Judge Richard Matsch had been totally on the up-and-up, nothing. But the stage was set, at least in the case of the McVeigh trial, and prosecutors did not have to make a serious attempt to destroy the double jeopardy-clause, this time around. Had a conviction of McVeigh not been the result of the trial, they could have made the same distinction between federal courts and state courts as they have between criminal and civil trials.

To assume that they would be wrong to make that distinction would most definitely be an accurate assumption, but just being wrong and violating their oath to uphold the Constitution has never stopped federal prosecutors before.

To understand exactly how this correlates with the trials of Tim and Terry you have to read the original indictment. The indictment appears to be the result of a concerted effort between state and federal prosecutors to deceive us and to ultimately — and we believe intentionally — violate and destroy some of our Constitutional rights. It has been our experience, as we have stated before, that many of these federal prosecutors have nothing but contempt for our Constitutional rights. They, with much legislative assistance from the Washington "District of Criminals," do anything and everything in their power to undermine our Constitution because the Constitution does not restrict the people, it restricts government.

It limits the powers of these self-anointed elitists, and they don't like it. The opportunities surrounding the Oklahoma City bombing case will not be ignored by these federal opportunists. Consider that the first part of the indictment against Tim and Terry lists 160 names of people killed in the bombing. The last part of the indictment lists eight more names of federal law enforcement persons who were killed in the bombing.

You might think that all's well. There were 168 known deaths and there are 168 names on the indictment. But when the names are cross-referenced that's just not the case. The names of those eight federal law enforcement personnel are already included in the list of 160 names. That means there are eight people who were killed in the bombing who are not included on the indictment. When we first discovered this discrepancy, we thought that perhaps those eight people were not federal employees and were not on federal property but that's not the case either.

At least three of those eight people were federal employees and were in the Murrah Federal Building when they were killed. When the prosecutors were brought to task on this issue they claimed that the names of those eight victims were accidentally excluded from the indictment.

Now, Bob's a sign painter and I'm a farmer, and neither of us has any college education. The first time we read the indictment we noticed the discrepancy. It took all of 10 minutes for a couple of workin' dudes to find a problem, and we weren't looking for a problem. We must remember that there were dozens of government attorneys and prosecutors, state and federal, working on this case, putting together this indictment. At least a kazillion years of law school and legal experience behind the dozens of eyes writing and reviewing the indictments over a period of months never noticed that they left eight names off the list of people killed in the bombing?

Is anyone naive enough to believe that lie? We knew from the very beginning that these names were intentionally left off the indictment so that the prosecutors would have their "ace in the hole." The prosecutors knew that, contrary to the reports by the media, the government's case against Tim was weak, at best, and against Terry its case was non-existent. The government realized that its chance of getting a conviction before any honest judge and any unbiased jury was slim to none. After all, the prosecutors know about all of the disinformation in the media, because many times they are the source of that disinformation. Lies to the media may influence public opinion and that biased public opinion may be brought into the courtroom through the jury, and lies and disinformation were not supposed to mean squat in a courtroom in front of an honest, experienced federal judge like Richard Matsch.

We all know now, however, that Judge Matsch did not allow Tim McVeigh to defend himself. It is likely that similar tactics are planned for Terry.

Was it a coincidence that all of these occurrences just "fell into place?" Is a coincidence that the stage has been set to violate double jeopardy? Is a coincidence that all of the brilliant state and federal prosecutors experienced the exact same "oversight" on the indictment? Isn't that kind of like a couple of dozen kids in the same classroom identically misspelling the same word on a test?

Is it a coincidence that the president added his little piece to the so-called anti-terrorism bill which severely limits the appeals power of federal judges in state court cases? Is it a coincidence that two days after we discussed this issue with defense investigators, in what we thought were private conversations, an article appearing in the *Daily Oklahoman* revealed "the plan" in part when it reported that "Oklahoma County District Attorney Robert Macy has talked of filing a 168-count murder charge — listing all of the victims — once he gets his turn at prosecuting the defendants."

"His turn at prosecuting the defendants."

How many "turns" will the government have in the future at prosecuting the citizens of this country for the same crime? As many "turns" as it takes to get a guilty verdict?

Actually, the federal indictment against Tim and Terry is only for the eight federal officers killed in the bombing. Even though the indictment lists the names of 160 people who were killed, the federal trials are for the deaths of those eight federal officers. The prosecutors obviously planned on trying both defendants the second time for the same offense in Oklahoma under state charges. Just in case the state prosecutors confronted a judge who can actually understand the original intent of the double jeopardy clause in the Constitution, eight names were intentionally not mentioned in the indictment with the intention of extracting a public outcry for "justice" for those victims whose names were ignored.

It would appear as if that move of deception was not necessary, at least in the McVeigh trial where conviction was a certainty as Matsch blocked McVeigh's attorneys from defending him. Still, nobody seems to be challenging the obvious intent to violate double jeopardy. Nearly all of the "TV attorneys" accept as perfectly legal being tried twice for the same offense as long as the person or persons being tried are not tried twice in the same jurisdiction

If one accepts that logic then one could only conclude that you could be tried in a U.N. court, federal court, state court, county court, city court and maybe even a township court or a citizens' common-law court for the same offense. What's the difference if your life or limb is put in jeopardy twice for the same offense or six times for the same offense in the same jurisdiction or in different jurisdictions?

Could one of those TV attorneys please show us where it makes that distinction in Article V in the Constitution? "Nor shall any person be subject for the same offense to be twice put in jeopardy of life or limb;" Just where in the double jeopardy clause does it mention an exception for jurisdictions? In the Declaration of Independence, our Founding Fathers declared "He has combined with others to subject us to a jurisdiction foreign to our Constitution, and unacknowledged by our laws; giving his Assent to their Acts of pretended Legislation:"

It would be patently unconstitutional to subject Tim and Terry to any criminal trial if the charges were directly or indirectly related to the Oklahoma City bombing, but that won't stop state prosecutors from trying. The prosecution cannot allow these two defendants to get off with a "not guilty" verdict because the feds would then have to admit that they have allowed the real perpetrators of this crime to escape. Under those circumstances it would not be difficult to prove "intent" on the part of many federal agents in positions of authority. Does anyone still think that eight names were inadvertently left off the indictment? Does anyone still believe that all of these things just coincidentally happened?

The timing of the president's "addition" to the anti-terrorism bill was so perfect that it might lead a thinking person to believe he had a hidden agenda of some sort. Of course, to a thinking "informed" citizen, his agenda is rather obvious. That's why there has been a concerted effort to withhold this information from YOU.

So the prosecutors left eight names off the indictment with the intention of writing an insurance policy for bringing the defendants back to Oklahoma, where insider Frank Keating is King, to a kangaroo court where a conviction would be certain. Their hope was that the public would demand that justice be served for the eight innocent souls who were not named at the previous trials.

To hell with double jeopardy! And, with blessings from the media, Clinton's little kicker in the anti-terrorism bill would deny the defendants their appeals process for having their Constitutional Rights violated in state court just like it was designed to do. No federal judge will dare interfere with King Keating's Kangaroo Court. But there will be five major roadblocks for the prosecution. Five immovable objects making certain that justice is actually served: Terry's lead attorney Michael Tigar, the authors of this book, the truth, Stephen Jones (we hope) and YOU!

Edmund Burke once said: "The only thing necessary for evil to triumph is for good men to do nothing." We wholeheartedly agree.

"We've learned a lot of lessons since the Kennedy assassinations. What is the truth? It's gonna be up to us as a people to band together and unite as a nation to get to the bottom of this. Let's not let another 30 years go by. For God's sake, No!"
— Michael Hinton (eyewitness to the Oklahoma City bombing)

We must remember that the price of Liberty is eternal vigilance and Liberty can never yield to government. Please get informed and stay informed. Please get involved and stay involved because THE RIGHTS YOU SAVE MAY BE YOUR OWN! •

CHAPTER 28: A CRY FOR HELP

The decision to write this chapter and to include the following information was not an easy decision to make. For all practical purposes, we assumed this book was completely finished with the exception of final editing. For well over a year, because of our concerns for the safety of the accused, we have not discussed publicly what you are about to read, although we have shared some of this information privately with close, trusted friends. After much thought and after many months of prayer, soul-searching and consideration, [co-author] Bob Papovich and I have concluded that we can no longer keep this information from the public forum. We will try to present this information in its chronological order and let you decide for yourself if there may be some things going on here that occurred specifically to keep us from discovering the truth, or if all of these things just happened by coincidence.

To put this entire situation into its proper perspective we must begin by going back briefly to May of 1995. Approximately two weeks after the bombing, while I was still in prison, Bob was busy on the telephone looking for help, information and maybe a few answers. He talked to many people while searching for informational assistance including Indianolis-based attorney Linda Thompson, the producer of *Waco: The Big Lie* videos. Although many people would consider Ms. Thompson a "far-out radical," we must remember that the Framers of the Constitution were considered extremely radical by at least nine out of 10 people during their era also. I don't think anyone could deny that Linda is, at the very least, a sincere American patriot, willing to sacrifice everything for the love of our country and our Constitution.

Among other things, Linda told Bob: "The next time you talk to Tim [McVeigh], run these names by him. Ask him who these guys are and where they are." One of those names was Louis "Jelly" West. At the time, Bob had no idea of the significance of that name, and had never heard the name before. Unfortunately, this would not be the last time he would hear that name.

On May 23, 1995, I was finally and officially released from prison after a 32-day incarceration. Coincidentally, it was the same day the feds had the Murrah Building imploded. "Keeping me in prison until the Feds could destroy the evidence" was an absolutely necessary clause in their insurance policy. The court's decision to keep me on a tether until the indictments were handed down on Tim McVeigh and Terry Nichols also played a very important role in keeping us away from Tim. As we have previously stated, after the indictments were handed down, all the rules changed.

During the summer of '95 we were visited by two of Tim's attorneys, Richard Burr and Robert Nigh. It seem that Bob Papovich had been writing Tim and "informing" him of the problems we had with some of the activities of his defense team. Apparently Stephen Jones considered it necessary to send his representatives to answer our questions about some of those "activities" and to tell us that Tim couldn't respond to our letters in writing because the defense team was challenging the prosecution's request for an analysis of Tim's handwriting. Many of their explanations made no sense, including the handwriting analysis excuse. The FBI already had dozens of letters written by Tim to his sister and to many friends, as well as letters to the editor in a few newspapers. Keep in mind, we are not in any way criticizing Rich Burr or Rob Nigh. At the time, it is unlikely that either of them were intimately familiar with the facts surrounding this tragedy or with the eventual direction of the defense "strategy."

In August 1995, immediately after my tether was removed, Bob and I traveled to Oklahoma City to converse with Mr. Tigar and with Mr. Jones and to try to get some inside information as to what was really going on out there. Our plans were to visit Terry and to visit Tim in an attempt to get to the bottom of this thing. Our first visit to Stephen Jones' office brought to our attention a very alarming fact of which we were formerly unaware. *Right there in Mr. Jones' office hung a plaque stating that Stephen Jones was the special counsel to none other than Oklahoma Gov. Frank Keating!*

Was this the same Gov. Keating who had made it perfectly clear that he would do anything and everything within his power as governor to block every non-federal government effort to investigate this crime? The same Gov. Keating whose résumé included bureaucratic positions in the FBI, Secret Service, Justice Department, and a variety of other government "intelligence" agencies? It seems that Tim's court-appointed attorney and Gov. Keating were old friends! The phrase "conflict of interest" immediately came to mind and, considering Frank Keating's publicly stated "presumption of guilt," conflict of interest is most certainly an understatement. Some, but by no means all, of the questions that started gnawing at our somewhat limited intellects were: "Whose idea was it to have this national tragedy take place in the secret-agent-man governor's state?" and, "Whose idea was it to appoint one of the governor's buddies to defend Tim McVeigh?"

Since this new information added considerable fuel to our flames of suspicion, our first private conversation with Stephen Jones was very enlightening and, at times, very heated to say the least. We expressed our displeasure about several issues during that discussion in August, including the suggested direction of potential defense strategies which Mr. Jones surprisingly shared with us. We asked Stephen if he may provide us with the opportunity to visit Tim, since it became apparent during our conversation that Tim was reluctant to tell his attorneys what, if anything, he might know about this tragedy.

We reasoned that it was unlikely Tim would trust any of them, considering that he didn't know any of them before they were assigned to represent him and that we didn't completely trust any of them either. We assured Mr. Jones that if we could get in to see Tim he would surely confide in us because he had no reason not to trust us. We were confident that we could discover the identities of the people responsible for setting Tim up to take the blame for this senseless act of terrorism if we could just get in to see him. We have since concluded that that was the wrong thing to say at the wrong time to the wrong person. Mr. Jones told us that it would be difficult to arrange visitation with Tim this trip but he would see what he could do about the possibility of our visiting Tim during our next trip to Oklahoma City.

We must say that Stephen Jones, above all else, has always been very responsive to us and very open with us, to the extent that he could be. He has never, at any time, been out of touch and has never shunned us or ignored us. For that we must compliment him. He may or may not have had a choice in the direction of the defense strategy and what inevitable fate was planned for his client, Timothy James McVeigh.

Soon after arriving home from Oklahoma City, I received a phone call from Tim. The conversation was brief and to the point. Tim told me that, if he could, he would prefer to defend himself. Being incarcerated in a federal penitentiary and kept in total isolation, he was obviously not in a position to do so. He also suggested that we stop writing for a while because all of his mail was being confiscated. Apparently, the information Bob was passing along to Tim in his letters was striking a nerve somewhere with someone.

Keep in mind also that, during that same time period, Tim and Terry received a hypodermic syringe and cigarette butts on their food trays, apparently from someone who was making a point that the two prisoners were not "out of reach." During that time period also, Terry's fingernails began turning black — which could indicate that he was being subjected to a slow poisoning which might also have been another warning. Immediately after the condition and Terry's suspicions were brought to the attention of his attorneys, the condition mysteriously "cleared up."

Our next trip to Oklahoma netted the same results as the first: No contact except during the court hearings. The fact that we had been led to believe we could visit Tim suggested that we were being given the runaround by Mr. Jones. Sometimes after the breaks for lunch or the mid-morning or mid-afternoon breaks — while everyone was still standing and mingling, before the judge came into the courtroom and while the attorneys weren't paying close attention to their client — we did converse with Tim reading lips and hand-signaling.

Some of our brief conversations were alarming, to say the least.

On one of those breaks, Bob told Tim that he absolutely had to call us and write to us. Bob said he should keep in contact so we would know what was going on and so we could at least attempt to monitor the situation.

Tim's response while shaking his head in a negative gesture and crossing his hands at the wrists was: "I can't. They have my hands tied." Some questions that immediately came to mind were; "Who has his hands tied? And why?" Keep in mind that nobody tried to keep us away from Terry. Terry doesn't know anything about this tragedy, so he's never really been a threat. Of course, elimination of Terry in any way whatsoever would've resulted in an automatic acceptance of "guilty as charged" by most members of the media and all government spokespersons. We believe it would be reasonable to conclude, looking at this situation objectively, that Tim does know something and many people in positions of high authority do not want that "something" revealed. We have always believed that Tim knows who set him up to take the blame for this tragedy.

When we returned home from our second trip to Oklahoma, we were somewhat frustrated by our inability to make formal contact with Tim. Although our certainty that Tim wanted to communicate was confirmed by our brief lip-reading sessions in court, we could not prove that which we knew to be true. If we could prove that Tim was being kept isolated against his wishes and that he was not allowed to communicate with anyone he could trust, that proof just might arouse the suspicions of some very inquisitive reporters. If those reporters started asking members of Tim's defense team, questions concerning Tim's isolation, their answers might make as little sense to those reporters as they did to us.

Particularly specious was their argument suggesting that if we talked to Tim, we may be subpoenaed to testify as to what was said during our conversations. Apparently, after being raided by over a hundred masked men, dressed in black, with fully automatic weapons, helicopters and attack dogs, after spending 32 days in a federal penitentiary, being followed by the feds, and who knows who else, for another three months, and walking through numerous airports, including the airport in Oklahoma City several times after my face had been plastered all over every TV news show, newspaper and magazine in the country, after months of government and media propaganda accusing me of being the "guru" behind the Oklahoma City bombing, and numerous life-threatening phone calls and letters, I was supposed to be afraid of a subpoena? You can see why our suspicions grew stronger.

We did keep in contact with Tim through Bob's letters, but Tim could not keep in contact with us. We traveled to Oklahoma again in late January, 1996, to attend more hearings and to visit with Terry and the defense teams.

During one of the breaks in court, Tim passed Bob a note through one of the investigators. We couldn't keep the note for all of the obvious reasons, obvious to the defense and prosecution, anyway. None of the reasons have ever been obvious to us. Since Bob couldn't keep the note, he tried his best to memorize it. He regrets not keeping it long enough to just copy it down word for word, line for line and symbol for symbol. Although he could not remember the message verbatim, he did remember the specific highlights and he did remember the message within the message. The note, as shown on the next page (p. 348), has been recreated by Bob as closely as he can remember it, and we can assure you that it is very close to the original.

We were reasonably sure that Tim was trying to send us a hidden message without being too tremendously obvious. Considering the wording and the double underlines, it was apparent that he was trying to tell us that the psychologists were already messing with his head. We believe the significance of the double line that Tim also put under "ongoing investigation" was an indication that the psychologists were, in fact, profiling the case inside Tim's head to fit the FBI's allegations. At the time he may have still had enough wherewithal to "cry for help." Unfortunately, at the time, we didn't know how to answer that cry. We can only pray that God will forgive us for our ignorance.

Before our last trip to Oklahoma, Bob wrote Tim and asked him some very crucial questions. He told Tim that he could answer our questions when we saw him in court the following week. The hearings were

A Mysterious Note

Note reproduced by Bob Papovich

This note is a facsimile of a handwritten note that Tim McVeigh passed to co-authors James Nichols and Bob Papovich. The co-authors were not permitted to keep the communication, so Papovich made it a point to memorize it, virtually word for word, and reproduce it, attempting to not only duplicate the precise wording, but the ancillary markings — showing emphasis in certain areas. The co-authors and others closely associated with the case have been attempting to decipher its contents since.

expected to last for two or three days because of the number of motions filed by both defense teams. A day or two before the hearings began the defense attorneys filed several more motions which assured us of at least three or four days of hearings, providing plenty of time for conversations during the breaks and more than ample opportunity for Tim to answer our questions.

We took a lunch break on the first day and then a mid-afternoon break, and that was it! We were informed that the rest of the sessions would be behind closed doors. We hardly even made eye contact with Tim and he certainly never had any opportunity to give us the answers we were looking for. We were caught completely by surprise. Did someone know what we had planned? Did that someone cut these public hearings short so we could not get answers to our questions? We became even more suspicious of an ever-widening conspiracy to make certain Tim was kept isolated, much more suspicious.

One of the many decisions eventually determined at those final hearings in Oklahoma City was the change of venue. Judge Richard Matsch decided that neither defendant could receive a fair and impartial trial in Oklahoma City (as if they could receive a fair and impartial trial anywhere) so they changed the location to Denver, Colo. Preparations would soon be made to transfer Tim and Terry from El Reno, F.C.I in Oklahoma, to Englewood, F.C.I. just out side of Denver.

Fortunately, our last night in Oklahoma City was spent with a friend who would be visiting Tim in the very near future. Bob asked that friend if he could ask Tim some questions the next time he had an opportunity to visit him, and the friend said that he would. The questions were:

1. Do you want us to keep writing?
2. Do you want to call us?
3. Do you want us to visit you in prison?

The next day we headed back home and didn't get in touch with our mutual friend in Oklahoma for nearly a week and a half.

On Saturday morning, March 9, 1996, Bob received a letter from Stephen Jones telling him that it was not in Tim's best interests for Bob to write or try to contact him in any way whatsoever. Everything from this time forward should first go through Mr. Jones. Basically, Mr. Jones said very politely what could've been said in two simple words. "PISS OFF."

The letter was dated March 6 and the envelope was postmarked March 7, indicating that the letter had been written and mailed late on March 6. The obvious mistakes in the letter indicated that the letter had been written under tremendous stress and anxiety.

A few hours after receiving the letter from Stephen Jones, Bob called our friend in Oklahoma to get the answers to our questions. Bob said the conversation went something like this: (almost verbatim)

Bob: "Hey! By any chance, did you get in to see Tim last week?"

Friend: "As a matter of fact, no. But I did get in to see him this week on Wednesday." (i.e., March 6)

Bob: "Did you have a chance to ask him those questions?"

Friend: "Yes I did, Bob. And the answer to all three was a definite YES! As a matter of fact, Tim filed a formal request through me to Stephen Jones for you and James to visit him."

Needless to say, we never received the request for visitation, and we find it unlikely that it ever left Stephen Jones' office, certainly not intended for our eyes anyway. Mr. Jones' letter and Tim's request created much turmoil on both sides of the ocean, so to speak.

We were now facing a dilemma: Do we stop writing Tim for fear that all of our suspicions are unfounded? If everything is on the up and up, we may just make the defense team's job even more difficult. But, if our concerns are correct, we cannot, in good conscience, ignore what we believe to be true and abandon a friend during a time of such enormous crisis

Needless to say, our position has not been a popular one and Tim has had few people in his corner throughout this ordeal, paid or unpaid, but sometimes you just have to ignore what is politically correct and do what is morally right. This situation definitely created some waves of anxiety and uncertainty on our side of the ocean. On the other side of the ocean, a storm was definitely brewing.

That storm would eventually become a full-blown hurricane.

Shortly after Tim filed his formal request for visitation that we were not supposed to know about, our good friend and investigative author, Michele Moore, informed us that Dr. Louis Jolyan West had been seen going in and out of El Reno Federal Corrections Institution. We wondered how Linda Thompson came by his name just two weeks after the bombing. Dr. West is most noted for his work with regard to the trial of Patricia Hearst, the newspaper heiress who was "kidnapped" in 1974 by the so-called Symbionese Liberation Army (SLA). While in "captivity," she helped commit a bank robbery. Dr. West testified for the defense in the Patricia Hearst trial after she "escaped" from the SLA. With the help, too, of famed attorney F. Lee Bailey, she was acquitted.

Dr. West, a psychiatrist and professor at UCLA, is also regarded as an expert on terrorist psychology and once stated that some terrorists have a "death wish" of their own; i.e., they will sometimes confess to a murder or murders they did not commit in order to be executed in order to make a political point. Could that be the case with Timothy James McVeigh?

In any event, rumor had it that Dr. West or some of his colleagues were there to "treat" McVeigh. It was being reported nationally that Tim was suffering from "bouts of depression." It appeared as if our worst suspicions were coming true. There was no longer any doubt about the meaning behind Tim's message within a message within the note he passed Bob in court. He was trying to tell us what they were doing to his mind while in total isolation.

There was no longer any doubt about his "cry for help." And there was no longer any doubt that Tim needed help, desperately. After Tim filed his request for visitation, it was reported that they sent in their ultimate mind-control agent, their "big gun," Louis "Jelly" West, and began their propaganda campaign, using the national media to set up Lee Harvey McVeigh for a "suicide."

We couldn't help but wonder just what was Dr. West's relationship to this tragedy before the fact? And, since he was notorious for his experiments with mind-altering drugs (on other people, of course) might he or someone else be administering some sort of drug to Tim?

Soon after all of these new and alarming bits of information came to our attention, Michele called us again. Being in Oklahoma and being extremely bright and very observant, Michele kept on top of things all the time. Nothing escapes Michele's scrutiny. Thank God for our meeting Michele, because without her help and without her keeping us up to date on everything that was going on in Oklahoma, we couldn't have possibly gathered enough information to write this book and, like the rest of the nation, would've been kept in the dark on many issues concerning this investigation. In turn, we have given Michele much information that was only available from persons intimately involved with the defendants and with the defense teams.

This time, Michele called to warn us it had been rumored that Tim and Terry were to be temporarily held in a new Federal Transfer Center in Oklahoma City on their way to Denver. She said the new transfer center had already recorded two inmate deaths which were ruled "suicides."

One of those suicide rulings is being challenged because of the apparent beating Kenneth Trentadue took while he struggled to "hang himself" with a sheet. The prison wanted to cremate the body and when the family objected someone at the transfer center tried to hide the marks and bruises with makeup before the body was shipped home for burial.

Mr. Trentadue's brother, being an attorney, became very suspicious when he heard of the desire to cremate the body. When the body arrived the family had their own mortician wash the body which lead to the discovery of many bruises, particularly around the feet and arms. It seems that Kenneth Trentadue, in his struggle to "commit suicide," repeatedly smashed his skull, crushing it in three places. He also managed to cut his own throat and burn himself repeatedly on the head and shoulders, and at the base of his spine with an electrical stun gun which apparently is issued to every prisoner when he enters that particular federal transfer center.

Kenneth Trentadue inflicted cuts, bruises and abrasions all over his own body, and then stomped his face with a boot before he somehow managed to hang his 19-inch neck from a plastic ceiling vent with a 23-inch braided sheet without even messing up his bed. If Mr. Trentadue actually did self-inflict all of those injuries and could somehow tie a knot and hang himself with an extra four inches of braided sheet in a brand-new state-of-the-art, supposedly hang-proof cell, it would seem that he missed his calling. He should have been a magician.

Recently a national nightly news program covered the Kenneth Trentadue case. You can rest assured that the feds will do everything in their power to sweep this issue under the carpet and, if not for the information you are now reading, the link to Lee Harvey McVeigh would never have been made public.

When Tim filed a formal request for visitation with people he could trust, and who refused to be intimidated by the feds, did someone get real nervous about what he might be able to tell those people concerning what was really going on in this tragedy? Were the wheels set in motion to eliminate McVeigh via publicized depression and ultimately a suicide

Fortunately, Michele Moore brought to our attention the "problems" within the transfer center. By the time we called Tim's defense team they had already been notified by Michele and some might argue that Michele is not an extremely popular person among those who may have intended on closing their eyes to a potentially sinister plan. Arguably, these notifications effectively stopped any perceived plan to have an instant trial, conviction and execution, all in one, just for the cost of a sheet. Plan "B", although not as efficient but just as effective as plan "A," would have to be put into action.

Keep in mind that Bob and I, at every opportunity, were complaining to the media that Tim's and Terry's civil rights were being violated. Terry was not being allowed any contact visitation from anyone, not even his wife and children. He was allowed no visitation other than immediate family, excluding close friends like Bob and Sandy. Tim was being kept isolated from everyone except immediate family, who could seldom visit because they lived in New York and Florida, and hostile journalists hand-picked by Stephen Jones.

In the spring of 1996 Tim and Terry were transferred from El Reno to Englewood. Soon after their transfer I received phone call permission requests from Englewood concerning Terry and Tim, and Bob received a request for Terry. The calls from Tim never came.

Soon after their transfer Stephen Jones had Tim on national prime time television giving a controlled interview to a popular reporter. Stephen Jones asked McVeigh about the conditions at Englewood. Was there an improvement over the conditions at El Reno?

Tim responded by saying that Englewood was 100 percent better. "Are you having any problems here." Mr. Jones asked. "No, they have resolved all of my problems," Tim said. In that instant, everything we had been saying for nearly a year about Tim's isolation and about his civil rights being violated lost all credibility. Was that really Tim talking, or was it Louis "Jelly" West or some other mind-control agent? There was little doubt in our minds about the answer to that question. The words were coming from Tim's lips but it was definitely not Tim talking.

The first time we attended a hearing in Denver it was apparent that Tim had a completely different attitude. He had several journalist "friends" in the courtroom with whom he made eye contact and acknowledged their presence with a friendly gesture and a smile. We can assure you, without any doubt, none of those journalists ever wrote anything "friendly" about Tim. Tim barely made eye contact with us, consequently we had no opportunity to converse with him in any way whatsoever.

Over the next few months Bob wrote Tim several times, although not as often as he had before receiving the letter from Stephen Jones. He consistently told Tim in his letters that our ability to help him was severely limited by his inability to help us. In every letter he told Tim to call us if he could. Bob even informed Tim of the most likely times to catch me at home when he called. The calls never came.

Finally, on Oct. 26, 1996, Bob wrote Tim to assure him that I had received his request to call and to assure him that I had approved the request and sent it back to the prison. We wanted to make absolutely certain that he knew his calls were approved on this end just in case he had been told something else. We also let Tim know that we had never received a request for visitation, so he would know who put the skids on that request without really telling anyone else who may read our letters that we knew a request was actually made. Since the intensity of our pursuit had been reduced considerably over those months during the summer and fall of '96, it appeared as if the intensity of the mind control paralleled our reduction.

In November of 1996, immediately after receiving Bob's letter, Tim unleashed another subtle "cry for help." Bob received a document from Englewood, dated Nov. 21, 1996, asking permission for Timothy McVeigh to call Bob's phone number. This was, undoubtedly, a message from Tim that he wanted to call but someone, somewhere was not allowing him to call. The fact that we were not receiving any calls from Tim was obviously not Tim's choice. He couldn't call us or write to tell us what was going on, so another phone permission request was the only way Tim had of contacting us and letting us know that it was not his choice to not call or write.

On Nov. 26, 1996, Tim wrote a letter to Phil Bacharack of the *Oklahoma Gazette*, and in that letter he made an attempt to pass us another note. Tim knew if he wrote a letter to us it would never leave the prison. But nobody would care if he wrote a letter to a reporter. The media may even be able to take something he wrote in that letter out of context and use it against him in some convoluted way. And that's exactly what they did.

They used his criticism of the slaughter of the innocent men, women and children in Waco at the hands of the FBI and BATF to confirm his "motive" for allegedly killing the innocent men, women and children in the Murrah Building.

Like Bob has said: "If Tim's criticism of the FBI and BATF could actually be considered a motive for blowing up the Murrah Building, considering our criticism of the FBI and BATF in this book, we'll be blamed for World War III." And so much for the b.s. excuse given to us by Tim's defense team that Stephen Jones didn't want Tim writing "us" because of their challenge to the prosecution's request for a handwriting analysis.

Tim wanted to make certain that we knew he was trying to contact us. In the letter to Phil he wrote, "The idea is that once the FBI can control the flow of information, they can then demonize their target. In my case, I have been sealed away in federal prison and denied most visitation and free communication."

Keep in mind that Tim formally requested permission to call Bob's number on Nov. 21. The letter to Bacharack was dated Nov. 26. This was his insurance policy that we would get his message. Any reporter receiving a handwritten letter from Timothy McVeigh would unquestionably make headline news instantly, all over the world.

Never, in Tim's wildest imagination, could he have ever dreamed that his letter would not surface publicly until April, 1997, just when jury selection for Tim's trial was about to begin, affording the media more fuel for the "Waco motive" theory which had lost its impact because it never really made any sense.

Again, we were effectively cut off at the pass. Again, Timothy James McVeigh's cries for help went unanswered. Again, we did not know how to answer those cries. Again, we can only pray that God will forgive us for our ignorance and that Tim will forgive us for our silence.

You can rest assured that this is not yet the final chapter in this tragedy. This book and especially this last chapter is finally an answer to that cry. With your help, your support and your love for our country we will do everything in our power to make certain that this tragedy in Oklahoma will not be FREEDOM'S END. We all need to pray that it's not too late. •

Terry Nichols, left, takes a nap in the living room of the home of co-author Bob Papovich, right.

Suspected Oklahoma City bomber Terry Nichols, left, sits with his first wife, Lana, far right, and a Papovich family friend, Gilda Baker.

Appendices

FACTUAL STATEMENT
IN SUPPORT OF PLEA PETITION

On December 15th and 16th I rode with Tim McVeigh from my home in Kingman, Az. to Kansas. There I was to receive weapons that Tim McVeigh told me had been stolen by Terry Nichols and himself. While in Kansas, McVeigh and I loaded about twenty-five weapons into a car that I had rented. On December 17th, 1994, I drove the rental car back to Arizona through Oklahoma and Oklahoma City. Later, after returning to Arizona and at the request of Tim McVeigh, I sold some of the weapons and again at the request of Tim McVeigh I gave him some money to give to Terry Nichols.

Prior to April 1995, McVeigh told me about the plans that he and Terry Nichols had to blow up the Federal Building in Oklahoma City, Oklahoma. I did not as soon as possible make known my knowledge of the McVeigh and Nichols plot to any judge or other persons in civil authority. When FBI agents questioned me later, about two days after the bombing and during the next three days, I lied about my knowledge and concealed information. For example, I falsely stated that I had no knowledge of plans to bomb the federal building. I also gave certain items that I had received from McVeigh, including a bag of ammonium nitrate fertilizer, to a neighbor of mine so the items would not be found by law enforcement officers in a search of my residence.

Michael Joseph Fortier

U.S. Department of Justice

Federal Bureau of Prisons

Federal Correctional Institution

El Reno, OK 73036

August 18, 1995

Bob Papovich
4516 Germania Rd.
Shover, MI 48472

Dear Mr. Papovich:

On Wednesday, August 16, 1995, you attempted to visit Terry
Nichols, register number 08157-031, a pre-trial inmate confined
at this facility. You were informed at that time you had not
been approved to visit Mr. Nichols.

In accordance with Bureau of Prisons policy, only immediate
family members will be placed on Mr. Nichols' approved visiting
list.

If you have any further questions regarding this issue, please
contact Mike Morris, Unit Manager, at 405-262-4875, extension
318.

Sincerely,

Sam Calbone
Associate Warden of Programs

U.S. Department of Justice

Federal Bureau of Prisons

Federal Correctional Institution

_____

El Reno, OK 73036

October 18, 1995

Robert and Sandy Papovich
4516 Germania
Snover, MI 48472

RE: NICHOLS, Terry
     Register Number: 08157-031

Dear Mr & Mrs. Papovich:

I am in receipt of your letter dated October 9, 1995, in which
you are requesting you and your wife be allowed visiting
privileges with Mr. Terry Nichols, a pre-trial inmate housed at
this facility.

As stated in previous correspondence from Mr. Sam Calbone,
Associate Warden, Federal Bureau of Prisons policy allows for
only immediate family member to be placed on pre-trial inmates
visiting list. This policy will continue to be followed.

If you have any further questions regarding this issue, please
contact Mike Morris, Unit Manager at 405-262-4875, extension 318.

Sincerely,

R.G. Thompson
Warden

U.S. Department of Justice

Bureau of Prisons
Federal Correctional Institution

9595 West Quincy Avenue
Littleton, CO 80123

April 4, 1996

Bob and Sandy Popovich
4516 Germania Road
Snover, MI 48472

RE: NICHOLS, Terry
    Reg. No. 08157-031

Dear Mr. and Mrs. Popovich:

The above-named inmate has submitted your telephone number for placement on the list of telephone numbers the inmate wishes to call. To allow such communication to occur at the earliest possible time, we have placed your names and telephone number on the inmate's telephone list.

As required by our procedures, the inmate has informed us that you are agreeable to such communication. If this is not the case, please let us know by completing the portion below and returning this letter. Upon your written request, we will remove your name and number from the inmate's telephone list. Absent this request, your name and number will be removed only upon request of the inmate or if the Associate Warden determines that the telephone communication poses a threat to institution security or good order, or poses a threat to others.

If you have any questions on this matter, please let me know.

Sincerely,

C. M. Strickland
Jail Administrator
(303)985-1566, Ext. 1400

****

We, _____, do not wish to receive telephone calls from the
     (Print Name)

above-named inmate. We request our telephone number be removed from this inmate's telephone list.

_____   _____
Date   Signature

_____   _____
Date   Signature

U.S. Department of Justice

Federal Bureau of Prisons

Federal Correctional Institution

FCI Englewood
9595 West Quincy Avenue
Littleton, Colorado 80123

November 21, 1996

Bob Papovich
4516 Germania
Snover, Michigan 48472

RE: MCVEIGH, Timothy
  Reg. No.: 12076-064

Dear Mr. Papovich:

The above-named inmate has submitted your telephone number for placement on the list of telephone numbers the inmate wishes to call. To allow such communication to occur at the earliest possible time, we need your approval to place your name and telephone number on the inmate's telephone list.

As required by our procedures, the inmate has informed us that you are agreeable to such communication. If this is the case, please let us know by completing the portion below and returning this letter. Upon your written request, we will add your name and number to the inmate's telephone list. Absent this request, your name and number will not be added. Once approved, your name can be removed at the request of the inmate or if the Associate Warden determines that the telephone communication poses a threat to institution security or good order, or poses a threat to others.

If you have any questions on this matter, please let me know.

Sincerely,

C.M. Strickland
Jail Administrator
(303) 985-1566 Ext. 1400

* *

I, _____, do wish to receive telephone calls from the
  (Print Name)

above-named inmate. I request my telephone number be added to this inmate's telephone list.

_____   _____
Date   Signature

JONES, WYATT & ROBERTS

ATTORNEYS AND COUNSELORS AT LAW
A PROFESSIONAL ASSOCIATION

114 EAST BROADWAY, SUITE 1100
POST OFFICE BOX 472
ENID, OKLAHOMA 73702-0472

STEPHEN JONES
ROBERT L. WYATT, IV
MICHAEL D. ROBERTS

TELEPHONE (405) 242-5500
FAX (405) 242-4556

JAMES L. HAN⬛
JULIA A. ⬛

March 6, 1996

Mr. Bob Papovich
4516 Germania
Snover, Michigan 48472

Dear Bob:

It was good to see you last week during the hearing.

Tim has given me copies of your letters and he has received them.

It is absolutely not a good idea for you to write to Tim or to see him or speak with him on the telephone. We have discouraged all contact by Tim with anyone who is remotely connected with the case outside of his family for the simple reason that we do not want those individuals to be harassed by the FBI, and we do not want some seemingly innocent statement taken out of context and exploited against him at the trial.

As Tim's friend, I would be grateful if you would accept my advice on this matter since it is in Tim's best interest and that you not write or contact him. This is an extremely difficult case and we do not want anybody injured any more than they already have and we certainly do not want to place Tim in any worse position.

If you feel that there is something absolutely essential to get to Tim, please communicate with me and I will see that he gets it.

Sincerely yours,

Stephen Jones

SJ:re
2\wp51\mcveigh\letters\papovich.306

SENT BY: ·   8-10-95 : 3:12PM ;U.S. ATTORNEY. WD/OK~   14052364741 ;# 2/

IN THE UNITED STATES DISTRICT COURT FOR THE

WESTERN DISTRICT OF OKLAHOMA

FILED

AUG 10 1995

ROBERT D. DENNIS, CLERK
U.S. DIST. COURT, WESTERN DIST. OF OKL

UNITED STATES OF AMERICA,	)
Plaintiff,	)
-vs-	)
TIMOTHY JAMES McVEIGH and TERRY LYNN NICHOLS,	)
Defendants.	)

No. **CR 95-11**

Violations: 18 USC § 2332a;
18 USC § 844(f);
18 USC § 1114;
18 USC § 1111; &
18 USC § 2(a)&(b)

I N D I C T M E N T

COUNT ONE
(Conspiracy to Use a Weapon of Mass Destruction)

The Grand Jury charges:

1. Beginning on or about September 13, 1994 and continuing thereafter until on or about April 19, 1995, at Oklahoma City, Oklahoma, in the Western District of Oklahoma and elsewhere,

**TIMOTHY JAMES McVEIGH
and
TERRY LYNN NICHOLS,**

the defendants herein, did knowingly, intentionally, willfully and maliciously conspire, combine and agree together and with others unknown to the Grand Jury to use a weapon of mass destruction, namely an explosive bomb placed in a truck (a "truck bomb"), against persons within the United States and against property that was owned and used by the United States and by a department and agency of the United States, namely, the Alfred P. Murrah Federal Building at 200 N.W. 5th Street, Oklahoma City, Oklahoma, resulting in death, grievous bodily injury and destruction of the building.

2.   It was the object of the conspiracy to kill and injure innocent persons and to damage property of the United States.

THE MANNER AND MEANS USED BY THE CONSPIRATORS TO FURTHER THE OBJECTS OF THE CONSPIRACY

Among the manner and means used by the defendants to further the objects of the conspiracy were the following:

3.   McVEIGH and NICHOLS planned an act of violence against persons and property of the United States.

4.   McVEIGH and NICHOLS selected the Alfred P. Murrah Federal Building and its occupants as the targets of their act of violence and McVEIGH attempted to recruit others to assist in the act of violence.

5.   McVEIGH and NICHOLS obtained and attempted to obtain the components of a truck bomb, including a truck, ammonium nitrate, racing and diesel fuel, detonation cord and other explosive materials.

6.   McVEIGH and NICHOLS used storage units to conceal the truck bomb components and stolen property.

7.   McVEIGH and NICHOLS used stolen property and its proceeds to help finance their act of violence.

8.   McVEIGH and NICHOLS made calls with a telephone calling card that they had acquired in a false name as a means of concealing their true identities and as a means of preventing calls from being traced to them.

9. **McVEIGH** and **NICHOLS** used different false names in business transactions as a means of concealing their true identities, their whereabouts and the true intent of their activities.

10. **McVEIGH** and **NICHOLS** constructed an explosive truck bomb, and **McVEIGH** placed it outside the Alfred P. Murrah Federal Building in downtown Oklahoma City, where he detonated the bomb.

OVERT ACTS

To further the conspiracy and to achieve its objectives, **McVEIGH** and **NICHOLS** committed and caused to be committed the following acts, among others, in the Western District of Oklahoma and elsewhere:

11. On or about September 22, 1994, **McVEIGH** rented a storage unit in the name "Shawn Rivers" in Herington, Kansas.

12. On or about September 30, 1994, **McVEIGH** and **NICHOLS** purchased forty fifty-pound bags of ammonium nitrate in McPherson, Kansas under the name "Mike Havens.".

13. In or about late September 1994, **McVEIGH** made telephone calls in an attempt to obtain detonation cord and racing fuel.

14. On or about October 1, 1994, **McVEIGH** and **NICHOLS** stole explosives from a storage locker (commonly referred to as a magazine) in Marion, Kansas.

15. On or about October 3, 1994, **McVEIGH** and **NICHOLS** transported the stolen explosives to Kingman, Arizona.

16. On or about October 4, 1994, **McVEIGH** rented a storage unit in Kingman, Arizona for the stolen explosives.

3

17. On or about October 16, 1994, **NICHOLS** registered at a motel in Salina, Kansas under the name "Terry Havens."

18. On or about October 17, 1994, **NICHOLS** rented storage unit No. 40 in Council Grove, Kansas in the name "Joe Kyle."

19. On or about October 18, 1994, **McVEIGH and NICHOLS** purchased forty fifty-pound bags of ammonium nitrate in McPherson, Kansas under the name "Mike Havens."

20. In or about October 1994, **McVEIGH and NICHOLS** planned a robbery of a firearms dealer in Arkansas as a means to obtain moneys to help finance their planned act of violence.

21. On or about November 5, 1994, **McVEIGH and NICHOLS** caused firearms, ammunition, coins, United States currency, precious metals and other property to be stolen from a firearms dealer in Arkansas.

22. On or about November 7, 1994, **NICHOLS** rented storage unit No. 37 in Council Grove, Kansas in the name "Ted Parker" and used the unit to conceal property stolen in the Arkansas robbery.

23. On or about November 16, 1994, **NICHOLS** rented a storage unit in Las Vegas, Nevada and stored, among other items, a ski mask.

24. On or about November 21, 1994 and prior to departing for the Philippines, **NICHOLS** prepared a letter to **McVEIGH**, to be delivered only in the event of **NICHOLS'** death, in which he advised **McVEIGH**, among other matters, that storage unit No. 37 in Council Grove, Kansas had been rented in the name "Parker" and instructed **McVEIGH** to clear out the contents or extend the lease on No. 37 by

February 1, 1995. **NICHOLS** further instructed **McVEIGH** to "liquidate" storage unit No. 40.

25. On or about December 16, 1994, while en route to Kansas to take possession of firearms stolen in the Arkansas robbery, **McVEIGH** drove with Michael Fortier to the Alfred P. Murrah Federal Building and identified the building as the target.

26. In early 1995, following **NICHOLS'** return from the Philippines, firearms stolen in the Arkansas robbery were sold and **McVEIGH**, **NICHOLS** and Michael Fortier obtained currency from those sales.

27. On or about February 9, 1995, **NICHOLS**, using currency, paid for the continued use of storage unit No. 40 at Council Grove, Kansas in the name of "Joe Kyle."

28. In or about March, 1995, **McVEIGH** obtained a driver's license in the name of "Robert Kling" bearing a date of birth of April 19, 1972.

29. On or about April 14, 1995, **McVEIGH**, using currency, purchased a 1977 Mercury Marquis in Junction City, Kansas.

30. On or about April 14, 1995, **McVEIGH** called the **NICHOLS** residence in Herington, Kansas from Junction City, Kansas.

31. On or about April 14, 1995, **McVEIGH** called a business in Junction City and, using the name "Bob Kling", inquired about renting a truck capable of carrying 5,000 pounds of cargo.

32. On or about April 14, 1995, **McVEIGH**, using currency, rented a room at a motel in Junction City, Kansas.

33. On or about April 15, 1995, **McVEIGH**, using currency, placed a deposit for a rental truck in the name "Robert Kling."

5

34. On or about April 17, 1995, **McVEIGH** took possession of a 20-foot rental truck in Junction City, Kansas.

35. On or about April 18, 1995, at Geary Lake State Park in Kansas, **McVEIGH and NICHOLS** constructed an explosive truck bomb with barrels filled with a mixture of ammonium nitrate, fuel and other explosives placed in the cargo compartment of the rental truck.

36. On April 19, 1995, **McVEIGH** parked the truck bomb directly outside the Alfred P. Murrah Federal Building, located within the Western District of Oklahoma, during regular business and day-care hours.

37. On April 19, 1995, **McVEIGH** caused the truck bomb to explode.

THE RESULTS OF THE CONSPIRACY

38. As intended by **McVEIGH and NICHOLS**, the truck bomb explosion resulted in death and personal injury and the destruction of the Alfred P. Murrah Federal Building, located within the Western District of Oklahoma. The following persons were present at the Alfred P. Murrah Federal Building on April 19, 1995, and were killed as a result of the explosion:

Names	Ages
Charles E. Hurlburt	73
John Karl Vaness III	67
Anna Jean Hurlburt	67
Donald Lee Fritzler	64
Eula Leigh Mitchell	64
Donald Earl Burns, Sr.	63

Norma Jean Johnson	62
Calvin C. Battle	62
Laura Jane Garrison	61
Olen Burl Bloomer	61
Luther Hartman Treanor	61
Rheta Ione Bender Long	60
Juretta Colleen Guiles	59
Robert Glen Westberry	57
Carolyn Ann Kreymborg	57
Leora Lee Sells	57
Mary Anne Fritzler	57
Virginia Mae Thompson	56
Peola Y. Battle	56
Peter Robert Avillanoza	56
Richard Leroy Cummins	55
Ronald Vernon Harding	55
LaRue Ann Treanor	55
Ethel Louise Griffin	55
Antonio C. Reyes	55
Thompson Eugene Hodges, Jr.	54
Alvin Junior Justes	54
Margaret Goodson	54
Oleta Christine Biddy	54
David Jack Walker	54
James Anthony McCarthy	53
Carol L. Bowers	53
Linda Coleen Housley	53
John Albert Youngblood	52
Robert Nolan Walker, Jr.	52
Thomas Lynn Hawthorne, Sr.	52
Dolores Marie Stratton	51
Jules Alfonso Valdez	51
John Thomas Stewart	51

Mickey Bryant Maroney	50
John Clayton Moss III	50
Carole Sue Khalil	50
Emilio Tapia-Rangel	50
James Everette Boles	50
Donald R. Leonard	50
Castine Deveroux	49
Clarence Eugene Wilson	49
Wanda Lee Watkins	49
Michael Lee Loudenslager	48
Carrol June Fields	48
Frances Ann Williams	48
Claudine Ritter	48
Ted Leon Allen	48
Linda Gail Griffin McKinney	47
Patricia "Trish" Ann Nix	47
Betsy Janice McGonnell	47
David Neil Burkett	47
Michael George Thompson	47
Catherine Mary Leinen	47
Sharon Louise Wood Chesnut	47
Ricky Lee Tomlin	46
Larry James Jones	46
Richard Arthur Allen	46
Harley Richard Cottingham	46
Lanny Lee David Scroggins	46
George Michael Howard	45
Jerry Lee Parker	45
Judy Joann Fisher	45
Diane Elaine Hollingsworth Althouse	45
Michael D. Weaver	45
Robert Lee Luster, Jr.	45
Peter Leslie DeMaster	44

8

Katherine Ann Finley	44
Doris Adele Higginbottom	44
Steven Douglas Curry	44
Michael Joe Carrillo	44
Cheryl E. Bradley Hammon	44
Aurelia Donna Luster	43
Linda L. Florence	43
Claudette Meek	43
William Stephen Williams	42
Johnny Allen Wade	42
Larry Laverne Turner	42
Brenda Faye Daniels	42
Margaret Louise Clark Spencer	42
Paul Gregory Broxterman	42
Paul Douglas Ice	42
Woodrow Clifford "Woody" Brady	41
Claude Arthur Medearis	41
Teresa Lea Lauderdale	41
Terry Smith Rees	41
Alan Gerald Whicher	40
Lola Renee Bolden	40
Kathy Lynn Seidl	39
Kimberly Kay Clark	39
Mary Leasure Rentie	39
Diana Lynn Day	38
Robin Ann Huff	37
Peggy Louise Jenkins Holland	37
Victoria Jeanette Texter	37
Susan Jane Ferrell	37
Kenneth Glenn McCullough	36
Victoria Lee Sohn	36
Pamela Denise Argo	36
Rona Linn Chafey	35

9

Jo Ann Whittenberg	35
Gilbert Xavier Martinez	35
Wanda Lee Howell	34
Saundra Gail "Sandy" Avery	34
James Kenneth Martin	34
Lucio Aleman, Jr.	33
Valerie Jo Koelsch	33
Teresa Antionette Alexander	33
Kim Robin Cousins	33
Michelle Ann Reeder	33
Andrea Y. Blanton	33
Karen Gist Carr	32
Christi Yolanda Jenkins	32
Jamie Lee Genzer	32
Ronota Ann Woodbridge	31
Benjamin Laranzo Davis	29
Kimberly Ruth Burgess	29
Tresia Jo Mathes-Worton	28
Mark Allen Bolte	28
Randolph Guzman	28
Sheila R. Gigger Driver	28
Karan Denise Shepherd	27
Sonja Lynn Sanders	27
Derwin Wade Miller	27
Jill Diane Randolph	27
Carrie Ann Lenz	26
Cynthia Lynn Campbell Brown	26
Cassandra K. Booker	25
Shelly Deann (Turner) Bland	25
Scott Dwain Williams	24
Dana LeAnne Cooper	24
Julie Marie Welch	23
Frankie Ann Merrell	23

10

Christine Nicole Rosas	22
Lakesha Levy	21
Cartney J. McRaven	19
Aaron M. Coverdale	5
Ashley Megan Eckles	4
Zackary Taylor Chavez	3
Kayla Marie Haddock	3
Peachlyn Bradley	3
Chase Dalton Smith	3
Anthony Christopher Cooper II	2
Colton Smith	2
Elijah Coverdale	2
Dominique R. London	2
Baylee Almon	1
Jaci Rae Coyne	1
Blake Ryan Kennedy	1
Tevin D'Aundrae Garrett	1
Danielle Nicole Bell	1
Tylor S. Eaves	8 months
Antonio Ansara Cooper, Jr.	6 months
Kevin Lee Gottshall II	6 months
Gabreon Bruce	4 months

All in violation of Title 18, United States Code, Section 2332a.

11

<u>COUNT TWO</u>
(Use of A Weapon of Mass Destruction)

The Grand Jury further charges:

On or about April 19, 1995, at Oklahoma City, Oklahoma, in the Western District of Oklahoma,

TIMOTHY JAMES McVEIGH
and
TERRY LYNN NICHOLS,

the defendants herein, did knowingly, intentionally, willfully and maliciously use, aid and abet the use of, and cause to be used, a weapon of mass destruction, namely an explosive bomb placed in a truck, against persons within the United States, resulting in death to the persons named in Count One, Paragraph 38 (which is expressly incorporated by reference herein) and personal injury to other persons.

All in violation of Title 18, United States Code, Sections 2332a and 2(a)&(b).

12

COUNT THREE
(Destruction by Explosive)

The Grand Jury further charges:

On or about April 19, 1995, at Oklahoma City, Oklahoma, in the Western

District of Oklahoma,

TIMOTHY JAMES McVEIGH
and
TERRY LYNN NICHOLS,

the defendants herein, did knowingly, intentionally, willfully and maliciously damage and destroy, aid and abet the damage and destruction of, and cause to be damaged and destroyed, by means of an explosive, namely, an explosive bomb placed in a truck, a building and other personal and real property in whole and in part owned, possessed and used by the United States and departments and agencies of the United States, that is, the Alfred P. Murrah Federal Building, 200 N.W. 5th Street, Oklahoma City, Oklahoma, causing, as a direct and proximate result, the death of the persons named in Count One, Paragraph 38 (which is expressly incorporated by reference herein) and personal injury to other persons.

All in violation of Title 18, United States Code, Sections 844(f) and 2(a)&(b).

13

COUNTS FOUR THROUGH ELEVEN
(First Degree Murder)

The Grand Jury further charges:

On or about April 19, 1995, at Oklahoma City, Oklahoma, in the Western District of Oklahoma,

TIMOTHY JAMES McVEIGH
and
TERRY LYNN NICHOLS,

the defendants herein, did unlawfully, willfully, deliberately, maliciously, and with premeditation and malice aforethought, kill, and aid, abet and cause the killing of, the following persons while they were engaged in and on account of the performance of their official duties as law enforcement officers:

Count	Name/Position	Agency Employed By
FOUR	Mickey Bryant Maroney Special Agent	United States Secret Service
FIVE	Donald R. Leonard Special Agent	United States Secret Service
SIX	Alan Gerald Whicher Assistant Special Agent in Charge	United States Secret Service
SEVEN	Cynthia Lynn Campbell-Brown Special Agent	United States Secret Service
EIGHT	Kenneth Glenn McCullough Special Agent	United States Drug Enforcement Administration
NINE	Paul Douglas Ice Special Agent	United States Customs Service
TEN	Claude Arthur Medearis Special Agent	United States Customs Service
ELEVEN	Paul G. Broxterman Special Agent	Department of Housing and Urban Development Office of Inspector General

14

All in violation of Title 18, United States Code, Sections 1114, 1111 and 2(a)&(b); and Title 28, Code of Federal Regulations, Section 64.2(h).

A TRUE BILL:

FOREPERSON OF THE GRAND JURY

PATRICK M. RYAN
United States Attorney

15

United States District Court

_____ Eastern _____ _____ DISTRICT OF _____ Michigan _____

In the Matter of the Search of
(Name, address or brief description of person, property or premises to be searched)

Green and white metal pole barn,
located at 3616 Van Dyke Road
Decker, Michigan

APPLICATION AND AFFIDAVIT
FOR SEARCH WARRANT

CASE NUMBER: **95 X 71775**

I _____ James Tritt _____ being duly sworn depose and say:

I am a(n) _____ Special Agent, Federal Bureau of Investigation _____ and have reason to believe
                                   Official Title

that ☐ on the person of or ☒ on the property or premises known as (name, description and/or location)

Attachment A

in the _____ Eastern _____ District of _____ Michigan _____
there is now concealed a certain person or property, namely (describe the person or property to be seized)

A 55 gallon blue plastic like drum, bearing the writing, "Flourish 6-14-6" or "Flourish 0-14-0
and its contents
which is (state one or more bases for search and seizure set forth under Rule 41(b) of the Federal Rules of Criminal Procedure)

property that constitutes evidence of the comission of a criminal offense

concerning a violation of Title _____ 18 _____ United States code, Section(s) _____ 844(f) _____ .
The facts to support a finding of Probable Cause are as follows:

See attached affidavit

Continued on the attached sheet and made a part hereof.   ☒ Yes   ☐ No

Signature of Affiant

Sworn to before me, and subscribed in my presence

Date 4/28/95   at _____
                       City and State

_____   _____
Name and Title of Judicial Officer   Signature of Judicial Officer

17. One person who lives near the Nichols farm said that, some-time in February, 1995, she and her family were awakened by a loud boom of such a magnitude that it shook the entire house. She was unable to determine the cause or location of the boom.

18. During the search of the Nichols' farm, conducted 4/21/95 through 4/24/95, observed inside the pole barn was a 55 gallon plastic like drum. The drum is blue. It has a lighter blue top and has white stenciled letters on it which read Flourish 6-14-6 or 0-14-0. This drum is full of an unknown substance. In addition, Special Agent Andrew Sluss advised me that the barrel has on it scratch marks that he recognizes as having been placed there by him during the search of these premises between 4/21/95 and 4/24/95.

19. Agent Sluss advised me that this barrel is the same as the barrel described in a search warrant for these same premises that is dated April 27, 1995. In the April 27 warrant the barrel is described as bearing the writing "Flourish 15-0-0." Agent Sluss advised me that the description in the April 27 warrant is incorrect, and that the correct description is that in paragraph 18, above.

20. Investigation conducted to date in Oklahoma City has deter-mined that fragments of blue and white plastic have been found throughout the crime scene, in many of the bodies of the victims, and on the roofs of buildings in the vicinity of the explosion. According to SSA James T. Thurman, these numerous fragments show evidence of having once formed the container or containers which held the high explosive mate-rial which caused the destruction of the Alfred P. Murrah Building.

21. During the search of Terry Nichols residence in Harrington Kansas on 4/22/95 and 4/23/95 four blue 55 gallon drums were seized.

James Tritt
Special Agent
Federal Bureau of Investigation

Duly sworn and Subscribed to before me this 28ᵗʰ day of April, 1995.

United States Magistrate Judge

(**United States District Court**

EASTERN —— DISTRICT OF —— MICHIGAN

UNITED STATES OF AMERICA

V.

JAMES DOUGLAS NICHOLS

CRIMINAL COMPLAINT

CASE NUMBER: 95-m-80361

(Name and Address of Defendant)

I, the undersigned complainant being duly sworn state the following is true and correct to the best of my knowledge and belief. On or about ___1992 through 1995___ in ___Sanilac___ county, in the ___Eastern___ District of ___Michigan___ defendant(s) did, (Track Statutory Language of Offense)

conspire with other persons, including TERRY NICHOLS and TIMOTHY MCVEIGH, to make and possess firearms, that is, destructive devices, that were not registered to them in the National Firearms Registration and Transfer Record, and that were made in violation of the provisions of Chapter 53 of Title 26, United States Code;

in violation of Title ___18 / 26___ United States Code, Section ___371 / 5861___ .

I further state that I am a(x) ___Special Agent, FBI___ and that this complaint is based on the following facts:

SEE ATTACHED AFFIDAVIT

A TRUE COPY

CLERK, U.S. DISTRICT COURT
EASTERN DISTRICT OF MICHIGAN

BY _____
DEPUTY CLERK

Continued on the attached sheet and made a part hereof: [x] Yes [ ] No

_____
Signature of Complainant

Sworn to before me and subscribed in my presence,

on ___MAR 2 5 1995___ at ___Milan, Michigan___
Date   City and State

MAGISTRATE JUDGE LYNN HOOE

LYNN V. HOOE, JR

Name & Title of Judicial Officer   Signature of Judicial Officer

UNITED STATES DISTRICT COURT
EASTERN DISTRICT OF MICHIGAN
SOUTHERN DIVISION

UNITED STATES OF AMERICA,

        Plaintiff,

-vs-

D-1 JAMES NICHOLS,

        Defendant.
_____/

CRIMINAL NO. 95-80361

HONORABLE: PAUL D. BORMAN

VIO: 18 U.S.C. §§ 2, 371
     26 U.S.C. §§ 5841, 5845,
           5861(d), 5871

MAGISTRATE JUDGE ROMNES

I N D I C T M E N T

THE GRAND JURY CHARGES:

COUNT ONE

(18 U.S.C. § 371; 26 U.S.C. §§ 5841, 5845, 5861(d) & 5871 –
Conspiracy To Possess Unregistered Firearms)

D-1 JAMES NICHOLS,

That, from approximately 1988 to and including April 21, 1995, in the Eastern District of Michigan, Southern Division, defendant JAMES NICHOLS did knowingly, wilfully, and intentionally combine, conspire, confederate, and agree with Terry Nichols, Timothy McVeigh, and other persons, whose names are both known and unknown to the grand jury, to possess firearms, specifically: destructive devices, not registered to any of the co-conspirators in the National Firearms Registration and Transfer Record, contrary to the provisions of Title 26, United States Code, Sections 5841, 5845, 5861(d), and 5871;

It was part of the unlawful conspiracy that the co-conspirators would experiment with various materials to manufacture destructive devices and detonate them on the Nichols farm, located at 3616 North Van Dyke Road, Decker, Michigan.

OVERT ACTS

In furtherance of the unlawful conspiracy, and to effect the objectives thereof, the co-conspirators committed at least one of the following overt acts, among others:

1. In approximately 1988, Terry Nichols and at least one other person constructed homemade bombs made out of diesel fuel.

2. In approximately 1992, JAMES NICHOLS, Terry Nichols, and Timothy McVeigh experimented in the manufacture and detonation of destructive devices made up of readily available materials such as brake fluid and diesel fuel.

3. In approximately 1994, JAMES NICHOLS and Terry Nichols made and stored grenades.

4. On April 21, 1995, JAMES NICHOLS possessed components of improvised explosive devices.

All in violation of Title 18, United States Code, Section 371.

COUNT TWO

(26 U.S.C. §§ 5841, 5845, 5861(d), & 5871 –
Possession of Unregistered Firearm)

D-1 JAMES NICHOLS,

That, on or about April 21, 1995, in the Eastern District of Michigan, Southern Division, defendant JAMES NICHOLS knowingly possessed a firearm, specifically: a combination of parts designed and intended for conversion into a destructive device and from which a destructive device could be readily assembled, which was not registered to him in the National Firearms Registration and Transfer Record as required by Title 26, Chapter 53 of the United States Code.

In violation of Title 26, United States Code, Sections 5841, 5845, 5861(d), and 5871.

COUNT THREE

(26 U.S.C. §§ 5841, 5845, 5861(d), & 5871;
18 U.S.C. § 2 — Possession of Unregistered Firearm)

D-1 JAMES NICHOLS,

That, in approximately 1992, in the Eastern District of Michigan, Southern Division, defendant JAMES NICHOLS knowingly possessed a firearm, specifically: a destructive device, which was not registered to him in the National Firearms Registration and Transfer Record as required by Title 26, Chapter 53 of the United States Code, and aided and abetted others in the same.

In violation of Title 26, United States Code, Sections 5841, 5845, 5861(d), and 5871; Title 18, United States Code, Section 2.

THIS IS A TRUE BILL

FOREPERSON

SAUL A. GREEN
United States Attorney

LYNN HELLAND
Assistant United States Attorney

ROBERT P. CARES
Assistant United States Attorney

Dated: 5/11/95

RECEIVED

UNITED STATES DISTRICT COURT
EASTERN DISTRICT OF MICHIGAN
SOUTHERN DIVISION

UNITED STATES OF AMERICA,

        Plaintiff,

    vs.

JAMES DOUGLAS NICHOLS
and TERRY NICHOLS,

        Defendants.

_____/

CRIM. NO. 95-80361

HONORABLE LYNN V. HOOE

MEMORANDUM OF LAW CONCERNING THE CHARGED OFFENSE

Defendants James Douglas Nichols and Terry Nichols have been charged in a criminal complaint with conspiring with each other and with other persons, including Timothy McVeigh, to make and possess unregistered destructive devices in violation of 18 U.S.C. § 371 and 26 U.S.C. § 5861. Defendant James Nichols faces a preliminary examination on this conspiracy charge before this Honorable Court. This memorandum explains the charge against James Nichols.

             *   *   *   *   *

Under federal law, it is unlawful for any person to possess or make destructive devices. Specifically, 26 U.S.C. § 5861(d) makes it illegal "to receive or possess a firearm which is not registered . . . in the National Firearms Registration and Transfer Record[,]" and 26 U.S.C. § 5861(f) proscribes "mak[ing] a firearm in violation of the provisions of" Title 26 of the United States Code. The term "firearm" employed in Title 26 is defined by 26 U.S.C. § 5845(a)(8) to include "a destructive device." The term "destructive device," in turn, refers to "any explosive, incendiary, or poison gas" bomb, grenade, or other similar device, as well as "any combination of parts either designed or intended for use in converting any device into a destructive device . . . and from which a destructive device may be readily assembled."[1] 26 U.S.C. § 5845(f).

"A homemade explosive device is a destructive device within the meaning of [26 U.S.C.] section 5845(f) even though all of its components may be possessed legally." United States v. Price, 877 F.2d 334, 337 (5th Cir. 1989). "Moreover, unassembled components fit within the definition of a destructive device if the defendant possesses every essential part necessary to construct an explosive device, and if those parts may be assembled readily." Id.; accord United States v. Greer, 588 F.2d 1151, 1157 (6th Cir. 1978), cert. denied, 440 U.S. 983 (1979). In this respect, the definition of a destructive device is broad, but its breadth does not give rise to any constitutional infirmity. Price, 877 F.2d at 337-38.

To establish the substantive offense of making or possessing a destructive device, the government must prove two elements: the defendant knowingly made or possessed a destructive device, and the

---

[1] The definition of the term "destructive device" contains a statutory exception for "any device which is neither designed nor redesigned for use as a weapon[.]" 26 U.S.C. § 5845(f). However, this exception "contained in the definition of destructive device should be treated as [an] affirmative defense[] rather than as part of the elements of the offense." United States v. Beason, 690 F.2d 439, 445 (5th Cir. 1982), cert. denied, 459 U.S. 1177 (1983). The defendant, therefore, has the burden of asserting and establishing the applicability of the statutory exception. Id. Moreover, the mere character of a destructive device can refute a defense based upon the statutory exception. See id. at 445-46 (although grenades purportedly were to be used for fishing, presence of BB pellets in grenades undercut reliance upon statutory exception).

device was not registered in the National Firearms Registration and Transfer Record.) United States v. Crawford, 906 F.2d 1531, 1534 (11th Cir. 1990). With regard to the first element, although the statute at issue -- 26 U.S.C. § 5861 -- does not contain an express mens rea requirement, the Supreme Court has held that some level of guilty knowledge on the defendant's part is necessary.) See Staples v. United States, 114 S. Ct. 1793, 1804 (1994) (setting forth mens rea requirement for offense of unlawful possession of unregistered machinegun). With respect to the second element, the government is not obliged to prove that the defendant knew the destructive device was unregistered. See United States v. Woodlan, 527 F.2d 608, 609 (6th Cir.), cert. denied, 429 U.S. 823 (1976); accord United States v. Freed, 401 U.S. 601, 607-10 (1971). Likewise, the government is under no obligation to demonstrate that the defendant knew that the device had to be registered in order to be lawfully possessed. See Woodlan, 527 F.2d at 609.

In this case, the government has not charged any substantive offense under 26 U.S.C. § 5861. Instead, Defendants James Nichols and Terry Nichols are charged with conspiring to make and possess destructive devices. This conspiracy charge merely requires proof of the following three elements: (1) an agreement to engage in the criminal activity of making or possessing unregistered destructive devices; (2) one or more overt acts to implement the agreement; and (3) the requisite intent to commit the substantive crime. United States v. Winslow, 962 F.2d 845, 851 (9th Cir. 1992). Thus, if the government can establish that Defendant James Nichols agreed with

3

a co-conspirator to knowingly make or possess a destructive device, and then undertook any overt act in furtherance of this agreement, Defendant James Nichols is guilty of the offense that is charged in the amended criminal complaint.

Respectfully submitted,

SAUL A. GREEN
United States Attorney

Robert P Cares

ROBERT P. CARES
Assistant U.S. Attorney

Christopher P. Yates

CHRISTOPHER P. YATES
Assistant U.S. Attorney
211 W. Fort Street
Suite 2300
Detroit, Michigan 48226

Dated: April 27, 1995

4

CERTIFICATE OF SERVICE

It is hereby certified that, on April 27, 1995, service of the government's Memorandum of Law Concerning the Charged Offense was made upon opposing counsel **by hand delivery** and by placing a copy of the Memorandum in a stamped envelope and depositing the envelope in the United States mail addressed to:

> Miriam Siefer, Esq.
> 2255 Penobscot Building
> Detroit, Michigan 48226

Patti Turczynski
PATTI TURCZYNSKI, Secretary
Office of the U.S. Attorney

UNITED STATES DISTRICT COURT
EASTERN DISTRICT OF MICHIGAN
SOUTHERN DIVISION

R̲E̲C̲E̲I̲V̲E̲D̲

MAY 2 .. :'95

COURT ADMINISTRATOR
EASTERN MICHIGAN

UNITED STATES OF AMERICA,

        Plaintiff,

vs.   CRIM. NO. 95-80361

JAMES DOUGLAS NICHOLS et al,   ʙᴜʀᴍᴀɴ

        Defendants.
_____/

ROBERT R. ELSEY   P24519
Attorney for Defendant
15324 Mack Avenue, Suite 207
Grosse Pointe Park, MI 48224
(313) 881-6055
_____/

THE DEFENDANT'S RESPONSE TO THE GOVERNMENT'S BRIEF OPPOSING THE DEFENSE MOTION TO DISMISS AND THE FURTHER REQUEST FOR DE NOVO REVIEW OF THE DETENTION ORDER AND SUPPLEMENTAL BRIEF TO THE PETITION FOR HABEAS CORPUS

        In response, the Defendant will recapitulate
salient points. The Defendant contends that the Government
has no jurisdiction to charge the Defendant as he was
charged in the original complaint or in the succeeding
indictment.

Issue Presented

        CAN THE GOVERNMENT IGNORE THE LIMITATIONS
        OF 26 USC 7801 THROUGH 7805 (a) WITH
        REFERENCE TO JURISDICTION AND FURTHER
        ATTEMPT TO AVOID THE CONSEQUENCES OF
        26 USC § 7805 BY ATTEMPTING TO INDICATE
        THAT THE PROSECUTION IS JUSTIFIED UNDER
        A GENERAL POWER TO TAX?

Discussion

The United States Government has indicated in its Response Brief that Defendant "At the threshold, ... misses the point of the statute." Government cites <u>United States v. Price</u>, 877 F2d 334 (5th Circuit, 1989). That particular case is totally inapplicable as it involves a <u>firearm dealer</u>. Due to the fact that it involves a firearm dealer, the case essentially conforms to the Defendant's theory to dismiss.

The Government also cites the <u>United States v. Greer</u>, 588 F2d 1151 (6th Circuit, 1978). That case is likewise particularly inapplicable as it also deals with someone who is a dealer in firearms. Further, under the analysis of the recent <u>United States v. Lopez</u>, 1995 Lexis 3039 (decided April 26, 1995), the case is also inapplicable on the law. Specifically, <u>Greer</u> deals with a dealer in firearms. Review of the legislative history of <u>Greer</u>, supra, demonstrates that the purpose of the statute was to strengthen and enhance the Omnibus Crime Control Act of 1968, 588 F2d at 1155. The recent decision in <u>Lopez</u> unequivocally held that a statute, to have Commerce Clause protection, must demonstrate a nexus to interstate commerce for purposes of jurisdiction; there must be a showing that a Defendant was involved in interstate commerce. With reference to the legislative history that accompanies § 5861, it must be demonstrated that the legislative history (or by the specific language of the Act itself) that § 5861 and its related parts are applicable to private acts of farmers who are not involved in interstate commerce and who are not even alleged to have been involved in interstate commerce. § 5861 contains no jurisdictional elements, per the requirement of Lopez, supra. Further, it must substantially affect interstate commerce if there were to be jurisdictional language.

Furthermore, United States v. Lopez, supra, specifically overrules United States v. Hale, 978 F2d 1016, and United States v. Pearson, 8 F3d 631. The logic for this is simply that the Court of Appeals (8th Circuit) both held that the lack of nexus with interstate commerce is irrelevant and, therefore, it upheld the District Court convictions in Hale and Pearson. In Hale and Pearson the statute under consideration is 18 USC 922, which is the very same statute involved in with the Lopez decision. The Supreme Court in Lopez specifically said 18 USC § 922 has no nexus to interstate commerce either by its legislative history or by actual words stated in the Act. The very language of Lopez reverses the specific language of Hale and Pearson.

The Government further attempts to indicate that the Commerce Clause is not adjudicative of the issue. It attempts to indicate that the general taxing power of the United States Government allows the government to prosecute the Defendant notwithstanding a lack of Commerce Clause connection. The Government cites United States v. Giannini 455 F2d 147 (9th Circuit, 1972). That case specifically involves the taxing power of the United States Government as does United States v. Tous 461 F2d 656 (9th Circuit, 1972) and United States v. Warin 530 F2d 103 (6th Circuit). These cases involving the taxing power are all inapplicable as they are referencing possession of firearms involved in actual transfers. The case before this Court at this time does not involve a transfer, but involves the private acts of an individual on his own property. Therefore, there is no transfer of a possessed material that would require the supervision of the Internal Revenue Service in terms of the excise tax.

Under 26 USC § 7805 (a) only the Internal Revenue Commissioner or the Secretary of Treasury has the power to say what is a transfer. There is no section in the Code of Federal Regulations which describes the private acts of the Defendant herein as a transfer under the taxing power or, alternatively, under the Commerce Clause power.

The Government contends that reliance on 26 USC § 7801 through 7805 (a) is misplaced. The Government's contention is simply misplaced. Apart from a contentious and illogical argument, the government offers absolutely no authority for its argument. The government asks this Article III Court to interpret the application of the Internal Revenue Code. The Supreme Court of the United States has specifically stated "...Congress has delegated to the (Secretary of Treasury and his delegates,) the Commissioner (of Internal Revenue), <u>not to the courts,</u> the task of prescribing all needful rules and regulations for the enforcement of the Internal Revenue Code, 28 USC § 7805 (a)". See specifically <u>National Muffler Dealers Association v. United States</u> 440 U.S. 478, 99 S Ct 1304 (1979). See also <u>United States v. Correll</u> 389 U.S. @ 307, 88 S Ct at 449.

The 6th Circuit specifically has indicated that 26 USC § 7401 through 7405 are jurisdictional. <u>United States v. One 1972 Cadillac Coupe</u> 355 F Supp 513 (1973).

See also 26 CFR Part 301.7805-1 and 301.7805 (c).

References also made to <u>Goulding v. United States</u> 957 F2d 1420 (7th Circuit 1992).

In that decision the 7th Circuit indicated that:

> "Congress has delegated to the (Secretary of the Treasury and his delegate,) the Commissioner (of Internal Revenue) not to the courts, the task of prescribing 'all needful rules and regulations for the enforcement of the instances specified.' <u>United States v. Borden Company</u> 308 US 188, 84 L Ed 181, 60 S Ct 182 (1939)."

5

In the Goulding decision the court indicated that the
statute **was** not complete by itself, since it merely declares
the **range** of its operation and leaves to its progeny the
means to be utilized in the effectuation of its command.
But it is the statute which creates the offense of the
willful removal... and provides the punishment for
violations. The regulations on the other hand, prescribe
the identifying language. Once promulgated, the regulations
called for by the statute itself have the force of law in
violations thereof in criminal prosecutions, just as if the
details had been incorporated into the congressional
language. The result is that neither the statute nor the
regulations are complete without the other, and only
together do they have any force. Effectively, therefore,
the construction of one necessarily involves the
construction of the other. In Goulding the charges in the
information were founded on a statute and its accompanying
regulations. Information was subsequently dismissed solely
because the allegations did not state an offense under the
statute as amplified by the regulations.

Again, in the context of criminal prosecution, the rule
of strict construction must be applied to an interpreting of
a statute and its regulation, United States v. Halseth 342
US 277, 936 L Ed 308, 72 S Ct 275 (1952); United States v.
Wiltberger (US) 5 Wheat 76, 95, 96; 5 L Ed 42, 43 (1820).

Conclusion

The Government has not provided an argument that is supported by case law or statute to justify the complaint or indictment and, therefore, dismissal is proper for lack of jurisdiction.

ROBERT R. ELSEY   P24519
15324 Mack Avenue, Suite 207
Grosse Pointe Park, MI 48224
(313) 881-6055

Dated: _____

PROOF OF SERVICE
The undersigned certifies that the foregoing instrument was served upon all parties to the above cause by ~~enclosing a copy thereof in the U.S. Mail, postage prepaid, in envelopes addressed to each of the attorneys of record herein at their respective addresses disclosed on the pleadings~~, on _____ 5-14 ____, 19 95

7

UNITED STATES DISTRICT COURT
EASTERN DISTRICT OF MICHIGAN
SOUTHERN DIVISION

F I L E

MAY - 8 1995

CLERK'S OFFICE
U.S. DISTRICT COURT
EASTERN MICHIGAN

UNITED STATES OF AMERICA,

           Plaintiff,   CASE NO. 95X71775

-vs-

3616 North Van Dyke Road
Decker, Michigan, (all buildings,
vehicles, and farm equipment on
premises or other conveyances),

           Defendant(s).
_____/

MOTION TO SEAL SEARCH INVENTORY AND AFFIDAVIT

NOW COMES the United States of America, by Saul A. Green, United States Attorney, and Robert P. Cares, Assistant United States Attorney, both for the Eastern District of Michigan, Southern Division, and respectfully requests that the search inventory and the affidavit in the above-entitled cause be sealed for the following reasons:

1. The affidavit contains a detailed, accurate description of evidence known in this case as of the date of the affidavit. The inventory contains a very detailed, descriptive list of the items seized from the described premises. The government is attempting to identify and interview all persons who might have pertinent information in this case. It is important to the investigation that the information so obtained be accurate, and not be tainted by a witness's desire for reward or fear of punishment. Release of the detailed information contained in the inventory and affidavit would make it easier for potential witnesses falsely to conform their testimony to the known evidence in the case, and would make it harder for the government to detect any such falsity.

2. The government anticipates future searches and future arrests in this case. Release of the detailed information contained in the inventory would indicate to any other involved individuals the types of material in which the government is interested, and would assist them in destroying evidence to avoid its discovery by the government.

WHEREFORE, the government respectfully requests that the returned search warrant and affidavit in this cause be sealed.

SAUL A. GREEN
United States Attorney

Robert P Cares

ROBERT P. CARES
Assistant U.S. Attorney

Dated: 5/8/95

UNITED STATES DISTRICT COURT
EASTERN DISTRICT OF MICHIGAN
SOUTHERN DIVISION

F L E

MAY - 8 1995

CLERK'S OFFICE
U.S. DISTRICT COURT
EASTERN MICHIGAN

UNITED STATES OF AMERICA,

           Plaintiff,

  -vs-

3616 North Van Dyke Road
Decker, Michigan, (all buildings,
vehicles, and farm equipment on
premises or other conveyances),

           Defendant(s).

_____/

CASE NO. 95X71775

ORDER TO SEAL

The Government having moved to seal certain documents and the Court being duly advised in the premises:

IT IS HEREBY ORDERED that said documents be sealed and maintained in a safe place and not be opened unless by further Order of this Court.

HONORABLE VIRGINIA M. MORGAN
United States Magistrate Judge

Entered: **MAY 8 1995**

United States District Court

_____Eastern_____ — DISTRICT OF _____Michigan_____

In the Matter of the Search of
(Name, address or brief description of person or property to be searched)

SEARCH WARRANT

reen and white metal pole barn,
ocated at 3616 Van Dyke Road
ecker, Michigan

CASE NUMBER: **95 X 71775**

TO: **Any Federal Agent** _____ and any Authorized Officer of the United States

Affidavit(s) having been made before me by _____ **James Tritt** _____ who has reason to
                                                            Affiant

believe that ☐ on the person of or ☒ on the premises known as (name, description and/or location)

See Attachment A.

F I L E

MAY - 8 1995

C... ...'S OFFICE
U.S. ... TRICT COURT
EASTERN MICHIGAN

in the ___Eastern___ _____ District of _____Michigan_____ _____ there is now
concealed a certain person or property, namely (describe the person or property)

A 55 gallon blue plastic like drum, bearing the writing, "Flourish 6-14-6" or "Flourish 0-14-(
and its contents

I am satisfied that the affidavit(s) and any recorded testimony establish probable cause to believe that the person
or property so described is now concealed on the person or premises above-described and establish grounds for
the issuance of this warrant.

YOU ARE HEREBY COMMANDED to search on or before _____ 5/1/95 _____
                                                                              Date

(not to exceed 10 days) the person or place named above for the person or property specified, serving this warrant
and making the search (in the daytime — 6:00 A.M. to 10:00 P.M.) (at any time in the day or night as I find
reasonable cause has been established) and if the person or property be found there to seize same, leaving a copy
of this warrant and receipt for the person or property taken, and prepare a written inventory of the person or property seized and promptly return this warrant to _____
                                                                    U.S. Judge or Magistrate
as required by law.

_____ 4/28/95 _____ at   **DETROIT, MICHIGAN**
.te and Time Issued   City and State

MAGISTRATE JUDGE THOMAS CARLSON   _Thomas A Carl..._
Name and Title of Judicial Officer   Signature of Judicial Officer

pr: 28/1995 | April 28, 1995 ≈ 4:50 p.m. in Green + white metal pole barn

ENTORY MADE IN THE PRESENCE OF

Special Agent Steven M. Overly

VENTORY OF PERSON OR PROPERTY TAKEN PURSUANT TO THE WARRANT

all attached

CERTIFICATION

I swear that this inventory is a true and detailed account of the person or property taken by me on the warrant.

Subscribed, sworn to, and returned before me this date.

U.S. Judge or Magistrate   5/8/95
                                   Date

Receipt for Property Received/Returned/Released/Seized

On (date) _April 28, 1995_

item(s) listed below were:
- ☐ Received From
- ☐ Returned To
- ☐ Released To
- ☒ Seized

Time: _5:00 p.m_

(Name) _James Nichols_
(Street Address) _3616 Van Dyke_
(City) _Decker, Mich_

Description of Item(s):

One - blue plastic like drum
Marked in white paint
"National AG
Flourish
6-14-6
55 US GAL
1760 FL OZ
208.2 LT"

end of list

Received by: _No one at Present_ (Signature)

Received from _Andrew Nichols_ (Signature)

Attachment A

A green and white metal pole barn, located at 3616 North Van
Dyke, also known as M-53, in Decker, Evergreen Township, Sanilac
County, Michigan. This locaion is located 1/4 mile north of
Deckerville Road on the east side of M-53. The house on the
property is a two-story wood frame farmhouse, white incolor.
East of the house is a wooden pole barn, faded red in color.
East of the wooden pole barn is a metal pole barn, which is white
with green trim. Southeast of the metal pole barn is a large
hip-roof style barn, red in color. The property also contains
three large metal grain bins and two above ground fuel storage
tanks. There is one common driveway which leads to the house and
by which all outbuildings can be accessed. The house sits
approximately 100 to 130 feet off the road. Neither the house
nor the mailbox contain an address.

United States District Court

Eastern _____ DISTRICT OF _____ Michigan _____

In the Matter of the Search of
<small>(Name, address or brief description of person or property to be searched)</small>

3616 North Van Dyke Road
Decker, Michigan
Including the ground and subsurface of the
premises and surrounding acreage
(approximately 800 acres)

SEARCH WARRANT

CASE NUMBER: 95 X 71671

TO: _____Any Federal Agent_____ and any Authorized Officer of the United States

Affidavit(s) having been made before me by _____Hilary Jenkins_____ who has reason to
<small>Affiant</small>

believe that ☐ on the person of or ☒ on the premises known as (name, description and/or location)
   See Attachment A.

in the_____Eastern_____ District of _____Michigan_____ there is now
concealed a certain person or property, namely (describe the person or property)

   See Attachment B.

I am satisfied that the affidavit(s) and any recorded testimony establish probable cause to believe that the person
or property so described is now concealed on the person or premises above-described and establish grounds for
the issuance of this warrant.

YOU ARE HEREBY COMMANDED to search on or before _April 30, 1995_
<small>Date</small>

(not to exceed 10 days) the person or place named above for the person or property specified, serving this warrant
and making the search (in the daytime — 6:00 A.M. to 10:00 P.M.) (at any time in the day or night as I find
reasonable cause has been established) and if the person or property be found there to seize same, leaving a copy
of this warrant and receipt for the person or property taken, and prepare a written inventory of the person or property seized and promptly return this warrant to _Duty U.S. magistrate judge_
<small>U.S. Judge or Magistrate</small>
as required by law.

April 21, 1995 at 6:54 pm   at   _DETROIT, MICHIGAN_
<small>Date and Time Issued</small>   <small>City and State</small>

DONALD A. SCHEER
U.S. MAGISTRATE JUDGE   _Donald A. Scheer_
<small>Name and Title of Judicial Officer</small>   <small>Signature of Judicial Officer</small>

DATE WARRANT RECEIVED	DATE AND TIME WARRANT EXECUTED	COPY OF WARRANT AND RECEIPT FOR ITEMS LEFT WITH
April 21, 1995	*April 23, 1995 10⁵*	*AT RESIDENCE*

INVENTORY MADE IN THE PRESENCE OF

N/A

INVENTORY OF PERSON OR PROPERTY TAKEN PURSUANT TO THE WARRANT

SEE ATTACHED SHEETS (2)

CERTIFICATION

I swear that this inventory is a true and detailed account of the person or property taken by me on the warrant.

Alfred M. Petran Jr. Special Agent, FBI

Subscribed, sworn to, and returned before me this date.

_____ _____
U.S. Judge or Magistrate   Date

Attachment A

3616 North Van Dyke, also known as M-53, in Decker,
Evergreen Township, Sanilac County, Michigan. The residence is
located approximately 1/4 mile north of Deckerville Road on the
east side of M-53. the house is a two-story wood frame
farmhouse, white incolor. East of the house is a wooden pole
barn, faded red in color. East of the wooden pole barn is a
metal pole barn, which is white with green trim. Southeast of
the metal pole barn is a large hip-roof style barn, red in color.
the property also contains three large metal grain bins and two
above ground fuel storage tanks. There is one common driveway
which lead to the house and by which all outbuilding can be
accessed. The house sits approximately 100 to 130 feet off the
road. Neither the house nor the mailbox contain and address.

The house is situated on approximately 800 acres of
unimproved land.

The search warrant is for the ground and subsurface of the
land identified above, including the surrounding 800 acres.

Attachment "B"

Materials include, but are not limited to, the following:

1. Fragmented pipe (metal and/or plastic pipe with end caps or enclosures) and/or suitable containers for the explosive;

2. Electrical or non-electrical fusing systems (wire, batteries, clocks, and burning-type fuses).

FEDERAL BUREAU OF INVESTIGATION
Receipt for Property Received/Returned/Released/Seized

Page __1__ of __2__

On (date) __04-23-95__

item(s) listed below were:
☐ Received From
☐ Returned To
☐ Released To
☐ Seized

Time: _____

(Name) __JAMES NICHOLS__
(Street Address) __3616 N. VAN DYKE__
(City) __DECKER, MICH__

Description of Item(s):

Col #	Item	Description
1-W	#1	Meal Ready to Eat wrapper (AW)
3-W	2	3 3/8 piece of metal x 3/4 (DW)
6-W	3	2 7/8 by 1 7/16 piece of metal (IW)
6-W	4	D cell battery (2 1/4 long) (JW)
6-W	5	2 7/8 x 1 7/8 piece of metal (KW)
8-W	6	1 1/2 x 2 7/8 piece of aluminum (CW)
9-W	7	top of sch lodg pan 2 1/2 diameter (BW)
10-W	8	2 x 3/4 piece of aluminum (DW)
11-W	9	1 1/2 x 1 3/4 piece of aluminum (AW)
12-W	10	bottom of aluminum can 2 diam (IW)
12-W	11	top of aluminum can 2 1/2 diam (KW)
13-W	12	pull tab from aluminum can (LW)
13-W	13	top of miller can folded over (AW)
14-W	14	crumpled aluminum 3/4 inch (FW)
14-W	15	1 3/4 diameter piece of metal (MW)
14-W	16	round part of pull tab (CW)
15-W	17	green crumpled metal 3/4 x 2 1/4 (BW)
17-W	18	bottom of aluminum can 2 1/4 diam (DW)
2-E	19	crumpled alum can w/ red & blue marking (TE)
4-E	20	crumpled aluminum can miller 1 1/2 folded over (YE)
6-E	21	crumpled aluminum 1 1/4 x 3 (BE)
7-E	22	piece of aluminum 1 1/2 x 3 1/2 (NE)
7-E	23	piece of metal 1 3/4 x 2 7/8 (LE)
4-E	24	crumpled aluminum can miller lite a HLC 2 x 1 7/8 (JE)
12-E	25	3 1/2 inch piece white metal with hole (DE)

Received by: _____
(Signature)

Received from ___Alfred Mobley Jr - SA FBI___
(Signature)

FEDERAL BUREAU OF INVESTIGATION
Receipt for Property Received/Returned/Released/Seized

Page __2__ of __2__

On (date) __04-23-95__

item(s) listed below were:
☐ Received From
☐ Returned To
☐ Released To
☐ Seized

Time: _____

(Name) __JAMES NICHOLS__

(Street Address) __3616 N. VAN DYKE__

(City) __DECKER, MICH__

Description of Item(s):

Col #	Item #	Description
12-E	26	2½ʺ crushed cylinder type item of metal (O E)
13-E	27	metal aluminum (looks like Alcan) 2¼ x 3/8 (P J E)
14-E	28	York - Series # tag dated 7/72 (K E)
15-E	29	crushed green metal tube 1¾ x 5¾ (Q E)
16-E	30	crumpled heavy aluminum 2¼ x 2 (W E)
16-8	31	crushed green 1¼ metal tube x 2¼ (Y E)

Received by: _____
(Signature)

Received from: _Alfred M Whitney-SA FBI_
(Signature)

Index